Jews in the Early
Modern World

Jews in the Early Modern World

Dean Phillip Bell

ROWMAN & LITTLEFIELD PUBLISHERS, INC.
Lanham • Boulder • New York • Toronto • Plymouth, UK

ROWMAN & LITTLEFIELD PUBLISHERS, INC.

Published in the United States of America
by Rowman & Littlefield Publishers, Inc.
A wholly owned subsidiary of The Rowman & Littlefield Publishing Group, Inc.
4501 Forbes Boulevard, Suite 200, Lanham, Maryland 20706
www.rowmanlittlefield.com

Estover Road, Plymouth PL6 7PY, United Kingdom

British Library Cataloguing in Publication Information Available

Library of Congress Cataloging-in-Publication Data

Bell, Dean Phillip, 1967–
 Jews in the early modern world / Dean Phillip Bell.
  p. cm.
 Includes bibliographical references and index.
 ISBN-13: 978-0-7425-4517-5 (cloth : alk. paper)
 ISBN-10: 0-7425-4517-2 (cloth : alk. paper)
 ISBN-13: 978-0-7425-4518-2 (pbk. : alk. paper)
 ISBN-10: 0-7425-4518-0 (pbk. : alk. paper)
  1. Jews—History—70–1789. 2. Jews—Social life and customs. 3. Judaism—
History—Medieval and early modern period, 425–1789. 4. Jews—Identity.
5. Judaism—Relations—Christianity. 6. Christianity and other religions—Judaism.
I. Title.
DS124.B46 2008
909'.04924—dc22

                                                                    2007006495

Printed in the United States of America

∞™ The paper used in this publication meets the minimum requirements of
American National Standard for Information Sciences—Permanence of Paper
for Printed Library Materials, ANSI/NISO Z39.48-1992.

For Juli, for everything

Contents

Illustrations

TABLES

Acknowledgments

This book has evolved over many years, and as I have thought about its contents and written its pages, I have benefited from wonderfully stimulating conversations with many different colleagues. I owe each of them a real debt of gratitude, for listening, correcting, criticizing (at times vigorously), and supporting me throughout this process.

I thank my colleagues at the Newberry Library, who have provided generous assistance for this and other projects over the past several years. This project could never have materialized without the assistance of my colleagues at Spertus Institute's Asher Library. In particular, many thanks go to Gail Goldberg, for her untiring efforts to track down more obscure articles and volumes than should be expected in the entire career of the most dedicated professional, and to Glenn Ferdman, director of the Asher Library, who literally rolled up his sleeves, guiding me through extensive rare book and map collections and reading an early draft of the manuscript.

This book has benefited from the insights of a wide range of students, friends, and colleagues. My students at Spertus have encountered many of the ideas in this book in various seminars over the years—they have provided me with encouragement and held me accountable for as much clarity and cohesion as I could deliver. I extend very special thanks to Professor Luke Clossey and the students in his undergraduate early modern world history survey at Simon Fraser University, Mandeep Bal, Denis Boko, Chad Cowles, Bailee Erickson, Stephen Greenfield, Lauren Ogston, Sasha Regehr, Anthony Sullivan, Lucas Van Meer-Mass, and Kenny Yen. They read quickly and commented extensively and constructively on the first full draft of the manuscript and helped improve the final product immeasurably. Alissa Tanzar, in her capacity as research assistant, provided similarly crucial feedback on the text; she also offered invaluable assistance in the collection and selection of images for the volume. Tony Doyle and Tracy Kostenbader labored extensively in preparing maps and images for the book, and I am appreciative of their very skilled efforts.

My colleagues Lynda Crawford, Bella Ehrenpreis, and Hal Lewis read and commented on the manuscript and challenged me to refocus and improve throughout. Brian Romer deserves special recognition for all his efforts in eliciting the idea for this book, soliciting marvelous feedback, and shepherding this volume through to publication. Without the support of my home institution, the Spertus Institute of Jewish Studies, and its president Howard Sulkin, this volume would never have become a reality. The volume is in many ways an attempt to bring together the rich resources of the Institute and to practice what has been a powerful vision of educational integration at Spertus.

In the end, this book would never have been possible in conception or execution without the support and love of my wife Juli and our children, Malkaya, Chanan, and Ronia. They listened patiently (if at times captively) to the ideas in the volume and were always willing to share me and my time with a project whose relevance to real life, or any life for that matter, was not always immediately clear. As always, Juli has been a partner in everything I do, and this work is as much attributable to her as to me and my pen.

Timeline of Events

400	Closing of Palestinian Talmud
499	Closing of Babylonian Talmud
500–1050	Early Middle Ages
632	Death of Muhammad
638	Islamic Conquest of Jerusalem
694–711	Judaism Outlawed in Spain
711	Arab Conquest of Spain
740	Conversion of Khazars
1050–1250	High Middle Ages
1084	Charter for Jews in Speyer, Germany
1096	First Crusade
1135–1204	Moses Maimonides
1144	Blood Libel in Norwich, England
1165	Forced Conversions in Yemen
1179	Third Lateran Council
1215	Fourth Lateran Council
1240	Disputation and Burning of Talmud in Paris
1250–1500	Late Middle Ages
1263	Disputation in Barcelona
1290	Expulsion of Jews from England
1286	Completion of *Zohar*
1368–1369	Massacres of Castilian Jews
1306	Expulsion of Jews from France
1348–1350	Black Death
1386	Formation of Polish-Lithuanian Commonwealth
1389	Massacres of Jews in Prague

1391	Persecution of Jews in Spain
1413–1414	Tortosa Disputations
1421	Expulsion of Jews from Austria
1432	Valladolid Synod
1453	Ottoman Conquest of Constantinople (now Istanbul)
1455–1522	Johannes Reuchlin, Christian Hebraist
1457	First Book Printed by Gutenberg
1462	Jewish Ghetto Formed in Frankfurt am Main
1465	Attack on Jewish Quarter in Fez
1469	Union of Castile and Aragon
1475	First Hebrew Book Printed
1475	Trent Ritual Murder Accusation and Trial
1492	Expulsion of Jews from Spain; Moors from Granada
1495	Expulsion of Jews from Lithuania
1496	Expulsion of Jews from Portugal
1506	Attack on New Christians in Lisbon
1516	Creation of Venetian Ghetto
1516	Ottoman Conquest of Israel
1523	David Reuveni in Venice
1528	First *Auto da fe* in New World
1531	Portuguese Inquisition Established
1538	Attempt of Jacob Berab to Reinstitute *Semikhah* (Rabbinic Ordination)
1541	Expulsion of Jews from Naples, Prague
1546	Death of Martin Luther
1553	Burning of Talmud in Italy
1554	Censorship of Hebrew Books in Italy
1555	Pope Paul IV Edict "Cum Nimis Absurdum," Enforcing Segregation of Jews
1556	Burning of Marranos in Ancona
1565	First Printing of *Shulhan Arukh*
1568	Construction of Synagogue by Portuguese Jews in Cochin
1570	Earthquake in Ferrara, Italy
1570	Attempted Expulsion of Jews from Venice
1571	Defeat of Ottomans at the Battle of Lepanto
1571–1648	Rabbi Leon Modena
1572	Death of Isaac Luria, Important Kabbalistic Thinker
1580	Council of Four Lands Formed in Poland
1603	Synod of German Jews
1607	Congregation of Portuguese Jews in Amsterdam Established
1614	Fettmilch Uprising in Frankfurt

1618–1648	Thirty Years' War
1624	Excommunication of Uriel da Costa
1639	Unification of Amsterdam Sephardic Congregations
1648	Chmielnicki Massacres
1648–1649	Expulsion of Ashkenazic Jews from Hamburg
1654	Jews Forced to Leave Recife with Portuguese Incursions
1654	Settlement of First Jews in New Amsterdam (Later New York)
1656	Reentry of Jews to England
1656	Excommunication of Baruch Spinoza
1665	Shabbetai Sevi Declares Himself the Messiah
1666	Conversion of Shabbetai Sevi to Islam
1670	Expulsion from Lower Austria
1670	Spinoza's *Tractatus Theologico-Politicus*
1670	Expulsion of Jews from Vienna
1675	Construction of Portuguese Synagogue in Amsterdam
1683	Turkish Siege of Vienna
1700	Rabbi Judah the Pious Leads a Large Group of Jews to Palestine

Introduction: Time, Space, and Perspective

You have just purchased—or most likely been forced to purchase—this book. While that fact alone does not obligate you to read what follows, it does entitle you to ask a few questions. What is this book about? Why was it written, and why now? And, what implications does it have; to be blunt, why should you care beyond the fact that you may be responsible for some of the material between its covers?

Obviously, I felt a need to write this book, and I believed that there was a useful purpose that I could serve in so doing. Therefore, I begin with a few thoughts about how this book might be of value and, in a sense, how it came to be. Books, like the research that hopefully underpins them, go through much iteration. The ideas for many good books travel rather circuitous and often extremely entertaining paths and many times assume a life and direction all their own. While I have consciously conceived of and shaped this volume, it has in a sense re-formed itself continually along the way.

This book is about the history and experiences of Jews in the period from 1400 to 1700. As we will see, what defined someone as a Jew could be a complicated question. Jews could be individuals who followed rabbinic law, who followed some version of laws and behavior stipulated in the Hebrew Bible, or who were simply accused of being Jews by non-Jewish authorities. Jews' experiences could be wide-ranging and diverse, and importantly, they are impossible to understand without reference to the broader non-Jewish societies in which the Jews themselves lived and traveled. Some of this complexity will emerge in the main body of this book. For now, we begin with a broader question of why the period between 1400 and 1700 has been selected and what holds it together: some real-life events, some theoretical sensibilities, some strange whims of a history professor turned administrator with nothing better to do than torture prospective students?

PERIODIZATION

To answer our question it may be helpful to think for a moment about what historians actually do or, better, frequently attempt to do. History is really about opinions and the process of investigation. While it takes the past as its subject, history is about much less and much more than events that previously transpired. Much less, because we can never really know the full story of the past—let alone the various interpretations and perspectives that existed as the events themselves unfolded—and much more, because what history does is help us to understand ourselves better. We come to terms with who we are as individuals and as a society by the types of questions we ask, the way we look at the world, and the answers and observations that we construct based on a limited pool of sources. While historians do in a sense manipulate the past, they are not generally charlatans or criminals,[1] as much as self-reflective patients in need of a form of therapy that can only be administered in a particular setting—one that pits or frames the present against the past, often with the hope of informing the future.

Historians approach their subject with the help—or at times hindrance—of particular theories or concepts, which are used to inform (presumably) careful reading or examination of a wide range of historical sources. Generally, historians are forced by the sheer volume of evidence, range of questions, and available methodologies to choose a particular topic, geographical region, or period of time in which to place their research. While years ago it was fashionable for historians to write grand narratives of large pieces of the past in almost encyclopedic fashion, over the past several decades historians have become narrower—perhaps more humble—in their approaches. Of course, not everyone agrees that the increasing micro approach to the past is necessarily a good thing; some contend that the observations of individual cases do not allow for broader application and may, in fact, falsely represent or jade how we interpret the past. What is more, "grand" narratives at times allow historians to compare the developments in different regions and to pose new questions to direct research and inquiry.

Perhaps the most important development in the study of history over the past century—more important some might argue than any philosophical or theoretical advances, or even than the discovery of new bodies of evidence with which historians can grapple—has been the penchant for dividing and re-dividing the past. Let me offer one example. It used to be that the "Renaissance" was seen as the harbinger of modernity, separating the gloom of a supposed "dark ages" from the light of a renewed flowering of human intellect and culture. In this model, history could be very neatly divided between Antiquity, the Middle Ages, and Modernity. But not everyone remained content with this division. After all, the Renaissance was still somewhat "traditional" and did not totally comport with later social, political, and religious developments associated with the scientific advancements beginning in the seventeenth century or the modern revolutions of the eighteenth. Slowly, by the end of the nineteenth century, the Renaissance, along with the Reformation began to form the beginning of a newly termed "early modern" period. But scholars, in what has come to be called the revolt of the medievalists (can we say that the medievalists were revolting?) and romantics, asserted that the Renaissance actually represented a step backward from the creative developments of the Middle Ages (as opposed to a pejoratively envisioned "Dark Ages"). Scholars began to uncover and explore various rebirths, or renaissances (notice the lowercase "r" unlike the uppercase "R" of the Italian Renaissance), beginning already in Europe at the end of the eighth century (Charlemagne and the Carolingians), in the tenth century (the Ottonians), and during the "Renaissance of the Twelfth Century," which sported significant commercial, technological, bureaucratic, and intellectual developments.

Periodization does matter. When we choose a particular set of dates within which to place our subjects or topics, we in a very real sense dictate how they will be read, interpreted, and preserved. Placing the early modern period in the fifteenth century, for example, steals some of the thunder of the sixteenth-century Reformation, ending the early modern period before the French Revolution leaves the impression of the previous century as more "traditional" than some would find convincing.

Having laid out the background and, in part, the case for careful attention to the question of why we study the past and how we divide it up, let's consider briefly various ways to think about the "early modern" period in general and specifically as it applies to Jewish history, the theme of this book.

EARLY MODERN?

The term "early modern"[2] came into historical use in the late nineteenth century.[3] It was more widely used in the 1940s[4] and became somewhat universal in European historiography by 1970, with early modern studies peaking in the 1980s.[5] Since its inception as a scholarly discipline, there has been important growth in the study of the early modern period. There are now, for example, several journals devoted to the topic, including the *Sixteenth Century Journal*, which added in 1998 the subtitle "The Journal of Early Modern Studies," and the *Journal of Early Modern History* begun in

1997. The articles and book reviews in these and a host of other publications reveal the explosion in the number of works exploring many different aspects of early modern culture, politics, religion, science, and economics around the globe. Not everyone will agree about when to end the Middle Ages or begin Modernity; therefore, most scholars these days will confess that there must have been something worth considering in between those two periods. Before I advance my own reassessment of the periodization question, it is instructive to review some general approaches to the question of how to define early modern.

One intriguing essay by the historian John Bossy cast the early modern period in the West between 1400 and 1700. Bossy pleaded that he had chosen 1400 as the starting point of his reflections, not because anything of great significance happened in that year, but rather because nothing did.[6] For him, however, the year reflected well a certain state in the history of what he called traditional Christianity.[7] By 1700, after the Protestant Reformation and the consolidation of Christianity into multiple but distinct denominations during the seventeenth century, Christianity (which Bossy defined very broadly as a society and culture, more than simply a religion) had changed in important ways. In 1400, Bossy asserted, "religion" connoted "a worshipful attitude to God or a respect for holy things," and as such was an attribute of individuals or communities. By 1700, however, "the Christian world was full of religions, objective social and moral entities characterized by system, principles and hard edges, which could be envisioned by Voltaire as cutting one another's throats."[8] Religion had become systematic and overarching, something beyond individuals. If, in 1400 religion was largely understood at the level of personal relations typified by "friendship or charity," by 1700 it had become more impersonal and focused more particularly on formal guidelines and rules for behavior.[9] In part, then, Bossy defined the early modern period as one in which a certain formalization or institutionalization of religion occurred. Such a formalization had great impact on many different political, cultural, and social issues.

We will have occasion, in what follows, to ask whether Bossy's assessment makes sense and whether or not it has value for understanding the course of Jewish history. At the outset, however, it should be noted that the early modern period has, until recently, largely been one discussed within the context of Europe and in reference to Christianity. That is no longer the case. In part, the spread of the idea of "early modern" as an important tool for considering the past is a result of the influence of Western history. In part it allows historians to differentiate traditional and modern society in general at times of significant societal and technological change—what some historians like to think of as an "acceleration of history."

For India, for example, one recent scholar has argued that there was an early modern history and that it was characterized by rapid and massive change in human organization and interaction with other humans and nature. According to this scholar, six characteristics defined society as early modern: the creation of global sea passages; the rise of a global world economy; the growth of large, stable states; the doubling of world population; intensified use of land; and diffusion of technologies.[10] Another scholar notes similar parallels for China and identifies population growth; a generally quickening tempo in the areas of history, communal activity, and political and intellectual change; the growth of "regional" cities and towns; the rise of urban commercial classes; religious revival and missionary movements (leading to religious reformations); rural unrest; and the decline of nomadism.[11]

For Eurasia more generally, a number of common developments have been isolated for the period between the first half of the fifteenth and the first half of the nineteenth centuries. These developments include territorial consolidation; administrative centralization and social regulation; and cultural integration.[12] Common themes in all these assessments include expanding population, the formation of centralized states, globalization, increased technology, and the revival and reassessment of religion.

A number of issues have been widely discussed by historians as being characteristic of the European early modern period. Central themes in early modern studies have included "civilizing processes" associated with the development of the state, the quest for authority and the nature and form of religious observance (termed by some **confessionalization**), and the continuity and development of traditional belief. One particularly important work, Theodore Rabb's slender volume *The Struggle for Stability in Early Modern Europe*, published more than thirty years ago, contributed a great deal to this discussion. Rabb examined the period from 1500 to 1700 in particular, noting that the period was characterized by a search for authority. Among the developments seen as central in this paradigm were as follows: the emergence of new royal and national administrative centralization; the development of international economic and military rivalries; religious Reformation as in the Protestant Reformation and the Catholic (Counter-)Reformation; and new intellectual and artistic accomplishments. In addition, two other fundamental changes have been seen as significant, and these form part of the foundation for this study, namely, rapid population growth and (in part, due to geographic mobility) changing patterns of social relations.[13]

Dating the Early Modern Period

How have historians dated the early modern period? In large part, the answer to that question depends on the focus and scope of the histories being written. In general European history, for example, the early modern period often begins with the year 1500—a very nice round number but also the eve of the Protestant Reformation—or in the mid-1450s, with the rising threat of the Turks against Europe or the innovation of the printing press. Generally, the early modern period ends with the French Revolution in 1789. But, in other contexts, dating differs. In German history, for example, the period frequently begins in the late 1470s with the rise of the Habsburg dynasty and ends in 1806 with the impact of Napoleon's incursions. German historians might even offer more varied and shorter durations of history, sometimes asserting that the period after the Thirty Years' War (1618–1648) marked a new phase. In the history of the Ottoman Empire, the turn of the fourteenth century, with the foundation of the Ottoman State, has usually been seen as the beginning of a period that ended at the end of the sixteenth century, with important political changes within the Empire. The beginning of the fifteenth century was also significant in Ottoman history. It was a period that witnessed important territorial growth during the reign of Bayezid I (1389–1402) as well as defeat at the hands of Timur, who had established a strong empire in central Asia and Iran, at the Battle of Ankara in 1402. In Chinese history, the beginning of the fifteenth century marked important naval expeditions west.[14]

How one draws the boundaries of any period depends a great deal on how one defines core social issues and on location. For example, modernity could be associated with the development of capitalism, the nation-state, particular demographic patterns, or certain religious or world outlooks. Even in these cases, however, there is not always a great deal of clarity, since there are obviously enormous regional variations and varying stages of development. Depending on how we define it, capitalism, for example, may have first developed in some areas in the nineteenth century, the sixteenth, or perhaps even the twelfth. Or, consider the uneven development of "nation-states" in the West. Were the burgeoning nation-states of England and France in the thirteenth century the beginnings of modernity, perhaps the consolidating Spanish and English monarchies of the sixteenth century, or even the development of national entities in Germany and Italy in the second half of the nineteenth century? In the field of demography historians have located the beginning of the "early modern" period in the middle of the fifteenth or the middle of the seventeenth century, but even this periodization could vary dramatically by region.[15]

While there are many ways to periodize the early modern period, there are enough significant changes around the beginning of the fifteenth century and the end of the seventeenth to give these dates strong consideration. Especially in Europe and the Ottoman Empire, these dates were extremely significant. They marked important political development, the resolution of major population shifts, significant economic transformations, and dramatic religious change. Although many different ranges of dates continue to be used for the early modern period, the period between 1400 and 1700 is becoming more frequently utilized. We ask now whether these dates make sense for the history of the Jews as well.

The Concept of Early Modern in Jewish History

How have Jewish historians approached the topic of the early modern? In traditional Jewish historiography, periodization is handled in rather broad strokes, perhaps best characterized as biblical, rabbinic, medieval, and modern. Even in such models the various periods are not always exact, with transition periods often blurring and blending one into the next. The reasons for recent and growing interest in further and more exact periodization may be related to ongoing discussions about what is modern and, by the way, what is medieval as well; by developments in other historical disciplines, which have increasingly parsed the past; and by a variety of contemporary scholarly and ideological orientations that have something to gain from re-dividing history in particular ways.

In a now classic article by the historian of modern German Jewry Michael Meyer, a variety of beginning points for modern Jewish history have been examined.[16] The historian Isaac Marcus Jost, for example, had indicated that 1740 was a logical beginning of modern Jewish history, for it was in that year that Frederick the Great ascended the throne. For the early nineteenth-century Jost, who was a traditionally educated Jew but one with sympathies for Enlightenment rationalism,[17] Frederick was the enlightened despot who awoke a spirit that led to civil equality. Jost saw in this period a decline of unquestioned rabbinic authority, a shift from the Jewish community as a separate social and political entity to one of a religious denomination, the increasing participation of Jews in German cultural and political life, and the onset of an age of spiritual liberalism.

Other historians saw matters differently. The early nineteenth-century and philosophically minded Austro-Hungarian Nachman Krochmal saw history as a series of cycles of growth, blossoming, and decay. For him, the most recent period of decline was epitomized by the Cossack persecution of the Jews in the middle of the seventeenth century; his own age, by contrast, was one of germination. The towering nineteenth-century Jewish historian Heinrich Graetz, whose impact continued well into the twentieth century, like the purveyors of general historical scholarship of his time, assigned a primary role in historical change to great individuals. For him, the beginning of modernity occurred with the figure of Moses Mendelssohn at the end of the eighteenth century.

The great eastern European historian of the late nineteenth and early twentieth centuries, Simon Dubnow challenged Graetz on many levels. He favored the designation of the French Revolution, with the opportunity for

Jews to gain citizenship, instead of the Jewish Enlightenment, or **Haskalah**, as the beginning of modernity. But Dubnow's pre-modern period stretched back into the late fifteenth century. Dubnow wrote, "The expulsion of the Jews from Spain brought about important changes in the life of the Jewish people, changes closely connected with the great events occurring at the same time in the life of the nations of Europe, and forming the dividing line between the Middle Ages and the Modern Epoch."[18] On the other side of the balance sheet he noted, "The second half of the XVIIIth century was a period of transition for the Jews, during which the old order of their lives gave place to the new."[19]

The father of Jewish social history in the twentieth century, Jacob Katz, found indications of important historical change before the eighteenth century. For Katz, the period between the sixteenth and eighteenth centuries witnessed a decline of rabbinic authority, the pursuit of secular education, a growing disregard of traditional Jewish norms, and increasing integration in the broader non-Jewish world. According to Katz, however, such tendencies were neutralized and did not completely break with Jewish tradition until the end of the eighteenth century, when the deviant became the norm. Other twentieth-century historians, such as Israel Abrahams, in his popular book *Jewish Life in the Middle Ages*, seemed to imply a certain vitality in the Jewish Middle Ages that was in fact somewhat supplanted by a more rigid rabbinic control and quest for religious conformity beginning in the sixteenth century and extending until the end of the eighteenth.[20] This curious tension in interpretation clearly has to do with how the various historians approached their topic and defined their terms. The observations of Katz and Abrahams may, however, lead in the same direction. Katz noted aberrance, but within a traditional framework that was not broken; Abrahams stressed the intellectual continuity and religious conformity of the religious codes, which he contrasted to the comparatively complex intellectual and cultural creativity of the medieval period.

Other modern scholars have cast the onslaught of modernity further back. The ardent Zionist Ben-Zion Dinur selected the year 1700, when Rabbi Judah the Pious led a thousand Jews to Palestine. The great scholar of Jewish mysticism, Gershom Scholem stressed that the Sabbatians of the late seventeenth century shattered traditional Judaism and reappeared later as leaders of the Reform movement. Salo Baron, the dean of Jewish Studies in America who held the first appointment in Jewish history at an American university, also focused on the seventeenth century. He emphasized the context of global historical changes.[21]

Dinur divided the history of Diaspora Judaism into eight periods: first stability (636–1096) and crisis (1096–1215); second stability (1215–1348) and crisis (1348–1496); and third stability (1496–1648) and crisis

(1648–1789).[22] Indeed, periodization by means of crisis or persecution has been very popular and much practiced. In this regard, the span of time from the Spanish expulsion until the Chmielnicki massacres of 1648 is often seen as a discrete period. Other scholars, like Leopold Zunz (1794–1886) in the nineteenth century, interested among other things in medieval literature, traced the persecutions of Jews under the Christian Church into the middle of the sixteenth century, with special emphasis on the Crusades and the pogroms associated with the Black Death in the middle of the fourteenth century. "The Middle Ages," Zunz wrote, "are the period of barbarism, that is, of the united sway of physical force, ignorance, and priestcraft."[23] Still others, like the contemporary historian Jonathan Israel, have paralleled such periodization. Israel has argued that after around 1570 the experience of Jews in Europe improved dramatically, and Jews became reabsorbed and tolerated in important ways.[24]

Writing from traditional, religious, and eastern European perspectives, many historians of the last century saw little novelty in the early modern period. Critical new approaches to the study of the past, combined with scholarly and popular interests in identity, popular culture, and the experience of Jews living under Islam, however, make it no longer possible to write a history of the early modern period as simply an appendage to the Middle Ages or a precursor being dragged unwillingly into modernity.

But simply because historians choose to carve up the past in certain ways is not reason enough to sanction such divisions. We must, therefore, ask about the value of dividing up an early modern Jewish history. Are the traditional categories of medieval and modern simply insufficient? Is the call of broader historical scholarship too great? Did anyone in the early modern period see him or herself differently? As we will see in the chapters that follow, the answer to each of these questions is clearly yes.

In the traditional division of Jewish history, the medieval period runs from the close of the Talmud through the *Haskalah*, or Jewish Enlightenment. Little attempt is made to differentiate the important, often regional, developments and variations within the Jewish experience. Rather, it is secularization, assimilation, and search for emancipation that mark off the modern period from all pre-modern Jewish history. Such a periodization, however, which assumes something of a general Jewish homogeneity before the modern period, does a great disservice to the richness, complexity, and dynamic of early modern Jews, who were in many ways not simply "medieval" or "modern." Indeed, the very fact that many of the central figures of the early modern period, such as the **Sephardic** statesman and exegete Isaac Abarbanel (1437–1508), the Italian historian Azariah de' Rossi (1511–ca. 1578), and the **Ashkenazic** historian and scientist David Gans (1541–1613), have been simultaneously appropriated as medieval and modern is a clear signal that the period under investigation is important, not simply as one of transition, but rather one that needs to be understood on its own terms.

One of the central issues holding this period together across various regions and that helps to make sense of many different internal and external developments is Jewish demography. Jews, especially in the Diaspora, have had a long history of migration and readjustment. It would be difficult to understand Jewish history without understanding the role of migration and dispersion. The period bounded in this study witnessed a very monumental series of transformations that affected not simply where the Jews lived but also how they formed communities, how they identified themselves and developed their cultures, and how they interacted with the non-Jewish people around them.

Significant population movements running from the middle of the fourteenth century until the end of the fifteenth century created new communities and ideas of and needs for community. The Black Death persecutions from the mid-fourteenth century scattered Jewish populations and further weakened the Jewish sense of security.[25] The persecutions of the late fourteenth century in Spain set the stage for the momentous movement of people and ideas with the expulsions from the Iberian peninsula at the end of the fifteenth and the beginning of the sixteenth century. The expulsion of Jews from many different states, provinces, and cities in the fifteenth century led to mass migrations eastward (Poland and the Ottoman Empire) that eventually transformed the nature and identity of Jewish history. The progress of the Ottoman Turks throughout the early fifteenth century and their massive population movements already in the middle of that century helped to create new Jewish communities and significantly affected the trajectory of Jewish history in an area that included the vast majority of world Jewry at the time.

By the beginning of the eighteenth century, on the other hand, many "modern" demographic patterns had been established, with the tremendous growth of Polish Jewry, the solidification of central and southern European Jewry, and the re-entry of Jews into places like England and their entrenchment in the New World. By the end of the seventeenth century, as the fortunes and the power of the Ottoman Empire declined so did the ascendancy of Sephardic Jewry.

THE SCOPE AND ORGANIZATION OF THIS BOOK

Many different sources are available for the study of medieval and early modern Jewish history. A wide range of non-contemporaneous scholarly works, or secondary literature, is available on a diverse array of topics. Many different kinds of primary sources, sources originating from the period being studied, are also available in printed editions and in numerous archives and document collections. For the topic under consideration it is important to note that both Jewish and non-Jewish sources are valuable in reconstructing the Jewish past. Various archival materials, such as court records, notarial documents, and tax lists can be supplemented by polemics, religious writings in the forms of biblical commentaries, sermons, and rabbinic **responsa**, as well as in literature, artistic representations, and legal documents. These sources exist in numerous languages, especially Latin and European vernaculars in the West, and Arabic, Greek, and other languages in the South and East. Hebrew sources exist from nearly every corner of the early modern world inhabited by Jews.

Many important and fascinating studies on a wide range of topics that fall in the period between 1400 and 1700 have been published, especially over the past several decades (see the bibliography and the suggestions for further reading). In part, this book is a synthesis of these materials, which often vary widely in their sense of periodization and focus, and which generally concentrate on topics within rather discrete geographic, ethnic, or cultural boundaries.

Given the considerations presented above, this book begins (in chapter 2) with a review of Jewish demography in the early modern period, for without an understanding of the nature and shifts in Jewish settlement and migration, it is difficult if not impossible to understand any other Jewish developments. Population and settlement forced Jews to develop or adapt certain communal institutions and structures, and this book next assesses the nature, scope, and variations of Jewish communal life. In addition to various communal structures, chapter 3 also explores the social structures of early modern Jewish communities.

There are many themes that could be used in organizing this book. Among the themes common to the early modern period discussed above are globalization; population growth; increased social stratification; economic development; the location of and challenge to authority (communal and religious); and increasing cultural interaction. Chapters 2 and 3 address the first four of these themes. For chapters 4 and 5 I have opted for the simple division of self and other. Both of these categories address the question of authority and cultural interaction, though from different perspectives.

The great theorist of early modern European history Michel de Certeau, in his compelling assessment of historical writing, argues for the centrality of selectivity and self on the one hand and separation on the other.[26] In writing their histories, de Certeau notes that all historians begin from present determinations and current events, which drive their readings and assessments of the past. Personal intentions and individual social outlooks inspire the type of research and the choice of historical topics that the historian selects, unconsciously organizing research and providing a framework for interpretation. The historian, indeed, begins his or her work by collecting and by setting aside documents. His or her perspectives inform how the historian reads but also how he or she decides what data to include and exclude. History is, in a sense, about limitations and so consequently about identities. In chapter 4, therefore, we focus on how Jews understood themselves and how they selected and crafted their society and culture. What did early modern Jews believe, how did they practice their religion, and how did they deviate from the norms articulated by the religious and lay leaders in their communities? This chapter also asks about the development and expression of Jewish cultural life more generally in order to gain insights about Jewish identity.

The flip side of history is, in a sense, otherness and alienation. History is simultaneously about differentiation and separation of the past and the present, even if the two are never completely severed in theory or practice. History, especially for the period that concerns us, is about the dead, but it seeks to make the dead come alive and speak to us. In this sense, the quest of history is to find meaning in the Other. In this regard, chapter 5 asks us to attempt to understand early modern Jews by considering their relations with non-Jews. Such relations were frequently negative, resulting in legal and social restrictions, as well as various forms of persecution such as expulsions and massacres. On the other hand, many times Jewish relations with non-Jews were either neutral or positive, with Jews engaging non-Jews socially, economically, intellectually, and even religiously. While not frequently documented in historical sources, such positive relations were important.

In the conclusion the primary findings of the previous chapters are summarized and assessed for what we can learn about the history of the Jews and the early modern period itself. Now we begin in chapter 1 with a brief overview of the history of the Jews in the Middle Ages. This is not intended to be a complete survey of a topic that is well developed and complex in its own right. Rather, background information is provided as context for understanding some of the early modern issues to be presented and as an opportunity to evaluate the various changes and continuities for early modern Jews and early modern Judaism that are considered in the subsequent chapters. Throughout this volume terms or concepts that may be unfamiliar to the general reader are bolded in the text and defined in the glossary.

NOTES

1. "Consider what might be unmasked by seeing the historian as criminal, historical practice as a kind of crime. What crimes do historians commit? They might

best be seen as thieves, as persons who practice a form of grave robbing. Renaissance grave robbers carried off bodies to sell to physicians for dissections, and historians also appropriate and dismember the past, absconding with the words of others to make their own classifications and to write new narratives. Even more than the inquisitors and judges of the criminal record, historians are likely to suborn witnesses, depriving them of their own integrity; at the worst they are even forced to answer historians' questions with words spoken in answer to other questions. From a slightly different perspective influenced by Foucault, the crime of history, like that of medicine, might be seen as originating in its construction as a discipline. Fulfilling the demands of their discipline, historians justify their little thefts, unveiling past derelictions and expropriating judicial secrets" (Edward Muir and Guido Ruggiero, eds., *History from Crime*, trans. Corrada Biazzo Curry, Margaret A. Gallucci, and Mary M. Gallucci [Baltimore, 1994], vii–viii).

2. Throughout this volume I have purposively assumed a global perspective. In part the decision to do so was informed by the simple demographic centrality of Ottoman Jewry, and in part it has been informed by the growing global approach to European history. One recent scholar, in a book focusing on early modern Europe, notes that even that work must more actively incorporate experiences in the Polish-Lithuanian Commonwealth and the Ottoman Empire. See Karen L. Taylor and James B. Collins, "Introduction: Interpreting Early Modern Europe," in *Early Modern Europe: Issues and Interpretations*, ed. James B. Collins and Karen L. Taylor (Oxford, 2006), 1.

3. Luke Clossey, "Early Modern World," in *The Berkshire Encyclopedia of World History*, ed. William Hardy McNeill et al. (Great Barrington, MA, 2005), 593.

4. Randolph Starn, "Review Article: The Early Modern Muddle," *Journal of Early Modern History* 6 (3) (2002): 297.

5. Starn, "Review Article: The Early Modern Muddle," 298, 301.

6. While the periodization of the early modern does vary considerably, the period 1400 to 1700 is receiving a good deal of focus. Consider, for example, the major four-volume undertaking being published by Cambridge University Press entitled "Cultural Exchanges in Early Modern Europe," each volume of which explores different themes between 1400 and 1700.

7. John Bossy, *Christianity in the West, 1400–1700* (Oxford, 1985), 3.

8. Bossy, *Christianity in the West*, 170.

9. Bossy, *Christianity in the West*, 171.

10. John F. Richards, "Early Modern India and World History," *Journal of World History* 8 (2) (Fall 1997): 197–209.

11. Joseph F. Fletcher, *Studies on Chinese and Islamic Inner Asia*, ed. Beatrice Forbes Manz (Brookfield, VT, 1995), 8–33.

12. Victor Lieberman, "Transcending East-West Dichotomies: State and Culture Formation in Six Ostensibly Disparate Areas," excerpts reprinted in *Early Modern Europe: Issues and Interpretations*, ed. James B. Collins and Karen L. Taylor (Oxford, 2006), 419–29.

13. Philip Benedict, "Introduction," in *Early Modern Europe: From Crisis to Stability*, ed. Philip Benedict and Myron P. Gutmann (Newark, DE, 2005), 16. And yet, despite these various issues, themes, and categories, early modernism remains difficult to define. Not everyone, in fact, agrees that the concept "early modern" is a useful

historical category. According to one scholar, "there is no universal 'pre-modernity,' but rather a wide range of societies with distinctive cultures and structures that went through their own historical development over centuries or millennia before and after Western contact. . . . 'Post-modernists' have therefore argued that 'modernization' is itself an illusion or myth, and it is essential variety and uniqueness of different societies that matters and should be central to social theory" (Jack A. Goldstone, "The Problem of the 'Early Modern' World," *Journal of the Economic and Social History of the Orient* 41 [3] [1998]: 251). This scholar dismisses the concept of early modern (1500–1850, while advancing the concept of advanced organic societies): "In other words, 'early modern' can mean almost nothing, or almost everything, and as such, is a wholly meaningless term. It developed out of the need to fill in a space in the Marxist theory of stages of history, where it fills the gap between feudalism and industrial capitalism in Europe by interpolating commercial practices that have been widespread from the earliest days of commerce, while erroneously concluding that those practices represent something new, something essentially Western, and something closely tied to the emergence of 'modern' societies. In fact, none of these latter propositions are valid. Thus the term 'early modern' is founded on a series of errors, and has no useful application to world history" (Goldstone, "The Problem of the 'Early Modern' World," 261).

14. Clossey, "Early Modern World," 592.

15. Ole J. Benedictow, *The Black Death, 1346–1353: The Complete History* (Wiltshire, UK, 2006; orig., 2004), 250–52.

16. Michael A. Meyer, "Where Does the Modern Period of Jewish History Begin?" *Judaism* 24 (1975): 329–38.

17. Michael A. Meyer, *Ideas of Jewish History* (Detroit, 1987), 175. And recently, see the introductory essay by Michael Graetz, "Zur Zäsur zwischen Mittelalter und Neuzeit in der jüdischen Geschichte," in *Schöpferische Momente des europäischen Judentums in der frühen Neuzeit*, ed. Michael Graetz (Heidelberg, Germany, 2000), 1–18.

18. Simon Dubnow, *An Outline of Jewish History*, 3 vols. (New York, 1925), 3:176.

19. Dubnow, *An Outline of Jewish History*, 3:268.

20. Dubnow, *An Outline of Jewish History*, 3:xxv, xxvi.

21. Meyer, "Where Does the Modern Period of Jewish History Begin?"

22. Ben-Zion Dinur, *Israel and the Diaspora* (Philadelphia, 1969), 66ff.

23. Leopold Zunz, *The Sufferings of the Jews during the Middle Ages*, trans. A. Löwy (New York, 1907), 26.

24. See his important *European Jewry in the Age of Mercantilism, 1550–1750*, 3rd ed. (London, 1998).

25. Whether or not the Black Death of the mid-fourteenth century is a classic example of the severe population declines associated with the end of the later Middle Ages or the beginnings from which the early modern population would rebound, it is certain that many historians have seen it as something of a watershed in the history of humanity. According to one of the most thorough scholars of this topic, Ole J. Benedictow, the Black Death had a wide range of significant impacts. Benedictow writes, "It should be clear that the Black Death was an event of great historical importance. It put its stamp on the economic and social scene, the living standards of the masses improved greatly, while the upper classes and social elites saw their in-

comes fall and their charmed way of life being undermined. It also put its stamp on the period's religious mentality and outlook on life.

"It hastened the development and transformation of European medieval society and civilization into its (early) modern historical form. By creating a great deficit of labour it speeded up economic, technological, social and administrative modernization, which especially in the capitalist centres in northern Italy and partly in Flanders found expression in a more secular and urban culture associated with the Renaissance. It also hastened the breakdown of feudal economic structures and mentalities and the rise of a prevailing dynamic capitalist market economy and concomitant innovative and dynamic attitudes and mentalities. Thus, the seeming paradox that late-medieval culture and mentality comprised both obsession with death and salvation, fascination with economic and social opportunities, and the secularization of economy and art" (Benedictow, *The Black Death*, 250–52).

26. See Michel de Certeau, *The Practice of Everyday Life*, trans. Steven Rendall (Berkeley, CA, 1984).

1

A Medieval Context

MEDIEVAL PRECEDENTS

Before we embark on an exploration of the early modern period, it is constructive to provide a brief overview of the experience of the Jews in the Middle Ages that may provide a partial context for the chapters that follow. Let's begin with the same **periodization** problem—when exactly were the Middle Ages? The answer to this question will be divided between the Christian and Muslim worlds.

The European Middle Ages have often been viewed as the Dark Ages—a period of intellectual decline and barbarism. Over the past century, however, scholars have come to understand the European Middle Ages as more than the middle ground between the rich cultural legacy of (Greek and Roman) Antiquity and the cultural rebirth of the Renaissance. The Middle Ages themselves now appear quite complex and vibrant. Historians of Europe now divide the Middle Ages into early, high (or central), and late periods. The high Middle Ages are now seen as a period in which religious life developed, commerce expanded, urban centers radiated, and cultural life flourished. At the height of the Middle Ages politics matured, with England and France developing into nascent nation-states. Even the early Middle Ages has become subject to increasing intellectual curiosity as new sources have been uncovered and old sources have been subjected to new and probing questions. As we saw previously in the introduction, historians now speak of multiple "renaissances" before the Renaissance—especially those occurring during the reign of Charlemagne and his successors in the late eighth and early ninth centuries, during the tenth-century reign of the Ottonian kings and during the entire twelfth century.

JEWS AND MEDIEVAL CHRISTIAN SOCIETY

The early Middle Ages (ca. 500–1050) in Europe were dominated by the fall of the Roman Empire and its division into the Latin West and the Byzantine East, and subsequently unification in the West under the Carolingians (with the important political consolidation of Charlemagne); a series of pro-longed barbarian invasions; the gradual expansion of Christianity; and the rise of Islam. Political turmoil and small Jewish population centers in much of the European West led to often harsh and quickly changeable legislation regarding the Jews. On the Iberian peninsula, for example, Visigothic (the Visigoths were Germanic tribesmen who overran Iberia in the early Middle Ages) and Christian legislation alternated between limited toleration and forced conversion and expulsion. The growth of Christianity, a religion that saw itself as growing out of but superceding Judaism, frequently led to at-tacks against the Jews and stifling legislation against the practice of Judaism. In addition, the relatively small economic opportunities of the early Middle Ages provided little room for Jewish entrepreneurial development. Some positive developments, however, indicated possible improvements for Jews. The rise of Islam in the East and in the South offered Jews an al-ternative reality and different opportunities.

The high Middle Ages (1050–1250) experienced extensive economic de-velopment in what has been termed the commercial revolution; dramatic urbanization; the advance of science and philosophy, and the founding of schools and universities; increased social mobility; and the increased role and bureaucraticization of the Church—leading to both standardization of practices and beliefs and, consequently, the emergence of heresy. The com-mercial and urban development of the period attracted Jews, whose popu-lation increased dramatically in some places, and revealed new opportuni-ties for Jews to work and earn livelihoods. The position of the Jews in an increasingly Christian environment ebbed and flowed. At times religious debates (in the form of polemic and disputations) and restriction domi-nated; at other times intellectual interest in Judaism accelerated, and more consistent legislation prevailed. Jews could be welcomed as boons to eco-nomic growth, as the famous charter in eleventh-century Speyer exempli-fies. At the same time, Jews could be subject to heavy taxation, discrimina-tion, periodic violent attacks, and increasing occupational restriction, so that during this period Jews were forced out of many professions and often had to practice pawn-broking or moneylending. While Jews have been car-icatured as the purveyors solely of these professions, there did exist a wide range of professions in which Jews operated throughout Europe. Neverthe-less, it is clear that there were significant and far-reaching restrictions on what Jews could do and where they could live.

The later Middle Ages (1250–1500) have typically been viewed as a period of increasing stagnation, decline, or crisis. War, violent feuds, and pestilence ravaged much of Europe; the economy shrank; and the papacy fell as nation-states emerged in northwest Europe. Europe, according to tradition, was waning. On the other hand, the later Middle Ages also witnessed the supposed rebirth of the Renaissance and set the tone for important economic, scientific, and religious developments beginning in the sixteenth century. The violence of the later Middle Ages has typically been seen as played out for the Jews in restrictive legislation, religious debates, pogroms, and expulsions. A series of thirteenth-century disputations demonized the Jews, who were accused of blasphemy and false belief. Numerous popular uprisings, along with more calculated attacks against the Jews during times of political or societal crisis, such as the Black Plague in the middle of the fourteenth century, led to expulsions and attacks against individual Jews and entire Jewish communities. In fifteenth-century Germany, for example, the Jews were expelled from many urban areas, just as they were expelled from entire countries during the later Middle Ages—1290 in England, 1306 (and again later after they had been readmitted) in France, and 1492 in Spain. While some historians connect growing nationalism and attempts at cultural, political, and religious homogeneity, there remained an intellectual interest in Jews and Judaism, and Jews did play an important role in the European expansion overseas. Just as in the earlier periods, developments could vary tremendously by region. As in other periods, the fate of the Jews depended upon local circumstances and must be examined in different contexts.

In the medieval Christian West, the position of Judaism was set on its path by the duality advocated by St. Augustine of Hippo already in the late fourth and early fifth century. On the one hand, Augustine saw the Jews as the rejected and superceded people of God; on the other hand, his doctrine of the witness, the idea that a remnant of Jews must survive to see their error at the end of days and witness the second coming of Jesus, lent a certain rationale to some form of, however limited, toleration. Throughout the medieval period, Jews were caught between the poles of grudging toleration, generally in the form of internal Jewish communal autonomy, and severe restriction and persecution, the allegedly deserved reward for what many believed were pernicious people fallen from grace and unable or, worse, unwilling to see Christ as God.

Christianity and Judaism

Early Christianity had important ties to Judaism. It arose within a particularly rich and diverse period of Jewish development and for some time coexisted alongside other Jewish sectarian systems. Indeed, according to the New Testament itself, Jesus did not claim to found a new religion, and he insisted that he did not intend to change the letter of the Law. At the same time, Christianity in order to define itself had to separate from Judaism. Emphasis, therefore, was placed on the supposed differentiation of "letter" or external meaning (Judaism, Old Testament) and "spirit" or internal meaning (Christianity, New Testament), and the belief that Christians were the new Jews, God's new chosen people.

The rejection or **supercession** of Judaism was central to Christian identity. As such, a certain anti-Judaism was endemic to Christianity. This position was no doubt strengthened by at times vigorous debates between Jews and Christians, and a variety of anti-Christian polemic on the part of Jews. Indeed, some Jews harbored negative descriptions of Jesus and throughout much of the Middle Ages seem to have considered Christianity, with its doctrine of the Trinity, a form of idol worship.[1] What is more, the early relationship between Judaism and Christianity was at times quite strained, particularly as Christianity was persecuted in the late Roman Empire, and Jews engaged in widespread proselytizing efforts of non-Jewish Romans.

Religious Polemics

There were numerous Jewish polemicists and apologists and several high profile formal religious debates throughout the Middle Ages. The disputation in Paris in 1240 was perhaps the first important medieval engagement. A similarly significant disputation occurred in 1263 in Barcelona, pitting the learned Rabbi Moses ben Nahman (Nahmanides) on one side and the Jewish convert to Christianity Pablo Christiani and several Dominican and Franciscan officials on the other. The dispute reflected well the growing interest in and use of Hebrew among some orders of the Christian Church in their attempts to convert the Jews. The Christian position was based upon passages of the Talmud and intended to demonstrate that the Messiah had already appeared, that he was human and divine, and that he died to atone for the sins of mankind. Nahmanides countered that some passages of the Talmud were to be taken literally, and these did not accommodate a Christological interpretation; other passages were to be taken allegorically, and so did not prove the Christian position either. Nahmanides also took opportunities to attack certain aspects of Christian dogma. The disputation was never formally concluded. Jews and Christians both claimed victory, though one thing is certain: Jews were forced to listen to a conversionary sermon in their synagogue, and despite secular promises of protection, Nahmanides felt threatened and left Spain for the Holy Land in 1267.

One text, the high medieval *Nizzahon Vetus* (Old Polemic, referred to in the following as NV), provides a good opportunity to see Jewish attempts at self-defense. The NV makes it clear that the Talmud is a correct and necessary supplement to the Torah. According to the author of the NV,

> The heretics [i.e., Christians] criticize us by saying that the Talmud distorts and spoils our entire Torah and prevents us from realizing the truth by leading us astray. The answer is that the Talmud is a fence and hedge around the entire Torah, for all the commandments are spread through the twenty-four books of the Bible, a little here and a little there, and one who learns a particular commandment is likely to forget it before he reaches the next.[2]

While Christianity is referred to as idolatrous,[3] Judaism is presented as the one true religion.

A very important exchange revolves around the discussion of Psalm 15. According to the Christians in the NV's polemic, Jews who loan money should not take money in the form of interest from gentiles, since in their reading the Psalm states that nobody should lend money at interest. According to the two parts of Psalm 15 cited by the straw Christian set up in the NV, "who shall abide in your tabernacle and who shall dwell in your holy hill? He who walks uprightly and works righteousness, and speaks the truth in his heart. He who does not gossip with his tongue. . . . [He who does these things] shall never stumble," and "he who does not lend his money at interest." The NV argues that gentiles may have been considered "brothers," since they are descendants of the biblical Esau, but they have since disqualified themselves and are now considered strangers, and indeed they define themselves as foreigners. The entire question of permissibility to loan to gentiles with interest revolves around the break in their descent, their lineage. Indeed, Christians are seen as rebellious people who helped to destroy Jerusalem. The fundamental opposition of Judaism and Christianity is here portrayed as based on biblical history.

Law and Politics

Christian relations with Judaism must be understood within the various, and at times, overlapping, contexts in which they were steeped. Different systems of law—Roman, Germanic, ecclesiastical, civic, and feudal—advocated a range of relations with and proscriptions against Judaism. Roman law, for example, had maintained something of an ambivalent position regarding the Jews. While Roman polytheism seemed to allow some toleration, Roman law and sensibilities looked askance at certain Jewish practices and beliefs, such as that of circumcision, which was often depicted as mutilation. Once Christianity penetrated Roman legislation, anti-Jewish sentiments often became embedded in legal culture and thinking. Any suspicion that Jews were exercising power over Christians led to anti-Jewish suspicion and restrictions.

The dual approach to Judaism and the Jews exemplified by Augustine meant that Jews were frequently under the protection of individual rulers and Church edicts. They were even seen as vulnerable people much like clerics and women, who were also not allowed to bear arms. On the other hand, Jews often suffered discriminatory legislation, public prohibitions, and occasional anti-Jewish violence, as during the Crusades and at other times, when Jews might be blamed for general societal ills. Jews were granted charters that allowed settlement, certain business, exemptions from some tolls, and the freedom to live according to Jewish laws; at the same time, such legislation outlined restrictions imposed on the Jews and their financial obligations. In a sense, Jews were treated as a form of property (they were labeled "serfs of the imperial chamber"), and they could serve as a whipping post when upstart burghers or cities wanted to assault their lords indirectly—generally those who protected the Jews—by attacking the Jews.

Social and Cultural Relations

In early Christian society the accumulation of wealth was often perceived negatively, and merchants and trade were consequently also not seen in a favorable light. As the West entered a period of commercial revolution beginning in the eleventh century, some of these perceptions began to change. But in a world where commerce was increasingly seen as useful, the Jews might be seen as competition. Slowly the scope of Jewish business was channeled into narrower bounds, as Jews were forced from formal participation in many occupations and were increasingly being forced into the difficult and despised area of moneylending. While charging interest on loans was seen as against biblical law and not appropriate for Christians, Jews were allowed to charge reasonable rates of interest, generally around 5 percent. For a variety of reasons, including that many debts were never repaid and ruling authorities frequently cancelled all debts owed to Jews, that figure was often much higher. Jews were, therefore, castigated as taking advantage of Christians, especially the poor. Jews truly were trapped in a difficult position. On the one hand, as the Church fought against usury the position of the Jews was seen as evil; on the other hand, as late medieval Christians themselves began to move into moneylending and found ways to open loan banks in some areas, the Jews were squeezed further from that profession as well. Similar tensions arose in the area of pawn-broking.

Emblematically, in the early eleventh century, the emperor Henry II expelled the Jews from Mainz, demonstrating the vulnerability of the Jews' situation and, perhaps, heralding a broader movement of exclusion in the high Middle Ages. Canon law frequently lumped Jews together with pagans and heretics, and legislated against social contact with them. Jews, like other groups perceived of as unsavory, such as lepers and prostitutes, were forced to wear distinguishing marks or clothing, and often areas of Jewish residence were restricted by local authorities—although it should be pointed out that Jews often sought close living proximity to one another for internal governing and religious reasons. Jewish quarters dotted German cities, and as early as the late eleventh century, the Jews in Speyer had their quarter separated by walls. The first official ghetto is generally dated to the second half of the fifteenth century in Frankfurt, though more or less permeable and separate living quarters existed for much of the Middle Ages.

Generally, Jews were not allowed citizenship, though we do possess records of Jews taking citizen oaths from time to time. Popular culture often took anti-Jewish tones; the fire was stoked by superstition, separation, and the inflammatory words of preachers, who presented Judaism as archaic and demonic. Traditional stereotypes, especially those that cast the Jews as magicians or sorcerers, thieves, ritual murderers, and blasphemers circulated widely in medieval Europe. The Crusades, which roused Christians against enemies in the Holy Land, also served to raise ire against non-Christians at home. Well-documented and horrific attacks against the Jews throughout Europe served as a starting point for the first crusade and, according to some historians, left an indelible mark on the history of the Jews in the West.[4]

Church law in the high Middle Ages could be rather antagonistic toward the Jews. During the Third Lateran Council of the Church (1179), previous Church laws legislating the activities of Jews and Muslims were repeated. Jews and Muslims, for example, were prohibited from having Christian servants or practicing usury. Although Jews were historically and theoretically protected by Church decrees from forcible conversion, according to the decrees of the Third Lateran Council, Jews who converted to Christianity were to be treated well. The Fourth Lateran Council (1215) prohibited Jews from taking immoderate interest, holding public offices, or making public appearances during Easter and Christian fast days. In addition, and most famously, Jews were to wear a yellow badge to distinguish themselves, converts to Christianity were ordered to desist from any Jewish practices, and interest on debts owed by Christians to Jews was to be cancelled. In the later Middle Ages, Christian conflict with Judaism became more pronounced, through anti-Jewish preaching and the attack on rabbinic literature, such as evidenced in a famous disputation in Paris in 1240. In part this increased conflict was due to growing Christian interest in Hebrew language and rabbinic interpretation of the Bible. In part it may have been related to various political and economic developments during the course of the thirteenth and early fourteenth centuries, for example, those related to the process of developing nation-states in western Europe.

It is important, however, not to assume that Jews lived only in seclusion, separated from the world around them. Alongside latent hostility and social isolation, we also find indications of integration. Jews not only spoke Hebrew, but they were also familiar with local vernacular languages. At times, they even copied Christian scholarly and literary formulae, such as in Moses Rieti's *Migdash Me'at*, which was modeled upon Dante's *Divine Comedy*. Even the often-cited polemicist Yom Tov Lipmann Mühlhausen in the fifteenth century conceded the value of secular and philosophical study, when he noted,

> Many of the degrees of wisdom can be found among the sages of Greece . . .
> and from this do not make the error that those degrees are forbidden, namely
> natural science and astronomy and philosophy, for these are branches of our
> faith and lead us to the love of His Blessed Name and fear of Him . . . and this
> is not Greek wisdom but the wisdom of all who are wise.[5]

Often Jews and Christians lived in close proximity, and they interacted in various ways on a daily basis. Some Jewish and Christian sources repeatedly prohibited Jewish and Christian sexual interaction as well as gambling, dancing, and dining together, suggesting that such encounters must have occurred on a regular basis. We know that Jews and Christians were involved with each other in business, and it is clear that Jews also borrowed money from Christians and that the presumption that moneylending was a one-way relationship is not tenable. Jewish and Christian relations could vary greatly by period and location, with local or regional customs often allowing some level of interaction. On the other hand, efforts to keep Jews and Christians separated, through restrictions on sale and consumption of wine or even milk, for example, indicate that Jewish and Christian relations were no simple matter.

The position of Jewish women in the medieval West in some ways reflected well the position of Jews in society more generally. One important scholar of medieval Jewish history and society, Avraham Grossman, has charted a trajectory of positive developments for the position of women in medieval Jewish European society. Women had certain expanded rights regarding divorce and against polygamy. They played an expanded and central role in the economic sector. What is more, there developed a certain relaxation on the prohibition of teaching women Torah, and women increased their participation in *mitzvot* (commandments) more generally. Indeed, women were often known for and praised for their piety and modesty. Legislation was developed to punish physically abusive husbands, the prohibition against marrying a woman who had had two husbands die was removed, and women themselves were allowed a certain degree of self-determination. Finally, even in the sphere of religious development, women gained a certain elevated status through kabbalistic thinking, which saw the feminine as fundamental in the structure of the world and the divine.

On the other hand, negative attitudes about women persisted, greater strictures relating to menstrual laws were developed, and particularly in Muslim lands, a greatly increased emphasis was placed on customs of modesty.[6] Like the Jews more generally in society, Jewish women played important communal and economic roles, had some freedoms and privileges, and yet were still restricted in numerous ways.

JEWS AND MEDIEVAL ISLAMIC SOCIETY

Jews under medieval Islam never suffered from the same general negative perceptions as in the Christian West. Despite regional variations and high medieval political instability, in medieval Islam multicultural environments, combined with active engagement in sciences and literature, led to something of an Islamic golden age for the Jews, at least according to most historical accounts. It has been primarily in the context of recent political developments that the once assumed positive views of Jewish life under medieval Islam have been seriously questioned.

Islamic Complexities

Islam arose within the context of medieval Byzantium and pre-Islamic Arabia, where there was a lack of centralized and organized authority. The story of Muhammad is too complex to review here. What we can say is that by the early 630s most of the Arabian tribes had accepted the prophetic mission of Muhammad, who was simultaneously a prophet, state builder, and social reformer. From the seventh century on, Islam spread from the Arabian Peninsula. Islam developed within an urban environment, and Muhammad recognized the influence of the more ancient monotheistic religions of Judaism and Christianity. The central text of Islam was an Arab work that gave attention and respect to aspects of Judaism and Christianity but also differentiated itself from those traditions. Muhammad became interested in further differentiating Islam from Judaism particularly when the Jews of Medina did not recognize Islam. He therefore fixed Friday as the holy day, abolished the leap year, and rejected certain dietary laws, while maintaining others.

Medieval Islam has generally been subdivided according to major invasions: in the seventh and eighth centuries the invasion of Arab Muslims; the invasion of the north and northeast steppe peoples, beginning with the Turkish migration in the tenth and eleventh centuries; and the great Mongol invasions of the thirteenth century. The "late Middle Ages" witnessed unsuccessful further penetration into Europe, though by the sixteenth century the Ottoman Empire was, under Suleyman the Magnificent, in many ways at the height of its culture and political power. While the Ottoman Empire expanded, it met stiff resistance on the borders of central Europe and was even defeated at sea by the naval forces of the Republic of Venice during the Battle of Lepanto in 1571.

Islam and Judaism

Islam developed with the written teaching of the prophet and was complemented by oral sayings and traditions known as **hadith**. Influenced by both Jewish and Christian legal sources, it also developed in a very specific cultural context. Islam was early on fraught with internal divisions of varying religious and political orientations (the effect of these divisions is still felt powerfully today). The ongoing conquests of Islam had the effect of reuniting a large segment of the Jews under one central, if external, authority. Jerusalem itself was taken in 638. By the early eighth century Islam spanned the region from India to the Pyrenees, containing some 90 percent of the total global Jewish population. Islamic success was often seen by Jews in messianic terms and divine retribution for harsh treatment of the Jews at the hands of Byzantines, Persians, and Western Christians.

For our purposes, the appearance and growth of the Ottomans is of particular importance. In the eleventh century political power passed from the Arabs to the Turks, and the Seljuk Turks dominated across Iran, eventually creating a small princedom after the defeat of a Byzantine force, laying the groundwork for the Ottomans. The Ottomans forged in response to Christian advances after the Crusades and Mongol invasions of the thirteenth century[7] and by the middle of the fifteenth century had created a vast and sophisticated empire.

Muslim domination had profound impact on the Jews. Muslims respected Jews as "People of the Book," and Jews were often treated better than Christians, who were also recognized as "People of the Book." Islam respected trade and urban lifestyle, and Jewish links along imperial commercial routes were encouraged, especially when Jews served as intermediaries in the trade between parts of Christian Europe and the Ottoman Empire. Unlike the vast restrictions frequently placed on Jews in the Christian West, Jews were involved in a rich and variegated range of professions. Jews were involved in crafts, as well as trade, moneylending, and state financing.

Under Islam, practice rather than belief was stressed, resulting in less concern with heretical thought and more toleration for other religions. Non-Muslim religions were clearly viewed as second rate and to be denigrated, but the proponents of such religions could still hold certain, if limited, rights. Of course the toleration of other faiths could vary dramatically depending upon local conditions. In fact, persecutions and massacres were not unknown in the Muslim world, as those in Granada in 1066 and those initiated by the Almohads in North Africa and Spain in the twelfth century indicate. In the end, pluralism often existed but never equality. This situation held in all lands under Muslim control.

Jews were forced to pay a poll-tax, experienced some economic restrictions, had to wear distinguishing clothing, and suffered certain other social limitations, though in general internal communal autonomy was respected. Jews, as *dhimmis*, or protected people, paid certain taxes, had to show Muslims respect, and were theoretically prohibited from bearing arms. The somewhat ambivalent position regarding Jews is well summarized in two Quranic passages:

> Those who believe, and those who profess Judaism, and the Christians and the Sabians, those who believe in God and the Last Day and act righteously, shall have their reward with their Lord; there shall be no fear in them, neither shall they grieve. (II, 62)

> Fight against those who do not believe in God or in the Last Day, who do not forbid what God and his Prophet have forbidden or practice the true religion, among those who have been given the Book, until they pay the poll-tax from their hand, they being humbled. (IX, 29)

The religious debate between Judaism and Islam was significantly different than that between Judaism and Christianity. For one thing, Muhammad did not claim divinity or messianic character. Like Jews, who claimed descent from the biblical Abraham through Isaac, Muslims claimed descent from Abraham via Ishmael. Islam was not described as the fulfillment of Judaism, even if Islam was to take priority. There were no grounds for blaming Jews for the prophet's death, as with Christianity. Muslims were also less inclined to combat non-Muslims within their own Islamic domain.

Islamic Law and the Jews

Under traditional Islamic legal rulings, most notably the seventh-century pact of Umar, Jews were forbidden to construct new synagogues or to hold public ceremonies and were to be separated and humiliated—rising in the presence of Muslims, not mounting on saddles, not bearing weapons, and constructing houses at a lower level than those of Muslims, for example. Jews were not to bear honorific titles or possess slaves, and they were theoretically banned from state service. In addition, Jews were to dress in a way that demarcated them as such—the yellow badge was, it should be kept in mind, developed in the lands of Islam before it made its way to Christian Europe. In practice, however, here and in other ways Jews at times had more flexibility in how they behaved and what they could do.[8]

Despite its emphasis on practice, Islam was not without its polemic against Judaism. Islam saw Judaism and Christianity as abrogated; Jews were charged with tampering with the Bible and distorting texts, and defectively transmitting historical events to downplay the significance of Muhammad and Islam. Muslims rejected certain anthropomorphic readings of Scripture attributed to Jews and Christians, and they also found references to Muhammad throughout both the Old and New Testaments. On the other hand, there were more doctrinal similarities than differences between Muslims and Jews. Despite two Jewish derogatory descriptions of Muhammad, as madman and as defective, and two Jewish polemical works against Islam (both penned by Jews from the Christian West), many important Jewish thinkers embraced a wide range of Muslim thinking and scholarship, and admired certain Islamic schools of thought and religious practices.

Social and Cultural Interaction

Despite social and religious restrictions, Jews living under the crescent nevertheless participated in a rich cultural and scholarly world, serving simultaneously as arbiters and proponents of science that had been absorbed from the Greeks through Arabic and then transmitted to the Latins. Jews translated important scientific and philosophical works, but they also engaged them and adjusted their theological views as a consequence. They discussed, if not always embraced, various Islamic philosophical schools, creating what has been seen as a golden age of Jewish intellectual life.[9] It is important to point out the highly influential Jewish scholars Saadia Gaon (882–942), Isaac Israeli (ca. 855–ca. 955), Solomon ibn Gabirol (ca. 1020–ca. 1057), Bahya ibn Pakuda (fl late eleventh century), and Moses **Maimonides** (1135–1204). These scholars flourished in and often borrowed from the Islamic intellectual pools in which they were steeped. Jews also adapted Islamic approaches to literature and textual interpretation, as in the works of Moses ibn Ezra (ca. 1055–after 1135), Abraham ibn Ezra (1089–1164), Judah Halevi (before 1075–1141), and Abraham ibn Daud (ca. 1110–1180). The Islamic mystical school of Sufism,[10] to give one example, was inspired by Greek philosophy and in turn influenced important Jewish thinkers such as Solomon Ibn Gabirol and Bahya Ibn Pakuda. Even Islamic religious customs left indelible marks on medieval Jews, as is evidenced by the infiltration of some Islamic apocalyptic strands.

There were numerous centers of Jewish and Islamic interchange. In the mid-tenth century, for example, Cordova became a great center of learning for Jews living in Islamic Spain. While other centers also existed, Cordova witnessed a flourishing and rich culture that affected a widely dispersed

Jewish population and demonstrated the possibility of Jewish intellectual engagement with Islamic culture and thought.

Under Islam, Jews were often integrated into broader economic life. In part this was due to Islam's relatively more positive attitude toward commerce than Christianity, the earlier advent of a middle class, a tradition of merchant scholars, as well as flourishing trade with wide world markets. Jews and Muslims were involved in business, even if both sides occasionally condemned interfaith partnerships. Although the image of a malevolent Jewish moneylender existed in Arabic literature, Jews generally lent money primarily within the Jewish community, and they borrowed with interest from Muslim moneylenders.

Jews under Islam often lived in close proximity to one another, and many neighborhoods were primarily Jewish, but we have only a few specific references to Jewish quarters. Even in Jewish neighborhoods half of the houses typically belonged to non-Jews. Jews throughout medieval Islam had considerable occupational diversification. Women entered the public work force in greater numbers in the thirteenth century; we find records of women owning possessions, and women of all classes appeared as owners of immovable property. As in the West during the high Middle Ages and later, Jewish women under Islam managed households and were frequently legal guardians and executors of estates. Although not in the mainstream of society and not generally possessing means outside of shared property, women invested in real estate, lent money, and entered business partnerships. They bought and sold textiles, jewelry, and other items. Women were involved in wedding affairs, midwifery, and healing, and practiced as wet-nurses and doctors, even if they did not possess formal training. Women also participated in textile production, brokerage, synagogue cleaning, and preparation of the dead for burial. We have some records of women working as scribes and even Bible teachers, and one who apparently taught Talmud.[11] On the other hand, the widespread practice of polygamy, some historians have asserted, reflected a weaker position of Jewish women under Islam than was developing under medieval Christianity.[12]

In Jewish society under Islam, social occupation alone did not determine social position. According to one *geniza* (referring to a storage area for ritual objects or texts that are no longer usable) document, there were five social levels: upper class; bourgeoisie of business men, professionals, and master artisans; lower middle class; mass of urban craftsmen and laborers; and peasants.[13] Social advancement was possible in this society. While some professions were despised by Muslims, and some by Jews, Jews were involved in a rich range of occupations. Over 450 occupations were referenced in the *geniza*, but Jews were particularly prominent in textiles (especially silk work and dyeing), the production of glass, metal work (mostly silversmithing), food trade, and the pharmaceutical profession. Jews practiced nearly every profession from vizier to blacksmith and tailor. They also worked within the Jewish community in various religious communal professions.[14] Jewish physicians were held in high regard, and many Jews functioned in state administration, especially in collecting taxed customs duties. It is generally argued that Jews held influential government positions out of proportion with the actual Jewish population.

A very small number of Jews successfully penetrated the upper echelons of Islamic society, particularly through service at court. Samuel ha-Nagid (993–1056), for example, fled Cordova during the Almoravid Berber conquest of 1013. Propelled into an important position at court of the Berber king in Granada because of his Arabic writing skills, he eventually held a great deal of political power. He headed the Muslim army from 1038 until 1056 and was also appointed the *nagid* (head of the Jewish community) of Spanish Jewry in 1027 by his co-religionists. He was both a poet and a *halakhic* (Jewish legal) expert and writer. In 1066 when large numbers of Jews in Granada were murdered, his family was toppled and his son murdered. Hasdai (the *Nasi*, or prince) ibn Shaprut (915–70) was likewise a gifted scholar and diplomat. In addition to skills as a translator, he possessed important medical skills and was conversant with Hebrew, Latin, and various European languages.

At times, socialization between Jews and Muslims appears to have been rather free. Mixed bathing was not forbidden, lenient rulings regarding Muslim consumption of animals slaughtered by *dhimmis* (protected people) could be found, and Muslims certainly dined in Jewish homes. There is some evidence that Muslims participated in Jewish and Christian religious holidays, festivities, and even sporting events with Jews and Christians.

Limitations

Jewish success and professional integration, however, could be met with widespread resistance and envy. Possibilities for peaceful co-existence—provided always that Jews and Christians were recognized as second class and inferior—sometimes evaporated in the midst of theoretical and actual restrictions and even persecutions. In the early twelfth century in Baghdad, for example, we learn that Jews were forced to wear yellow badges on their headgear and neck, a necklace upon which was engraved the term *dhimmi* and a belt at the waist. Jewish women were also required to wear specific and identifying clothing and marks. The Jews were, at times, supervised by unsavory Muslims and subjected to mob derision and attacks. A persecution of Christians in North Africa and Spain in 1012 turned against Jews as well. While Islam theoretically rejected forcible conversion, there were conversions to Islam by prominent Jews throughout the medieval period.

OTHER CONTEXTS

In the Middle Ages we have some evidence, often anecdotal in nature, about individual Jews and Jewish communities in independent territories and even in parts of Asia and the Far East. There may have been some Jews already in India at the time of the destruction of the Second Temple in the first century of the Common Era. There are clearly references to Jews in India from Talmudic and medieval sources. There is legend among the Jews of India, or Bene Israel, that sometime between 1000 and 1400 Bene Israel were discovered in villages and taught the fundamentals of Judaism. In China, there is some documentary evidence of Jews by the eighth century, and foreign travel accounts from the ninth century list Jews, Muslims, and other foreigners amidst the Chinese population. Indeed, in the ninth century there is a contemporary report from an Arab geography indicating international Jewish merchants, called Radhanites, who traveled between Europe, the Mediterranean, the Middle East, and into India and China.[15] While these were probably never extremely large communities, they were significant, and they point both to the dispersion and to the mobility of Jews throughout the Middle Ages.

Perhaps the most well-known and intriguing group of Jews outside the boundaries of Christianity or Islam were the Khazars. The Khazars were of Turkish origin, and they flourished between the seventh and tenth centuries on the periphery of the Byzantine Empire, in the area of the Black Sea. The Khazars appear to have practiced Islam for some time but during the eighth century are said to have converted to Judaism. There is not a great deal of evidence for this conversion, aside from some scattered documents and later descriptions. The Khazars were clearly on the decline by the tenth century, the victims of growing Russian incursions. Nonetheless, the Khazars are an intriguing chapter in medieval Jewish history.[16]

CONCLUSIONS

The Middle Ages for the Jews could be defined internally, based on the developments within the various Jewish communities, or externally, dependent upon the multifaceted events and orientations of the broader world in which the Jews lived. At times these different Middle Ages interacted; at other times their paths seem not to have crossed.

The Jewish Middle Ages witnessed the increasing complexity of community, which included the formation of laymen as powerful leaders. A whole host of communal legislation emerged, just as Jews partook in wider non-Jewish cultural development, simultaneously absorbing the cultures around them and adopting them to their own needs and world-view.

The Middle Ages witnessed the closing of the *Mishnah* (the Oral Law), with local case law and custom beginning to take precedence in the myriad of Jewish settlements around the globe. Relatively small Jewish populations at times flowered into important population centers as Jews increasingly fell under Muslim rule and, despite numerous restrictions, played important functions in Christian society as well. Judaism as a religion was frequently contested or rejected in the East and West; the Talmud was debated and burned, segregation expanded, and Jews were subject to highly charged and changeable political conditions, such as the massacres of 1348 and expulsions in the wake of growing nationalism. At the end of the Middle Ages Jews began a migration eastward into Poland and Russia and took more direct roles in burgeoning international trade; after the expulsion from Spain in 1492, many Jews made their way into the Ottoman Empire as well.

Under both medieval Christianity and Islam, Jews were a much-discussed people, who were central in the self-definition of both Christians and Muslims. For the Middle Ages the vast majority of Jews lived under Islam, and they had, as at times they did under Christian rule, a good deal of internal freedom and even prospects of social and economic success. In both cases, however, Jews were seen as either second-class citizens or as aliens who were generally tolerated but who were subject to a range of personal and communal restrictions and plagued by occasional eruptions of violence and persecution.

In many important ways the position of the Jews remained consistent into the early modern period. Jews faced similar challenges and employed time-tested strategies as they negotiated the external world. Rapid changes were just around the corner as the world entered the early modern period. Significant population shifts and new religious and cultural world-views helped shape an early modern Jewry that was somehow both traditional and transformed. We now turn to a fuller examination of that world.

NOTES

1. See Jacob Katz, *Exclusiveness and Tolerance: Studies in Jewish-Gentile Relations in Medieval and Modern Times* (New Jersey, 1983; orig., 1961).

2. David Berger, ed. and trans., *The Jewish-Christian Debate in the High Middle Ages* (Philadelphia, 1979), no. 245, p. 230.

3. Berger, *The Jewish-Christian Debate*, no. 210, p. 206.

4. See Robert Chazan, *European Jewry and the First Crusade* (Berkeley, CA, 1987), who does not find the Crusades to have been quite such a watershed.

5. Hayyim Hillel Ben-Sasson, ed., *A History of the Jewish People* (Cambridge, MA, 1994; orig., 1976), 624.

6. See Avraham Grossman, *Pious and Rebellious: Jewish Women in Medieval Europe*, trans. Jonathan Chipman (Hanover, NH, and London, 2004), 273–81.

7. See Halil Inalcik, *The Ottoman Empire: The Classical Age 1300–1600* (London, 2000; orig., 1973).

8. For the complete text of the pact of Umar, see Norman A. Stillman, *The Jews of Arab Lands: A History and Source Book* (Philadelphia, 1979), 157–58.

9. See Barry W. Holtz, ed., *Back to the Sources: Reading the Classic Jewish Texts* (New York, 1984), as well as the work of Colette Sirat, *A History of Jewish Philosophy in the Middle Ages* (New York, 1985).

10. See Raymond P. Scheindlin, "Merchants and Intellectuals, Rabbis and Poets: Judei-Arabic Culture in the Golden Age of Islam," in *Cultures of the Jews: A New History*, ed. David Biale (New York, 2002), 347–48; 357 regarding its impact on Bahya ibn Pakuda; 360 regarding the appeal of Sufi brotherhoods for certain Jews.

11. See Scheindlin, "Merchants and Intellectuals," 346.

12. Grossman, *Pious and Rebellious*.

13. See, for example, Scheindlin, "Merchants and Intellectuals," 326.

14. See Mark R. Cohen, *Poverty and Charity in the Jewish Community of Medieval Egypt* (Princeton, NJ, 2005).

15. See Douglas Morton Dunlop, "Rhadanites," in *Encyclopedia Judaica*, 16 vols. (Jerusalem, 1971–1972).

16. For an overview, see Douglas Morton Dunlop, "Khazars," in *Encyclopedia Judaica*, 16 vols. (Jerusalem, 1971–1972). Among the growing literature, see the older work of Bernard D. Weinryb, "The Beginnings of East-European Jewry in Legend and Historiography," in *Studies and Essays in Honor of Abraham A. Neuman, President, Dropsie College for Hebrew and Cognate Learning, Philadelphia*, ed. Meir Ben-Horin, Bernard D. Weinryb, and Solomon Zeitlin (Leiden, Netherlands, 1962), 445–502; and the provocative work of Norman Golb as reflected in his "Exploring the Cairo Geniza for New Light on the History of the Jews of Medieval Europe," in *Cairo's Ben Ezra Synagogue: A Gateway to Medieval Mediterranean Life*, ed. Jacob Lassner (Chicago, 2001), 25–39.

2

Settlement and Demography

While demographic information is notoriously difficult to secure for pre-modern history, and all the more so for the history of the Jews since Jews did not often record the kinds of information about population that we would find helpful today, there are traces of information in travelogues, non-Jewish records (such as court, tax, and notarial documents), and even in various Jewish chronicles and communal ledgers. Grappling with Jewish demography in the early modern period is very difficult but extremely rewarding. Jewish settlement and migration patterns affected all aspects of Jewish existence, and the better we understand the various trends and developments the more sense we will be able to make of the Jewish history of this period. Drawing from a wide range of materials, this chapter sketches the key areas of Jewish settlement, presenting broad regional patterns as well as more detailed analyses of select individual Jewish communities.

EARLY MODERN JEWISH DEMOGRAPHY:
A GLOBAL PERSPECTIVE

Before we consider more specific examples of Jewish settlement, it is helpful to take a more global look. One traditional approach has been to divide Jewish population since the high Middle Ages between Jews who were **Ashkenazic** and Jews who were **Sephardic**. While the term Ashkenazic really refers to German Jews, it is also used more broadly to refer to the majority of Jews living in central and eastern, as well as parts of western, Europe. Sephardic Jews in this evaluation are from Spain and the entire Iberian peninsula, parts of Italy (especially the south), and the Ottoman

Empire. Many far-flung communities or settlements, such as those that existed at times in India, China, and the New World, were largely comprised of Sephardic Jews who were involved in international trade.

In the later Middle Ages the vast majority of Jews were Sephardic. Ashkenazic populations grew, however, while the number of Sephardic Jews either declined or remained stagnant in large part due to declining social and economic conditions and the waning of the Ottoman Empire by the end of the early modern period. By 1500 a third of the global Jewish population was Ashkenazic, a number that increased to half by 1700. After the eighteenth century, especially with the Jewish population explosion in eastern Europe and decline of Ottoman Jewry, Ashkenazic Jewry became ascendant (see table 2.1).

Jews were an extremely small minority in their host societies. Throughout the Middle Ages, large Jewish communities may have accounted for between 1 and 3 percent of the total population. One scholar estimates that Jews may have numbered around 1 percent of the total European population, or 450,000 out of forty-four million at the beginning of the fourteenth century.[1] In a society where a city of 10,000 inhabitants was enormous, one would not expect to find many large Jewish population concentrations. In fact, it is unlikely that the total Jewish population even reached 1 percent in medieval France, Italy, and the Holy Roman Empire. In Italy, for example, in 1300 there were approximately 50,000 Jews out of a total population of eleven million.

There were, however, some extremely large communities in the early modern period. Prague had 6,000 Jews in 1600 and over 11,500 by 1702, comprising almost 29 percent of the population. In the Ottoman Empire, Constantinople and Salonika each held an excess of 20,000 Jews in the middle of the sixteenth century. By the 1560s half of Safed's 10,000 people were Jewish.[2] In other areas absorbed by the Ottoman Empire large and long-standing Jewish populations could also be found. In Algiers, in North Africa, there were 8,000 to 9,000 Jews in 1600, a number that had at least doubled from a century before and that would increase by at least another quarter in the century to follow.[3] And while not of the same magnitude,

Table 2.1.   World Jewish Population: Sephardic and Ashkenazic

Date	Number of Jews (in millions)	Sephardic (percentage)	Ashkenazic (percentage)
1300	1.5	93	7
1500	1.5	67	23
1650	1.7	59	41
1700	2.0	50	50

Source: Raphael Patai, *Tents of Jacob: The Diaspora—Yesterday and Today* (New Jersey, 1971), 79.

Table 2.2. Jewish Population Centers with More Than 2,000 People

City (alphabetical)	Century
Adrianople (Edirne)	16
Alexandria	15
Algiers	16, 17
Amsterdam	17
Cairo	15, 16
Cracow (Cracow-Kazimierz)	16, 17
Crete (Candia)	17
Damascus	15, 16, 17
Ferrara	16
Fez	15, 16, 17
Frankfurt am Main	17
Istanbul	15, 16, 17
Lemberg (Lvov)	17
Lublin	17
Mantua	16
Messina	15
Palermo	15
Posen (Poznan)	16, 17
Prague	17
Rome	16, 17
Safed	16, 17
Salonika	16, 17
Seville	14
Smyrna (Izmir)	17
Toledo	14, 15
Venice	17

other Jewish communities were also significant in their size and influence. In Italy, Mantua and Ferrara were innovative cultural centers that had 2,000 Jews, perhaps as much as 20 percent of the total population. For a list of Jewish communities with at least 2,000 people during the early modern period, see map 2.1.

Major Population Shifts

The early modern period witnessed significant shifts in population in the West. Spain and Portugal, which boasted rather large Jewish populations throughout the later Middle Ages, expelled or converted their Jews, dislocating more than 150,000 Jews, many of whom traveled to Italy and then eventually on to the Ottoman Empire. The Italian Jewish population therefore swelled, at least temporarily, early in our period, even as the Iberian communities were drained. The migration is clear when we learn that there

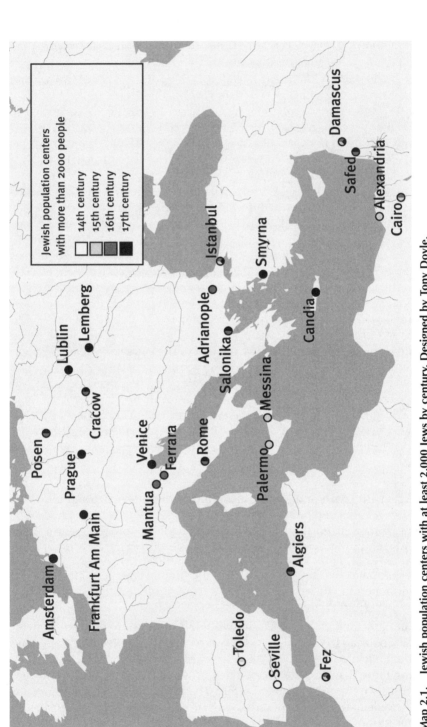

Map 2.1. Jewish population centers with at least 2,000 Jews by century. Designed by Tony Doyle.

were 2,500 to 3,000 Jewish families in Istanbul (previously Constantinople) before the Spanish expulsion, and 8,000 by 1553.

The settlement patterns in many regions could vary dramatically over time. In Italy, historians now isolate two major periods in the history of Jewish settlement. During the first phase, thousands of Jews settled throughout a vast region in the south. A second phase ensued in the sixteenth century in the wake of expulsions from Spain and Sicily. In this period, Jews became more intensively concentrated, particularly in major cities and especially in the north.[4] (See map 2.3.)

Much of central Europe maintained earlier medieval Jewish population levels, but the Jewish population in eastern Europe began to increase dramatically by 1500. Poland-Lithuania probably had 5,000 Jews in 1300, approximately 1 percent of the population. By 1490, however, that number had risen to 30,000, a full 3 percent of the total population, in about sixty different communities.[5] By 1575 there may have been between 120,000 and 150,000 Jews in Poland, out of a population of seven million.[6] (See table 2.3.) According to one estimate the Jewish population in Poland rose from 50,000 to 500,000 between 1501 and 1648.[7] Poland, therefore, may have accounted for 30 percent of world Jewry in the middle of the seventeenth century and 44 percent by the end of the eighteenth century.[8] Some have estimated that the Jewish population may have been a full 5 percent of the total Polish population by the middle of the seventeenth century. The proportion of Jews was particularly significant in the cities, where it may have been 10–15 percent in Poland and 20 percent in Lithuania.[9] In the sixteenth century Jews resided in 194 of 1,076 cities. By the middle of the seventeenth century that number had risen to 400.[10]

JEWISH POPULATION AND SETTLEMENT IN EUROPE

Iberia in the Fifteenth Century

The Jewish population of Iberia (Spain, Portugal, and Navarre) was large and culturally significant throughout the Middle Ages and into the early modern period. The Jews in medieval Iberia under Muslim rule had a remarkable cultural renaissance. Jews were numerous here, and in some

Table 2.3.	Major European Jewish Populations in 1600
Germany	35,000–40,000
Italy	25,000–35,000
Poland	approx. 150,000

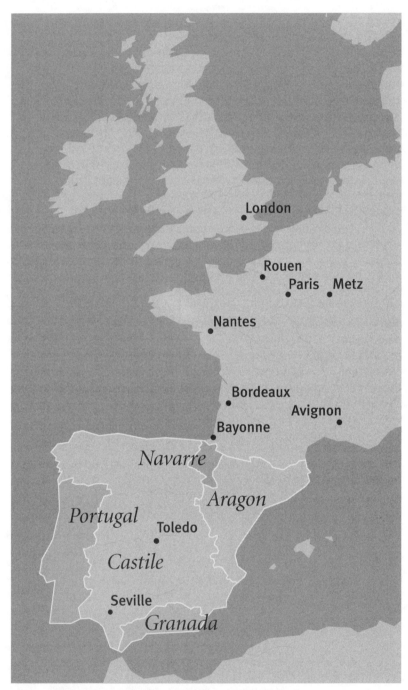

Map 2.2.   Spain and Western Europe. Designed by Tony Doyle.

towns may have constituted 6 to 20 percent of the population.[11] At the end of the thirteenth century there were about 3,600 Jewish families in Castile, or 20,000 individuals, a mere 0.4 percent of the total population. The population in Aragon was comparable but constituted a higher percentage (2 percent). Many large communities, such as Toledo, had only 200 to 400 Jewish families.[12]

There were increases in the first half of the fourteenth century, however, and in many cities with Jewish populations, Jews might have constituted more than 10 percent of the total population. In Avila and Tudela, for example, Jews may have comprised 30 percent of the population, with the total general population rarely exceeding 5,000 people.[13] Because population information is difficult to glean, the estimate of the Jewish population in Spain at the start of the fourteenth century ranges wildly but is generally taken to be around 150,000. The migration of Jews expelled from France at that time may have added significantly to the Jewish population in Spain.

In areas of Spain (as in Italy and France) it is likely that as much as 60 percent of the general population was decimated by the mid-fourteenth-century Black Death,[14] and the Jewish population clearly suffered from this devastation as well. Jews were affected by the plague and were also the targets of attacks by Christians, who either blamed the Jews for the plague or saw this as an opportunity to strip the Jews of their possessions. In some areas, such as the centralized states of Portugal and Navarre, the Jews appeared less vulnerable to such attacks.[15] In other places, however, large numbers of Jews were killed, even when there were attempts by some Jews to both reestablish their communities and secure the condemnation of anti-Jewish activities. In Valencia, for example, more than 250 Jews were killed and in Barcelona 400 in pogroms.[16]

While the scant information we possess might appear to suggest that certain Jewish population centers remained constant or even grew during the period of the plague, it now seems certain that such population statistics were more the result of migration from other areas where Jews were being persecuted. The number of Jewish households in Mallorca, for example, increased from 333 in 1343 to 516 in 1350. This was more than a 50 percent increase, at a time when Jews were dying from the plague and anti-Jewish attacks. The most likely explanation for such a population increase is that many survivors of attacks in Barcelona, Cervera, and Tarrega as well as other places sought refuge in Mallorca, swelling the Jewish population.[17] Besides decreasing the total Jewish population, the Black Death attacks also affected Jewish settlement, scattering the population in Castile and Aragon into smaller towns and more rural areas.

The Jewish population took another major hit at the end of the fourteenth century. In 1391 a wave of anti-Jewish massacres and campaigns decimated the Jewish population. Many Jews were killed and many more forcibly converted to Christianity. While some Jews reverted to Judaism within the next two decades, a large number remained Christians. After these forced conversions the large communities in cities like Seville, Toledo (which may have had more than 8,000 Jewish residents until a large massacre in 1368–1369), and Burgos declined, and much of Castilian Jewry was spread across smaller rural communities, often with less than fifty Jewish families each.[18]

The formation of Spain as a nation occurred in the early modern period. Late medieval Spain had been torn between two major and competing kingdoms, the crowns of Aragon and Castile. Aragon was a confederation of Catalonia, Valencia, and Aragon, independent territories that had their own laws and customs. Catalonia contained bustling seaports, and despite varying political and legal structures, the kingdom as a whole was rather mercantile and cosmopolitan. Castile, on the other hand, was more pastoral, and it was greatly affected by both the plague and the Reconquest. Here the Church exercised great authority. It was not until the 1469 union of Ferdinand and Isabella that the two crowns were effectively joined. (See map 2.2.)

Throughout the course of the fifteenth century, Jews and their communities faced many significant challenges. In the early fifteenth century, for example, the Jews of Saragossa were attacked after vicious sermons by a leading clergyman. While the community numbered approximately 200 Jewish families for most of the fifteenth century, the continuity was more the result of the ongoing migration of Jews from other parts of Spain.[19]

The expulsion from Spain at the end of the fifteenth century helped swell the ranks of Jewish communities in other places, such as Portugal and even Navarre, where the Jewish population of 3,550 taxpayers was 3.5 percent of the total population.[20] In Navarre a range of political developments, some international in scope, affected Jewish settlement.[21]

The majority of the 120,000 Jews living in Castile migrated to Portugal in 1492.[22] Perhaps 20,000 Andalusian Jews set out for North Africa, and quite a few, perhaps 12,000, reached Tlemcen, between Algeria and Morocco, though a quarter of those may have died from plague.[23] As many as 100,000 Spanish Jews converted to Christianity, joining the 30,000 *conversos* who had already converted earlier in the century.[24] During the first part of the early modern period, the Jewish settlement of Spain had gone through many and vast changes. What emerged was a large migration of Jews fleeing expulsion and persecution and the creation of an enormous pool of *conversos* (also known as New Christians, **Marranos**, or anusim), who would have a major impact on early modern Jewish history, even if they were not considered Jews by many in the Jewish world.

Italy

Jews have resided in Italy at least since the second century BCE. Despite various regional expulsions during the course of the Middle Ages and early modern period, the Jewish population was, at times, quite robust. (See map 2.3.) Throughout the high Middle Ages, southern Italian Jewish life predominated. In the early thirteenth century, under the culturally eclectic rule of Emperor Frederick II, there were probably 1,500 Jews each in Palermo, Apulia, and Campania. The famous Rabbi Obadiah of Bertinoro, in his travel letters of the late fifteenth century, noted some 850 Jewish families in Palermo and 400 in Messina.[25]

At the end of the fifteenth century as many as 40,000 Jews were expelled from Sicily and Sardinia, which were under Spanish domination (a fate repeated in Naples at the very beginning of the sixteenth century).[26] As a result, after the beginning of the sixteenth century, Jewish settlement in Italy shifted north to important urban areas. Throughout the early modern period the Jewish community in Rome remained large and important. Let's examine the situation first in Rome and then in some of the major northern communities, such as Venice.

Perhaps the most central and longest-standing Jewish community in Italy was the one found in Rome. While the Roman Jewish population was in decline, the community was buoyed by the infusion of immigrant Jews. Immigration came typically from other parts of Italy at times of various regional expulsions.[27] By the end of the first quarter of the sixteenth century, there were 373 Jewish families, or more than 1,770 Jews, living in Rome, constituting more than 3 percent of the total population, a proportion that kept pace with the dramatic general population increases in Rome at the time. By century's end, with almost 117,000 people in the city, there were more than 3,500 Jews.[28] The average Jewish household size was 4.77.

The history of Jewish settlement in Venice underlines the development of one type of Jewish community in early modern Italy. Jews were first mentioned in Venice at the end of the eleventh century. There was significant immigration of Jews from the Levant and from Germany in the thirteenth century, and Jews were tolerated to some degree for their commercial and moneylending work. There were, however, many restrictions on Jews, especially for those residing in the city and to some extent even in Venetian territories. At the end of the fourteenth century Jews had to wear special badges and, later in the fifteenth century, hats of various color. Throughout the later fifteenth century they were the subject of often virulent anti-Jewish sermons. Throughout the sixteenth century there were attempts to expel the Jews of Venice. The Jews, however, managed to survive such decrees. By the middle of the sixteenth century there were 900 Jews out of a population of more than 150,000 who were involved in various mercantile enterprises. By

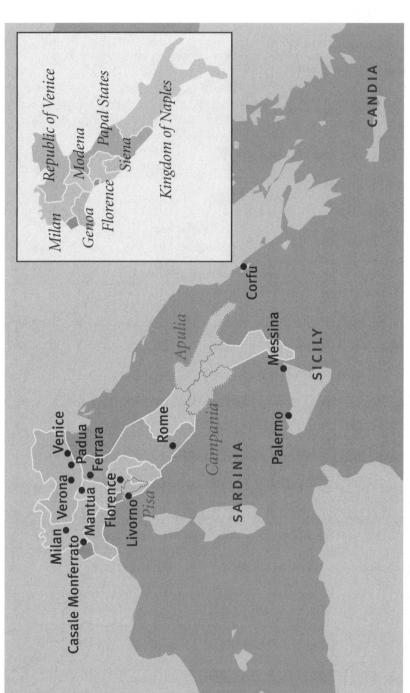

Map 2.3. Italy. Designed by Tony Doyle.

the middle of the seventeenth century that number had grown dramatically to 4,800 (although the general population remained steady at 150,000).[29]

The Venetian Jewish population by the beginning of the seventeenth century was rather diverse, constituted by three different nations of Ashkenazic, Ponentine, and Levantine Jews. The situation had been further muddied with the arrival of Jews and Marranos after the Spanish expulsion. In 1516 the Jews of Venice were segregated in a special ghetto. The ghetto, which was extremely congested, had been expanded to include an "old" ghetto in 1541 and a "newest" ghetto in 1633–1636; each of these expansions developed around the various national backgrounds of the multiethnic Jewish community.

There were other significant northern Italian Jewish population centers as well. Bologna, for example, had between 800 and 900 Jews; Padua and Casale Monferrato had 600–700 each; Florence had 500; and Verona, which left some very valuable communal documents from this period, had 400.

Outside of the major cities, Italian Jewish population was regional and often quite complex. Here we consider the examples of the Duchy of Milan and the cities of Pisa and Livorno. In the sixteenth century in the Duchy of Milan, Jews settled in towns that were the centers of economic life for the surrounding villages.[30] Because they were banned from settling in the capital city of Milan, Jews settled in a ring of outlying suburbs and smaller cities in order to remain keyed in to the commercial activity of the city. When, in 1566, Jews were forbidden to lend money, Jewish settlement patterns apparently began to shift, especially as Jewish bankers looked to migrate from the Duchy. The small outlying Jewish settlements eventually dissolved, with Jews remaining in four main communities, as well as two smaller communities.

Pisa and Livorno were among the most densely settled Jewish centers in Tuscany, an area where Jews constituted 1.25 percent of the total population and were dispersed in some two dozen small settlements in the last quarter of the sixteenth century. There were ninety-four Jews in Pisa by the last quarter of the sixteenth century,[31] but that number increased dramatically to 500 by 1615, before declining throughout the first half of the seventeenth century.[32]

In Livorno (Leghorn), the development of the Jewish settlement mirrored that of the general society. The newly formed Livorno Jewish community had 134 Jews after the first decade of the seventeenth century and 711 by 1622, comprising 10 percent of the population. The population continued to grow during the seventeenth century.[33]

Caught between Italian expansion, waning Byzantine authority, and growing Turkish invasions, there were few Italian-dominated Balkan and Greek Jewish communities of any great size. One exception was Candia (Crete), which in 1627 boasted something like 600 Jewish families, or 2,500 to 3,000 Jews.[34] Corfu, in the early sixteenth century under Venetian

Table 2.4.   Jewish Populations in Pisa and Livorno

Pisa		Livorno	
Year	Population	Year	Population
1570	94	1610	134
1613	441	1622	711
1615	500	1642	1,145
1632	357	1645	1,250
1643	341	1738	3,476

rule, may have had 200 or 300 Jewish families, but this was out of a population of some 40,000 people.[35] The island of Zante, occupied by Venice in 1482, also had a little more than 200 Jews in the first quarter of the sixteenth century.[36]

The Jewish settlement in Italy reflected the influence of foreign politics and internal Italian territorial divisions. The early modern shift of the Jewish population to the north led to concentrated settlement in some major cities as well as regional areas in central and northern Italy. The total number of Jews did not increase dramatically in the early modern period, despite short-term spikes with the migration of Spanish Jews eastward. Nevertheless, Italian Jewry was a culturally rich population that affected early modern Jewish life and many corners of the non-Jewish world as well as through Jewish participation in trade, the arts, and science.

Germany

The first solid evidence of Jewish settlement in Germany comes from the early Middle Ages. By the beginning of the fourteenth century, German Jewry was of notable size. (See map 2.4.) The Black Death persecutions of the middle fourteenth century, however, played havoc with the Jewish settlement patterns in Germany and stunted what might have been greater growth. Only in the southeast—Bohemia, Moravia, Styria, Slovenia, and Austria, though apparently not for lack of outbreaks of the plague[37]—did Jewish settlement continue uninterrupted through the mid-fourteenth-century pogroms. Some scholars have argued recently, and rather convincingly, that the number of Jews killed has been overestimated. Many Jews were forced to leave their home towns, but often they settled in close-by areas and in many cases were allowed to return several years later, even if under more disadvantaged conditions. In all, something like 240 Jewish settlements were re-established by century's end.

Nonetheless, it remains clear that new Jewish settlement was stymied after this period. Of the settlements mentioned in the sources between 1350 and 1519, half had already existed before 1250. It was primarily in the

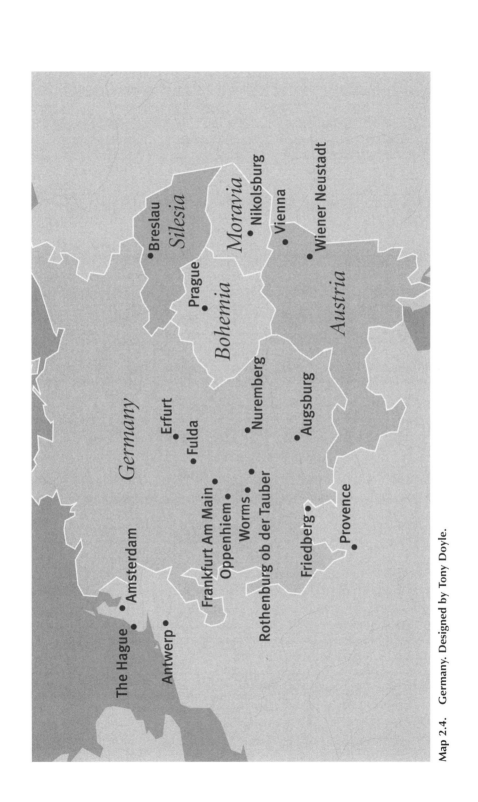

Map 2.4. Germany. Designed by Tony Doyle.

southwest that there was a substantial number of new Jewish communities formed after 1350.

In the later Middle Ages, the largest Jewish populations were in the cities of Regensburg and Prague, which at different times may have been home to 600 Jews. Smaller, but still significant, communities of over 300 Jews could be found in Augsburg, Breslau, Erfurt, Nuremberg, Oppenheim, Rothenburg ob der Tauber, and Wiener Neustadt, though most of these communities were expelled before the end of the fifteenth century. There also existed some smaller communities of up to 300 Jews spread across Germany. The largest concentration of Jewish settlements in Germany was in the center, south center, and east. Almost a third of the total settlements could be found in the older settlement areas of Thuringia, Hesse, Franconia, and Upper Palatinate.

By the beginning of the seventeenth century, the Jewish population was still only 35,000–40,000 people (0.2 percent of the total population). An important portion of the Jewish population was in the southeast, especially in Prague, but later in the century in Vienna, Nikolsburg, and Schnaittach as well, accounting for more than a third of the German Jewish population. In the northeast and the north, the Jewish population remained restricted. Despite some population increases related to participation in regional trading fairs, there were several massive expulsions at the end of the fifteenth and sixteenth centuries. Nonetheless, some new communities did develop in the north and northwest during the seventeenth century, where older restrictions were lifted or where economic development promoted Jewish settlement. The Jewish communities in and around Hamburg, for example, grew dramatically during the seventeenth century. Central Germany remained a most important population center for Jews, with probably more than a third of all German Jews residing there. Frankfurt am Main, Worms, Friedberg, and Fulda all boasted important Jewish communities throughout the early modern period. A small, but burgeoning, southwest Jewish population began to form during the sixteenth century, with a large number of village communities throughout the seventeenth century and forward.

By the end of the Thirty Years' War in 1648 there were some 60,000 Jews out of a total imperial population of around twenty million.[38] Jews remained excluded from many areas, and there were new expulsions, most notably from Lower Austria in 1670. In addition to generally consistent populations in the southeast and center of Germany, the northeast Jewish populations grew considerably, setting the stage for very significant Prussian growth during the course of the eighteenth century.

Let's examine Jewish settlement in one of the more significant German Jewish communities, Frankfurt am Main. (See figure 2.1.) In the eleventh century there had been mention of Jews conducting trade in Frankfurt am Main. Throughout the Middle Ages the fate of the Jews ebbed and flowed,

Figure 2.1. Frankfurt. Ballino-Zalti, 1567. From the Muriel Yale Collection of Rare and Antique Maps of the Holy Land and Ottoman Empire of the Asher Library, Spertus Institute of Jewish Studies.

Table 2.5. **Frankfurt am Main Jewish Population**

Year	Population
1463	110
1520	250
1569	900
1580	1,200
1600	2,200
1610	3,000

and bustling business was cut short by pogroms, massacres, and expulsions. Three-quarters of the 200 Jews resident in 1241 were massacred and Jewish houses demolished. The community redeveloped, was wiped out during the Black Death massacres, and re-formed again in 1360. The Jewish population in Frankfurt grew significantly from the middle of the fifteenth century until 1610, just before the Fettmilch uprising (1614), when the Jews represented more than 10 percent of the total city population. In many ways, the fate of the Jews and the population growth mirrored the more general blossoming of the city as a regional trading center. (See table 2.5.)

The German Jewish population was amongst the largest in early modern Europe. Many medieval settlement patterns remained in force in the early modern period, even as Jews began to settle in new areas in the north and in more rural settings in the southwest. There were some very important Jewish population centers in early modern Germany, but most of German Jewry was spread across central Europe in small to middle-sized communities that frequently formed regional associations.

The Netherlands

While it is known that there had been modest Jewish presence and developments in the Netherlands throughout the high and late Middle Ages, there is very limited information about Jewish settlement in the Netherlands until the sixteenth century, when some significant communities, especially of converted Jews returning to Judaism, began to develop, first in Antwerp and then, in the seventeenth century, in Amsterdam.

Portuguese Jews, or Marranos, settled in Antwerp and developed brisk business in the sixteenth century. They were accorded various privileges, and despite an edict of expulsion and the emigration of most of the Marranos, a small community of Portuguese Jews remained. In 1571 there were eighty-five Jewish families and seventeen bachelors; by 1666 there were still sixty-five bachelors listed.[39]

Within the political complexities that pitted the northern provinces of the Netherlands against Spain, many Jews were attracted to Amsterdam, where there was some degree of real religious liberty, as long as religious practices were kept private. In the early seventeenth century a small group of Sephardic Jews settled in Amsterdam, and under the direction of a German rabbi, Uri ha-Levi from Emden, developed a small community. By 1607 there was a congregation (Beth Jacob) of some fifteen Jews at the home of the prominent Jew Jacob Tirado. A second congregation (Neveh Shalom) was established in 1608 with Isaac Uziel serving as rabbi. Ashkenazic Jews settled in Amsterdam in the 1620s. They developed at a much slower rate and were largely poor and dependent upon the Sephardic Jews. After midcentury the number of Ashkenazic Jews began to grow dramatically. Polish Jews formed a separate community with their own congregation and customs.

Until after the middle of the seventeenth century, more Portuguese Jews in Amsterdam had been born in foreign lands than in the Netherlands, with particularly large groups from certain areas in Portugal and Spain, but also from Venice and Livorno in Italy, and parts of eastern France. By 1639 the community was hard to miss, with some 1,000 members. By 1650 the combined Sephardic and Ashkenazic population was around 3,000; by the early eighteenth century that number doubled but was becoming more significantly Ashkenazic. In the last quarter of the seventeenth century, Jews made up close to 4 percent of the population, making Amsterdam one of the largest and most important Jewish communities in Europe. At the end of the seventeenth and the beginning of the eighteenth century, other Jewish communities developed. In The Hague, for example, the first synagogue was consecrated in 1698.

The influence of Amsterdam Jews was global. Many were involved in international trade and in Dutch expansion in the New World. Amsterdam Jews maintained close contact with other leading Jewish communities in Europe and were steeped in a complex religious and political environment.

England and France

While not huge in total numbers, Jews remained in England and in France at various times during the early modern period despite medieval expulsions and ongoing settlement restrictions. In the thirteenth century there was a significant and vibrant Jewish population in England. It has been estimated that some 16,000 Jews were expelled from there in 1290. Although Jews were officially banned from England, there were pockets of Marranos during the early modern period, though even that small group was wracked by internal dissension and began to decline at the end of the sixteenth century.[40] A variety of factors, including increasing philo-semitism, political transformation, religious radicalism, and economic development, came together to create an atmosphere of possible readmission for the Jews in the middle of the seventeenth century. While Menasseh ben Israel (see chapter 5) is among the best-known personalities to advocate for the Jews' return in the middle of the seventeenth century, readmission was not a foregone conclusion or easily achieved. Indeed, Menasseh did not himself live to see the actual fruits of his labors, as the Jews were admitted a year after his death. At the very end of 1656, a house was rented in London for use as a synagogue, and slowly other components of a community were secured, setting the groundwork for the Jewish community to develop. It was initially a community of Portuguese Jews, very similar to and connected with the communities in Hamburg and Amsterdam. Marranos from Amsterdam, Hamburg, Livorno, and southern France began to assemble in London, which possessed some thirty-five heads of house by 1660. The community set roots and by 1663 had drafted its own ordinances (*ascamot*), based on those in Amsterdam and Venice.

The Jewish population in France in the thirteenth century hovered around 50,000 and was nearly 100,000 at the time of the early fourteenth-century expulsion, according to one estimate.[41] But that number was radically reduced with the expulsion and, during the course of the fourteenth century, after numerous political consolidations, additional expulsions, and attacks. In 1350 Jews were reauthorized to live in the kingdom, this time for a period of twenty years.[42] Despite generous privileges and the extension of this settlement permission, few Jews returned since they appeared to have opportunities for settlement only outside the confines of lands supervised directly by the king. The once thriving settlement of Jews in Provence, for example, was expelled in 1498, less than twenty years after royal annexation.[43] Indeed, throughout the royal domains very little Jewish settlement survived into the sixteenth century.[44] Some Jewish settlements continued, especially in Comtat Venaissin and Avignon.[45] In 1358, for example, there may have been 1,000 Jews living in Avignon under the authority of the popes.[46] The population of such papal Jews, however, never exceeded 2,500–3,000, and after 1569–1570, despite a failed expulsion attempt, many Jews left the area.[47]

A population of Jews also developed further east in the city of Metz at the end of the sixteenth century and in Lorraine. The Metz Jewish population grew from twenty households in 1595 to 480, or 1,900 individuals, by 1717 (out of a total population of 26,516).[48] (See table 2.6.)

Table 2.6.   Metz Jewish Population

Year	Population
1595	82
1637	350
1717	1,900

Throughout the seventeenth century a few small Jewish settlements were authorized in Lorraine, but they were generally the object of hostile reactions and dismantled quickly. By the 1720s, however, seventy-three families were authorized to remain in the Duchy, providing the base for an important development during the eighteenth century.[49] Jews also resided in nearby Alsace, which was under German rule for much of the early modern period.

There were also some significant pockets of Marranos in the New World possessions of the French crown (though "Jews" were not officially tolerated) and in Bordeaux,[50] where "Portuguese" merchants settled important enclaves. In late 1684, ninety-three Portuguese Jewish families in Bordeaux, from among the several hundred, deemed not useful to French commerce were ordered to leave within one month.[51] Small Portuguese Jewish population centers also existed in other parts of France, notably in Bayonne, Labastide, Peyrehorade, Dex, Rouen, and Paris, as well as in Nantes.[52] On the eve of the French Revolution there were still approximately 40,000 Jews living in France, despite formal prohibitions.[53]

The Jewish and Marrano communities in early modern England and France were small but involved in broader international concerns. French Jews were involved in important continental and international trade. The debate over readmission of the Jews in England was much discussed across Europe and had a variety of religious, political, and economic implications.

Poland

By the end of the early modern period, Polish Jews had become the most populous in Europe and perhaps in the world. The Jewish settlement in Poland was naturally affected by general political conditions, and we begin here with a review of Polish development in the early modern period. Various and previously divided territories, including Silesia (west), Great Poland (north), Little Poland (south), and Mazovia (east), were reunited by the last Piast dynasty ruler Casimir III (Casimir the Great) in the middle of the fourteenth century. In 1569 Poland was united with Lithuania to form a large and ambitious commonwealth that also included the Ukraine.[54]

The Polish state was extremely heterogeneous. Various ethnic and religious groups coexisted, often quite peacefully, in an environment that has been seen as rather tolerant. Six different languages—Latin, Polish, German, Russian, Hebrew, and Armenian—were used in official documents and, until the Catholic Reformation's closing of ranks in the seventeenth century, several Christian denominations, as well as Judaism and Islam, seem to have been fairly well tolerated.[55] While much of Poland was rural well into the sixteenth century, Jews seem to have settled in urban areas, certainly in the

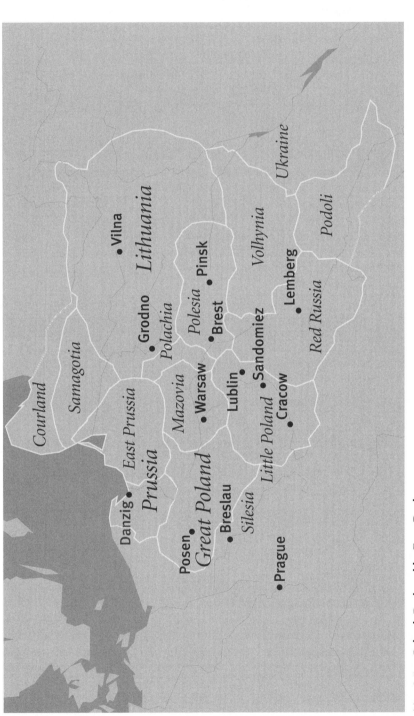

Map 2.5. Poland. Designed by Tony Doyle.

early phases of Polish Jewry; rural Jewry expanded more dramatically after the persecutions of the mid-seventeenth century.[56] In time, Jewish settlement was explained and seen almost as divinely ordained, since *po lin* in Hebrew meant literally "here rest,"[57] an apparent divine directive for Jewish settlement in Poland.

The earliest record we have of a Jew in Poland comes from the early eleventh century.[58] Jewish migration to and development within Poland grew during the high and later Middle Ages, and in the fourteenth century there was a significant increase of Jewish settlements. In the border area between Poland and Germany, in Silesia, the number of Jewish settlements grew from seven in the thirteenth to thirty-two in the fourteenth century. Fourteenth-century Breslau may have had between 130 and 140 Jewish heads of house.[59] There were communities in Cracow and possibly also Posen (Poznan), Sandomierz, Lemberg (Lvov), Brest-Litovsk, and perhaps Warsaw as well.[60] In the fourteenth century, Jewish cemeteries could be found near Sandomierz and Cracow,[61] marking these communities as important regional centers.

Late medieval population setbacks due to pogroms and anti-Jewish inflammatory preaching led to periodically tenuous Jewish settlement. However, steady streams of immigration from German-speaking lands due to city and regional expulsions fed the Jewish population numbers in Poland. While there is not a great deal of evidence to fill out the details of this migration, there are some indications of the trend eastwards: in evidence of individual Jewish settlements,[62] letters of privilege, and the derivation of German place names for Jews listed in communal or tax records. The Jewish settlement of Poland seems to have taken more extensive root during the fifteenth century. Before that time there are records of Jewish residence in nine or ten locations (not counting Silesia); in the fifteenth century that number ballooned to sixty-three and further to 198 in the sixteenth century.[63] Once established, general toleration, professional opportunity, and natural growth also helped the Polish Jewish community to increase.[64]

It should be noted that Jews also migrated into western Europe from Poland, especially during and after the latter half of the seventeenth century.[65] This migration was due to worsening economic conditions and persecution in Poland and burgeoning opportunities in the West, where some governments were beginning to be more receptive to Jews, such as in Brandenburg.[66] While large numbers of Jews settled, even if temporarily, in border towns such as Danzig, where there may have been 400–500 Polish Jews, many others migrated further into western Europe and even the New World.[67] Due to persecutions, many Jews in the area around Posen petitioned for entrance into Silesia in the 1650s, which by the end of the century possessed a large Polish population.[68] In late seventeenth-century Moravia, almost 20 percent of the Jews were immigrants from Poland,[69] and many Polish Jews made their way to Hamburg and Amsterdam. While not always received positively by the non-Jewish civic authorities or even the Jewish communities themselves, in many cases these Polish Jews established a significant presence and many large communities.[70] Polish Jews scattered across Germany, with the largest concentrations in Prussia.[71]

During the fifteenth century most Jews lived in western Poland, dispersed in forty different locales, with large populations in Cracow, Posen, and Lemberg.[72] In the sixteenth century migration moved to the east, especially into Red Russia (Galicia). Eventually, by the mid-eighteenth century, two-thirds of Poland's Jews were settled in the east,[73] population growth having been fueled by expulsions and persecutions in the west and new economic opportunities in the east.

Based on tax payments, scholars have presented a wide range of population statistics for the middle sixteenth century—from 100,000 to 300,000, depending on how many people one counts per tax amount paid.[74] Most scholars seem to agree that there were 450,000 Jews in the Polish-Lithuanian Commonwealth in the middle of the seventeenth century. Some have maintained that as many as 180,000 Jews died in the mid-seventeenth-century massacres,[75] so that by the last quarter of the century, estimates range from 180,000 to 350,000,[76] accounting for perhaps a third of the total world Jewish population. The most extensive population growth took place in eastern and southeastern regions of Poland-Lithuania.

As in Germany, Jewish population in individual towns could range from one or two to several dozen families.[77] Because of various settlement restrictions, Jewish population centers spread along major economic corridors. Some cities were particularly large. In 1570 on the outskirts of Lublin there were 1,035 Jews (20 percent of the total population) and by 1602, 2,000.[78] Kazimierz, in extreme southern Cracow, and Lemberg each grew rapidly at the end of the sixteenth and the beginning of the seventeenth century, and each had more than 4,500 Jews by the middle of the seventeenth century (the former more than 2,000 by the last quarter of the sixteenth century).[79] Kazimierz survived tension-filled internal community strife to become a major Jewish center. In the last quarter of the century it is estimated that 1,000 Jews in Kazimierz died of the plague, however, leading to the abandonment of the Jewish quarter by most inhabitants.[80] In Lemberg, two communities emerged on either side of the city walls. Inside the walls, 352 Jews lived in twenty-nine houses, while 559 Jews lived in fifty-two houses outside the walls by the middle of the sixteenth century.[81]

In some cases there were complex ties between communities. After facing forced conversion or expulsion at the end of the fifteenth century, Jews were allowed to return to Brest-Litovsk in 1503. By 1566 there were 156 Jewish-owned houses, approximately 20 percent of the total in the city. Many Jews were heavily involved in trade but some even in agriculture. Some 16 percent of the real estate was owned by Jews. Despite various attacks and hardships during the seventeenth century, there were still 525 Jews (not counting children under eleven) in the city in 1676.[82] A dozen Jewish families (60–75 Jews) from Brest-Litovsk established the Jewish community in Pinsk (Belarus) in 1506, when they chose to settle there rather than return to Lithuania after Jews were allowed to return from the expulsion[83] (ironically Pinsk was incorporated into Lithuania some fifteen years later). By 1566 there were more than 275 Jews, or 7 percent of the total city population. That number grew to 1,000 (20 percent) by the middle of the seventeenth century, before many thousands of Jews were murdered during the Chmielnicki massacres (see chapter 5).

There were a number of other significant Jewish population centers in early modern Poland. Consider Grodno and Posen, for example. The Jewish population in Grodno, in Belarus, accounted for 17 percent of the total city population by the middle of the sixteenth century. In 1560 there may have been 1,000 Jews in Grodno, and by the end of the eighteenth century it was the largest Jewish population in Lithuania behind Vilna.[84] Posen, later partitioned into Prussia, was also a great center of Polish Jewry. The western Polish city possessed 3,000 Jews, a full 10 percent of the total city population, and 137 Jewish houses by the end of the sixteenth century.[85] Despite total population decreases during the course of the seventeenth century, the proportion of Jews to non-Jews in the city actually increased to 15 percent as the general city population decreased.[86]

By the end of the early modern period, Poland was home to a large and vibrant Jewish population, with many influential centers that would help to fashion modern Jewish identity. (See table 2.7.)

Table 2.7. Jewish Populations in Select Polish Cities

City	Early Modern Population Peak
Cracow-Kazimierz	4,500
Lemberg	4,500
Posen	3,000 (10–15% of city total)
Grodno	1,000 (17%)
Lublin	2,000 (20%)
Pinsk	1,000 (20%)
Brest-Litovsk	525 (20%)

JEWISH POPULATION AND SETTLEMENT IN THE OTTOMAN EMPIRE AND THE ISLAMIC LANDS

The Ottoman Empire

The Jewish population and settlement of the Ottoman Empire was complex. (See map 2.6.) In part this complexity was due to the widespread settlement patterns and relations that had existed before the Ottoman state formed. Jews throughout Anatolia and the Balkans, for example, were primarily Greek-speakers, and they maintained their own unique Jewish identities and customs. Some of the Jewish populations that would be subsumed under Ottoman rule were quite large. Under the Mamelukes, whom the Ottomans later displaced in many regions in the Middle East, there may have been 40,000 Jews each in Egypt and Syria according to some estimates.[87] A late fifteenth-century traveler, for example, estimated around 5,000 Jews in Fustat-Cairo alone.[88]

In part, however, the complexity of Ottoman Jewish settlement was also determined by Ottoman political and religious policy. The addition of Ashkenazic and Sephardic Jews from Europe during the course of the fifteenth and sixteenth centuries combined with various Ottoman settlement policies and led to diverse and heterogeneous Jewish communities. Some of these communities were quite large by early modern standards, when a very large city might have no more than 10,000 inhabitants.

Ottoman Jewry through much of the early modern period was not only diverse but also very large and extremely significant. The seventeenth-century Venetian scholar, Rabbi Simhah Luzatto noted, "The main center of the [Jewish] nation is in the land of the Turkish sultan, not merely because Jews have always been dwelling there but also because Jewish émigrés from Spain hastened there."[89]

The Ottomans were famous for their policies of forced movement of people. *Sürgün*, exiling or resettling, is at its root a term for exile, persecution, and expulsion. However, in practice, the term reflected a process that could be utilized for punishment of crimes as well as a method for colonizing or resettling conquered areas within the Empire.[90] The process, or at least the result of the process, was described rather positively by the Jewish historian Elijah Capsali, who wrote,

> The Jews gathered together from all the cities of Turkey, both far and near, each person coming from his own place, and the community gathered in Constantinople in its thousands and its tens of thousands. The heavens helped them, too, and the king provided them perfect estates and houses filled with all kinds of goodness. The Jews resided there with their families and their clans; they were fruitful and swarmed and multiplied, and the land was full of them. From that day on, whenever the king conquered a place where there were Jews, he

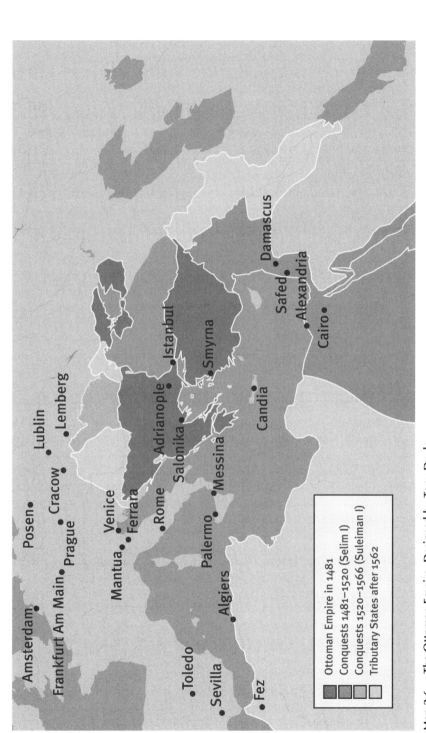

Map 2.6. The Ottoman Empire. Designed by Tony Doyle.

Ottoman Empire in 1481
Conquests 1481–1520 (Selim I)
Conquests 1520–1566 (Suleiman I)
Tributary States after 1562

would immediately shake them up and drive them from there—and dispatch them to Constantinople, the seat of his kingdom, and he would pick them up and cuddle them for ever. Now, since the Jews feared the Lord, he provided them with houses filled with all kinds of goodness in a place where formerly, at the time of the King of Byzantium, there were only two or three congregations, the Jews increased in numbers, becoming a people with more than communities, for the land could not support them altogether—for their property was overwhelming.[91]

As this passage hints, the Ottoman authorities redrew the boundaries and scope of Jewish communities, making a tremendous impact on the governance of the Jewish communities themselves. Such changes were not limited to the capital of Istanbul (Constantinople; see figure 2.2), as there were times of other forced, and significant, migrations within the Empire. In 1522, for example, some 150 Jewish families were exiled from Salonika and resettled in Rhodes.[92] After the Ottoman defeat of Belgrade in 1521 and Buda in 1524, thousands of Jews from these areas were resettled throughout the Empire, especially in Edirne, Izmir, Salonika, as well as Istanbul.[93] In October of 1576, an order was given for a thousand "rich and prosperous" Jews from Safed to be relocated to the city of Famagusta in Cyprus. Within about a year and half the order had been revoked.[94]

A German traveler from the mid-sixteenth century, Hans Dernschwam, described his experiences in the Ottoman Empire. He included some observations about the Jews, writing,

You will find in every town innumerable Jews of all countries and languages. And every Jewish group sticks together in accordance with its language. And wherever Jews have been expelled in any land they all come together in Turkey as thick as vermin; speak German, Italian, Spanish, Portuguese, French, Czechish, Polish, Greek, Turkish, Syriac, Chaldean, and other languages besides these.[95]

In Constantinople (Istanbul), in particular, he wrote that the Jews were thick "as ants" and that there were more than twice as many Jews as Christians— over 15,000 Jewish men alone. He noted that there were forty-two or more synagogues in Constantinople, divided by nationality.[96] Of Salonika, he wrote that there were more Jews even than in Constantinople, around 20,000.[97] Still, Dernschwam seems to have taken some consolation in the fact that "the Jews are despised in Turkey as they are anywhere else; possess no estates although many own their own homes."[98]

Dernschwam was not mistaken. Salonika and Istanbul had developed into major Jewish population centers. By 1519 there were 3,143 Jewish households and 930 tax-paying bachelors in Salonika, together comprising more than half of the total city population.[99] In 1477 there were 1,647 Jewish households in Istanbul, something akin to 11 percent of the total number of

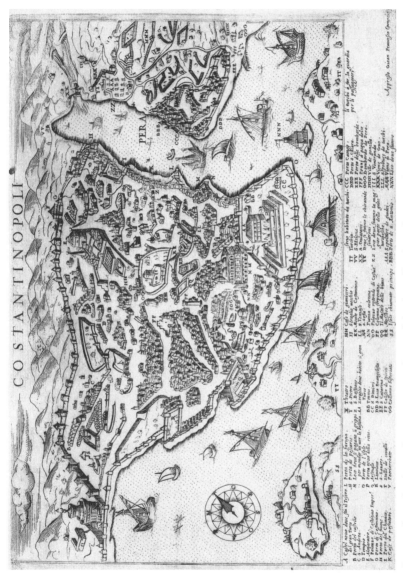

Figure 2.2. Constantinopole. Camocio, 1572. From the Muriel Yale Collection of Rare and Antique Maps of the Holy Land and Ottoman Empire of the Asher Library, Spertus Institute of Jewish Studies.

city households (probably the same percentage as in 1520–1530, when there were 1,647 Jewish households compared with 5,162 Christian and 9,517 Muslim).[100] In 1540 that number had actually decreased to 1,522, though it still constituted an immense Jewish community.

Ottoman expansion in the Middle East during the second decade of the sixteenth century had far-reaching consequences for Jewish population in those areas. While some have suggested that a third of the 300,000 residents of Israel were Jewish in the sixteenth century, it is difficult to confirm the veracity of this assertion.[101] In any event, during the course of the sixteenth century some large Jewish settlements did evolve, with Jews traversing to the Holy Land for a host of reasons—some religious, some related to business or personal matters, and some the result of the massive Spanish expulsion that seemed to usher in a messianic opportunity.

Ottoman governance of Israel led to the establishment of four (and later five) primary administrative districts—Jerusalem, Gaza, Nablus, and Safed.[102] While many districts were relatively small in size, they could be rather complex in ethnic makeup, with Jews from North Africa, Provence, and Syria, for example. In some districts, Jewish population was centered in key cities; in others it was spread across various rural areas. In the district of Safed, for example, Jews settled in the city as well as in surrounding villages, which often served as places of refuge during times of persecution and pestilence.

The Jewish population in Jerusalem underwent growth with the Ottoman conquest. According to Ottoman registers, the 199 Jewish households of 1525/1526 grew to 224 by 1538/1539, 324 by 1553/1554, and corresponding to the developments in much of Israel, had shrunk again to 237 by 1562/1563.[103] In sixteenth-century Jerusalem there were six different communities, the most visible being those of the Ashkenazim, Sephardim, Musta'rab, and North Africans (there were also settlements of Ethiopians and Karaites).[104]

There were other significant population centers in the ever-expanding Ottoman Empire. In Damascus by the middle of the sixteenth century there were 503 Jewish households, and in Buda in Hungary there were 122 Jewish households in 1562/1563. Throughout the early sixteenth century there was a significant Jewish settlement in the southern Balkans and western Anatolia. The historian Avigdor Levy notes seven major Jewish centers: Patras (252 Jewish households); Thebes (126); Trikkala (181); Edirne (231 and later growing by 1568/1569 to 553); Valona (528, but declining sharply); Bursa (117; also with dramatic increases by 1571/1572); and Rhodes (144).[105] There were also more than twenty other towns with Jewish populations of between twenty-one and ninety-one households.[106] Cultural prominence was still held in Aleppo, Baghdad, Cairo, Alexandria (which, according to the late fifteenth-century traveler Rabbi Meshullam ben Rabbi Menahem of

Volterra, included 4,000 Jewish householders; though another traveler, Berti-noro, noted only twenty-five families and two old synagogues),[107] and Rashid.[108] Baghdad had, indeed, been home to an enormous Jewish popu-lation in the Middle Ages. In the middle of the thirteenth century there were 36,000 Jews in the city, with sixteen different synagogues.[109]

Jewish settlement in Ottoman lands was complex, depending as it did on existing, pre-Ottoman conditions and the political maneuvers of the Ot-toman state. Throughout most of the early modern period, Jews living un-der Islamic Ottoman suzerainty comprised the largest portion of world Jewry. These Jews lived in a multivalent world and maintained some im-portant contact with European Jews. Letters from the Ottoman Empire en-couraged Jewish co-religionists in Europe to make their way East. Already in a letter from the late fifteenth century, one such writer addressed "the Ashkenazic communities in Schwaben and the Rhine Valley, Steiermark, Moravia, and Hungary to tell them of the goodness of this land [Turkey]."[110]

North Africa

North Africa had a long and rich, if at times complicated, history of Jewish settlement. Many Jews immigrated to North Africa during the ter-rible persecutions of 1391 in Spain. One example was the important *ha-lakhic* scholar, Rabbi Isaac ben Sheshet Perfet, known as Ribash. Ribash was born in Barcelona in 1326. There he studied with leading rabbinic au-thorities. In 1370 he was arrested under false charges. After his release he moved to Saragossa and then in 1385 to Valencia. In 1391 he made his way to Algiers, although some residents there refused refuge to Spanish emigrants. In the end, some 30,000 Jews of various backgrounds may have settled in North Africa.[111]

There were some very large Jewish communities in North Africa. In Al-giers, for example, Jewish population estimates range from 1,000 to 5,000 out of a population of 60,000–100,000 in the sixteenth century. In the sev-enteenth century that number seems to have grown to 8,000–9,000 and even 10,000–12,000 by the end of the century.[112] Fez in Morocco was also a bustling Jewish center, where in the early seventeenth century, one chron-icler writes that 10,000 Jews, mostly expelled from Spain, occupied the *mel-lah* (Jewish quarter).[113] One Christian correspondent living in Fez noted that the city contained 50,000 residents, 4,000 of them Jews who lived in their own walled-in quarter.[114] As in other Islamic lands, the Jewish popu-lation was very diverse, containing Berber Jews, Arabic-speaking Jews, Span-ish Jews from Castile and Aragon, Spanish Jews originating from Muslim Spain, and Jews and New Christians from Portugal.[115]

The emigrations of Jews and *conversos* had a significant impact on local Jewish culture. Indeed, many of the scholars in Fez were émigrés. It was newly transplanted Jews who also established the first Hebrew printing press there in 1516. The combination of various ethnic and regional backgrounds and religious traditions could lead to complex communal structures and internal communal conflict.

Iran

The two most powerful Islamic states in the early modern period were the Ottoman and the **Safavid** empires. In the Iran of the Shiite Safavid Empire, the position of the Jews was at times very difficult, and Jews were not granted the same degree of freedoms and opportunities as in the Ottoman lands.[116] Iran, which was engaged in frequent battles with the Ottomans, was also viewed by European powers as a bulwark against Ottoman expansion. Not only European military assistance but also European anti-Jewish mentalities made their way into Iran.[117] The rise of Shiite clerics to prominent power in the later sixteenth century increased religious restrictions on Jews and pressures to convert to Islam. Forced conversions were, in fact, instituted under Shah Abbas II (r. 1642–1667).[118] In the early modern period, there were significant Jewish populations in the cities of Isfahan and Kashan, with 600 Jews in the former and 1,000 in the latter in the mid-seventeenth century. Unlike the tolerant Ottoman regime, Jews in Iran experienced a more repressive environment. Not surprisingly, most Jews who survived this difficult time immigrated to Baghdad, under Ottoman rule.[119]

JEWISH POPULATION AND SETTLEMENT AT THE EDGES OF THE WORLD

The New World

New Christians, or Marranos, had made their way to Spanish America probably already with Christopher Columbus and later Cortes. There has, in fact, been some speculation about whether Columbus was himself from New Christian descent. While not all New Christians would have been secretly practicing Judaism, some apparently were, and many parts of the New World became havens for Marranos. Not surprisingly, therefore, the Inquisition was established in the New World early, by the 1520s, and continued in operation in various areas throughout the early modern period.[120] Some scholars have speculated that there were more Spanish Crypto-Jews than Spanish Catholics in Mexico City by the middle of the sixteenth century. This may explain why the Inquisition was introduced there in 1571. While we do not have accurate population numbers, Marranos seem to have been rather prosperous in Mexico. They were engaged in all aspects of colonial trade. They appear to have maintained communication with Jews in Europe and the Near East and developed vibrant communities.[121]

With Dutch incursions into northeast Brazil in the first half of the seventeenth century, the stage was set for further Jewish settlements in the New World. Jews flocked to parts of the New World from the Netherlands and from other places because of fairly tolerant Dutch religious policies. The mid-seventeenth-century council minutes book of the Jews in Brazil, for the congregations Zur Israel and Magen Abraham, list well over 150 males (who were probably heads of house).[122]

In 1638 a group of 200 Jews arrived in Dutch Brazil. It has been estimated that by 1645 half of the 1,500 Europeans living in Dutch Brazil were Jews. Even after many Jews died or returned to the Netherlands during the war with Portugal, there may still have been about 650 Jews (1650). When the Portuguese regained Brazil in 1654, Dutch and Jews were to leave within three months. As a result, Jews moved to other parts of the New World or returned to the Netherlands.

The first, and in many respects most significant, Jewish settlement developed in Recife. Some Jews moved from Recife to Curacao and quickly established the foundations of a community under the tolerant eye of the Dutch, who had conquered the island in 1634. (See map 2.7.) The community imported Rabbi Josiau Pardo from Amsterdam and established a community governing structure. By 1636 Jews in Recife had already constructed a synagogue, and they established schools and formulated communal legislation.[123] Jews were involved in many different professions, including crafts, trade, the sugar industry, tax farming, and the slave trade.

The Dutch position in Recife, however, was always tenuous, and when the Dutch were run out in 1654, the Jews of Recife had to move quickly. Many Jews returned to Amsterdam; some tried their luck throughout the Caribbean, and a few made their way to New Amsterdam (later New York). The twenty-three Jews who sought refuge in New Amsterdam faced initial restriction and did not initially develop into a significant community until the 1680s. In parts of New Netherland (modern-day New York Tri-State area extending just south of the Delaware Bay) that were conquered by the English in the mid-1660s, Jewish settlement became entrenched. By the beginning of the eighteenth century there were 200 to 300 Jews in the area, a number that would grow tenfold by the Revolutionary War. Most Jews who settled here in this period were of Portuguese descent. Communities were eventually established in Montreal, Newport, New York, Philadelphia, Charleston (South Carolina), and Savannah. Jewish cemeteries, whose presence indicates more formal and larger communities, were established in Newport in 1678 and New York in 1682.[124]

Perhaps as important as their actual numbers in settlement was the influence of Jewish Scripture on the European immigrants to the New World.

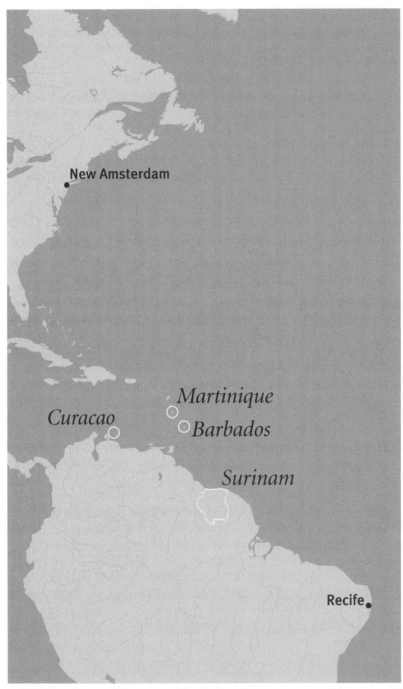

Map 2.7.   The New World. Designed by Tony Doyle.

Much of Puritan ideology in North America was based on social and religious concepts culled from the Hebrew Bible. Indeed, the Pilgrims saw themselves as Israelites escaping persecution and establishing themselves as God's Chosen People in a new land.[125]

Another successful Jewish settlement was in Surinam. Jews moved there beginning in the 1630s, with several waves of settlement. By the end of the 1660s more than 500 Jews, owning some forty sugar plantations and thousands of slaves, resided there. That number grew to 2,000 by the early eighteenth century. By the last quarter of the century the Jews of Surinam had built a school in addition to a synagogue.

Small enclaves of Portuguese New Christians also existed in Argentina, then under Portuguese rule. We do not know how many may have practiced Judaism, but we do know that there were at least ninety-six of the 2,000 residents of Buenos Aires in 1620. Of this group, thirty-four were farmers, twenty-five were artisans, and fourteen were sailors.[126]

In some important ways the Caribbean environment was relatively favorable, at least in areas that were governed by the Dutch and English. The Dutch, in particular, encouraged Jewish settlement and economic development, particularly in the face of Spanish and Portuguese hostility and economic encroachment. They even agreed to recognize Jews as Dutch citizens in the event they were captured by the Spanish. The Dutch West India Company found the Jews particularly useful, especially given Jewish initiative to develop new businesses and cultivate various goods. Barbados was something of a success story for Jewish settlement. Three hundred Jews lived there in 1679. Jews were involved in a range of commercial ventures and also cultivated sugar and coffee. The community appears to have been quite strong in the eighteenth century. The Jewish community of Martinique, under the rule of the French, numbered fewer than 100 in the late seventeenth century at the time that the restrictive Black Code was circulated (see chapter 5).[127] Well into the early eighteenth century, there may still have been enough Jews for a *minyan* (ten adult men required for prayer services) there, but by the end of the century there was no significant presence.[128] Still, given stark colonial conditions and Spanish and Portuguese pressure, many Jewish settlements were small and short-lived.

India and China

Some late medieval and early modern sources mention the presence of at least some Jews in India.[129] (See map 2.8.) The Jewish community in Shingly (near Cochin) apparently dissolved during the period 1341–1505, though sixteenth-century legislation that indicated that Jewish soldiers would not fight on Saturdays testified to ongoing existence of pockets of Jews in India.[130] European Jews corresponded with these Jews well into the seventeenth century.

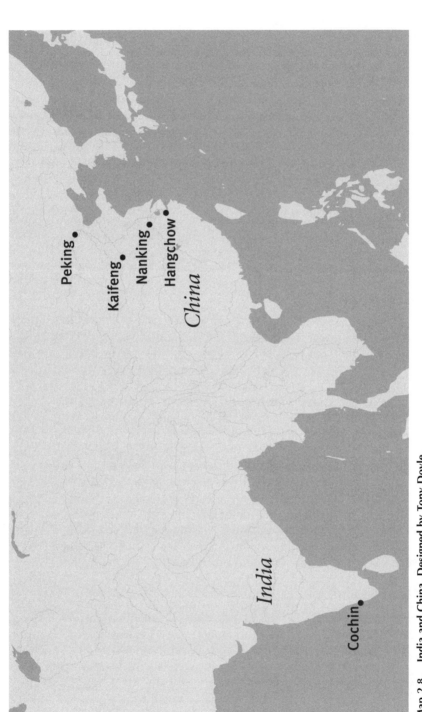

Map 2.8. India and China. Designed by Tony Doyle.

According to Edward Terry, writing in the early seventeenth century, and based on the two and a half years he spent in India as chaplain to Sir Thomas Roe,

> Now, for the inhabitants of Indostan, they were anciently Gentiles, or notorious idolaters, called in generall Hindos; but ever since they were subdued by Tamberlaine, have beene mixed with Mahometans. There are besides many Persians and Tartars, many Abissines and Armenians, and some few almost of every people in Asia, if not of Europe, that have residence here. Amongst them are some Jewes, but not beloved, for their very name is a proverbe or word of reproach.[131]

Early Portuguese expeditions to India encountered apparently indigenous (or at least long-settled) Jews, but Portuguese and Spanish Jews also made their way to India as the Portuguese established a secure economic presence. As such, Jews in India were largely under the authority of the Portuguese who had an important commercial position and who legislated stringently against them, as well as against other local groups.[132] Indeed, by the 1540s there were calls for the establishment of an Inquisition in Goa, in southwest India, to search out New Christians suspected of **Judaizing**.[133]

The Jews along the Malabar Coast in Cochin (southern India) had been granted religious freedom by local rulers. Throughout the sixteenth century we have documents indicating a Jewish presence in Cochin, where a synagogue was constructed in 1568. The synagogue clearly borrowed architectural elements and religious practices from Hindu temples.[134] Religious toleration for Jews continued later under Dutch rule, beginning in the early 1660s and stretching through the eighteenth century. This environment attracted a wide range of Jews from throughout Europe and the Ottoman Empire, with many important Jewish merchants settling in or using Cochin as a base of operations.

Jews also made their way in the sixteenth century to northern India, then under Mogul rule. Later, when England played an important economic role in this part of India, a number of Portuguese Jews from England became active in international trade, especially in the trafficking of precious stones.

A similar, if smaller scale, incursion of Jewish merchants occurred in China. As in India, some apparently long-standing Jewish residence combined with the settlement of Jewish traders to create a newsworthy and far-flung network of Jews involved in international trade. Already in the middle of the sixteenth century there were rumors of Jews living in China. Some rumors were transmitted via European travelers; other evidence includes laws that allegedly mentioned Jews along with Moors and Gentiles.[135] At the beginning of the seventeenth century, the travel account of Matteo Ricci indicates that there may have been 1,000 Jews in Kaifeng.[136]

Prolonged absence of contact with other Jewish communities, however, led to increasing internal dissolution of Chinese Jewish communities.[137]

Jews had apparently lived in China for generations and there was some speculation among Europeans that these Jews were part of the Ten Lost Tribes.[138] This was similar to legends circulating about members of the Ten Lost Tribes in South America.[139] Menasseh ben Israel, like other Jews, apparently accepted a belief that the mention of "Sinim" in the book of Isaiah (49:12) referred to Jews living in China, even if many exegetes had interpreted the language as meaning simply "the land of the South."[140]

Internal Chinese memory was equally vague about the timing of the arrival of Jews in China; some sources suggested hundreds of years previous, to the period of Tamerlane or some 400 years earlier at the time of Ghengis Kahn.[141] It appears that Jews may have settled in Kaifeng some time between the middle of the tenth and first quarter of the twelfth century, perhaps coming from India or somewhere in the Middle East.[142] There is some evidence that Jews were living in other areas as well,[143] perhaps Hangchow, Peking, and Nanking.[144] (See map 2.8.) The synagogue in Kaifeng was destroyed in the later part of the first half of the seventeenth century by a terrible flooding of the Yellow River that may have taken as many as 300,000 Chinese lives.[145] About a decade later construction of a new facility was begun,[146] suggesting something of a resilient community. At this time, according to one survivor, there were a couple hundred Jewish families.[147] Apparently, at that time, a very powerful Jewish officer held an important position in the Middle Army.[148]

While not statistically impressive, the existence of Jewish settlements in "remote" parts of the world revealed the far-flung network of early modern society, to which Jews contributed a great deal. It also raised questions about the possible dispersion of Ancient Israelites, who, it was believed, would gather at the end of days to usher in the messianic era.

THE COMPLEXITIES OF JEWISH SETTLEMENT

It is important to distinguish between Jewish settlements and Jewish communities. Simply because Jews settled in a particular area does not mean that together or individually they constituted a "community" (see chapter 3). Suffice it to say that, throughout our period, especially in some parts of central Europe, there were large numbers of Jewish settlements in which a single or several Jews or Jewish families settled in a particular area for particular purposes, often trade or some other economic role. In many cases a local lord or prince or even a city council issued a contract whereby an individual Jew or group of Jews were allowed to live in the area for a set number of years. While the number of years could vary quite a bit, the number was often between two and ten. The contract specified what kinds of business Jews might conduct as well as any other privileges that they might be granted and restrictions and monies they were responsible to pay.

Jewish settlement was affected by a wide range of external factors, including political stability, economic change, and religious conflict. Throughout the early modern period Jews, like other minority groups, were sometimes encouraged to settle in frontier regions or new cities with the prospect of certain privileges, related especially to religious practice, citizen rights, and economic freedom. Such was the case in 1588, for example, when the town of Zamosc granted a group of Sephardic Jews a settlement privilege.[149]

Regional and Geographically Disperse Communities

In parts of central Germany arrangements with non-Jewish authorities forced Jews to form something of a regional association to meet various social and religious needs. Such arrangements, like the contracts upon which they were based, could be quite fragile. By the end of the early modern period, some rather large rural Jewish settlements had taken hold and blossomed. There are even some examples of villages in southern Germany and in eastern Europe in which more Jews inhabited the village than Christians and where Jews and Christians shared various structures of communal governance.

In many other areas Jewish settlement was also a regional in addition to a local affair. While the Jewish population in Rome, for example, continued to grow in the sixteenth century—from 1,500 in midcentury to 3,500 by the end of the century—the population in the broader Roman district was enormous, with 12,500 Jews residing in eighty different local communities.[150] In late medieval Sicily, some 35,000 Jews, more than in the entire mainland combined, were spread across twenty different locations, especially Palermo, Syracuse, and Messina.[151] In the Lemberg region of Poland, which included Lemberg and seventeen smaller towns, the Jewish population was around 10 percent of the total in the later sixteenth century.[152] In fifteenth-century Germany there were more than 1,000 places with Jews. Of that number, however, more than 50 percent had only one or two Jewish families. Less than one third had up to ten Jewish families, and only 6.6 percent had up to twenty families. There were only forty communities with more than 150 Jews and only twenty-four with more than 300 Jews. Jewish settlement in late medieval and early modern Germany remained quite diffuse. Within fifty kilometers of the town of Heidelberg, for example, there were eleven Jewish settlements; within fifty kilometers of Nuremberg, thirty-eight; and within fifty kilometers of Frankfurt am Main, thirty-six.

Urban Population Centers

Despite these examples of "rural" or geographically disperse Jewish communities, which could be replicated in other areas, including the Ottoman Empire, most Jews remained urban dwellers. In fifteenth-century Germany, 73 percent of Jews resided in cities and another 11.5 percent in small cities. Only 15 percent lived in villages. There were, of course, a wide range of Jewish settlements and communities with something more than a handful of Jews and something much less than the thousands or even hundreds of Jews found in some major cities.

Larger Jewish settlements could accommodate more formal structures of community organization and governance (see chapter 3). Some Jewish communities developed into very large Jewish population centers, with thousands of Jews living in a single geographical region. This was particularly true in southern Italy and Spain in the fourteenth and fifteenth centuries, the Ottoman Empire in the sixteenth century, and eastern Europe in the seventeenth century. In central Europe, Prague was perhaps the largest Jewish population center, accounting for a third of the total city population by the beginning of the seventeenth century.

In many of these cases, it is more appropriate to speak of Jewish communities in the plural. As we have seen, Jews divided themselves by various criteria, from religious customs, countries of origin, vernacular languages spoken, and so forth, so that multiple communities of Jews might exist side by side, and at times in conflict, even within the same city.

Settlement Policies and Restrictions

Jewish populations could be highly changeable due to a variety of internal and external conditions. In some communities rigid Jewish restrictions were placed on the settlement of other Jews. In part, such restrictions allowed for control over communal affairs and the guarantee that resident Jews would have certain professional opportunities or even monopolies. In rabbinic discussions of exclusion of settlement, the *herem ha-yishuv*, theoretical and practical issues could be involved. One of the leading *halakhic* authorities of the late fifteenth century, Rabbi Joseph Colon in northern Italy, noted,

> If [a resident] is able to "close the door" in front of [a new immigrant] and keep him from entering, it is of course obvious that he has this right. Would you want rather to argue that the local citizen is kept at ground level while the foreigner rises to the highest heavens? Just as [the outsider] is trying to use the governing authority to gain entrance against the will of the city's residents, so too [the residents] may stop him by recourse to the governing authority. . . . Who is the person so lacking in intelligence that he would err in this? Anyone

who suggests [otherwise] is in error; any judge who would rule [differently] is no judge![153]

While not every rabbinic authority agreed that such a monopoly on settlement was legal or warranted, the restriction on settlement was widely practiced. In 1623 the Lithuanian Jewish Council decreed that "no [Jew] from another country shall be allowed to establish a residence in any Lithuanian province without the knowledge and consent of the [Jewish] head of the province."[154] The authority for such a declaration was based both on precedence in Jewish law and the granting of such rights by the non-Jewish authorities.

After the expulsion from Spain there were examples of Jewish communities unwilling to allow the émigrés to settle in their community. In some communities, such as Amsterdam and Hamburg, the flow of poor eastern European refugees was most unwelcome. Their ragged appearance and customs offended the resident Jews, who were also afraid that their presence would be seen unfavorably by the civic authorities. Such cases, however, were rare exceptions. In general, Jewish communities were fairly hospitable to foreign Jews and also maintained poor boxes for local poor, itinerant poor, and the poor of the Holy Land.

In some cases, residence was granted to outside Jews upon the payment of certain fees or on the provision that the new resident would have limited occupational choices. Such restrictions were common in many late medieval Polish Jewish communities. For those that were not granted residence, only limited time in the community was allowed. As in many communities, in Cracow, for example, foreign Jews were allowed to remain in the city for no more than three days.[155]

Restrictions on Jewish settlement were also in part dictated by external conditions, particularly at times when there was agitation in the general populace to expel the Jews or when local or territorial rulers were implementing various policies. In early sixteenth-century Kiev, for example, King Sigismund III prohibited Jews from permanent settlement or the acquisition of real estate in the city.[156] Throughout central and eastern Europe various cities successfully secured the privilege of not tolerating Jewish residence, the privilege of *non tolerandis Judaeis*, as they did in Warsaw in 1527.[157] While such legislation was, as the name suggests, generally directed specifically at the Jews, other similar legislation restricted the rights or settlement of a variety of non-native people. In the middle of the fifteenth century in Poland, for example, King Casimir IV authorized that "no Lombard, Nuremberger, Scot, Englishman, or Jew shall enjoy the liberties of the city."[158]

While Jewish settlement could be rather tenuous, with anti-Jewish restrictive legislation in force in many places and with the threat of expulsion hanging over the Jews like the sword of Damacles, expulsions might often be temporary or never enforced. The Venetian expulsion of 1571, for example, was never carried out—though in this case the political muscle of the Sultan's court (which was concerned to protect the rights and business of its Jews) assured that Jews would continue to be tolerated in Venice.[159] Equally important, the expulsion of the Jews from one area often opened up new areas of settlement, as evidenced by the exodus of Jews from Germany in the later Middle Ages to destinations in Poland and Italy. In some areas, competing princes at times opened their territories to the Jews in hopes of economic benefit. By the end of the sixteenth century, Jews were being admitted into areas that had previously never granted Jews settlement rights. Hamburg, in northern Germany, for example, became an important Jewish center. For further discussion of expulsion, see chapter 5.

Living Quarters

Throughout the medieval and early modern periods, Jews tended to live in a particular area, quarter, or street within a city. Often this was voluntary because of Jewish religious rites and sense of community. In Poland, for example, Jews often lived together in a Jewish street, but specific living quarters were not strictly superimposed upon them.[160] In most cases, such streets were not much different than any other streets but were organized by general ethnic or occupational divisions within the city. At times the non-Jewish neighbors on these Jewish streets were often artisans from lower social levels.[161] Increasingly at the end of the Middle Ages and at the beginning of the early modern period, Jews were formally segregated. In the mid-fourteenth century, Jews in Venetian-controlled Negroponte were confined to a Jewish quarter.[162] By the end of the fifteenth century, the Jews of Cracow were collected in "the Jewish city of Kazimierz," a grouping of a few specific streets that were gated off from the non-Jewish city.[163]

In some cases, where more complex social and religious populations interacted, such as in Spain, Jews could be separated into special quarters in the same way that other groups, notably Muslims, were. Such arrangements, especially when imposed, could lead to complex rules about property ownership and relations between owners and lessees. In Trujillo, for example, when Jews were forced into a new quarter, it was established that the community would have to purchase houses within the quarter that individual Jews did not buy or could not afford. If Jews (and Muslims) owned houses outside the new quarter and Christians were prepared to buy these houses, they would have to be sold at the price assessed by special officials.[164]

In the Middle Ages European Jews often lived squarely in the center of town, close to the markets, where they conducted business and, ironically, close to the center of religious control, the Church.[165] In Germany, when Jews were expelled and readmitted to certain cities they were often moved from such choice locations to less favorable parts of the city.

Forced ghettoization first developed in the early modern period. The Jews in Frankfurt were sequestered into a ghetto in 1462, although the most well-known ghetto was established in 1516 in Venice. The term "ghetto" was coined when the Jews of Venice were relocated to a foundry no longer in use. The Italian term for casting metal was "gettare," the foundry was known as "il gettaro," and so the new residence of the Jews became known as the ghetto. This name stuck and has had an intriguing history of its own.[166] Although somewhat surprised by the move, some Jews tried to see the forced segregation positively. They referred to the ghetto as their *get*, in Hebrew their bill of divorce, from the Christian society that surrounded them.

Often restrictions were in place regarding when Jews could come and go from the ghetto, and at times penalties were given to those who transgressed such rules. At the same time, the creation of the ghetto forced Jews to create new boundaries of community and, in communities with complex patterns of migration and people of multiethnic background, to interact in new ways. In Venice, for example, the ghetto expanded twice from its original boundaries and included a diverse range of Jews from various ethnic and geographical regions, each group inhabiting a particular part of the ghetto.[167]

But even the most formal ghettos, replete with walls and gates, were incredibly more permeable than was once believed. In some cases, Christians either owned houses in the ghetto or resided there themselves. At the very least, Christians visited the ghettos frequently for various economic and, at times, more nefarious purposes. The Venetian ghetto was a magnet for tourists as well as local Christians doing business or gambling.

In some places Jews lived both within and outside of the Jewish quarter. A French writer from late seventeenth century described the situation of the Jews in Morocco in the following terms:

> They dress in the Arab fashion, but their cloaks and caps are black in order to be distinguishable. In Fez and Marrakesh, they are separated from the inhabitants, having their quarters apart, surrounded by walls, the gates of which are guarded by men set by the king so that they can conduct their business in peace and sanctify their Sabbath and their other holidays. In the other cities, they are mixed with the Moors. They traffic in nothing other than merchandising and their trades. There are several of them who are quite rich, who do not bear themselves any higher than the least of them. They are in correspondence with Jews who live in Europe and who send them with the consent of the consuls arms and munitions.[168]

In seventeenth-century Posen there were 2,795 Jews in the Jewish quarter, but another 335 resided outside the Jewish quarter.[169] The ghetto in Florence was built downtown near the slaughterhouse. Owned by the Grand Duke, it included seventy-five units—twenty-four shops, a synagogue, an inn, and forty-four varying-sized apartments.[170] In 1632 there were 390 Jews in the ghetto and 549 (from ninety-seven families) by 1642. But some Jews also lived and worked outside the ghetto. In 1642 there were seven shops outside the ghetto, and in 1657 twenty-seven Jews lived outside the ghetto while 470 lived inside.[171] Throughout the kingdom of Navarre many Jews lived in specially designated quarters. But in some cities, such as Pamplona and Tudela, Jews lived inside and outside the Jewish quarter, and in Corella Jews lived in every neighborhood of the village.[172]

Length of Settlement and Migration Patterns

Lacking solid and consistent information, it is hard to estimate how long Jews lived in a particular area or where they went when they left. The information we do have seems to indicate that some Jews maintained a more long-term residence than historical accounts generally reveal. Even so, however, Jews frequently were forced to move at some point in their lives. According to the Augsburg (southern Germany) tax lists from 1438, twenty-four Jews resided and paid taxes in Augsburg. The average length of residence in Augsburg was twelve years. Only one of the taxpayers had resided in Augsburg over thirty years, two over twenty, five over fifteen, five over ten, nine over five, and only two under five. Similar patterns seem to have held for other mid-sized German Jewish communities. In Nuremberg, twelve of the sixteen money-handlers listed in 1489 belonged to the three families who had been in the community for twenty to twenty-eight years and were important enough to be significantly involved in city business outside of the Jewish community.[173]

While we do not know the migratory patterns of most Jews, and while the travel patterns of Jews could vary considerably, we do have some information about the movements of some particularly wealthy businessmen, luminary rabbinic figures, and occasionally, the travels of more ordinary Jews recorded in Jewish and non-Jewish sources. Given the generally dispersed nature of Jewish life in early modern times and the far-flung networks of business and family, many Jews traveled extensively. Some Jews traveled great distances, for example, Sephardic businessmen involved in international trade, those suffering from the Spanish expulsion of the late fifteenth century, or Jews who left Europe for Israel for religious reasons. Nonetheless, most Jewish travel was regional in nature and related to family visits, such as weddings or births, or business.

Travel Patterns of Individual Jews: Exempla

Let us consider now some examples of the movements of more famous Jews. Rabbi Jacob Weil, the leader of the Augsburg community, first settled in Bamberg and, finally, permanently in Erfurt no later than 1443 but was, according to family tradition, buried in Nuremberg.[174] Rabbi Joseph Colon, one of the great legal scholars of the fifteenth century, was born in Chambery, France, and could trace his lineage back to the great Jewish exegete Rabbi Solomon ben Isaac (**Rashi**). Colon was something of a wanderer, living in Mainz, where he may have studied with the famous Rabbi Jacob Molin (Maharil), and he served as rabbi in Mantua, Pieve di Sacco, Mestre, and Bologna. He died in Padua around 1480. Rabbi Moses Mintz, a cousin of Rabbi Yehudah Mintz of Padua, was a student of Rabbi Zalman Katz, a rabbi in Nuremberg. He studied at a number of *yeshivot* (Talmudic academies) and with important rabbinic scholars, such as Rabbi Israel Isserlein and Rabbi Zalman Yaant of Italy, though we do not know when he crossed over into Italy. Mintz left Würzburg after the expulsion of the Jews from that city in 1450, after which he moved on to Mainz. He left Mainz in 1462 after persecutions against the Jews and made his way to Landau, then Ulm (1464), Bamberg (1469), Nuremberg (1473), and finally to Posen (1474), one of the first great rabbis to settle there. It is unclear whether or not he died on the way to Israel, but certainly he had entertained the notion of moving there. In each of these cases, the frequent movement was primarily regional in nature.

Other Jews, especially Marranos and Jews fleeing the Inquisition, might have more complicated but telling migratory patterns. Consider, for example, the itinerary of Dona Gracia Nasi, Samuel Pallache, as well as the great Jewish scholars Isaac Abarbanel and Solomon Ashkenazi. Dona Gracia Nasi (ca. 1510–1569) was of Marrano background and was known as a stateswoman and a great patroness. She was probably of Spanish origin, born with the Christian name Beatrice de Luna. She was the daughter of a Portuguese royal physician. In 1528, at the age of eighteen, she married Francisco Mendes, also a Marrano of distinguished Jewish lineage. Mendes and his brother created a thriving business in precious stones and spices in Lisbon and Antwerp. But Gracia's husband died in 1536, leaving her a widow in her midtwenties. Shortly after the death of her husband, she left Portugal with her family, briefly for England and the Netherlands. She became embroiled in numerous family intrigues, revolving around her fortune and involving non-Jewish authorities.

Gracia next settled in Venice, where she was denounced as a Judaizer (a Christian secretly practicing Judaism) by her sister Reyna, who was seeking to acquire a larger portion of the family fortune. After the intervention of Turkish authorities, she was freed. Gracia next settled in Ferrara where she likely practiced openly as a Jew. She continued to be involved in Jewish communal affairs, but as anti-Jewish hostilities were rising on the peninsula, she left for the Ottoman Empire. After traveling through parts of the Empire, including Salonika, she settled in Istanbul in 1553 and became known for her business acumen, conducting trade throughout Europe and the Ottoman Empire. In addition to the vast sums she expended on philanthropy, she was also involved in some political activity, such as the Jewish boycott of the port of Ancona after the burning of twenty-six Marranos who openly returned to Judaism. Her influence extended to the Holy Land, where she endowed a *yeshivah* (Talmudic academy) in Tiberias.

A Marrano diplomat, Samuel Pallache also moved around a great deal during his life. Pallache was born in Fez in Morocco in the middle of the sixteenth century. His grandparents had been expelled from Spain at the end of the fifteenth century. Pallache resided in Madrid and worked for the Spanish crown ostensibly as a Catholic, and he may also have been something of a spy, pirate, and double agent, perhaps even in the service of the Ottomans. He later worked in commerce and diplomacy in the Netherlands (Amsterdam and The Hague), where he was an openly practicing Jew. Pallache was simultaneously involved in many facets of early modern business and politics,[175] in a sense exemplifying the tenuous position of Jews in the early modern period.

Or, consider the example of the famous Jewish exegete and statesman, Isaac Abarbanel (1437–1508). Born in Lisbon, Abarbanel became a wealthy and influential figure in Spain and then in various other communities after the expulsion. After service to the Portuguese crown, he escaped a charged political environment and re-established his profession in the service of the Spanish monarchs Ferdinand and Isabella in 1484. After failing in attempts to have the 1492 expulsion edict reversed, Abarbanel himself made for Valencia and then Naples. Again Abarbanel entered court service, but after the French attack on Naples, he moved to Messina and then Corfu, before returning to Naples in 1496. Seven years later, Abarbanel settled in Venice, where he completed a number of his scholarly works, and he was later buried in Padua.

One final example is Solomon Ashkenazi (ca. 1520–1602), who was likely of German lineage, despite being born in northern Italy. He studied medicine at Padua and later assumed a position as court physician in Cracow. Solomon moved to Istanbul in 1564 and later played an important role in the peace negotiations between the Ottoman Empire and Venice in the 1570s, as well as in other political conflicts.[176]

The wide extent of Jewish movement, both voluntary and forced, was extremely significant in the early modern period, as it had been throughout the Middle Ages. Such movement shaped the nature of Jewish communities and created intricate networks through which Jews communicated.

COMPLEX AND MULTIETHNIC COMMUNITIES:
THE EXAMPLES OF HAMBURG AND SAFED

While the terms for congregation and community could often be used in the same sense, there had been important distinctions in the concepts since the Middle Ages. In medieval Egypt, for example, we find diverging congregations following variously the rites of Babylonian and Palestinian Jews.[177] In the early modern period, the distinctions between various Ashkenazic and Sephardic groups, each with a range of ethnic, national, or ritual distinctions, made some Jewish societies extremely complex and somewhat internally divided. Here we consider the cases of Hamburg in Germany and Safed in the land of Israel.

Hamburg, Germany

Jewish settlement in Hamburg developed significantly only after the beginning of the seventeenth century. Between 1550 and 1600, the city's population doubled from 20,000 to 40,000 and increased again to 75,000 by the early eighteenth century.[178] At any given time, 50 percent of this population was comprised of immigrants, typically from the Netherlands during the period of 1550–1650. Later immigrants came from other parts of Germany, especially Lower Saxony.[179]

In the midst of religious factionalism in seventeenth-century Europe, the booming city of Hamburg became an important test case for the limits of religious toleration. Beginning in the 1550s, a wide range of immigrants, including Italian Catholics, Sephardic Jews, and Calvinist Dutch, had brought the wealth and skills necessary to transform Hamburg into a major commercial center.[180] Whereas the largest immigrant group, Lutherans, could be relatively easily integrated into the city's infrastructure, the position of religious minorities was more complex and at times much more volatile. Well into the nineteenth century the Jews' relationship to the city was subjected to numerous strains and attempts at expulsion, and remained contractual, based upon short-term arrangements with the city.[181] A tension between maintaining religious uniformity and economic viability continually pitted the Lutheran clergy, burghers, and city leadership, in the form of the Senate, against each other.

The position of the Jews in Hamburg was complicated by the fact that a few miles west, the town of Altona, under the jurisdiction of the counts of Schaumburg and later, after 1640, the kings of Denmark, provided extraordinary toleration of religious minorities in an attempt to siphon off business from Hamburg. Already in 1600, Altona provided freedom to Jews, Calvinists, Catholics, Mennonites, and after the middle of the eighteenth century, even to Christian sectarians.[182] Indeed, Altona rapidly expanded from a hamlet of ten to fifteen houses in 1567 to a small town of around 3,000 by 1664 (and 12,000 by 1710). Many religious minorities took advantage of the religious freedoms provided in the city but continued to maintain residence or close business contacts in Hamburg.[183] East of Hamburg, similar privileges were granted to Jews and Mennonites in Wandsbek. That locale, however, never grew into a large town.

Portuguese Jews

As in Amsterdam, Portuguese Jews in Hamburg dominated in the Jewish settlement during much of the seventeenth century. The Portuguese maintained a privileged status unlike that of the German Jews, who were expelled in midcentury. The Portuguese shared the protection of the ruling Senate that was lavished upon other early merchant communities, such as the English and the Dutch.

In 1603 the Hamburg burghers demanded heavy taxes on the Iberian community and called for the expulsion of its Jewish members. The Senate refused to recognize any Jews in the city, though by 1606 it reluctantly had to acknowledge the existence of seven Jewish families and two unmarried Jewish brokers.[184] By 1610 there were 116 Portuguese Jews in the city, who advocated vociferously on their own behalf, noting their influence with the Spanish authorities and the effect that might have on Hamburg trade.[185] The city council opposed an expulsion, largely because of the important economic contributions of the Jews, many of whom were very influential in local and regional finance. In fact, some Jewish financiers helped to found the Bank of Hamburg in 1619. In light of this, as well as the pending invitations of the Portuguese to the competing cities of Emden, Stade, Altona, and Wandsbek, and after consultation with the theological faculty at Jena and Frankfurt an der Oder, the Senate provided the Portuguese community an initial two-year contract in 1612.[186] The contract was composed of seventeen articles that defined the rights and privileges of the Portuguese.

Like the Dutch and English communities, the Portuguese accepted a protected status in return for the annual payment of 1,000 Marks. Indeed, an April 1649 mandate recorded that nobody should insult those "who are here of the resident foreign nations, be they English, French, Netherlandish, Portuguese or other."[187] The Portuguese were admonished to live modestly and peacefully, in return for freedom to trade and the right to conduct financial transactions in the city. The Portuguese, like other religious minorities, were restrained in public religious displays—they were not permitted to have a synagogue or cemetery or to practice circumcision.[188] Indeed, later attempts to build a synagogue in 1660, 1668, and 1672 were rigorously opposed.[189]

Despite later relaxation of restrictions, there existed a good deal of anti-Jewish animus throughout the seventeenth century. The influential

Lutheran pastor Johannes Müller, for example, asserted that toleration of the Jews contributed to the decay of Lutheranism in Hamburg. In a 1649 essay, he complained of the noisy and extravagant religious ceremonies of the Jews; he also maintained that Jews defiled the Christian Sabbath, insulted Christian women, and possessed generally poor morals. These concerns and arguments, however, did not sway the Senate, which was more concerned that the Jews, who maintained important trade relations, might leave the city. The results were new ordinances and the continued growth of the Portuguese community, which by 1660 numbered 600.[190] The toleration of the Portuguese Jews has been tied to a number of issues, including the fashioning of Hamburg as a Zion of the north;[191] the influence of the mercantile elite in the city; the anti-Catholicism of the city; relationships with foreign powers;[192] and the influence of several powerful individual Jews.[193]

The prospects and size of the Portuguese community in Hamburg, however, declined rapidly by the end of the century. The special levies of the later seventeenth century, combined with increasing unrest, tended to undermine the vitality of the Portuguese community. The Portuguese Jews in 1692 numbered only 300,[194] then dwindled even further to twenty-seven taxpayers by 1732. Eventually most Portuguese made their way back to the Netherlands.[195] By contrast, by 1710, German Jews began to acquire similar privileges to those previously enjoyed by the Portuguese alone,[196] and by the end of the eighteenth century, the Jewish community numbered 6,300 Ashkenazic Jews and only 130 Sephardim.[197]

Ashkenazic Jews

The settlement and development of Ashkenazic Jews in and around Hamburg took a rather different course than that of the Portuguese Jews in the seventeenth century. A 1583 petition by an Ashkenazic pearl dealer, in the name of twelve Jewish families, to settle in the city was rejected.[198] There is some speculation that this Jew, whose petition was later rejected again, as well as additional individuals, eventually settled around Hamburg, for in 1574 the Count Adolf of Schaumburg issued a *Schutzbrief* (letter of protection) to four Jews providing settlement rights in Altona and Ottensen.[199]

By 1612, Ashkenazic Jews had negotiated the first general privilege in Altona. A second contract of 1614 granted general privileges for sixteen families.[200] In return, the Jews were to pay 100 **Reichsthaler** per head and an annual *Schutzgeld* (protection fee) of ten Reichsthaler.[201] The smaller settlement of Jews in Wandsbek was initiated in 1621 with four families from Altona and confirmed with a privilege dated November 10, 1637.[202]

Although under the protection of the rulers of Altona, many Jews continued to be attracted to the life and opportunities of Hamburg.[203] An undated list, presumably from the 1620s, indicates that there were seventeen protected Jews in the region, eight living in Altona and nine in Hamburg.[204] In 1671 the Ashkenazic Jews in Hamburg, Altona, and Wandsbek formed a three-community federation as proposed in 1669 by the Frankfurt chief rabbi Aaron Koidonover.[205]

Ashkenazic Jews in Hamburg were generally of more modest means and social standing than their Portuguese co-religionists, the richest serving as jewelers and small moneylenders and the poorest as craftsmen and laborers. Indeed, there is record of eighteen German Jews in Hamburg in 1652, recorded as "servants of the nation," that is, domestic servants of the Portuguese Jews.[206] In the anti-Jewish climate of 1648–1649, the Ashkenazic Jews were officially expelled from the city, although they later returned in 1657–1658.[207] By the 1660s, there were forty to fifty Ashkenazic families in the city.[208] As it attained privileges similar to that of the Portuguese Jews in the early eighteenth century, the Ashkenazic population grew rapidly to 600 taxpayers by 1730, with no fewer than fourteen unofficial synagogues and forty-one schools.[209]

The Jewish community in early modern Hamburg was complex. Portuguese and German communities existed side by side, both inside the city and in separate communities in smaller towns in close proximity. But these communities were very different in terms of religious customs and social and economic status. While not an enormous Jewish population center, the situation in Hamburg points to a number of important issues that faced early modern Jewish communities.

Safed, Israel

Hamburg was not the only complex and multiethnic community and certainly not the most important. In Italy and under the far-flung rule of the Ottomans, numerous Jewish communities developed as conglomerates of various congregations and ethnic nationalities. Waves of immigration from Iberia, Italy, and throughout the Empire itself, combined with a wide range of business relations with Jews from central and eastern Europe as well as from all parts of the Mediterranean, to make many Ottoman Jewish communities extremely diverse.

We have already seen something of the impressive scope of the communities in Istanbul and Salonika. Safed in the Upper Galilee, provides another instructive example. It grew into an extremely important Jewish city in the sixteenth century—important not only for the large population that sprouted there but also, as we will see later in this book (chapter 4), for the significant religious and cultural developments that emerged there as well. In the late fifteenth century the Jewish community of Safed and its environs numbered about 300 families and was well protected by local rulers. The community witnessed the immigration of Spanish Jewish refugees at the time of the Spanish expulsion and with the Ottoman conquest in 1516. Although there were only half as many Jews and Muslims in Safed in the early 1520s, there were equal numbers by the late 1560s.[210] In 1525 there were 233 Jewish households; 1555–1556, 719 plus sixty-three bachelors; 1567–1568, 945 plus twelve bachelors; and 1596–1597, 904 including ninety-three bachelors, eight religious officials, and sixty-four disabled persons.[211]

The complexion of the Jewish communities in Safed was complicated and multicultural. The 719 Jewish householders in 1555–1556 were from various ethnic backgrounds: Spanish (from Castile, Seville, Aragon, Catalonia, Cordova); Portuguese; Musta'rab; Italian (including groups from Calabria and Apulia); **Maghrebi**; Ashkenazi; and Hungarian. Previously, Jews from Provence had been in Safed, and other sources provide evidence of some Jews from Sicily, Bosnia, Romania, Kurdistan, and Yemen.[212] (See table 2.8.)

At times, this complicated environment led to tense ethnic relations among the Jews. As one rabbinic discussion, that of Moses di Trani, revealed, the solutions that the Jews devised were not always sufficient or universally accepted. Di Trani writes,

> The congregation in a certain city made an agreement that whoever came to the city [Safed] if both he and his father were born in Italy, even though his grandfather came from Portugal or Castile or Aragon or some other kingdom, he should belong to the Italian congregation. And if his father was born in one of the forementioned kingdoms, though he himself was born in Italy he should belong to [his father's] kingdom, and the same principle applied to all the nations. Upon this **haskamah**'s [ordinance's] renewal, the Aragonese congregation raised objections, saying that it was not right that someone who is [really] Aragonese, or from another kingdom, should be considered Italian simply because he and his father were born in Italy.[213]

At stake were not only finances, money paid in taxes by congregants, but also ethnic identity and the political balance that came from maintaining and increasing particular population groups.

Table 2.8. Ethnicity of Safed Jewish Community, 1555–1556

Ethnic Background	Population
Spanish	334
Portuguese	143
Musta'rab	98
Italian	74
Maghrebi	20
Ashkenazi	20
Hungarian	12

CONCLUSIONS

Jewish population and settlement patterns in the early modern period could be highly volatile. While some areas experienced significant and long-term continuity, such as in parts of the Ottoman Empire, most Jewish settlements changed dramatically over time because of a wide range of external conditions and Jewish migration. While pockets of Jews could be found in nearly every part of the globe, it was in central and eastern Europe and throughout the broad reaches of the Ottoman Empire that the majority of Jews resided. Significant numbers of Jews from western and central Europe in the later Middle Ages migrated, en masse, east to the Ottoman Empire and Poland. For the early part of the early modern period, the majority of Jews lived under Ottoman rule, continuing the long medieval tradition of Jews living under Islam, but also incorporating large numbers of Jews as the Ottoman state expanded greatly. While the late medieval settlement of Jews in Poland was slim, the Polish Jewish population was becoming dominant by the end of our period, a trend that would continue into and help to define the modern period of Jewish history.

While almost impossible to offer broad generalizations, there are a few things we can say about Jewish population and settlement in the early modern period. First, Jews tended to live in close proximity to one another, even when they were not formally segregated into a ghetto. The reasons had to do with community building and the need for certain social, religious, and even economic functions (see chapter 3). Nonetheless, it appears that Jews continually engaged with the non-Jews in whose midst they lived, often with social as well as business implications. Second, throughout our period there could be serious restrictions placed on Jewish settlement in any given area. There were many legislative attempts by various levels of the non-Jewish authorities to limit or to eliminate Jewish settlement. Formal decrees of *non tolerandis* or of *sürgün* combined with at times violent expulsions and pogroms to remove Jews from broad areas. On the other hand, changing demographics, politics, and economic situations sometimes created new opportunities for Jewish settlement. But it was not simply external conditions that dictated Jewish settlement. With Talmudic and medieval rabbinic precedents, Jews themselves regulated the size and makeup of their own communities and decided who was allowed to stay and under what conditions.

Given the vast movement of Jews throughout the early modern period as well as the diverse experiences, backgrounds, and customs that Jews took with them, it should not be too surprising that many Jewish settlements, especially the large settlements, were far from homogenous. Jews of varying ethnic, national, and cultural backgrounds formed complex and at times tension-filled communities. In these cases it is perhaps better to talk about Jewish communities within communities. On the other hand, settlements beyond a single location might themselves form a broader community as well. The interplay between various Jewish groups, and at times local non-Jewish authorities, could lead to conflict as well as to coalescence (see chapter 3).

Finally, while it is difficult to establish the length of Jewish residence in any one particular location, we do get a sense that, in many cases, individual Jews might remain in a particular geographical area for extended periods of time. Nonetheless, Jews were among the most mobile of people in our period, as the migratory and travel paths of some well-known individuals indicate. While such mobility could lead to difficulty in community development and structure, it was also important as a survival technique, and early modern Jews showed a great deal of tenacity and ability to adapt to changing conditions. This was, perhaps, the primary reason that Jews were able to survive in so many and frequently changing diasporas. As we noted at the beginning of this book, the population and movement of the Jews really lay at the foundation of the early modern Jewish experience. As we will now see, the complexities outlined in this chapter had significant reverberations in the community structures, cultural developments, and relations with non-Jews that developed in the early modern period.

NOTES

1. Anna Foa, *The Jews of Europe after the Black Death* (Berkeley, CA, 2000), 8.

2. Jonathan Israel, *European Jewry in the Age of Mercantilism, 1550–1750*, 3rd ed. (London, 1998).

3. Maurice Eisenbeth, *Le judaïsme nord-africain* (Paris, 1932), 147ff.

4. Robert Bonfil, *Jewish Life in Renaissance Italy*, trans. Anthony Oldcorn (Berkeley, CA, 1994).

5. *Encyclopedia Judaica*, 16 vols. (Jerusalem, 1971–1972).

6. Israel, *European Jewry*.

7. Simon Dubnow, *History of the Jews in Russia and Poland from the Earliest Times Until the Present Day*, trans. I. Friedländer, 3 vols. (Philadelphia, 1916–1920), 1:66.

8. Zenon Guldon and Jacek Wijaczka, "The Accusation of Ritual Murder in Poland 1500–1800," *Polin* 10 (1997): 99.

9. Haim Hillel Ben-Sasson, "Poland: Internal Jewish Life," in *Encyclopedia Judaica*, 16 vols. (Jerusalem, 1971–1972).

10. Guldon and Wijaczka, "The Accusation of Ritual Murder in Poland 1500–1800," 100.

11. Norman A. Stillman, *The Jews of Arab Lands: A History and Source Book* (Philadelphia, 1979), 54, citing Ashtor.

12. Foa, *The Jews of Europe*, 75.

13. Foa, *The Jews of Europe*, 76.

14. See Ole J. Benedictow, *The Black Death, 1346–1353: The Complete History* (Wiltshire, UK, 2006; orig., 2004), 382–84.

15. See Benjamin R. Gampel, "A Letter to a Wayward Teacher: The Transformation of Sephardic Culture in Christian Iberia," in *Cultures of the Jews: A New History*, ed. David Biale (New York, 2002), 426.

16. Simon R. Schwarzfuchs, "Spain: Conversos," in *Encyclopedia Judaica*, 16 vols. (Jerusalem, 1971–1972).

17. See Benedictow, *The Black Death*, 281.

18. See Schwarzfuchs, "Spain."

19. Haim Beinart, "Saragossa," in *Encyclopedia Judaica*, 16 vols. (Jerusalem, 1971–1972).

20. Dean Phillip Bell, *Sacred Communities: Jewish and Christian Identities in Fifteenth-Century Germany* (Leiden, Netherlands, and Boston, 2001), 242.

21. See Benjamin R. Gampel, *The Last Jews on Iberian Soil: Navarrese Jewry 1479–1498* (Berkeley, CA, 1989), 14.

22. Jane Gerber, *The Jews of Spain: A History of the Sephardic Experience* (New York, 1992), 139.

23. Gerber, *The Jews of Spain*, 148.

24. Gerber, *The Jews of Spain*, 140.

25. Elkan Nathan Adler, ed. *Jewish Travellers: A Treasury of Travelogues from Nine Centuries*, 2nd ed. (New York, 1966), 210, 214.

26. The influence of the Spanish monarchs spread, not only within Iberia (where the Jews were forcibly converted in the early sixteenth century) and Spanish Italian strongholds, but also to the Holy Roman Empire, where imperial marriage arrangements apparently included assurances that Jews would be expelled.

27. Bernard Dov Cooperman, "Ethnicity and Institution Building among Jews in Early Modern Rome," *AJS Review* 30 (1) (2006): 119–45.

28. Cooperman, "Ethnicity."

29. See Cecil Roth, *History of the Jews in Venice* (New York, 1975), 106–7.

30. Orly Caroline Meron, "Demographic and Spatial Aspects of Jewish Life in the Duchy of Milan during the Spanish Period, 1535–1597," in *Papers in Jewish Demography 1989*, ed. U. O. Schmelz and S. DellaPergola (Jerusalem, 1993), 37.

31. Lucia Frattarelli Fischer, "Urban Forms of Jewish Settlement in Tuscan Cities (Florence, Pisa, Leghorn) during the 17th Century," in *Papers in Jewish Demography 1989*, ed. U. O. Schmelz and S. DellaPergola (Jerusalem, 1993), 48.

32. Frattarelli Fischer, "Urban Forms," 55.

33. Frattarelli Fischer, "Urban Forms," 56.

34. Salo Baron, *A Social and Religious History of the Jews*, vols. 16–17, 2nd ed. (Philadelphia, 1976–1980), 17:71.

35. Baron, *A Social and Religious History*, 17:81–82.

36. Baron, *A Social and Religious History*, 17:84.

37. See Benedictow, *The Black Death*, 221–24 (and for Poland, which also seems now to have been widely affected by the plague, see 218–21).

38. See J. Friedrich Battenberg, *Die Juden in Deutschland vom 16. bis zum Ende des 18. Jahrhunderts* (Munich, 2001), 52.

39. See Simon R. Schwarzfuchs, "Antwerp," in *Encyclopedia Judaica*, 16 vols. (Jerusalem, 1971–1972).

40. Cecil Roth, *A History of the Jews in England* (Oxford, 1941), 143–44.

41. Esther Benbassa, *The Jews of France: A History from Antiquity to the Present*, trans. M. B. DeBevoise (Princeton, NJ, 1999), 27; on the larger number, see Foa, *The Jews of Europe*, 8.

42. Benbassa, *The Jews of France*, 22–23.

43. Benbassa, *The Jews of France*, 25. There may have been around 20,000 Jews there at the time—see Foa, *The Jews of Europe*, 8.

44. Benbassa, *The Jews of France*, 25.

45. Benbassa, *The Jews of France*, 41.

46. Salo Baron, *The Jewish Community: Its History and Structure to the American Revolution*, 3 vols. (Philadelphia, 1942), 3:106; see also Cooperman, "Ethnicity."

47. Benbassa, *The Jews of France*, 43.

48. Benbassa, *The Jews of France*, 58.

49. Benbassa, *The Jews of France*, 59.

50. Benbassa, *The Jews of France*, 48.

51. Frances Malino, *The Sephardic Jews of Bordeaux: Assimilation and Emancipation in Revolutionary and Napoleonic France* (Alabama, 1978), 5.

52. Foa, *The Jews of Europe*, 180.

53. Benbassa, *The Jews of France*, 71.

54. Bernard Weinryb, *The Jews of Poland: A Social and Economic History of the Jewish Community in Poland from 1100 to 1800* (Philadelphia, 1973), 4.

55. Iwo Cyprian Pogonowski, *Jews in Poland: A Documentary History* (New York, 1998), 15, 16.

56. Baron, *A Social and Religious History*, 16:120.

57. See Haya Bar-Itzhak, *Jewish Poland: Legends of Origin: Ethnopoetics and Legendary Chronicles* (Detroit, 2001); and Hillel Levine, *Economic Origins of Antisemitism: Poland and Its Jews in the Early Modern Period* (New Haven, CT, 1991), 33.

58. Jerzy Wyrozumski, "Jews in Medieval Poland," in *The Jews in Old Poland, 1000–1795*, ed. Antony Polonsky, Jakub Basista, and Andrzej Link-Lenczowski (London, 1993), 13.

59. Weinryb, *The Jews of Poland*, 309.

60. Weinryb, *The Jews of Poland*, 26.

61. Weinryb, *The Jews of Poland*, 26.

62. Especially of noted rabbinic personalities and court Jews—see Weinryb, *The Jews of Poland*, 30–31.

63. Weinryb, *The Jews of Poland*, 31.

64. Weinryb, *The Jews of Poland*, 115–16.

65. See Moses Shulvass, *The Jews in the World of the Renaissance*, trans. Elvin I. Kose (Leiden, Netherlands, 1973).

66. Shulvass, *The Jews in the World of the Renaissance*, 15, 20, 27.

67. Shulvass, *The Jews in the World of the Renaissance*, 23.

68. Shulvass, *The Jews in the World of the Renaissance*, 25–26, 40.

69. Shulvass, *The Jews in the World of the Renaissance*, 46.

70. See, for example, Shulvass, *The Jews in the World of the Renaissance*, 34, 47, where he notes 13–15 percent of the Amsterdam Jews were Polish—see also 48–49 regarding the conflict between earlier Ashkenazic immigrants and Lithuanian Jews in the 1650s. See also Daniel Swetschinski, *Reluctant Cosmopolitans: The Portuguese Jews of Seventeenth-Century Amsterdam* (London, 2000).

71. Shulvass, *The Jews in the World of the Renaissance*, 39.

72. Weinryb, *The Jews of Poland*, 116.

73. Weinryb, *The Jews of Poland*, 117.

74. Zenon Guldon and Karol Krzystanek, "The Jewish Population in the Towns on the West Bank of the Vistula in Sandomierz Province, 16th–18th Centuries," in *The Jews in Old Poland, 1000–1795*, ed. Antony Polonsky, Jakub Basista, and Andrzej Link-Lenczowski (London, 1993), 323.

75. Guldon and Krzystanek, "The Jewish Population," 325.

76. Guldon and Krzystanek, "The Jewish Population," 328.

77. Edward Fram, *Ideals Face Reality: Jewish Law and Life in Poland, 1550–1655* (Cincinnati, 1997), 20.

78. Shiomshon Leib Kirshenboim, "Lublin," in *Encyclopedia Judaica*, 16 vols. (Jerusalem, 1971–1972).

79. Fram, *Ideals Face Reality*.

80. Arthur Cygielman, "Cracow (Kazimierz)," in *Encyclopedia Judaica*, 16 vols. (Jerusalem, 1971–1972).

81. Avraham Rubinstein, "Lvov (Lemberg)," in *Encyclopedia Judaica*, 16 vols. (Jerusalem, 1971–1972).

82. Nathan Michael Gelber, "Brest-Litovsk," in *Encyclopedia Judaica*, 16 vols. (Jerusalem, 1971–1972).

83. Mordekhai Nadov, "Pinsk," in *Encyclopedia Judaica*, 16 vols. (Jerusalem, 1971–1972).

84. Dov Rabin, "Grodno," in *Encyclopedia Judaica*, 16 vols. (Jerusalem, 1971–1972).

85. Dov Avron, "Poznan (Posen)," in *Encyclopedia Judaica*, 16 vols. (Jerusalem, 1971–1972).

86. Avron, "Poznan (Posen)."

87. See Baron, *A Social and Religious History*, 17:163.

88. Baron, *A Social and Religious History*, 17:163.

89. Quoted in Joseph R. Hacker, "Jewish Autonomy in the Ottoman Empire: Its Scope and Limits. Jewish Courts from the Sixteenth to the Eighteenth Centuries," in *The Jews of the Ottoman Empire*, ed. Avigdor Levy (Princeton, NJ, 1994), 158.

90. See Joseph R. Hacker, "The 'Sürgün' System and Jewish Society in the Ottoman Empire during the Fifteenth to the Seventeenth Centuries," in *Ottoman and Turkish Jewry: Community and Leadership*, ed. Aron Rodrigue (Bloomington, IN, 1992), 2.

91. Quoted in Hacker, "The 'Sürgün' System," 6–7.

92. Hacker, "The 'Sürgün' System," 27.

93. Bernard Lewis, *The Jews of Islam* (Princeton, NJ, 1984), 124.

94. See Stillman, *The Jews of Arab Lands*, 295–96; Avigdor Levy, ed., *The Jews of the Ottoman Empire* (Princeton, NJ, 1992), 28.

95. Jacob Marcus, *The Jew in the Medieval World: A Source Book, 315–1791* (Cincinnati, 1938), 412.

96. Marcus, *The Jew in the Medieval World*, 413.

97. Marcus, *The Jew in the Medieval World*, 413.

98. Marcus, *The Jew in the Medieval World*, 412.

99. Levy, *The Jews of the Ottoman Empire*, 6.

100. Lewis, *The Jews of Islam*, 118.

101. Abraham David, *To Come to the Land: Immigration and Settlement in Sixteenth-Century Eretz-Israel*, trans. Dena Ordan (Tuscaloosa, AL, 1999), 2.

102. David, *To Come to the Land*, 1.

103. David, *To Come to the Land*, 60.

104. David, *To Come to the Land*, 72.

105. Levy, *The Jews of the Ottoman Empire*, 11. For a general overview, see also Stanford J. Shaw, *The Jews of the Ottoman Empire and the Turkish Republic* (New York, 1991), 37–40.

106. Levy, *The Jews of the Ottoman Empire*, 11–12.

107. Adler, *Jewish Travellers*, 222.

108. Levy, *The Jews of the Ottoman Empire*, 13.

109. Compare this to 43,000 Christians with fifty-six churches; Baron, *A Social and Religious History*, 3:78.

110. Cited in David, *To Come to the Land*, 13.

111. Hirsch Jacob Zimmels, "Isaac ben Sheshet Perfet," in *Encyclopedia Judaica*, 16 vols. (Jerusalem, 1971–1972). See also Gampel, "A Letter to a Wayward Teacher," 428.

112. See H. Z. Hirschberg, *A History of the Jews in North Africa*, 2 vols. (Leiden, Netherlands, 1974–1981), especially vol. 2.

113. Hirschberg, *A History of the Jews in North Africa*, 2:194.

114. Stillman, *The Jews of Arab Lands*, 287.

115. See Baron, *A Social and Religious History*, 17:254.

116. Lewis, *The Jews of Islam*, 151.

117. Habib Levy, *Comprehensive History of the Jews of Iran: The Outset of the Diaspora*, ed. Hooshang Ebrami, trans. George W. Maschke (Costa Mesa, CA, 1999), 259–63.

118. Levy, *Comprehensive History of the Jews of Iran*, 287.

119. Levy, *Comprehensive History of the Jews of Iran*, 288–89.

120. Martin A. Cohen, "Latin America: Colonial Period," in *Encyclopedia Judaica*, 16 vols. (Jerusalem, 1971–1972).

121. Seymour B. Liebman and Harold Lerner, "Mexico: Colonial Period," in *Encyclopedia Judaica*, 16 vols. (Jerusalem, 1971–1972).

122. Arnold Wiznitzer, *The Records of the Earliest Jewish Community in the New World* (New York, 1954), 50–52, see 48–50 regarding officers.

123. Here and below, see Arnold Wiznitzer, "Brazil: Colonial Period," in *Encyclopedia Judaica*, 16 vols. (Jerusalem, 1971–1972).

124. See "Colonial American Jewry, 1654–1776: English Period, 1664–1776," in *Encyclopedia Judaica*, 16 vols. (Jerusalem, 1971–1972).

125. See Abraham I. Katsh, "Colonial American Jewry, 1654–1776: Dutch Period, 1654–1664," in *Encyclopedia Judaica*, 16 vols. (Jerusalem, 1971–1972).

126. Fred Bronner, "Argentina: Colonial Period," in *Encyclopedia Judaica*, 16 vols. (Jerusalem, 1971–1972).

127. Mordechai Arbell, "Jewish Settlements in the French Colonies in the Caribbean (Martinique, Guadeloupe, Haiti, Cayenne) and the 'Black Code,'" in *The Jews and the Expansion of Europe to the West, 1450–1800*, ed. Paolo Bernardini and Norman Fiering (New York, 2001), 294.

128. Arbell, "Jewish Settlements in the French Colonies in the Caribbean," 295.

129. Nathan Katz, *Who Are the Jews of India?* (Berkeley, CA, 2000), 32–33.

130. Katz, *Who Are the Jews of India?* 37.

131. William Foster, ed., *Early Travels in India 1583–1619* (Oxford, 1921), 307–8.

132. Katz, *Who Are the Jews of India?* 48.

133. Here and below, see Walter Joseph Fischel, "India: Early Phase," in *Encyclopedia Judaica*, 16 vols. (Jerusalem, 1971–1972).

134. Katz, *Who Are the Jews of India?* 40, 42.

135. Michael Pollak, *Mandarins, Jews, and Missionaries: The Jewish Experience in the Chinese Empire* (Philadelphia, 1980), 24.

136. Pollak, *Mandarins, Jews, and Missionaries*, 8.

137. Pollak, *Mandarins, Jews, and Missionaries*, 11.

138. Pollak, *Mandarins, Jews, and Missionaries*, 24–25.

139. See Pollak, *Mandarins, Jews, and Missionaries*, 44.

140. Pollak, *Mandarins, Jews, and Missionaries*, 49.

141. Pollak, *Mandarins, Jews, and Missionaries*, 55, 58.

142. Pollak, *Mandarins, Jews, and Missionaries*, 60.

143. Pollak, *Mandarins, Jews, and Missionaries*, 62.

144. Pollak, *Mandarins, Jews, and Missionaries*, 64–65.

145. Pollak, *Mandarins, Jews, and Missionaries*, 68–69.

146. Pollak, *Mandarins, Jews, and Missionaries*, 69.

147. Pollak, *Mandarins, Jews, and Missionaries*, 70.

148. Pollak, *Mandarins, Jews, and Missionaries*, 71.

149. Weinryb, *The Jews of Poland*, 136.

150. See Shulvass, *The Jews in the World of the Renaissance*.

151. See Bonfil, *Jewish Life in Renaissance Italy*.

152. See Fram, *Ideals Face Reality*.

153. Quoted and translated in Cooperman, "Ethnicity," 142.

154. Baron, *A Social and Religious History*, 16:12.

155. Weinryb, *The Jews of Poland*, 158.

156. Yehuda Slutsky, "Kiev: The Jewish Community before 1667," in *Encyclopedia Judaica*, 16 vols. (Jerusalem, 1971–1972).

157. Avraham Rubinstein, "Warsaw," in *Encyclopedia Judaica*, 16 vols. (Jerusalem, 1971–1972).

158. Baron, *A Social and Religious History*, 16:19.

159. See Benjamin Arbel, *Trading Nations: Jews and Venetians in the Early Modern Eastern Mediterranean* (Leiden, Netherlands, 1995).

160. Weinryb, *The Jews of Poland*, 43.

161. Weinryb, *The Jews of Poland*, 81.

162. Baron, *A Social and Religious History*, 17:74.

163. Weinryb, *The Jews of Poland*, 82.

164. Haim Beinart, *Trujillo: A Jewish Community in Extremadura on the Eve of the Expulsion from Spain* (Jerusalem, 1980), 15–16.

165. See, for example, Weinryb, *The Jews of Poland*, 81–82.

166. See Benjamin Ravid, "From Geographical Realia to Historiographical Symbol: The Odyssey of the Word *Ghetto*," in *Essential Papers on Jewish Culture in Renaissance and Baroque Italy*, ed. David B. Ruderman (New York, 1992), 373–85; see also Foa, *The Jews of Europe*, 139.

167. See Roth, *History of the Jews in Venice*, 60–71.

168. Stillman, *The Jews of Arab Lands*, 304.

169. Adam Teller, *Living Together: The Jewish Quarter of Poznań in the First Half of the Seventeenth Century* (Hebrew) (Jerusalem, 2003), 47.

170. Teller, *Living Together*, 51.

171. Fischer, "Urban Forms," 57.

172. Gampel, *The Last Jews*, 14–15.

173. See Michael Toch, "The Jewish Community of Nuremberg in the Year 1489: Social and Demographic Structure" (Hebrew), *Zion* 45:60–72.

174. *Encyclopedia Judaica*, 16 vols. (Jerusalem, 1971–1972), 16: 385–86.

175. See the recent biography, Mercedes Garcia-Arenal and Gerard Wiegers, *A Man of Three Worlds: Samuel Pallache, a Moroccan Jew in Catholic and Protestant Europe*, trans. Martin Beagles (Baltimore, 2003).

176. See Cecil Roth, "Ashkenazi, Solomon," in *Encyclopedia Judaica*, 16 vols. (Jerusalem, 1971–1972). See also Arbel, *Trading Nations*.

177. See S. D. Goitein, *A Mediterranean Society: An Abridgement in One Volume*, rev. and ed. Jacob Lassner (Berkeley, CA, 1999), 95ff.

178. Joachim Whaley, *Religious Toleration and Social Change in Hamburg 1529–1819* (Cambridge, UK, 1985), 10.

179. Whaley, *Religious Toleration and Social Change in Hamburg*, 10.

180. Whaley, *Religious Toleration and Social Change in Hamburg*, 10.

181. Whaley, *Religious Toleration and Social Change in Hamburg*, 11.

182. Whaley, *Religious Toleration and Social Change in Hamburg*, 35.

183. Whaley, *Religious Toleration and Social Change in Hamburg*, 36.

184. Whaley, *Religious Toleration and Social Change in Hamburg*, 73.

185. Whaley, *Religious Toleration and Social Change in Hamburg*, 74.

186. Whaley, *Religious Toleration and Social Change in Hamburg*, 74.

187. Hermann Kellenbenz, *Sephardim an der unteren Elbe: Ihre wirtschaftliche und politische Bedeutung vom Ende des 16. bis zum Beginn des 18. Jahrhunderts* (Wiesbaden, Germany, 1958), 47.

188. Whaley, *Religious Toleration and Social Change in Hamburg*, 75.

189. Whaley, *Religious Toleration and Social Change in Hamburg*, 78.

190. Whaley, *Religious Toleration and Social Change in Hamburg*, 79.

191. Whaley, *Religious Toleration and Social Change in Hamburg*, 194–95, 198.

192. Jutta Braden, *Hamburger Judenpolitik im Zeitaliter lutherischer Orthodoxie (1590–1710)* (Hamburg, Germany, 2001), 161–63.

193. Braden, *Hamburger Judenpolitik*, 169.

194. Whaley, *Religious Toleration and Social Change in Hamburg*, 79.

195. Whaley, *Religious Toleration and Social Change in Hamburg*, 80.

196. See Heinz Mosche Graupe, ed., *Die Statuten der drei Gemeinden Altona, Hamburg und Wandsbek: Quellen zu jüd. Gemeindeorganisation im 17. u 18. Jahrhundert*, 2 vols. (Hamburg, Germany, 1973), 1:25, regarding the earlier legislation of May 28, 1697.

197. Whaley, *Religious Toleration and Social Change in Hamburg*, 73.

198. Whaley, *Religious Toleration and Social Change in Hamburg*, 81.

199. Graupe, *Die Statuten der drei Gemeinden Altona, Hamburg und Wandsbek*, 1:13.

200. Graupe, *Die Statuten der drei Gemeinden Altona, Hamburg und Wandsbek*, 1:15.

201. Graupe, *Die Statuten der drei Gemeinden Altona, Hamburg und Wandsbek*, 1:15.

202. Graupe, *Die Statuten der drei Gemeinden Altona, Hamburg und Wandsbek*, 1:29.

203. Whaley, *Religious Toleration and Social Change in Hamburg*, 81; Graupe, *Die Statuten der drei Gemeinden Altona, Hamburg und Wandsbek*, 1:15.

204. Graupe, *Die Statuten der drei Gemeinden Altona, Hamburg und Wandsbek*, 1: 15–16.

205. Graupe, *Die Statuten der drei Gemeinden Altona, Hamburg und Wandsbek*, 1: 17–18.

206. Whaley, *Religious Toleration and Social Change in Hamburg*, 81.

207. Braden, *Hamburger Judenpolitik*, 178; Graupe, *Die Statuten der drei Gemeinden Altona, Hamburg und Wandsbek*, 1:25; See also Glückel of Hameln, *The Memoirs of Glückel of Hameln*, trans. Marvin Lowenthal (New York, 1977).

208. Whaley, *Religious Toleration and Social Change in Hamburg*, 81.

209. Whaley, *Religious Toleration and Social Change in Hamburg*, 92.

210. David, *To Come to the Land*, 97–98.

211. David, *To Come to the Land*, 99.

212. David, *To Come to the Land*, 112.

213. David, *To Come to the Land*, 113; see also Solomon Freehof, *A Treasury of Responsa* (Philadelphia, 1963).

3

Community and Social Life

Now that we have learned something about the characteristics of Jewish settlement in the early modern period and the significant demographic changes and challenges that Jews faced, it is time we turn to consider the nature and structure of early modern Jewish communities. Not surprisingly, the nature and development of Jewish communal and social structures was affected in large measure by the size, continuity, and limitations imposed upon Jewish communities and settlements.

This chapter offers an overview of early modern Jewish communal structures, noting basic similarities as well as important differences. The tools of community governance, such as formal charters or "constitutions," and the primary "leadership" positions, such as the rabbi and *parnas*, are presented. This chapter also examines tensions and polarities within Jewish communities and how they may have been reflective of other social developments. While we know that many communities were highly oligarchic, this chapter traces the patterns and meanings of Jewish social organization, with special emphasis on the range of Jews' professions and occupations. While not always visible in communal documents, the position of women in early modern Jewish society is given attention in this chapter, noting their important and multifaceted contributions that often extended beyond the private and undocumented.

THE NATURE OF JEWISH COMMUNITY

What was Jewish community and specifically what was a Jewish community in the early modern period? As modern sociology has taught us, communities

can be variously defined entities that reflect many different kinds of relationships.[1] Such relationships can be dynamic and changeable, making community a rather fluid concept.

Traditional historians, such as Yitzhak Baer, the great scholar of medieval
Spanish Jewry, envisioned the Jewish community as a living organism that
was simultaneously religious and secular and that was both unique to its
context and part of a broader community of Jews, Israel.[2] No matter how it
is theorized, most historians contend that the Jewish community in the Diaspora was something of a voluntary community, dependent upon the consent of its members.[3] Early modern Jewish community was also something
of a partnership but not a partnership that was easily dissolved.

While the nature and even function of early modern Jewish communities
could vary widely, many communities shared similar needs, organizing
principles and governance. Traditionally, a Jewish community was defined
as a court. The community also functioned as a religious association that
provided ritual services (including burial and care of the sick) and provi-
sions. In the Ottoman Empire, in particular, where various ethnic Jewish
groups existed side by side, the center of a community was a congregation,
and most congregations were leery of ceding too much power to the centralized *kehilla* (community) of a city.[4]

It is, in fact, no easy task to define Jewish community, especially in the
myriad of settings in which Jews lived during the early modern period.
There were many different types of communities. While we have seen large
Jewish population centers in major cities in the last chapter, we also visited
thinly dispersed Jewish populations outside of cities and in rural areas.
Community might extend to include the city in which Jews lived together,
along with outlying suburban areas or smaller nearby communities, but
community might also be reflected in the association of a number of *kehillot*
(communities) within a particular region, the region (*medinah*) itself, or
even an entire country.

Early modern Jewish communities were simultaneously defined from
within and without. They might be formed by adherence to particular customs, by geographical location, by economic or political expediency, or
even by the dictates of external authorities (local, territorial, or national/im-
perial). Jewish communities might borrow from the non-Jewish communal
organization surrounding them, even as uniquely Jewish elements were
present and specific Jewish needs were addressed.

How one became a member of a community could vary tremendously. In
some places, communal membership began with the settlement in an area,
the purchase of a house, or the conducting of a certain level of business.
Communal membership meant tax obligations and, for some, communal
service duties as well. At times, decisions on who could be admitted to a
community were made by the members of the Jewish community them-

selves;[5] at other times, such decisions were dictated by the policies of the non-Jewish authorities that governed the Jews.[6] Membership in the community, however, could extend beyond mere residence. For purposes of taxation, individuals no longer living in a particular city might be obliged to contribute to that community's financial burdens or might be responsible for business taking place outside of the specified community.

The Jewish community of the early modern period was often granted a good deal of autonomy to deal with internal matters. In Poland, for example, King Casimir IV (1447–1492) granted a privilege in 1453 that gave Jewish leaders the authority to judge legal cases between Jews. The same privilege allowed Jews to slaughter cattle according to Jewish law and noted that Jews could not be taken to Christian ecclesiastical courts.[7] Jews living in Ottoman lands were also granted a good deal of internal autonomy through the use of a *millet* (administrative) system, intended for religious minorities. The system extended Ottoman administrative practices into the Jewish communities.[8]

COMMUNITY GOVERNANCE

The early modern Jewish community was in a certain sense a "state" within a "state," and subsequently it was governed in accord with limitations placed on it by external authorities as well as by specific principles based on traditional *halakhic* (legal) literature and local customs and ordinances. The actualization of these principles occurred through the work of individuals in various communal positions and through a host of communal institutions.

Governing Organs: The Community Council and Other Communal Positions

Jewish communal governance was shaped, on the one hand, by Jewish legal precedents and, on the other, by various Jewish historical experiences and the environments in which they lived. The individual community was governed by a council, comprised generally of wealthy and scholarly[9] members of the community and convened to initiate and regulate communal policy, as well as to protect the community and its interests in economic, judicial, and diplomatic concerns. The members of the council were elected by majority vote and sworn to secrecy. Often only a select group of wealthy and distinguished families served in such offices.[10]

The number of members on the council varied from community to community, as did the exact procedures for electing members. Many communities appointed between seven and fourteen council members.[11] The communal organization of sixteenth-century Cracow-Kazimierz in Poland, for example, was concretized with a communal ordinance in 1595.[12] According to that ordinance, the community was governed by five heads (*roshim*), five notables (*tovim*), and fourteen members of the council (*kahal*). The community of Salonika was governed administratively by a central committee of seven lay leaders. A general assembly, or **mahamad**, represented the Jews living in various parts of the city and was responsible for electing committees.[13] In Amsterdam after 1639, the *mahamad* or council was nominated each year from among the wealthiest 20 percent of the population by the preceding seven members. The constitution and governance of the Amsterdam community (like others such as Livorno, Hamburg, and London) were based on the model of other communities, especially Venice, which had a great deal of influence throughout the Jewish settlements of the Netherlands and the Dutch colonies of the New World, as well as the Portuguese community in Hamburg.

In Amsterdam, as in other communities, the council wielded considerable authority, at times rather autocratically. The constitution of the combined Amsterdam communities in the seventeenth century began with the following *haskamah* (agreement):

> The Mahamad will have authority and superiority over everything. No person may go against the resolutions taken and made public by the said Mahamad nor sign papers to oppose it. Those who do will be punished with **herem**. Therefore it is ruled that the Mahamad which serves every year has to be supreme in the governing of the kahal and the nacao and its dependencies. . . . Above all they will see to it that the order of the Mahamad be obeyed and executed, for thus it behooves the good government, peace, and tranquility of this **Kahal Kados**. May God bless her.[14]

Like other communal councils, the scope of the Amsterdam *mahamad*'s activities was broad. It oversaw various charitable organizations and regulated synagogue worship, behavior, and seating (with various distinctions and seating based on social status and age). The council also oversaw communally run education and the sale of meat, a significant issue in many Jewish communities. The council maintained authority to punish individuals for social ills, from gambling and prostitution to more general improprieties such as marriages without parental permission. Community leaders could wield substantial power and lobby for their own individual gain and yet be held personally responsible for the vicissitudes facing the community, for example, the payment of ransom for co-religionists held in captivity.[15]

Community councils were often thinly veiled oligarchies, such as in Cracow-Kazimierz by the end of the sixteenth century.[16] The trend toward oligarchic and strong lay leadership had, however, already begun in the later Middle Ages. In early fourteenth-century Worms, for example, the *parnasim* were chosen for life appointments and gained the exclusive right to appoint their successors. In some places, lay communal leaders even began to operate their own courts of arbitration.[17]

The Complexities of Communal Governing

Some communities were extremely complex in their governance. In the multiethnic community of Venice, for example, differing committees and procedures governed the German, Spanish, and Levantine communities.[18] While these various communities maintained their own committees and functions, they also shared some broader communal functions, particularly as carried out in the pan-communal banking and assessment committees.

Regardless of the complexity or size of the Jewish community, the community had to engage members in a wide range of functions in order to run efficiently. Among the employees, some were paid but most were voluntary. The positions included the rabbi, *parnasim* (these lay leaders could go also by various other names)—chiefs (*roshim*), best men (*tovim*), trustees (*ne'emanim*)—and various other officials (*gabbaim*), tax assessors, community scribe, and beadle (*shammash*), whose duties included summoning people to prayer services.[19]

Many communities also had an honorary official known as the *shtadlan*, who served as something of a liaison to the external authorities. The *shtadlan* evolved in some places into the court Jew, the fiscal agent who served the growing financial needs of the lavish courts of absolutist rulers.[20] In this capacity, especially in central Europe, prominent Jews held monopolies on state tax collection and provided valuable financing, supplies, and economic advice. Many smaller ruling courts also employed Jewish factors. The court Jew was not new to the early modern period—there were many medieval examples in both Christian and Muslim lands. In the early modern period, however, with significant economic development, court factors gained new importance. Jews became heavily involved in court life, and examples of assimilating tendencies can be found. Nevertheless, recent scholarship indicates that most court Jews remained essentially tied to their communities, often times defending the Jewish communities and contributing to the religious life of the community through the sponsorship of learning and charity.

No matter how assimilated or how many privileges individual court Jews secured for themselves or their communities, court Jews were still Jews and suffered anti-Jewish suspicions and prejudice. Court Jews formed part of something of an aristocracy within the Jewish world, often intermarrying with other court Jewish families and creating important and influential dynasties.

In the Ottoman Empire, Jewish lay leaders also maintained important and often complex relationships with the non-Jewish authorities. They were responsible for petitioning the government and defending their communities. While the role of the *shtadlan* was not exactly parallel in the Ottoman Empire, there are many examples of Jews functioning in a similar role, though generally in a more local than national role.[21] As in central Europe, lay leaders fought edicts of expulsion and were frequently put in danger of prison or held accountable for communal tax obligations that were not met.[22] In Egypt the medieval position of the **nagid**, something like a local governor or territorial head of state, was affected by the various political intrigues at the local, regional, and imperial levels.[23] Traceable back until the eleventh century in this form (though the word is biblical in origin, with meaning as well in the Babylonian Jewish academy), the position seems to have operated intermittently until the early part of the sixteenth century and the conquest by the Ottomans.[24] In Fez after the sixteenth century, the *nagid* was the Jewish representative at the court and chosen by the ruler with the agreement of the Jewish community. The *nagid* could be very powerful, and the position, like many other offices, at times became hereditary.[25]

Jewish communities also appointed individuals with ritual responsibilities, such as cantors, preachers, *shohetim* (ritual slaughterers), and educators (these might be communal servants, teaching poorer children, as opposed to the tutors of the wealthier families).[26] Communities, especially larger ones, also employed individuals in other professions, such as communal physicians. Frankfurt civic authorities, for example, granted the Jewish community in 1631 the privilege of retaining a communal physician.[27] The Jews of Posen were similarly permitted to appoint a communal physician in 1631 with a set annual salary and a contract for three years with exemption from all taxes.[28]

Serving the Jewish community were various societies or brotherhoods that often appeared to resemble Christian fraternities or civic guilds. Most important in many communities was the burial society, the **hevra kadisha**, which gained new heights and levels of organization during the course of the sixteenth century.[29] One of the oldest such brotherhoods developed in Prague in the 1560s.[30] Other associations or welfare societies also developed more fully in the early modern period. In Frankfurt, Rabbi Akiva Frankfurt established a welfare society and fund in 1597. In the seventeenth century we find evidence of these organizations providing care for the sick,[31] and by the end of the seventeenth or beginning of the eighteenth century, almost every important town in central Europe had a hospital for the sick and poor.[32]

Rules and Procedures for Office Holding

In theory the Jewish community was something of a democracy with strict stipulations for voting and holding office. Election procedures varied by community but often involved either a direct vote of taxpaying males or the work of a board of elections. In Rome, the *fattori* (three chief officials), rabbis, and Board of Sixty met in the synagogue to choose by lot the treasurer for a three-year period. The same group also elected two *parnasim* for a six-month period. They would be responsible for the community money and goods.[33]

In practice, many communities were run by a few wealthy or prominent individuals, who formed something of an early modern Jewish oligarchy.[34] In late fifteenth-century Navarre, for example, six families from the city of Tudela provided sixteen of the twenty-nine community officials. In other communities, those holding communal positions did come from a diverse social and professional background. Much in line with the oligarchic nature of the communities themselves, the voting procedures could be highly manipulated and, despite much legislation to the contrary, could be based on lineage, wealth, or social connections.

In theory the length of tenure of office was generally one year; practically, however, officers were not typically removed from office so long as they continued to fulfill their duties. Elections often required the additional approval of the external civil or ecclesiastical authority and often stipulated that the person elected pay an election fee and take an oath of fealty to the civil authority.[35] Often a festive celebration or meal, and frequently additional payments to the non-Jewish overlords, accompanied the appointment.[36] In some cases, individual officials rotated into various communal positions. The communal ordinance of late sixteenth-century Worms, for example, stipulated that councilmen rotated on a monthly basis to the position of *parnas* of the month, **parnas ha-hodesh**.

The combined Minute Book of the congregations Zur Israel of Recife and Magen Abraham of Mauricia, Brazil, from 1648 to 1653, provides a glimpse at the appointment of communal officials in the New World. The Book specifies that the *mahamad* was composed of four *parnasim* and one *gabbai*, with two *parnasim* being elected on **Shabbat ha Gadol** and two in addition to the *gabbai* on *Rosh ha Shannah*, each for one-year terms. The regulations permitted the election of anyone, including relatives, provided that they did not serve together.[37] Men who had been converted (circumcised) in Brazil were not to be considered for office for one year, "so that they may become more conversant in matters pertaining to Judaism."[38] Elections were conducted using a ballot-box; decisions were to be made by majority vote,[39] but the decisions were kept secret until announced in the synagogue.[40] As in other communities, there were fines for those who refused the office.[41]

Service on the council was expected from those elected. There were some restrictions placed on service. Certain relatives, for example, were forbidden from serving simultaneously. According to the third *haskamah* of the Amsterdam constitution, "In one mahamad will not be elected a father together with his son, a brother with a brother, a grandfather with a grandson, an uncle with a nephew, a father-in-law with a son-in-law, cousins in the first degree, a brother-in-law with a brother-in-law. Neither can a relative in these degrees cast a ballot in favor of such a relative nor judge an issue which concerns him."[42] Women and unmarried men were excluded from serving on the *mahamad*, though there were exceptions for bachelors in the seventeenth century. The preferred age for *parnasim* was forty, while for various *gabbaim* it ranged between twenty-eight and thirty-eight. If anyone declined the position, he was subject to monetary fines and restrictions on synagogue honors. In Rome, for example, anyone who declined to serve as treasurer after being elected was to pay a monetary fine.[43] Protests by individuals attempting to avoid such service were generally in vain.[44]

The Rabbi

Throughout history, Jewish religious leaders performed particular legal (*halakhic*) functions and answered questions regarding religious law. In theory, the ordination of rabbis finds a proof text in the biblical Moses laying his hands on Joshua as his successor and on the seventy elders solicited to assist with governing the Israelites. The process of ordination, or *semikhah*, had had a long history in Judaism but ostensibly came to a formal end with the destruction of the governing body of the **Sanhedrin** in the second century CE. Nonetheless, individuals of particularly high learning were recognized as religious authorities and perhaps continued to be ordained throughout the Babylonian and Palestinian academies of the early Middle Ages and into the high Middle Ages. During the period of the scholars known as *geonim*, an exilarch or *rosh golah* gave license for some to arbitrate legal cases. *Geonim* could appoint a variety of officials, including scribes, public worship leaders, judges, and teachers.

Throughout the Middle Ages religious authorities were known by different terms and had a wide range of powers. In **Sephardic** lands, the rabbi was generally known as the *hakham*, or learned one. The process of ordination was renewed in Ashkenaz in the fourteenth century, and an attempt to restore *semikhah* was made in Safed in the late 1530s (see below).

In fifteenth-century Italy and Germany, the power and authority of the rabbi was institutionalized by the process of rabbinic ordination. The rite has been compared by some scholars to the ordination of Catholic priests or the granting of a university doctoral degree.[45] But the rabbi was not only a scholar; he was simultaneously a judge and religious leader who was granted the power to punish religious or communal transgression through excommunication.[46]

In fact, there existed different types of rabbis and rabbinic authority in the early modern period.[47] Important distinctions need to be made be-

tween the leading and prestigious rabbis of the age and the majority of
other lesser rabbinic figures.[48] The "non-professional" rabbi, known as
semikhat haver or *rav*, was granted this title after the completion of a number of years of study. He possessed a range of communal and legal authority, but he could not function in cases of marriage or divorce. He paid taxes
and was usually engaged in business. In early modern Poland, there existed
a religious official known as the preacher, or *darshan*, who was not fully a
rabbi but who delivered sermons to the congregation.[49]

The authoritative rabbi for the community, on the other hand, was a rabbinic scholar who maintained an academy (that is, he had the privilege of
instruction) and had authority in all ritual matters. He could appoint ritual
slaughterers and inspectors, send inspectors to other communities,[50] deliver
public speeches, and perform many important communal religious functions, such as marriages, divorce, *halizot*, and the administration of oaths to
widows in order to collect the money guaranteed in the *ketubot* (marriage
contracts). These authoritative rabbis could also serve as judges in courts of
arbitration, either in colleges or by themselves. Generally such courts were
composed of three rabbis, and the head of this court was termed the *av bet
din*. Some communities had more than one such rabbi, who was generally
invited by the community, had lived in the community for many years, or
was appointed by another prominent rabbi. A community could not be
forced to accept a rabbi, however.[51]

Rabbis were generally compensated in some way for their services. In
Worms the rabbi was provided with housing, given certain honors, and exempted from general and property taxes. In other communities, the rabbi
signed a multiyear contract and was paid an annual salary, generally from
community coffers or the pocketbooks of wealthy lay leaders. According to
a rabbinic contract from Verona, Italy, from the mid-sixteenth century, the
rabbi was selected by two lay leaders. The rabbi's primary functions were related to teaching—the rabbi's full schedule was delineated—as well as en-
acting communal excommunications. According to the contract,

> He will not be allowed to teach more than seven hours a day at most, and the
> rest of the time left to him, he shall persue and involve himself with matters
> which are to the benefit of the holy community, to chastise, to set aright, and
> to punish those who behave wrongly, to direct them in the way of ethics, and
> to strengthen those who study [Torah] and to require to learn, by any means at
> his disposal. And he shall be required, upon the request of the Holy Congre-
> gation of Verona or of the majority of the leaders at the time, to enact or to ban
> or to agree to whatever matter or edict [they may ask], provided that it is cor-
> rect and proper for the general good.[52]

In return for his services, the rabbi was to be paid an annual salary from the
charity box.[53]

Since the fifteenth century, and especially during the course of the six-teenth century, the rabbinate was professionalized in the sense that the rabbi became an official paid and appointed by the community, frequently lead-ing to limitations on rabbinic power. One scholar has argued that the pro-fessionalization, with the accompanying fees charged by rabbis for their ser-vice, fostered an increase in divorce within the Jewish communities. While critical of some of the language associated with professionalization, the em-inent historian of early modern Polish Jewry Adam Teller notes that the de-cline in rabbinic power and corresponding increase in the power of lay lead-ers in sixteenth-century Poland mirrored more general societal changes. Teller writes, "The declining power of the central authority and correspon-ding rise in the status of the nobility in Poland was mirrored by a decline in the power of the centralized rabbinate in favour of the individual commu-nities and the refashioning of the rabbinate as a form of semi-honorary of-ficial post, like those held by the Polish nobility." This development led to what Teller refers to as an actual "deprofessionalzing" of the rabbinate and a corresponding reduction of rabbinic political power within the Jewish community.[54] Of course individual rabbis, depending on their learning and individual skills, might hold a great deal of power and carry much influence.

The entire issue of ordination and the recognition of rabbinic titles itself was much discussed throughout the early modern period. In Venice in the early seventeenth century, an extensive ordinance was instituted that allowed all those who until that time had "attained the name Rabbi or Fellow . . . having ascended shall not descend, and their honor shall remain in place, of being called by the name Rabbi or Fellow upon ascending to read the Law."[55] Such rabbis, however, were not to be involved in communal affairs. They were expected "only to teach the laws of the Forbidden and the Permitted, and to issue excommunications on the basis of the mandates of the author-ities."[56] No rabbi was to have the authority to grant the title of rabbi or fel-low without the authority being first granted to him by the "distinguished heads and governors of the province." The ordinance went on to stipulate age requirements and procedures for those coming from outside Venice.

The position and function of the rabbi in Ottoman lands seems to have been very similar. The rabbi was engaged and could be dismissed by the lay leadership. He was involved in *halakhic* decision-making as well as educa-tion. His individual powers and role, of course, often depended greatly on his own personal prowess and personal and scholarly repute.[57]

Rabbis might be appointed as heads over entire regions. In Poland, chief rabbis who headed regional courts were appointed by regional councils.[58] Ottoman rulers did the same thing throughout the fifteenth and sixteenth centuries, though because of their heterogeneous communities they faced an even more difficult task.[59] After the movement of the Jews to Istanbul, Rabbi Moses Capsali was appointed as chief rabbi, though it remains unclear whether his position was empirewide or limited to Istanbul. Capsali was clearly the leading and final authority within Istanbul.[60] After Capsali, Rabbi Elijah Mizrahi became the leading rabbi in Istanbul. Given the waves of migration and increasing diversity, however, his authority does not appear to have extended beyond the city and was perhaps even limited there as well.[61] The appointment of a chief rabbi does not appear to have survived after Capsali, and the tax that Jews originally paid for the installation of the chief rabbi became a more general tax in turn for the privilege of self-governing their communities.[62] In Europe varying attempts were made by non-Jewish authorities to appoint a chief rabbi of a particular region or nation. This, it was assumed, would assist in the management of the community and the collection of taxes. Such attempts occurred in sixteenth-century Germany but do not appear to have been long-lasting.

The *Herem* (Excommunication)

Throughout the early modern period there was a palpable and growing tension between lay and rabbinic leaders in many communities. One important communal area that seemed to reflect this tension was the writ of excommunication (*herem*)[63] intended to punish individuals who deviated from communal norms or legislation. In Venice, legislation dictated that rabbis were central in the excommunication (and absolution) process as well as in the administration of oaths.[64] While the rabbis generally had to issue the excommunication—so reserving important power—many communal constitutions indicated that the rabbi could do so only with the approval, or even instigation, of the lay community council.[65]

The *herem* was intended to be a means of social and religious separation from the community. In an age in which Jews were forced by external society to remain within the Jewish community, viewed as a corporate entity, or to convert to the host community's religion, the *herem* was an incredibly powerful form of coercion. Jews under various forms or levels of *herem* were subjected to different restrictions, ranging from restrictions from participating in communal worship to securing kosher meat. The *herem* was also a social tool, and individuals who were excommunicated were not allowed to interact with other members of the community. While capital punishment was generally beyond the purview of the Jewish community, the community did have authority for other sorts of punishment, such as the imposition of monetary fines.[66]

Criticism of the Rabbis and Inter-Rabbinic Relations

In addition to attempts at controlling individual rabbis, the position of the rabbi in general was subject to criticism, especially when some rabbis appear to have been politically motivated or were less scrupulous than they should have been in their decision-making or in their personal behavior. The rabbis were open to a range of criticism, as the memoirist Glückel of Hameln, one of the few audible Jewish female voices from the pre-modern period, indicated throughout her work. In one case she discussed, in a rather humorous play on words, rabbinical court dishonesty or, better, swindling.[67] Frequently, in fact, she favored a personal piety and morality to formal or institutionalized religion.

Tensions between would-be rabbinic leaders and between rabbis and members of community councils could run high. The community in Breslau, for example, complained to Rabbi Jacob Weil in fifteenth-century Augsburg that a rabbi tried to force his authority on the community, without being invited to serve as the community rabbi.[68] A similar case occurred in Nuremberg in the fifteenth century, pitting two competing rabbis and their followers against one another and escalating into behaviors that challenged not only the honor of the rabbis themselves but also the cohesiveness of the entire Jewish community.[69]

Rabbinic leaders, especially in large communities, might oppose one another, but they might also unify and strengthen the rabbinate. According to a late sixteenth-century rabbi from Salonika, for example, "When influential Jews join together, they are strong enough to provide the leadership needed in this city. They have not previously had this strength, fearing those who, without grounds and in violation of Jewish law, informed about their money to the authorities. But when many are joined and united, they are far stronger than when they are separate and scattered."[70]

A curious and important episode, which highlights the promise of rabbinic cohesion but the inability to forge rabbinic agreement, in Jewish history occurred in 1538 when Rabbi Jacob Berab in Safed convened twenty-five rabbis in that city, who then appointed him as chief rabbi. In turn, Berab ordained four other rabbis, including Joseph Caro, author of the famous legal code the *Shulhan Arukh*. Berab had relied on a ruling of the medieval authority Moses **Maimonides** who noted, "If all the Palestinian sages would unanimously agree to appoint and ordain judges, then these new ordinants would possess the full authority of the original ordained judges."[71] Berab had not secured the agreement of the rabbis in Jerusalem, however, who in turn refused to recognize Berab's appointment and in effect ended the restoration of *semikhah*. According to the Jerusalem scholars,

This agreed proclamation of theirs cannot stand without our agreement, namely, ours the humble ones of the flock in Jerusalem. For though we are few in number compared to them, nevertheless, we are not mere reed-cutters. Besides the sanctity of this place (Jerusalem), there is an added consideration, in that the matter of ordination is in the hands of all the sages of the holy land, as Maimonides has written.[72]

Community Governing Tools

Communal legislation was dictated and approved by the rabbinate and the lay leadership; however, methods were in place for publicizing expectations of adherence among the entire community. According to a statute from early seventeenth-century Venice, for example, "The present statute was made public and called out, with the consent and in the presence of all the rabbis of the community, God preserve them, and in the presence of the entire community, adults and children, with an open ark and with the sound of the **shofar** and black candles. May God be with all Israel. Amen."[73]

The power of the communal regulations was to be absolute. The councilmen were charged to actuate the regulations but were themselves to be bound by the regulations. In Recife the regulations were read publicly and agreed to by each member. The Book concludes,

> The Gentlemen of the Mahamad shall not add to or violate any of these Eschamot [*haskamot*]. And if such action happens to become necessary, they shall have to give an account to the Kahal. And in case the Gentlemen of the Mahamad violate, diminish or increase them, they shall be subject to a fine of a hundred florins. And if there is any doubt about the interpretation of these Eschamot, they shall call for explanation upon the Gentlemen who prepared them. And the said Eschamot shall be read twice a year, on Sabbath agadol [*Shabbat ha Gadol*] and on the holiday of Suckot [**Sukkot**].[74]

The Jewish community had various governing tools at its disposal, such as the ability to control rent and to grant virtual monopolies in certain professions or businesses. As we saw in chapter 2, the community could also regulate settlement, and there were many cases of Jews being turned away from the community for fear of business competition, fear of negative perceptions on the part of external authorities, or simply because of internal tensions.

Another form of communal governance was the various records and assemblies (local or regional, occasionally even "national") of the Jewish communities. The Jewish community legislated through ordinances, or *takkanot* (sometimes in the form of sumptuary laws that dictated proper dress and behavior), and recorded these laws as well as various transactions and events in community ledgers (*pinkasim*). **Memorybooks**, which recorded the deaths of community members, often the wealthiest or most influential, also recorded various bits of communal lore and legend as well. Customs books similarly recorded local and regional practices, while codifying various communal practices.[75] Jewish communities, then, could be defined in many ways and possessed important governing structures, offices, and tools.

Regional Councils

Although the individual local community, especially before the end of
the fourteenth century, came to regard itself as an autonomous jurisdic-
tional area, communities often joined together to enact specific regulations
or to judge particular legal cases. Throughout the Middle Ages there were a
number of important rabbinic synods that attempted to create centralized
authority and legal observance. Of particular importance were the combined synods of the three German Rhineland communities Speyer, Worms,
and Mainz. Between 1196 and 1250 ordinances were discussed and approved regarding a broad array of topics such as trial procedures, debts, taxation, the ban of excommunication, sumptuary laws, synagogues, and relations with non-Jews. Such synods continued throughout the fourteenth and
fifteenth centuries. In Germany a number of landed or regional Jewries developed in the early modern period. Often these landed Jewries mirrored
broader territorial structures and served both Jewish and German purposes.
In Germany, several centralized courts and tax collection centers developed
during the course of the late sixteenth and early seventeenth centuries.

In Spain an assembly of Jewish communal representatives from Castile
met in the city of Valladolid in the early fifteenth century and passed a series of *takkanot*.[76] The primary role of Abraham Bienveniste, who was the
rabbi of the Court, added a certain legal sanction to the proceedings as the
assembly sought to establish some level of uniformity in communal legislation. The articles of the legislation treated topics such as taxation, sumptuary laws, and the election of judges and officials.

In Poland, centralized councils mirrored general economic development
(as reflected in annual fairs and settlement patterns). These centralized
councils allowed for regular meetings of the various constituent communities, often at set times of the year, but also when emergency situations arose.
The Council of the Province of Lithuania, for example, worked closely with
the three or four largest member communities to provide leadership and
practical protection during times of crisis.[77] Some communities were particularly important in these regional assemblies. The community of Brest-
Litovsk was primary in the Council of Lithuania. In the early years of the
council, nearly half of the meetings took place there, and council legislation
demarcated Brest-Litovsk as the community that had the privilege of sign-
ing legislation first. As might be expected, the community exercised particularly powerful control over some of the social and economic decisions of
the council.[78]

The Jewish National Parliament, or *seym*, that was convened in 1579 by
King Stephen Bathory reflected the structure of the broader Polish *seym*. The
seym was initially called the Council of Four Lands (though it included
three to five regions at any one time until the middle of the seventeenth

century),[79] and it gradually became the primary political body for the autonomous Jewish population in Poland.[80] Generally, it did not include rabbis, though rabbis appear to have met separately to discuss pressing *halakhic* concerns.[81] A Supreme Rabbinic Tribunal also served as a national body, even as local communities governed their own affairs.[82] In the Ottoman lands as well, different towns appointed members to represent communal interests in meetings of broader concern.[83]

Courts

Jewish courts were central to the operation of the community. Courts, which could be religious as well as lay, existed at various levels and with different functions and foci. In Cracow-Kazimierz, for example, three different law courts were established for varying levels of cases.[84] Throughout Poland, a complex system of courts was established, with the Council of the Four Lands standing as a kind of supreme court. According to the admittedly idealistic last chapter of Nathan of Hannover's chronicle *Abyss of Despair*,

> Justice obtained in Poland just as in Jerusalem before the destruction of the Temple. There were courts in every town, and if people did not care to try their case before the court of their own town they could go to a nearby court. And if they did not care to try their case before a nearby court, they could go to a superior court, for in every province there was a higher court. . . . If, however, different communities, through their leaders, would start litigation among themselves, in order to try their case they would have to appear before the leaders of the Four Lands—may their Rock and Redeemer guard them—who met twice a year.[85]

It is clear that throughout the early modern period Jews also had recourse to non-Jewish courts. At times Jews were involved in litigation with non-Jews. At other times, and for a variety of reasons, Jews believed that they would receive a fairer trial in a non-Jewish setting. Still, such recourse to non-Jewish authority could be dangerous to the Jewish community, opening as it might internal matters to external scrutiny. Therefore, it is not surprising that the synod of German Jews held at Frankfurt in 1603 began by legislating against Jews taking legal cases to Gentile courts:

> It is common offense among the people of our generation to refuse to obey Jewish law and even to compel opposing litigants to present themselves before secular courts. The result is that the Holy Name is profaned and that the Government and the judges are provoked at us. We have therefore decided that anyone who sues his neighbor in secular courts shall be compelled to free him from all the charges against him, even though the Courts decided in favor of the plaintiff.[86]

In Venice, Jews were discouraged generally from becoming involved with non-Jewish rulers or courts. According to a statute from 1617, "No one bearing the name of Israel, whomsoever, man or woman, child or adult, shall take the liberty, by himself, of coming before any magistracy of this city, or of interfering in any matter pertaining to the community, the heads and governors of the province, unless summoned and ordered to do so by the heads of the governors of the province, acting in the community's name."[87]

In the Ottoman Empire, just as in Europe, non-Jewish legal courts were frequently discussed in rabbinic writing. Despite some general concerns, Jews frequented Muslim courts when there were cases between Jews and non-Jews regarding civil law and commercial needs.[88] Cases between Jews, however, were banned from non-Jewish courts.[89] The primary reasons for this restriction were related to the perception of a certain superiority of Jewish law and Jewish courts, the concern that Muslim law court decisions might transgress Jewish law, the attempt to keep influential individuals from developing strong Ottoman relations and then lording over the Jewish community, the desire to avoid any harm to the reputation of the Jewish community, and the aversion of punishment not sanctioned by Jewish law.[90] Occasionally rabbis did allow the use of Muslim courts, especially when it came to the implementation of Jewish court decisions, the proof of property titles, and criminal offences.[91]

Taxation

In many ways taxation was a communal institution, and much of the community structure was related to assessing and collecting taxes. Most tax money, however, was paid out to the non-Jewish authorities, and very little was generally available to reinvest in the Jewish community itself.

There were different methods of tax assessment: a declarative method, in which each individual would declare his taxable possessions under oath but without itemizing them; a committee assessor method, whereby an elected committee of assessors would assess each individual's taxable wealth; or a combination of the first two methods, in which individual declarations would be reviewed by a committee of assessors.[92]

In Germany, taxes were generally collected according to property, not by head, unless extraordinary taxes were levied on the community. Usually, taxes were collected once a year.[93] The taxes of the community were either paid individually or, more typically, pooled as a communal unit, with the Jewish community responsible for assessing and administering the collection.[94] Although not generally encouraged, individuals were sometimes allowed to arrange their own taxes with the civil authorities. Small suburban communities were generally incorporated with the closest large community and treated as an economic unit.[95]

Certain objects were exempted from taxation.[96] Objects from which income was generated or potentially generated were taxable, but houses typically were not taxed in Germany unless they were rented or put up for sale. Despite the complaints of wealthy community members, vacant houses were generally considered exempt. Still, in times of emergency, all houses might be assessed. Fields and vineyards were taxed, but traditionally only about half of their real value was taxed because of the high rate of overhead associated with their possession.

Precious articles of a personal nature, such as cups and jewelry, were generally not taxed. Diamonds and precious stones, however, were not exempt. Ordinary household items and wardrobes were not taxed, but they could be assessed if placed for sale, since they would generate income. Books were generally exempt in order to encourage their production and purchase. Donations were tax exempt.

Some individuals were exempt or partially exempt from taxation, including Talmudic scholars (particularly after the thirteenth century), orphans, elementary school teachers, scribes, servants, unemployed or retired people, transients, or those exempted by the civil authorities.[97] Even these exempted or partially exempted persons, however, would be taxed in emergency situations or when an extraordinary tax was levied on the community. Much, however, depended on the custom of the region. In the Rhineland, for example, Talmudic scholars were not exempted from taxation.

In Recife various goods were taxed. Dry and other goods from Holland and other foreign ports were to be taxed at three-quarters per 100 "from the gross proceeds here obtained."[98] "Cash, gold, silver, jewels or pearls, amber, or similar things which go or come for business shall be taxable at three per thousand."[99] Sugar, tobacco, and even negroes were taxed a standard rate per volume.[100]

Taxation was imposed on the Jews from outside their communities, frequently by the emperor, king, or state.[101] In the Ottoman Empire, as a Muslim state, Jews were forced to pay a poll-tax that simultaneously guaranteed them protection and a certain level of internal autonomy.[102] The annual tax was divided by taxpayer income and was imposed on adult males.[103] The tax could be imposed on individuals, families,[104] or congregations, but the entire aggregate payment came from the community as a whole.[105] The state apparently encouraged the unification of various communities in this process, and the tax also served an important census-taking capacity.[106]

In some cities, a Jew who left the community might still be held responsible for paying the poll-tax to the city.[107] Various other taxes were also imposed on the Jews. These included a rabbi tax; an annual tax for the privilege of appointing a chief rabbi;[108] certain levies related to war; a tax on cultivated land and a separate tithing on vineyards, orchards, and crops; a courier tax; a livestock tax and a grazing ground tax; an army supply tax; and taxes in support of the palace, court, and police commander.[109]

In Navarre, Jews were charged special imposts upon the arrival of the monarch as well as various royal taxes, an (annual) sales tax, and special taxes related to the civil war raging in the late fifteenth century.[110] Jews in the main Navarrese city of Tudela paid taxes to royal and municipal authorities but also to ecclesiastical authorities, especially related to the practice of viticulture.[111] In parts of Poland, Jews were obligated to pay a tax to support the feeding of animals in the royal zoo, especially the lions and leopards![112]

Variations

At times, multiple communities might develop within one geographic area. This was especially true in more heterogeneous communities in Italy and the Ottoman Empire but might occur in other places as well when competing congregations clashed over customs or personalities. In Navarre, for example, after the expulsions from Spain, many Jews made their way to cities within the neighboring kingdom. Eventually these Jews, along with the native Navarrese Jews, were forcibly converted, but in the meantime, they had formed their own rather distinct communities. This led, in some cases, to internal Jewish communal friction.[113] Even in the often smaller and less complex communities of central and western Europe, conflicts might arise. In Amsterdam and Hamburg, for example, separate Sephardic and **Ashkenazic** communities developed, often with much tension (see chapter 2). Even in the same city, we find many examples of separate congregations. In Lemberg, for example, the two congregations had separate synagogues, *mikvaot* (ritual baths), and charitable institutions.[114]

Until the late fifteenth century, the Roman Jewish community was relatively homogenous in terms of the origins of individual members. After that time, however, the community became more diverse. By 1461 there were separate synagogues for non-Roman Italian Jews, Roman, German, French, and Catalan Jews.[115] Such divisions became particularly apparent when it came to religious rites and liturgy, which varied by ethnicity.[116] At the same time, however, there could be a good deal of fluidity between synagogues, and most controversies had to do with more practical sorts of matters such as property and rent.[117] In addition, Roman Jews were more likely than many other Jews to marry Jews of different ethnic backgrounds. As the historian Kenneth Stow writes, "The frequency of Roman Jews marrying those of different ethnic origins reinforces the impression that the 'melting pot' in Rome was on a brighter flame than were interethnic frictions. . . . The high outmarriage rates in Rome are especially indicative of ethnic amalgamation."[118]

Some cities developed competing congregations that were at times fueled by varying religious customs, ethnic makeup, or social standing. Early in the nascent Amsterdam community three congregations developed. Administrative systems were put into place to create a broader communal organization. In 1622 a governing body, the ***imposta***, was established. It was run by six *deputados* and two *parnasim* from each of the congregations. By 1639 the communities were united into a central congregation, even though differences continued to be evident. The new, merged community was governed by a *mahamad* or council of seven who were elected by the fifteen *parnasim* of the communities being dissolved. New communal statutes were drafted.

Communal Institutions

The Synagogue

In addition to communal positions, various communal institutions were significant in the early modern period.[119] Perhaps no edifice characterized the Jewish community more than the synagogue.[120] In many early modern Jewish communities, formal synagogues did not exist. They might be clandestine buildings revealing on the outside very little of their internal nature and function. They might be located in private homes. No matter the form, the existence of a synagogue was a key determinative factor in the existence and perpetuation of a community. The synagogue was a legislative center, where edicts could be read and excommunications decreed. It was more than simply an administrative center or a religious house of worship; it was a central community gathering space. The synagogue and the proper decorum within it were often the subject of various communal edicts and legislation.[121] The construction or even repair of the synagogue often required non-Jewish approval and was frequently the subject of intense debate in the various city councils and pulpits.

With the growing diversity in some multiethnic Jewish communities, separate synagogues often emerged based on "national" or ethnic background or religious customs. In seventeenth-century Venice, according to one witness, on the holiday of **Simhat Torah**, "many maidens and betrothed young women mask themselves, in order not to be recognized, and go to see all the synagogues . . . with people of all nations mingling: Spaniards, Levantines, Portuguese, Germans, Greeks, Italians and others, all singing in accordance with their particular custom."[122] This is a rather cosmopolitan image, and it illustrates what Jewish identity meant in the early modern period as well as how the various ethnicities and their communities interacted. An additional example of this was the complex Jewish community of Istanbul, where Jews gathered from very diverse backgrounds: native inhabitants of Greece and Byzantium, but also Jews from central Europe (especially from

Bavaria, Hungary, and Austria) and Italy, as well as a wide range of Sephardic Jews. Generally such ethnic communities had their own leadership, synagogue, confraternities, and coffers. In many cases they were independent communities within the same city, though in some cases they formed a larger Jewish communal superstructure headed by a rabbi or board of rabbis.

In Damascus, according to an early sixteenth century rabbi, Moses Bassola d'Ancona, the Jews numbered

> about 500 households. They have three synagogues which are beautifully built and adorned—one for the Sefradim, one for the native Jews, and one for the Sicilians. . . . There is also another synagogue at the end of the town called "Unb." A mile outside of Damascus there is a place called Jawbar, where there is a community of Arabic-speaking Jews numbering about sixty households. There is a very handsome synagogue there, the like of which I have never seen.[123]

At times, internal division had more to do with social conflict. In Kazimierz, in the early sixteenth century, conflict arose between two prominent families, leading for a time to the development of two separate fully autonomous communities, both recognized by the king. Each had its own communal religious and governing structure.[124]

Partially in response to the explosion of Ashkenazic immigration after the Thirty Years' War (1618–1648), the merger agreement of the Sephardic communities in Amsterdam placed precise restrictions on the affiliation of its members. According to the second *capitolo*,

> No one of the Portuguese or Spanish Jewish *natie* who until now has observed their religion in their Church or Synagogue as well as those who in the future will arrive from abroad and join them may separate himself from the Church or Synagogue and community in order to pray or congregate with ten or more persons.
>
> Much less that any one of them form or keep another Church without approval and explicit consent of the Gentlemen Burgomasters, after consultation with the Parnasim or Elders of that time.
>
> That no one of those who break with the aforesaid Church may go and pray outside their community in one of the other Jewish-Churches, whether German or Polish.[125]

This was the only statute of the *kahal* that was ratified directly by municipal law.[126]

The architecture of the synagogue often shared the structure and look of the general architecture surrounding it. In part this was due to the fact that Jews did not want, or were not allowed, to have the synagogue stand out. At times the synagogue was designed by non-Jewish architects, as was the case in Amsterdam, where the synagogue fit into the city landscape very neatly. The Sephardic synagogue of 1639 seems to have been based on other local galleried buildings such as the Remonstrant church (constructed in 1629) and the Lutheran church (1632–1633). The Ashkenazic synagogue of 1670–1671, with connected *mikvah* and caretaker residence, was influenced or designed by the municipal architect Daniel Stalpert and clearly reflected the appearance of other Dutch religious institutions of the period.

The later Sephardic synagogue of 1671–1675 was, however, a more magnificent undertaking, costing huge sums of money and drawing quite a lot of attention. (See figure 3.1.) According to an English traveler in 1680, writing in the language of the time, "Jewes, who are verie considerable in the trade of this citie have two synagogues, one whereof is the largest in Christendom, and as some say in the world, sure I am, it far exceeds those in Rome, Venice, and all other places where I have been." Atypically, this synagogue rose above the Jewish quarter's surroundings and measured some thirty-eight by twenty-six meters inside, holding 2,000 seats. The synagogue boasted seventy-two large windows, large Ionic columns, and stately *bimah* and ark, in places replicating a 1642 model of Solomon's Temple.

The construction of a synagogue could be a very cohesive experience, but it could also unearth internal tensions and discord. When the Scola Tempio in Rome burned in 1549, some in the community refused to sign the agreement to contribute to its rebuilding. A notarial document indicates that some community leaders argued that such people should be forced to do so by the *bet din*, but the community appears to have backed off, passing around the cup for voluntary alms instead.[127]

Decorum within the synagogue reflected communal regulations and norms but was also in a sense a theater upon which communal social hierarchies were played out. In Recife, the Minute Book notes, "Nobody may change his seat under the penalty of six florins in his first attempt to do so. The second time, he shall be subject to the fine imposed by the Gentlemen of the Mahamad."[128] Synagogue seating was highly political, and seating, as in early modern churches, revealed a great deal about social position and economic prosperity. Often the sale of seats was recorded in community records. In Worms, for example, we find the following:

> Mrs. Johit and her husband Leib Honik transacted a Kinian Sudar to sell a seat in the men's section of the synagogue. This is the seat between the stone pillar and the seat in which Leib Honik sits. The Honiks sold this seat to R' Haim, including the stender [lectern] attached to the stone pillar. Also included was the right to recite the *Amidah* behind the rabbi. The condition was stipulated that Leib, the members of the family, and anyone else sitting in this seat would enter and exit by way of the seat of R' Haim. The parties also agreed that R' Haim would not be permitted to place a lectern beside his seat. Rather he would sit without a lectern.[129]

Figure 3.1. Bernard Picart, *The Dedication of the Portuguese Synagogue in Amsterdam*. Ceremonies et coutumes religieuses de tous les peuples du monde/représentées par des figures dessinées de la main de Bernard Picard; avec une explication historique et quelques dissertations curieuses, vol. 1 (Amsterdam, 1723), between 122 and 123. From the Collection of the Asher Library, Spertus Institute of Jewish Studies.

Synagogue seats could be hotly contested and reflected social status; they were frequently the subject of rabbinic discussions.[130]

Other Communal Institutions

Various communal institutions existed to serve the religious and social needs of community residents. Jewish communities had ritual baths (*mikvaot*), community ovens, and cemeteries, as well as study halls and dance houses (the latter might be located within the confines of the synagogue itself). In some cases there were societies for dowering poor brides. In Venice in 1613 a Society for the Dowering of Brides was created. The society was composed of fifty members, each of whom paid fifty ducats. Membership, passed on as an inheritance, benefited girls from the most important Sephardic communities. The Society was imitated in other places as well, notably in Amsterdam.

The existence of such societies was not at all restricted to Sephardic Jews, as the case of Abraham Calfon in Venice attests. He left 8,000 ducats to the German Fraternity for the Dowering of Brides.[131]

In many communities there was a benevolent society or **gemilut hasadim**. This society provided a wide range of social services, related to care for the sick and burial of the dead, and it often mirrored similar efforts in non-Jewish confraternities.[132] In Rome, the regulations of the society dictated the organization, structure, and leadership of the society, including office holders and official duties.[133]

Although education was increasingly brought under communal direction in the early modern period, the older arrangement of a private tutor continued, especially among the wealthier classes. For a complete discussion of Jewish education, see chapter 4.

SOCIAL RELATIONS

The towering historian of Polish Jewry, Bernard Weinryb, estimated that in Poland 15 percent of the Jews earned wages, salaries, or fees; the rest were business entrepreneurs. Probably 10 percent of the Jews were poor and 7 percent very rich.[134] As these numbers indicate, there was a broad "middle class" that constituted the bulk of most communities. Indeed, some communities, such as that in Rome, appear to have been remarkably homogenous, at least in terms of economics.[135] Often, however, Jewish communal structure could be very hierarchical and oligarchic. Different classes existed within Jewish communities, based generally upon wealth and rabbinic learning. In Bohemia, four different classes were recognized, including homeowners with unlimited rights to conduct trade; leaseholders with limited trading rights; tenants without trading rights; and servants without any legal rights.[136]

Nevertheless, due to the restrictions imposed on and the privileges cultivated by Jews externally, some scholars maintain that class status was never a concrete development in early modern Jewry. Jewish communities remained rather fluid socially, although they were not really societies of equality.[137] Notwithstanding such fluidity, there were clearly various signs of status and privilege in the communities, including honors and seating in the synagogue and the range and variation of tax assessments.[138]

The notion of honor became for Jews, as it did for non-Jews of the period, very important. As the German memoirist Glückel of Hameln indicated and as the fortunes and careers of the court Jews revealed, honor was of considerable importance in early modern Germany. Glückel mentions the term honor frequently. In addition to being associated with wealth and proper recognition, it was also related to refinement of character and a certain sense of nobility.[139]

In Constantinople, the Jewish population was divided along both financial and ethnic lines. Fifty-seven percent of the tax-paying members of the Sephardic congregation belonged to the upper and middle tax brackets, while 43 percent belonged to the lowest. Among Ashkenazic Jews, however, only 8 percent belonged to the upper two brackets, and 92 percent belonged to the poorest. Of course, the wealth breakdown could vary greatly by community. In late medieval Egypt into the sixteenth century, Jewish society was indeed stratified by social class, but social class was not always nor necessarily determined by an individual's occupation. According to the medievalist S. D. Goitein, there were five different social levels: upper class; an upper and lower bourgeoisie that included businessmen, professionals, and master artisans; an upper and lower middle class; urban craftsmen and laborers; and peasants.[140] Goitein writes,

> The **Geniza** records are remarkable for the great number of occupations and the high degree of specialization and division of labor apparent in them. The terms for about 265 manual occupations have been identified thus far, as against 90 types of person engaged in commerce and banking and approximately the same number of professionals, officials, religious functionaries, and educators. This total of around 450 professions exceeds by far the listed professions for all other pre-modern cities thus far known.[141]

The same sources reveal a diverse array of professions in which women were engaged as well.[142]

In many areas of central Europe there was a marked increase in the impoverishment of the Jewish communities and in the number of poor Jews by the end of the early modern period. By the early eighteenth century in Germany, the majority of Jews were of the poorer classes, with perhaps only 20 percent well off and 25 percent comparable to the German middle class. In the eighteenth century it is estimated that 10 percent of the German Jewish population was made up of vagrants and itinerants, and that number ballooned to 25 percent in parts of south and central Germany. While such impoverishment was related to general social and economic conditions, the number of poor in Germany rose due to waves of migration from Poland after the persecutions of 1648. Other events, such as the Thirty Years' War, which engulfed much of central Europe from 1618 until 1648 and that had significant associated clashes especially in the Netherlands, might create opportunities for some Jewish merchants, but they also created hardships and down-turned fortunes, as they did for the population at large.

Often poorer Jews were not only at a disadvantage within the Jewish community; they might also be the target of non-Jewish exclusionary policies. In Frankfurt am Main, for example, in the midst of major social upheavals at the beginning of the seventeenth century, the city authorities drafted a proposal to expel the sixty poorest Jewish families. This was in response to a more radical proposal to expel all the Jews but the twenty wealthiest families.

Ethnicity and Social Class

In Amsterdam and Hamburg similar social and economic disparity existed between the established and well-to-do Portuguese Jews and more recent Ashkenazic immigrants, many of whom served the Portuguese community and were heavily dependent upon its largesse. In Amsterdam there was often little attempt to distinguish between German and Polish Jews, even though those groups formed their own communities with differing rites. Even the elevated status of one of the leading members of the early Portuguese community, such as Rabbi Uri ha-Levi, an Ashkenazic rabbi from Emden, was not enough to guarantee special rights to his non-Portuguese descendants. In 1700 communal leaders argued,

> Nothing is on record of any obligation on our part to extend to the . . . descendants [of Uri Halevi and his son Aron] the right to membership which they claim our congregation owes them; and even if this were the case (which it clearly is not), the communal officials of that period ought to have realized that it was not appropriate that these people continue on in our congregation, for they should have recognized that these people did not harmonize with our own people, as far as their customs are concerned.[143]

In part, such divisions could be attributed to internalized senses of ethnicity and the importance of blood purity that the former Iberian Jews inherited. In part, the Sephardic Jews feared that the low economic status of the

Ashkenazic Jews placed the Jewish community in a dangerous position with Christian and secular authorities.

The ex-*conversos* who made up the Jewish community in Amsterdam were reluctant to accept a convert to Judaism whose father was not Portuguese. In 1671 it decided that an Ashkenazic spouse of a Portuguese woman could not be accepted in the community or buried in the Portuguese Jewish cemetery; the same applied to offspring from the marriage. In 1697 it decided that even Portuguese males who married Jewish women not of the nation would lose member rights. In 1657 the *mahamad* prohibited "**tudescos** [referring to German Jews], Italian Jews and mulattos" from attending the communal school.

Often poor and in need, the Germans of Hamburg were seen as something of a public nuisance in need of separation and restriction. Several rulings from the community protocol book illustrate the concern over this growing problem. While charity for this segment of the poor was clearly needed and recognized, an important distinction was made between personal and communal responsibility and support.[144] Indeed, the communal leaders were careful to distance themselves from the poor Ashkenazim, many of who served as maidservants and who leveraged their positions to gain a foothold in the community. According to one proscriptive decree, "It should be further known that an ordinance was made, that those Tudescas [German Jewesses], who serve as members of our nation, should not marry in order to establish themselves (settle) in this city. In the event that they marry here, they must live outside [of the city]. They should not be given permission to settle in this city."[145] Nonetheless, it is clear that many poor Germans continued to remain in the city.[146] In some cases, the Portuguese community attempted to dictate the settlement of Ashkenazic Jews within Hamburg and beyond the city limits in surrounding communities not technically under its own jurisdiction.[147]

Criminal Activity and Internal Fighting

Given the changing social makeup of the Jewish communities, the rise of crime and Jewish criminals has been attributed to early modern developments. While the entire topic is a sensitive one, it now appears that there were serious crimes committed by Jews against other Jews and, perhaps, more surprisingly, against non-Jews as well.

Particularly in Germany, the study of such criminality has not always been welcome, especially since the Holocaust. Nevertheless, we have evidence of Jews involved in shady business and even of significant Jewish robber bands, some noted for stealing Church property, especially Church altars. Some Jews were accused, at times with some justification, of counterfeiting currency. In part, the growing impoverishment of Jews in Germany, especially after the sixteenth century, may explain this occurrence. The Frankfurt synod from the early seventeenth century was, in fact, careful to legislate against "wicked Jews who engage in trade of counterfeit coins," against anyone who borrowed wares or money from Gentiles with the intention of not paying for them or against anyone purchasing wares known to be stolen.[148] Already in Spain at the end of the fifteenth century, there were cases of coin clipping involving Jews.[149] In fifteenth-century Valencia, there were cases of theft and various forms of fraud committed by Jews.[150]

In Germany, Jews were accused of purse cutting and house robbery, as well as the desecration of churches. In some cases, Jews were notorious bandits or members of famous robber bands.[151] In mid-fifteenth-century Lemberg, a certain Jewish tax farmer (an individual who paid a fee to the government and then was given authority to collect the taxes in a particular area) was accused of collaborating with a gang of Jewish thieves, and there are examples in Poland of sophisticated Jewish robber bands that attacked both Jews and non-Jews.[152]

The problem of Polish Jewish criminal activity has been discussed by one recent scholar, who writes,

> Such was not the case in other matters of observance, particularly when money and/or power was involved. The religious prohibition against stealing from non-Jews was unequivocal by the sixteenth century, although Talmudic rabbis had argued over the source of the measure. By mid-seventeenth century, however, the problem of Polish Jews stealing from non-Jews had become so acute that Rabbi Me'ir ben Abraham Zak quipped, "In our great sins the thieves and robbers have multiplied [so much] that we can no longer count [them]." With a play on a Talmudic phrase, he claimed that most thieves of the day were Jews.[153]

But Jews stole from other Jews as well, as the 1595 ordinances of the Cracow community appear to indicate.[154] Dishonesty was also attributed to some rabbis, who either purchased their positions or used their power to collect money, such as through exorbitant fees charged for bills of divorce or through rendering decisions based on payments.[155] Among Polish Jews there were cases of fraud (as in the selling to Jews of non-kosher meat), domestic violence, and even murder.[156] One Jew in Warsaw was accused of stealing money and on two separate occasions of beating a Jewish woman.[157] Such deviations, however, are generally seen by historians, as they were by contemporary early modern Jews, as rather dramatic exceptions to a very high level of religious and moral behavior among early modern Polish Jews.[158]

Tensions between individuals occasionally ran high. There are many early modern examples of fights between Jews, frequently within the confines of the synagogue itself. In Rome in November 1551, a brawl erupted between members of the Ashkenazic community. *Halakhic* force was used to get individuals to reconcile.[159] While there is not a great deal of evidence of Jewish criminality in fifteenth-century Spain, there are reports of some isolated incidents, including homicide among Jews and violent attacks within the synagogue.[160] Such violence at times spilled out into the Jewish quarter and Jewish homes. In Hamburg, one individual was fined for violating "the law in the synagogue, in loud and disrespectful ways, against the *gabbai*."[161] He was admonished to behave better. On another occasion, "in the synagogue after the end of prayer services" two individuals "exchanged words and would have come to blows if they had not been separated by several people present. Both were judged guilty because of the injury to the respect of the synagogue, in the worst way, and required to make public apology before the *teva*. Since they carried this out, further punishment was dispensed with."[162]

While not a pleasant chapter in Jewish history, it is clear that there was some internal violence perpetrated among early modern Jews themselves. Judah, the son of the famous Salonika rabbi Samuel de Medina, for example, was killed by a hired assassin because of his ruling against a particular Jew. The same was true of one of the sons of the Salonika rabbi Joseph ibn Lev. Leon Modena, of Venice, reports the murder of his son Zebulun, who apparently got tangled up in the wrong crowd.[163] Familial feuds often spilled into the synagogue or the community more generally. In Spoleto, in the spring of 1480, a banker named Moses di Ventura was attacked by two Jews.[164] In late fifteenth-century Trujillo, two Jews were accused of having caused the death of a third, and a feud between the families escalated and drew the attention of non-Jewish authorities.[165]

Family

The size of Jewish families in the early modern period could vary quite a bit. Often, Jewish demographics mirrored those of the larger society in which the Jews lived. At times, multiple generations lived together in singles houses, creating an extended kinship relationship that helped to define Jewish society and community. In large German cities, three or four different families lived in each house, each house having been subdivided.[166] In Rome, the typical Jewish family was composed of two generations. The family functioned as a cohesive economic unit, with women having clearly defined rights.[167] The average Jewish family in Rome appears to have had no more than 4.3 children.[168]

Family, in the early modern period as now, could be a complicated concept. Tensions as well as relations could vary tremendously by region and for a host of individual personal reasons. Often familial relations spilled over into more general communal concerns as well. At times individual wills tell us a great deal about internal family dynamics.[169]

For many years historians believed that pre-modern families were less emotional and loving than they are today. New studies, however, demonstrate conclusively that families, and especially parents and children, were engaged in extremely loving relationships. To give one example, a certain Rachel, a widow living in Jerusalem, wrote to her son in Cairo, "My dear son, may the Rock and Redeemer keep thee, I am very worried because I have not received any letter from thee for such a long time. . . . And let me know fully always about thy health. The saying 'Out of sight, out of mind' is not always correct. For a mother who has experienced pain does not do so. She does not forget the pain she suffered with her child."[170] A similar concern was expressed by a wife writing to her husband from Prague in 1619 in the midst of war. "I have been ever grieved because I have not heard a word from you for seven weeks, where you are in the world, especially in such a situation as that which we have now."[171] Recalling a child who died during the Black Death, one Spanish Jewish father tenderly lamented, "This stone is a memorial / That a later generation may know / That 'neath it lies hidden a pleasant bud / a cherished child."[172]

One rabbinic **responsum** from Joel Sirkes in sixteenth-century Poland throws interesting light on the care felt by early modern Jewish parents for their children as well as for the way in which Jewish women were treated in rabbinic deliberations. According to this case a woman placed her child in a crib and went to sleep. When she awoke the child was dead in her arms. According to a servant, the child was brought to the mother for nursing during the night. The mother had no recollection of this but wanted to do penance in case the story was true, this apparently being the second time such a thing had happened. Rabbi Sirkes ruled that the mother was not liable for she was not aware that the child was with her. Nevertheless, the death could not be overlooked, and the mother was responsible for a certain level of penance.

> She should therefore fast forty consecutive days, exclusive of Sabbaths and holidays. During these days she should eat no meat and drink no wine, even at night. She should not sleep with pillows or blankets. Afterward, she should fast on Mondays and Thursdays for at least a full year. . . . She should not fast, however, during a time when she is pregnant or nursing but must make up these days afterward. She should wear no jewelry during the entire year, including Sabbaths and holidays. She must stay away from parties, gatherings and weddings. She should humble her heart in contrition, recite the confessional prayers in Yiddish, and pray that the Lord forgive her.[173]

Women

Women were integral members of the Jewish community and family.[174] In addition to domestic matters, it is clear that women were engaged in business, often together with their husbands but also as business heads, especially when they were widows. In sixteenth-century Rome, as in other places, we know that women owned and disposed of property.[175] In Rome, Jewish women worked in a range of activities from banking to embroidery. They held their own profits and maintained full control of their husbands' estates until their dowries could be resolved. In short, women in Rome had a certain degree of "economic leverage," something that gave them already a much better social and communal standing in western Europe since the high Middle Ages.[176] Given this power, women often controlled negotiations for engagement and marriage and were quick, when necessary, to refuse potential husbands they opposed.[177]

There is more information about Jewish women in early modern Europe than Jewish women living in the orbit of Islam. More restricted than in the Christian West, Jewish women were subjected to similar limitations imposed on Muslim women. Women, in particular, were often the target of sumptuary laws establishing how women could be dressed and appear in public. Yet women seem to have had some significant roles even under Islam. There were, to be sure, famous and influential women, such as Dona Gracia Nasi, who we met earlier in chapter 2. While the little information we have typically reflects women's private household roles, women at times had a significant degree of personal freedom. Already in the Middle Ages, women were part of the work force, and women of all classes apparently owned immovable property. Women throughout the medieval and early modern periods were involved in various forms of business and commerce, and women did travel, even if their economic life was restricted. Despite various impediments, women apparently did appear in court proceedings.[178]

In early modern Poland, women did receive informal education, often in the home environment. But a significant amount of literature was available to them explicating various biblical topics and instructions on religious rituals and commandments.[179] As the historian Moshe Rosman notes of the situation in Poland,

> The texts aimed at women, and popular among them, display a virtually complete internalization of the fundamentals of religious faith and categories, including those that are male-oriented. Women's prayers display a highly developed concept of a personal, immanent God who is accessible and merciful. Judging from women's liturgy and religious literature, they were familiar with biblical cosmogony and cosmology.[180]

Polish women's prayer life was probably more home-centered and private than the public synagogue worship of men. When they did gather for prayers, the service was specifically for them and led by other women.[181] By the sixteenth century, however, Polish synagogues more frequently included women's sections, thus institutionalizing to some extent women's attendance.[182] Throughout Europe it has been argued that a certain "women's German" developed, a special form of Yiddish that allowed women access to moralistic and liturgical works. Whether or not such Yiddish works were in fact intended for women and whether or not women were involved in the broad world of rabbinic learning, there clearly were some women who had remarkable literary or scholarly careers. More than that, some women were even on occasion permitted to perform certain religious functions. In Italy, for example, one woman received license, albeit temporary, to perform ritual slaughter.[183]

Women were clearly the subject of a good deal of rabbinic writing in the early modern period. The voices of women have been much more difficult to hear directly, and only a few sources were penned by women themselves. Still, there are examples in the historical sources of remarkably accomplished and well-known Jewish women in the early modern world. One such woman was Sara Copia Sullam, who was born in Venice in 1590, where she received a liberal arts education. Sara developed significant skills in Hebrew, Greek, and Latin and was known as an outstanding Italian poetess, who could also perform on the lute and harpsichord. Leon Modena wrote to her, "To my most illustrious Lady, my very esteemed Patroness, Sara Copia Sullam! Your Excellency, who has found me worthy of her beautiful and noble conversation, is by virtue of her exquisite manners, her numerous virtues and talents, far ahead of her age and sex, dear to men of taste as well as to those who understand and cultivate Italian poetry."[184]

Sara held a rather distinguished position among Jews and Christians as well as local and visiting scholars. Almost in the fashion of the eighteenth- and nineteenth-century salons, Sara hosted a wide range of intellectuals, some of whom sought to convert her to Christianity. In rebuffing such attempts, Sara displayed a remarkable breadth of learning and tremendous resolve in her faith. In one case, she wrote, "I do not know that there is to be found in Holy Scripture another autograph written by the hand of God than the Decalogue, to which I cling with my faith and also with works as much as in my power. . . . You will attain the immortality which you preach so eloquently, if you observe your Christian teaching as well as I observe the law of Judaism."[185] In upbraiding her would-be converter, she wrote further, "You would have acted wisely if in this case, especially when you are engaged in a controversy with a Jewess, you had consulted an expert, because 'ruach' means originally nothing else than atmospheric wind or the air which we breathe; thus it can clearly be seen how incorrect are the conclusions drawn by you from that word."[186]

Glückel of Hameln is perhaps the most famous early modern Jewish woman due to the popularity and scope of her Yiddish memoirs. Glückel was born in Hamburg in 1646 or 1647 as one of six children of Judah Joseph Leib, a trader and notable of the German-Jewish community, and the businesswoman Beila, daughter of Nathan Melrich of Altona. When Glückel turned twelve years old she was betrothed to Hayyim, the son of the trader Joseph ben Baruch Daniel Samuel ha-Levi (Segal), and known as Joseph Goldschmidt or Joseph Hamel, who was a few years older than her.

When Glückel wrote her memoirs her children ranged in age from two to twenty-eight, and she was clearly writing for herself, as she noted, as much as for them.[187] Glückel wrote the first four books and the opening sections of book 5 in 1689; the rest of book 5 was composed in the 1690s, book 6 in 1702, book 7 in 1715, and the final paragraph in 1719.[188] Her work helps to illustrate several important developments reflected in early modern autobiographical writing.

As the innovative historian Natalie Davis notes, the memoirs are in a very real sense a book of moral tales and religious injunctions, shaped by major life cycle events.[189] But they were also much more. Glückel was a gifted storyteller, with the capacity to shape her narrative very consciously and with great poignancy. As Davis argues, "The storyteller can move into the way others remember the past and change it merely by introducing an unexpected detail into a familiar account. Everything depends on the skill of the teller, on how she or he takes the stories from the 'collective treasury of legends or everyday conversation' and puts them into play."[190]

Glückel detailed her reasons for writing at the very beginning of the memoirs:

> In my great grief and for my heart's ease I began this book the year of Creation 5451 [1690–1691]—God soon rejoice us and send us His redeemer! . . . I began writing it, dear children, upon the death of your good father, in the hope of distracting my soul from the burdens laid upon it, and the bitter thought that we have lost our faithful shepherd. In this way I have managed to live through many wakeful nights, and springing from my bed shortened the sleepless hours.[191]

Much of Glückel's memoirs were based on her own experiences and what she had heard from family. In addition to firsthand impressions, there was a large and varied group of morality tales, both Jewish and non-Jewish, that Glückel had likely heard and read and then reassembled into her narrative. These tales transcended any specific context or historical event. However, when combined with stories of her own past, they took on dramatic and very relevant qualities.

We know about women's lives through other sources as well. Many rabbinic responsa, for example, dealt with questions related to marriage and marital relations. In an uncertain age where men involved in international commerce might be away from home for long periods of time, or where Jews traveling might be killed on the highway, the very real question arose regarding whether and under what circumstances women whose husbands had not returned home could remarry. In an era of extensive travel the mere fact that the husband disappeared was not generally proof enough that a divorce could be granted. Only with reliable witnesses regarding the husband's death could a woman remarry.

The responsa also frequently discuss other issues related to marriage. While rabbinic law required witnesses to a marriage proposal, some rabbinic authorities discounted such "testimony" when it appeared to have been forced or constructed. In these cases, women were not considered bound by the arrangement and were not required to have a divorce. In one such case, the Polish rabbi Joel Sirkes concluded that the testimony was not submitted satisfactorily at the appropriate time in front of a duly constituted court. He noted,

> We are not concerned lest the rumor of marriage should spread and be generally accepted, since the testimony was almost immediately rejected and the community would correctly assume that the court found the accusation without foundation. We cannot require a divorce merely in order to make the matter amply clear to all that they are not married, since this would disqualify L. [the woman] from marrying a priest and would create a situation where girls would be vulnerable prey for wicked blackmailers who might only start a rumor of marriage to require a divorce.[192]

Marriage was an important social act that was particularly significant for the upper-middle-class and upper-class world of the court Jews. The Yiddish memoirist Glückel of Hameln provided a good deal of information on the marriage patterns and arrangements of her children across central and western Europe. As an example, consider how Glückel described the engagement of her sister Hendle.

> At that time my sister Hendle, of blessed memory, became engaged to the son of the learned Reb Gumpel of Cleves. She received 1800 **Reichsthalers** as her dowry, in those days a handsome sum, more than anyone had ever dowered in Hamburg. Naturally her match was considered the most important in all Germany, and the whole world admired its excellence and the size of the dowry.[193]

Relations between early modern men and women could be quite passionate, not simply forced and pre-arranged relationships. According to one Renaissance-era letter from Ferrara, Salamone Candia of Verona declared to his soon to be bride,

> My most sumptuous and honoured bride. . . . How can I live, how can I control my limbs, now that I am parted from my heart? For without thee I am nothing but a painted man. All company, however delicious, seems to me a solitude while I am not with thee. All song changes to lamentation; all sweetness to bitterness; spring to winter; dawn to eve; laughter to crying. Without

thee, eating is punishment; sleeping a labour; to lie down is weariness; to rise up is anguish.[194]

The role of women and gender relations could be quite complex in the early modern period. There are some very interesting documents from the Roman archives that help to illustrate these complexities.

In early May of 1536, Rosetta, the wife of Angelo di Salomone took an oath to the effect that she would not curse or berate her husband ("or do anything else that is improper") and not embarrass him or raise her voice against him in the marketplace. If she had a disagreement she would speak to him modestly. If she violated the oath she would be assessed a monetary fine, part of which would go to the Apostolic Chamber. The husband, for his part, however, swore not to anger his wife; if he did, Rosetta was to inform Rabbi Abramo.[195]

The arbitration of a marital dispute in Rome also sheds some light on the legal rights of women. According to arbitration from late 1536 between Sabato di Raffaele and his wife Laura, Laura agreed to provide a list of items she took when she left her husband's house, in return for a payment of twenty sc and a guarantee from the husband not to strike her while she was at her father's house. As long as Laura was at her father's house, Sabato could not force her to return, and she was exempt from all marital duties. If there was to be reconciliation between husband and wife it must be mutual. The document ended, however, that if "she does return, then he is freed from his guarantee and may beat her in the way women, virgins and proper girls are hit."[196]

This particular case is further documented. In early June of 1539 an agreement was reached whereby Laura would return to her husband, and they would live peacefully, and she would behave properly. Laura agreed that her father and brothers would not strike Sabato on the hands. For his part, Sabato agreed to give Laura a dowry contract of 100 sc and that neither he nor his relatives would beat her. In addition to issues treating inheritance, the document ends as follows: "Sabato may not berate his wife with charges that [would justify] divorce, calling her a whore or lewd and so forth. Any time he calls her a whore, he will be fined 1 sc. Sabato will also refrain from striking Laura his wife, except at appropriate moments, when he may strike her occasionally and punish her with a light strap."[197]

The issue of impotence was significant in the early modern sexual economy. Frequent stories about cures for "tied knots" abound in various literature. One document from Rome in January of 1551 details the saga of one man, who had his knot undone by a gentile through (magical?) means.[198] Marital relations could become strained or used as justification for those seeking divorce. According to a document from late August 1538, which is typical of such incidents, we find that a certain woman testified that "she can no longer stand her husband. He is not a man, as far as she is concerned, but is like a eunuch. She wants a son to bury her; and since he has no strength, for his strength has waned, and he is impotent, she no longer wants him, and rejects him. She said in front of us 'I do not want him because he has become unbearable.'" The husband, for his part insisted that there was no truth to this accusation and was prepared to bring witness that he was potent.[199] This and the examples above reveal that women were active participants and had real power in early modern Jewish society. Despite the dearth of sources, Jewish women must be featured prominently in any historical account of this period.

PROFESSIONS AND OCCUPATIONS

Jewish professional involvement depended a great deal on local contexts and on restrictions imposed by non-Jewish authorities. Early modern Jews tended to be heavily involved in particular occupations, though the range of professional involvement could be incredibly diverse. In Amsterdam during the second half of the seventeenth century, for example, Portuguese Jewish men assumed important roles in the sugar, tobacco, and diamond industries of the New World. Amsterdam Jews had other occupations as well. For the early modern period, 3.9 percent worked in retail (as grocers, butchers, etc.); 6.8 percent in professions (from barber surgeons, physicians, and professors to teachers); and 6.8 percent as laborers (coral and diamond polishers, hat-makers, packers, musicians, painters, tobacco workers, etc.).[200]

Throughout the early modern period, Jews might turn up in surprising professions. In the Ottoman Empire there were examples of Jews working as miners, seamen, porters, and even farmers. In Germany, there are examples of Jews working as cannon-makers and engineers as well as prostitutes.[201] Jews in Mantua, Italy, were famed for their work in theater. In Navarre, a more regionally unique enterprise for Jews, one of ancient provenance, was viticulture.[202] Throughout early modern Poland, Jews were involved in managing estates, and many owned or managed inns, selling liquor.[203] In Warsaw there were Jewish brewers and distillers.[204] Jewish taverns were apparently quite common in Poland. In Belaya Tserkov, for example, there were seventeen Jewish taverns, as compared to 100 Jewish houses.[205] Important scholarship has now emerged detailing the Jewish work in the taverns and the taverns as locations for social and economic interchange and discrimination.

As in every community of reasonable size, Jews were employed within the Jewish communities. They worked in a range of positions, including as rabbis (who also moonlighted as scribes, judges, marriage brokers, and also moneylenders), scribes, beadles, and *shohetim*.[206] Within their own communities Jews worked as educators, butchers, and in some places bakers. In Constantinople, they were also meat processors, cheese- and wine–makers, and millers.

In much of the early modern period, Jews were involved in moneylending. Since the Middle Ages the ban on European Jews participating in craft professions governed by the guilds meant that moneylending was one of the few occupations consistently open to Jews. In the early modern period, as Christians developed mechanisms to establish loan banks and lend money to other Christians, Jews were squeezed further from the one area of work that had been left open to them, even if it was a profession that roused the enmity of poor Christians forced to seek the Jews' service.[207] While Jews did loan money to a wide range of Christians, the profession in Navarre, instructively, was in the hands of a relatively small cadre of individuals.[208]

As they were in the Middle Ages, Jews were frequently involved in medicine. In Italy as in many other places, including Poland and the Ottoman Empire, Jews were respected and much sought after physicians, even if they were often prohibited from formally matriculating at medical universities and restricted from attending to Christian patients. Under Ottoman rule some Jews were able to penetrate into court circles, especially through their skills and services as physicians. Jews were heavily involved in medicine. In the sixteenth century, the percentage of Jewish doctors rose from 25 to 47 percent, peaking by the early seventeenth century at 66 percent.[209] The Italian Jew, Jacopo of Gaeta, for example, was Mehmed II's chief physician and a trusted adviser, head of the treasury, and eventually, vizier. Although he converted to Islam shortly before he died, most of his success was as a professing Jew. Joseph Hamon, to give another example, served as the personal physician to Selim I, whom he accompanied into battle. Hamon also served an important role as a representative of and advocate for the Jewish community. According to an account from 1571, the Ottoman sultan extended special privileges and exemptions to a certain Jewish scholar and physician; the sultan exempted "the physician and his seed after him, both male and female, and also their children forever, (making them) eternally and definitely exempt from all kinds of taxes and burdens of government and toll, tribute, and custom and servitude to rulers."[210]

One Muslim writer from the fifteenth century wrote very respectfully of his Jewish teacher. "I have heard recently," he noted, "that he has finally attained the chief medical post in Tlemcen. He is an intimate member of the entourage of the ruler of that city. However due to his intelligence and good sense he does not get involved in anything that has to do with government." The student continued, "I ask Allah Exalted to let him die in the faith of the prophet Muhammad—may Allah bless him and grant him peace."[211]

In Navarre, Jews were at times involved in the sale or rental of land. Unlike in most parts of the early modern world, Jews in Navarre apparently owned land, either absolutely, through fixed payments to a permanent owner, or through rental.[212] Some Jews were therefore not surprisingly involved in agriculture. While Ottoman Jews might own land, they do not appear to have been heavily involved in its cultivation.[213]

In the New World Jews were involved in agriculture and plantation life, in many cases owning significant numbers of slaves. In general, while some early modern Polish Jews were involved in the agricultural sector, that involvement was limited to the cultivation of small gardens (Jews were banned from owning farm land)[214] and animal husbandry.[215] In extreme western Poland and Silesia there are examples of Jews engaged in agriculture, and Jews from Poland and Lithuania, as well as Germany, traded in horses and cattle.

In many places early modern Jews were involved in commerce, more international in some areas and more local in others. The Jews in frontier regions of Poland were important conduits for the trafficking of goods from Russia into the West. Jews were particularly involved in the important Polish river trades.[216] The Jews of Lemberg[217] were important mediators of trade between the Ottoman Empire and the West, just as the Jews in Danzig (Gdansk) were active in a wide range of economic markets and curried goods between East and West. Jews were regular and important participants in a host of fairs held throughout central and western Europe.[218]

Amsterdam Jews were engaged in trade with Italy and Constantinople. Following the general developments of the city and taking advantage of their own skills and far-flung networks, especially in the New World, many Jews in Amsterdam (81 percent) were engaged in commerce (71.9 percent as merchants). During the second half of the seventeenth century, Portuguese Jews were increasingly involved in speculation and trade in bills of exchange and insurance.

In central and eastern Europe Jews who left the urban areas often took with them into the countryside urban professions or urban business sensibilities. In Germany, Jews introduced door-to-door peddling in the countryside.

Jews were frequently participants in state and court administration. They served as court factors and provisioners in early modern Germany. Jewish migrants from the West brought important administrative skills and served in numerous capacities within the Ottoman state related to the collection of taxes, banking, supplying of the army, and commerce at the local, regional, and international levels.[219] Joseph Nasi (ca. 1524–1579)[220] became a particularly influential statesman in the Empire and advised the sultan in numerous ways, particularly regarding European politics and relations.[221] Jews in the Empire were merchants and also played significant roles in the management of customs houses and docks and as tax farmers. In the later fifteenth century the most important tax farms around the city were held by

Jews.[222] Jews, especially Jews in Egypt, were also heavily involved in this professional arena.[223] Jews, even Jewish women, appear to have been key political advisers and states administrators.[224]

In early modern Poland, Jews were often quite successful as leaseholders, or **arendars**, on nobles' estates, though this was an occupation much discussed and at times strictly legislated within the Jewish communities.[225] Often this particular function stirred anti-Jewish animus among the populace.[226] Jewish work in this area met restriction and legislation from the national assembly. In 1538 a formal resolution of the *Sejm* declared, "We herewith prescribe and ordain that henceforth and for all future times those in charge of the collection of our revenues must without exception be members of the landed nobility professing the Christian faith." What is more, the resolution continued, "We decree that it be unconditionally observed that no Jew be entrusted with the collection of state revenues of any kind, for it is unseeming and runs counter to the divine law that such persons be allowed to occupy any position of honor and to exercise any public function among the Christian people."[227]

Even when restricted from certain guild professions, it was possible to find some Jews employed in those trades—such as gold- and silver-smithing, brewing, and silk embroidering. At times guilds included both Jews and Christians. The guild of dealers in *romaneschi* clothes in Rome, for example, stipulated regulations for both Jewish and Christian members.[228] Evidence of Jewish butchers in Poland abounds, and a document of the Kazimierz butchers' guild, limiting the number of Jewish butchers to four, indicates that Jews were recognized in that profession at some level.[229] In some frontier regions, where guild restrictions were not particularly strong, Jews also moved into artisan trades.[230] In Amsterdam, as well, Jews also found employ in occupations that were not subject to the strict control of the guilds, such as engraving, gem cutting, and metal extracting.

Early modern Jews were frequently involved in the textile industry. Jews in Moravia were particularly renowned for trade in clothing and general involvement in the textile industry. Ottoman Jews were known for involvement in manufacture and the textile industries. Jews brought some technical skills with them in the production of textiles and weapons.[231] Approximately a thousand Jewish families worked in the wool industry in Salonika; many Jews also worked in textiles in other places, such as Safed and Istanbul.[232] In Navarre, sandwiched north between Aragon and Castile on the Iberian Peninsula, a large number of Jews were involved in clothing manufacture, as tailors, hosiery-makers, weavers, furriers, and curtain sewers.[233] In some Italian areas Jews were famous tailors.

In early modern Poland Jews, especially very poor ones, made and sold hats and collars, as they did in Cracow.[234] There were Jewish tailors and shoemakers in Lemberg, and in Warsaw at the very beginning of our period there is evidence of Jewish tailors and furriers. There were also examples of Jewish tanners and glaziers, among other artisans in Poland [235] and in the Ottoman Empire.

Jews were also involved in a variety of emerging industrial enterprises.[236] In Salonika Jews were involved in silver mining; in Rhodes, sulfur mining; and in Corinth, making alum.[237] Amsterdam Jews became particularly engaged in the silk industry, where a Jew, Manuel Rodrigues de Vega, was an innovator. As in Italy and Constantinople, Jews in Amsterdam were involved in printing. Imanoel Benveniste, who emigrated from Venice in the 1640s, printed some sixty-five works, including the *Midrash Rabbah*, the **Mishnah**, Isaac Alfasi's *Halakhot*, and between the years 1644 and 1648, the Talmud. Joseph Athias was also a very accomplished printer, responsible for prayerbooks and a famous edition of the Bible. He also experimented with copper plates. In Italy, Jews were involved in various work with printers and Christian Hebraists (Christian scholars studying Hebrew; see chapter 5).

It is impossible to generalize about early modern Jewish professions. Jews in some places were known for their work in particular areas, and despite restrictions in many places, Jews did manage to engage in a wide range of occupations. Jews, who often took their professional skills with them when they migrated, showed remarkable resiliency in adapting to the world around them.

CONCLUSIONS

Early modern Jewish communities could be complex and defined in varying ways. Jewish communities could be local as well as regional and organized around Jewish law and custom yet subservient to non-Jewish authorities. At its heart, however, the Jewish community was an association that bound Jews together for a range of religious as well as social, cultural, economic, and political reasons.

Given the diversity of early modern Jewish communities, it should not be surprising that their governance could also be divergent and complex. While varying tremendously, most communities, regardless of their size, had generally similar governing structures and tools. Communities were run by lay councils and a range of officials, from scribes to tax assessors. As with the different lay positions, there were distinctions or gradations within the rabbinate itself. At times this situation led to conflict between communal leaders and rabbis and among the rabbis themselves. Throughout the early modern period the rabbinate was frequently the site of contested authority. Some scholars have alternately proposed that the rabbinate was being professionalized or "de-professionalized." In either event, tensions over the location and expression of authority frequently erupted in the early modern Jewish world; such tensions could be seen clearly in the debate over the authority, and use of, excommunication.

In the early modern period Jewish communities had rules about the powers associated with communal office and the methods for electing individuals (always men, and generally adult married men) to these positions. While the community was generally and theoretically ruled by majority vote, many communities were simply thinly veiled oligarchies dominated by particularly wealthy, learned, or otherwise influential individuals or families. The governance of the community, while typically held within the community itself, could not always withstand the attention or desires of external non-Jewish authorities who wanted to control the community, particularly in their efforts to facilitate the collection and payment of taxes.

Many different governing processes and tools were utilized by early modern Jews. Regional councils, courts of law and arbitration, as well as various methods of tax assessment and collection existed. A wide range of social institutions could be found, such as welfare and dowering societies, and more physical communal institutions, such as synagogues and *mikvaot*, each providing important services and outlets within the Jewish community.

Despite the fact that most Jewish communities were rather small, the internal social and economic dynamics could be extremely complicated. This was especially the case when Jews of differing ethnic background circulated in the same cities or regions. Social stratification and social tensions existed within the Jewish communities as they did in the non-Jewish communities surrounding the Jews. Periodically, large numbers of poor Jews began to appear because of down-turned economic conditions, persecution, and forced migration. Throughout the early modern period we find evidence of growing vagabondage as well as crime committed by Jews. Such crimes, while clearly the exception, could be directed against fellow Jews as well as non-Jews.

The tremendous range of social stations within the communities was also clearly reflected in the range of professions and occupations practiced by Jews. While pre-modern Jews have stereotypically been seen as moneylenders and pawn-brokers—generally forced into these poorly perceived professions because of intense and restrictive legislation—Jews were also involved in a rich array of work that defies any easy categorization. There certainly were some professions that appear to have been common in certain regions, tailors in parts of Italy, for example. There were some areas of endeavor that appear to have had rather un-proportionately large or renowned Jewish participation, such as medicine or international commerce. Even where Jews were barred from engaging in certain trades, particularly when local guilds were strong, we can often find evidence of at least some Jews taking up the profession. There are, in fact, very few professions for which we cannot identify at least some Jews—we have, for example, evidence of Jewish soldiers, cannon-makers, and even prostitutes. In this context it is important to point out that Jewish women also engaged in a wide range of professions. Even when we do not have documentation, it appears that women engaged in business and were more involved in public affairs than was once assumed.

In the end, early modern Jewish communities could be very different, responding to a host of internal and external conditions. At the same time, however, there were many key characteristics that made early modern Jewish communities quite similar. Now that we have seen something of the formal structures of Jewish community and society, it is time to turn our attention to the development and expression of Jewish identity as evident in Jewish religion and culture and in Jewish engagements with the non-Jewish world.

NOTES

1. See Dean Phillip Bell, *Sacred Communities: Jewish and Christian Identities in Fifteenth-Century Germany* (Leiden, Netherlands, and Boston, 2001), 148ff.

2. See Israel Yuval, "Heilige Städte, heilige Gemeinden—Mainz als das Jerusalem Deutschlands," in *Jüdische Gemeinden und Organisationsformen von der Antike bis zur Gegenwart*, ed. R. Jütte and A. P. Kustermann (Köln, Germany, 1996), 91–92.

3. For the Ottoman Empire, see Avigdor Levy, *The Jews of the Ottoman Empire* (Princeton, NJ, 1992), 46ff.

4. Levy, *The Jews of the Ottoman Empire*, 48.

5. See Stefan Litt, *Protokollbuch und Statuten der Jüdischen Gemeinde Friedberg (16.–18. Jahrhundert)* (Friedberg, Germany, 2003), 230 (in the Hebrew, 45) regarding the position of "foreign Jews."

6. See Bell, *Sacred Communities*, 174–76.

7. Bernard Weinryb, *The Jews of Poland: A Social and Economic History of the Jewish Community in Poland from 1100 to 1800* (Philadelphia, 1973), 35.

8. Levy, *The Jews of the Ottoman Empire*, 42–43.

9. Wealth seems to have been the more important qualification.

10. They are called by a variety of names in the sources: *parnasim, gabbai, ma'arichim, ba'alai hoda'ot*.

11. Typically seven, according to Menahem Elon, *Jewish Law: History, Sources, Principles*, trans. Bernard Auerbach and Melvin J. Sykes, 4 vols. (Philadelphia, 1994; orig., 1973), 2:728.

12. See M. Balaban, "Die Krakauer Judengemeinde-Ordnung von 1595 und ihre Nachträge," *Jahrbuch der Jüdisch-Literarischen Gesellschaft* 10 (1913): 296–310; 11 (1916): 88–114; Bernard D. Weinryb, "Texts and Studies in the Communal History of Polish Jewry," *Proceedings of the American Academy for Jewish Research* 19 (1950): 77–98.

13. Levy, *The Jews of the Ottoman Empire*, 69.

14. Daniel Swetschinski, *Reluctant Cosmopolitans: The Portuguese Jews of Seventeenth-Century Amsterdam* (London, 2000).

15. See Swetschinski, *Reluctant Cosmopolitans.*

16. Arthur Cygielman, "Cracow (Kazimierz)," in *Encyclopedia Judaica,* 16 vols. (Jerusalem, 1971–1972).

17. Kenneth R. Stow, *Alienated Minority: The Jews of Medieval Latin Europe* (Cambridge, MA, 1992), 166.

18. See David Joshua Malkiel, *A Separate Republic: The Mechanics and Dynamics of Venetian Self-Government 1607–1624* (Jerusalem, 1991), 61ff.

19. See Shlomo Eidelberg, *R. Juspa, Shammash of Warmaisa (Worms): Jewish Life in Seventeenth Century Worms* (Jerusalem, 1991), 18.

20. See Selma Stern, *The Court Jew: A Contribution to the History of the Period of Absolutism in Central Europe* (Philadelphia, 1950).

21. See Leah Bornstein-Makovetsky, "Jewish Leadership and Ottoman Authorities during the Sixteenth and Seventeenth Centuries," in *Ottoman and Turkish Jewry: Community and Leadership,* ed. Aron Rodrigue (Bloomington, IN, 1992), 90–91, 93–94.

22. See Bornstein-Makovetsky, "Jewish Leadership and Ottoman Authorities," 108–9.

23. Eliezer Bashan (Sternberg), "Nagid," in *Encyclopedia Judaica,* 16 vols. (Jerusalem, 1971–1972).

24. See S. D. Goitein, *A Mediterranean Society: An Abridgement in One Volume,* rev. and ed. Jacob Lassner (Berkeley, CA, 1999), 85.

25. Bashan (Sternberg), "Nagid."

26. See, for example, Goitein, *A Mediterranean Society,* 106–17.

27. See Jacob Marcus, *Communal Sick-Care in the German Ghetto* (Cincinnati, 1947), 27ff.

28. Marcus, *Communal Sick-Care,* 34. Certain tax exemptions were common among the rabbis. See, for example, regarding Poland in the seventeenth century, Salo Baron, *A Social and Religious History of the Jews,* 2nd ed., vols. 16–17 (Philadelphia, 1976–1980), 16:288.

29. Marcus, *Communal Sick-Care,* 63.

30. Marcus, *Communal Sick-Care,* 68.

31. Marcus, *Communal Sick-Care,* 70.

32. Marcus, *Communal Sick-Care,* 86.

33. Kenneth Stow, ed., *The Jews in Rome,* 2 vols. (Leiden, Netherlands, 1995), 1:18 (no. 48).

34. See Stefan Rohrbacher, "Die jüdischen Gemeinden in den Medinot Aschkenas zwischen Spätmittelalter und Dreißigjährigem Krieg," in *Jüdische Gemeinden und ihr christlicher Kontext in kulturräumlich vergleichender Betrachtung von der Spätantike bis zum 18. Jahrhundert,* ed. Christoph Cluse, Alfred Haverkamp, and Israel J. Yuval (Hanover, Germany, 2003), 459.

35. Eidelberg, *R. Juspa,* 20; on elections in Friedberg more generally, see Litt, *Protokollbuch,* 384–85 (in the Hebrew, 154).

36. Eidelberg, *R. Juspa,* 20–21; Litt, *Protokollbuch,* 424.

37. Arnold Wiznitzer, *The Records of the Earliest Jewish Community in the New World* (New York, 1954), 59.

38. Wiznitzer, *The Records of the Earliest Jewish Community,* 59.

39. Wiznitzer, *The Records of the Earliest Jewish Community,* 60.

40. Wiznitzer, *The Records of the Earliest Jewish Community*, 59.

41. Wiznitzer, *The Records of the Earliest Jewish Community*, 61.

42. Swetschinski, *Reluctant Cosmopolitans*, 190–91.

43. Stow, *The Jews in Rome*, 1:18 (no. 48).

44. Stow, *The Jews in Rome*, 2:660–61 (no. 1535).

45. According to Isaac Abarbanel—quoted in Robert Bonfil, "Aliens Within: The Jews and Antijudaism," in *Handbook of European History 1400–1600: Late Middle Ages, Renaissance and Reformation*, vol. 1, ed. Thomas A. Brady Jr., Heiko A. Oberman, and James D. Tracy (Leiden, Netherlands, 1996), 284.

46. Bonfil, "Aliens Within," 286–87.

47. See Mordechai Breuer, "The Position of the Rabbinate in the Leadership of the German Communities in the Fifteenth Century" (Hebrew), *Zion* 41 (1–2) (1976): 52.

48. Breuer, "The Position of the Rabbinate," 66.

49. Moshe Rosman, "Innovative Tradition: Jewish Culture in the Polish-Lithuanian Commonwealth," in *Cultures of the Jews: A New History*, ed. David Biale (New York, 2002), 539.

50. See Bell, *Sacred Communities*, 158.

51. Bell, *Sacred Communities*, 180ff.

52. Robert Bonfil, *Rabbis and Jewish Communities in Renaissance Italy*, trans. Jonathan Chipman (London, 1993; orig., 1979), 331.

53. Bonfil, *Rabbis and Jewish Communities*, 332.

54. Adam Teller, "The Laicization of Early Modern Jewish Society: The Development of the Polish Communal Rabbinate in the 16th Century," in *Schöpferische Momente des europäischen Judentums in der frühen Neuzeit*, ed. Michael Graetz (Heidelberg, Germany, 2000), 333–35, 349.

55. Malkiel, *A Separate Republic*, 175.

56. Malkiel, *A Separate Republic*, 175–76.

57. Levy, *The Jews of the Ottoman Empire*, 48.

58. Edward Fram, *Ideals Face Reality: Jewish Law and Life in Poland, 1550–1655* (Cincinnati, 1997), 41.

59. Levy, *The Jews of the Ottoman Empire*, 53.

60. Levy, *The Jews of the Ottoman Empire*, 54–55.

61. Levy, *The Jews of the Ottoman Empire*, 56–57.

62. Levy, *The Jews of the Ottoman Empire*, 58–59.

63. Inappropriate or deviant behavior might be punished in any number of ways, especially through banning of synagogue or ritual participation or fines—see Dean Phillip Bell, "Confessionalization in Early Modern Germany: A Jewish Perspective," in *Politics and Reformations: Studies in Honor of Thomas A. Brady, Jr.*, ed. Peter Wallace et al. (Leiden, Netherlands, forthcoming), as well as Litt, *Protokollbuch*, 367–68 (in the Hebrew, 143–44).

64. See Malkiel, *A Separate Republic*, 193–94.

65. See Bell, "Confessionalization in Early Modern Germany."

66. See Yosef Kaplan, "The Place of the Herem in the Sefardic Community of Hamburg during the Seventeenth Century," in *Die Sefarden in Hamburg I*, ed. Michael Studemund-Halevy (Hamburg, Germany, 1994), 63–88.

67. Glückel of Hameln, *The Memoirs of Glückel of Hameln*, trans. Marvin Lowenthal (New York, 1977), 30, 90f.

68. Jacob Weil, *Sheelot u-teshuvot* (Jerusalem, 1958–1959; orig., 1549), responsum no. 146.

69. Bell, *Sacred Communities*.

70. Marc Saperstein, *Exile in Amsterdam: Saul Levi Morteira's Sermons to a Congregation of "New Jews"* (Cincinnati, 2005), 227.

71. Aaron Rothkoff, "Semikhah: Controversy on the Renewal of the Semikhah," in *Encyclopedia Judaica*, 16 vols. (Jerusalem, 1971–1972).

72. Solomon Freehof, *A Treasury of Responsa* (Philadelphia, 1963), 106.

73. Quoted in Malkiel, *A Separate Republic*, 29.

74. Wiznitzer, *The Records of the Earliest Jewish Community*, 72–73.

75. See Dean Phillip Bell, *Jewish Identity in Early Modern Germany: Memory, Power, and Community* (Aldershot, UK, 2007).

76. Here and following, see Eleazar Gutwirth, "Towards Expulsion: 1391–1492," in *Spain and the Jews: The Sephardi Experience 1492 and After*, ed. Elie Kedourie (London, 1992), 62–65.

77. Haim Hillel Ben-Sasson, "Council of the Lands: Structure of Leadership," in *Encyclopedia Judaica*, 16 vols. (Jerusalem, 1971–1972).

78. Nathan Michael Gelber, "Brest-Litovsk," in *Encyclopedia Judaica*, 16 vols. (Jerusalem, 1971–1972).

79. Fram, *Ideals Face Reality*, 43.

80. Iwo Cyprian Pogonowski, *Jews in Poland: A Documentary History* (New York, 1998), 75.

81. Fram, *Ideals Face Reality*, 43.

82. Pogonowski, *Jews in Poland*, 77.

83. Levy, *The Jews of the Ottoman Empire*, 50.

84. Cygielman, "Cracow (Kazimierz)."

85. Jacob Marcus, *The Jew in the Medieval World: A Source Book, 315–1791* (Cincinnati, 1938), 207; Nathan of Hannover, *Abyss of Despair: The Famous 17th Century Chronicle Depicting Jewish Life in Russia and Poland during the Chmielnicki Massacres of 1648–1649* = *Yeven metzulah*, trans. Abraham J. Mesch (New Brunswick, 1983), 119–20.

86. Louis Finkelstein, *Jewish Self-Government in the Middle Ages* (New York, 1924), 257.

87. Malkiel, *A Separate Republic*, 198–99.

88. Aryeh Shmuelevitz, *The Jews of the Ottoman Empire in the Late Fifteenth and the Sixteenth Centuries: Administrative, Economic, Legal, and Social Relations as Reflected in the Responsa* (Leiden, Netherlands, 1984), 50–51.

89. Shmuelevitz, *The Jews of the Ottoman Empire*, 68.

90. Shmuelevitz, *The Jews of the Ottoman Empire*, 70.

91. Shmuelevitz, *The Jews of the Ottoman Empire*, 73.

92. Eric Zimmer, *Harmony and Discord: An Analysis of the Decline of Jewish Self-Government in Fifteenth-Century Central Europe* (New York, 1970), 31f.

93. Four days were particularly prominent: January 1, May 1, November 11, and December 25, though often the payment could be given in two installments.

94. Bernhard Rosensweig, "Taxation in the Late Middle Ages in Germany and Austria," *Diné Israel: An Annual of Jewish Law, Past and Present* 12 (1984–1985): 65. See also his *Ashkenazic Jewry in Transition* (Waterloo, Ontario, 1975).

95. Moses Mintz, *Sheelot u-teshuvot* (Jerusalem, 1990–1991), responsum no. 1.

96. Mintz, *Sheelot u-teshuvot*, responsum no. 133. The issues discussed in this paragraph are based upon Zimmer, *Harmony and Discord*, and Rosensweig, *Ashkenazic Jewry in Transition*.

97. Zimmer, *Harmony and Discord*, and Rosensweig, *Ashkenazic Jewry in Transition*.

98. Shmuelevitz, *The Jews of the Ottoman Empire*, 73.

99. Shmuelevitz, *The Jews of the Ottoman Empire*, 73.

100. Shmuelevitz, *The Jews of the Ottoman Empire*, 73–74.

101. A similar range of taxes were paid by Polish Jews as well. See Baron, *A Social and Religious History*, 16:293ff.

102. See Shmuelevitz, *The Jews of the Ottoman Empire*, 84ff.

103. Shmuelevitz, *The Jews of the Ottoman Empire*, 85.

104. Shmuelevitz, *The Jews of the Ottoman Empire*, 85–86.

105. Shmuelevitz, *The Jews of the Ottoman Empire*, 110.

106. Shmuelevitz, *The Jews of the Ottoman Empire*, 87, 88.

107. Shmuelevitz, *The Jews of the Ottoman Empire*, 90.

108. Shmuelevitz, *The Jews of the Ottoman Empire*, 93.

109. Shmuelevitz, *The Jews of the Ottoman Empire*, 92–105.

110. See Benjamin R. Gampel, *The Last Jews on Iberian Soil: Navarrese Jewry 1479–1498* (Berkeley, CA, 1989), 63–65.

111. Gampel, *The Last Jews*, 67.

112. See Balaban, "Die Krakauer Judengemeinde-Ordnung von 1595 und ihre Nachträge," 304.

113. See Gampel, *The Last Jews*, 110ff.

114. Avraham Rubinstein, "Lvov (Lemberg)," in *Encyclopedia Judaica*, 16 vols. (Jerusalem, 1971–1972).

115. Stow, *The Jews in Rome*, 1:xxxv.

116. Stow, *The Jews in Rome*, 1:xxxix.

117. See Stow, *The Jews in Rome*, 1:xl–xlii.

118. Stow, *The Jews in Rome*, 1:xliv–xlv.

119. See also Bell, "Confessionalization in Early Modern Germany." See more generally Arye Maimon, Mordechai Breuer, and Yacov Guggenheim (eds.), *Germania Judaica. Volume III: 1350–1519, Part 3* (Tübingen, Germany, 2003), 2081ff.

120. See Sabine Ullmann, *Nachbarschaft und Konkurrenz: Juden und Christen in Dörfern der Markgrafschaft Burgau* (Göttingen, Germany, 1999), 154 for Binswagen.

121. See Litt, *Protokollbuch*, 272 for Friedberg (in the Hebrew, 73–74), as well as 394ff (in the Hebrew, 161ff).

122. Quoted in Malkiel, *A Separate Republic*, 230.

123. Norman A. Stillman, *The Jews of Arab Lands: A History and Source Book* (Philadelphia, 1979), 289.

124. Cygielman, "Cracow (Kazimierz)."

125. Swetschinski, *Reluctant Cosmopolitans*, 190.

126. Swetschinski, *Reluctant Cosmopolitans*, 190.

127. Stow, *The Jews in Rome*, 1:362–63 (no. 880).

128. Wiznitzer, *The Records of the Earliest Jewish Community*, 66.

129. Eidelberg, *R. Juspa*, 100.

130. See Nisson E. Shulman, *Authority and Community: Polish Jewry in the Sixteenth Century* (New York, 1986), 104–5.

131. Cecil Roth, *History of the Jews in Venice* (New York, 1975), 180.

132. See, for example, Elliot Horowitz, "Families and Their Fortunes: The Jews of Early Modern Italy," in *Cultures of the Jews: A New History*, ed. David Biale (New York, 2002), 586ff. See also Maureen Flynn, "The Charitable Activities of Confraternities," reprinted in *Early Modern Europe: Issues and Interpretations*, ed. James B. Collins and Karen L. Taylor (Oxford, 2006), 101–20.

133. See Stow, *The Jews in Rome*, 2:733–34 (no. 1693).

134. Weinryb, *The Jews of Poland*, 70.

135. Stow, *The Jews in Rome*, 1:xvii.

136. According to Mordechai Breuer.

137. Jacob Katz, *Tradition and Crisis: Jewish Society at the End of the Middle Ages*, trans. Bernard Dov Cooperman (New York, 1993; orig., 1958), 172–78.

138. Katz, *Tradition and Crisis*, 176.

139. Bell, *Sacred Communities*.

140. See Goitein, *A Mediterranean Society*, 221, 222.

141. Goitein, *A Mediterranean Society*, 232.

142. Goitein, *A Mediterranean Society*, 237ff.

143. Miriam Bodian, *Hebrews of the Portuguese Nation: Conversos and Community in Early Modern Amsterdam* (Bloomington, IN, 1997), 130.

144. Isaac Cassuto, "Aus den ältesten Protokollbuch der Portugiesisch-Jüdischen Gemeinde in Hamburg: Übersetzung und Anmerkungen," in *Jahrbuch der Jüdisch-Literarischen Gesellschaft* 6 (1908): 1–54; 7 (1909): 159–210; 8 (1910): 227–90; 9 (1911): 318–66; 10 (1912): 225–95; 11 (1916): 1–76; 12 (1920): 55–118—here at 6:35.

145. Cassuto, "Aus den ältesten Protokollbuch," 6:38.

146. Cassuto, "Aus den ältesten Protokollbuch," 6:41.

147. Cassuto, "Aus den ältesten Protokollbuch," 10:249.

148. Finkelstein, *Jewish Self-Government*, 261.

149. Haim Beinart, *Trujillo: A Jewish Community in Extremadura on the Eve of the Expulsion from Spain* (Jerusalem, 1980), 37–39.

150. Jose Hinojosa Montalvo, *The Jews of the Kingdom of Valencia from Persecution to Expulsion, 1391–1492* (Jerusalem, 1993), 175–77.

151. See Otto Ulbricht, "Criminality and Punishment of the Jews in the Early Modern Period," in *In and Out of the Ghetto: Jewish-Gentile Relations in Late Medieval and Early Modern Germany*, ed. R. Po-chia Hsia and Hartmut Lehmann (Cambridge, UK, 1995), 49–70; and Rudolf Glanz, *Geschichte des niederen jüdischen Volkes in Deutschland: eine Studie über historisches Gaunertum, Bettelwesen und Vagantentum* (New York, 1968).

152. Weinryb, *The Jews of Poland*, 90.

153. Fram, *Ideals Face Reality*, 54.

154. Fram, *Ideals Face Reality*, 55.

155. Fram, *Ideals Face Reality*, 56–58.

156. Fram, *Ideals Face Reality*, 59–60.

157. Weinryb, *The Jews of Poland*, 89.

158. Fram, *Ideals Face Reality*, 60.

159. See Stow, *The Jews in Rome*, 2:486 (no. 1168).

160. See Montalvo, *The Jews of the Kingdom of Valencia*, 173, for example.

161. Cassuto, "Aus den ältesten Protokollbuch," 6:39.

162. Cassuto, "Aus den ältesten Protokollbuch," 7:3.

163. Leon Modena, *The Autobiography of a Seventeenth-Century Venetian Rabbi: Leon Modena's* Life of Judah, ed. and trans. Mark R. Cohen (Princeton, NJ, 1988), 118ff.

164. Horowitz, "Families and Their Fortunes," 595.

165. Beinart, *Trujillo*, 28.

166. J. Friedrich Battenberg, *Die Juden in Deutschland vom 16. bis zum Ende des 18. Jahrhunderts* (Munich, 2001), 52.

167. Stow, *The Jews in Rome*, 1:xii–xiii.

168. Stow, *The Jews in Rome*, 1:xviii.

169. Stow, *The Jews in Rome*, 1:375 (no. 909).

170. Franz Kobler, ed., *A Treasury of Jewish Letters: Letters from the Famous and the Humble*, 2 vols. (London, 1952), 2:364, 366–67.

171. Kobler, *A Treasury of Jewish Letters*, 2:465.

172. Quoted in Ivan G. Marcus, *The Jewish Life Cycle: Rites of Passage from Biblical to Modern Times* (Seattle, 2004), 195.

173. Joel Sirkes, in Shulman, *Authority and Community*, 122–23.

174. There is now a great deal of literature on Jewish women in this period (see the overview in Judith Baskin, ed., *Jewish Women in Historical Perspective* [Detroit, 1991], as well as the intriguing work by Claudia Ulbrich, *Shulamit and Margarete: Power, Gender, and Religion in a Rural Society in Eighteenth-Century Europe*, trans. Thomas Dunlap [Boston and Leiden, Netherlands, 2004]) and in early modern studies more generally (see, for example, the various essays reprinted in James B. Collins and Karen L. Taylor, eds., *Early Modern Europe: Issues and Interpretations* [Oxford, 2006], including those by Merry Wiesner and Natalie Davis).

175. Stow, *The Jews in Rome*, 1:xi.

176. See Avraham Grossman, *Pious and Rebellious: Jewish Women in Medieval Europe*, trans. Jonathan Chipman (Hanover, NH, and London, 2004); Stow, *The Jews in Rome*, 1:lxv.

177. See Stow, *The Jews in Rome*, 1:lxvi–ii, regarding the *me'un*, or refusal.

178. Here and above see the discussion of women in Goitein, *A Mediterranean Society*, 439–67.

179. See Rosman, "Innovative Tradition," 552ff.

180. Rosman, "Innovative Tradition," 553.

181. Rosman, "Innovative Tradition," 554.

182. Rosman, "Innovative Tradition," 559.

183. Horowitz, "Families and Their Fortunes," 598.

184. Kobler, *A Treasury of Jewish Letters*, 2:438.

185. Kobler, *A Treasury of Jewish Letters*, 2:446–47.

186. Kobler, *A Treasury of Jewish Letters*, 2:446.

187. See Natalie Davis, *Women on the Margins: Three Seventeenth-Century Lives* (Cambridge, MA, 1995), 6; for a more formal background, see 8ff.

188. Davis, *Women on the Margins*, 30.

189. Davis, *Women on the Margins*, 31.

190. Davis, *Women on the Margins*, 7.

191. Davis, *Women on the Margins*, 1.

192. Sirkes, in Shulman, *Authority and Community*, 171–72.

193. Glückel of Hameln, *The Memoirs*, 10.

194. Kobler, *A Treasury of Jewish Letters*, 2:378.

195. Stow, *The Jews in Rome*, 1:6–7 (no. 17).

196. Stow, *The Jews in Rome*, 1:34 (no. 93).

197. Stow, *The Jews in Rome*, 1:151–52 (no. 394).

198. Stow, *The Jews in Rome*, 2:450–52 (no. 1089).

199. Stow, *The Jews in Rome*, 1:114–15 (no. 308).

200. See Swetschinski, *Reluctant Cosmopolitans*.

201. Regarding Jewish prostitutes, see for example, Horowitz, "Families and Their Fortunes," 599.

202. Gampel, *The Last Jews*, 24.

203. Fram, *Ideals Face Reality*, 26; see also Hillel Levine, *Economic Origins of Antisemitism: Poland and Its Jews in the Early Modern Period* (New Haven, CT, 1991).

204. Weinryb, *The Jews of Poland*, 68.

205. Baron, *A Social and Religious History*, 16:269.

206. Weinryb, *The Jews of Poland*, 69.

207. Weinryb, *The Jews of Poland*, 61.

208. Gampel, *The Last Jews*, 36.

209. Rhoads Murphey, "Jewish Contributions to Ottoman Medicine," in *Jews, Turks, Ottomans: A Shared History, Fifteenth through the Twentieth Century*, ed. Avigdor Levy (Syracuse, NY, 2002), 65.

210. Steven Bowman, *The Jews of Byzantium (1204–1453)* (Alabama, 1985), 327.

211. Stillman, *The Jews of Arab Lands*, 288.

212. Gampel, *The Last Jews*, 25.

213. Baron, *A Social and Religious History*, 17:198.

214. Fram, *Ideals Face Reality*, 28.

215. Fram, *Ideals Face Reality*, 27.

216. Pogonowski, *Jews in Poland*, 70. See also Baron, *A Social and Religious History*, 16:230ff.

217. Rubinstein, "Lvov (Lemberg)."

218. See, for example, Baron, *A Social and Religious History*, 16:235ff.

219. Levy, *The Jews of the Ottoman Empire*, 25.

220. Levy, *The Jews of the Ottoman Empire*, 32–33. See also Cecil Roth, "Nasi, Joseph," in *Encyclopedia Judaica*, 16 vols. (Jerusalem, 1971–1972).

221. Daniel Goffman, "Jews in Early Modern Ottoman Commerce," in *Jews, Turks, Ottomans: A Shared History, Fifteenth through the Twentieth Century*, ed. Avigdor Levy (Syracuse, NY, 2002), 15. See also Baron, *A Social and Religious History*, 17: 199–201.

222. Levy, *The Jews of the Ottoman Empire*, 23.

223. Levy, *The Jews of the Ottoman Empire*, 23, 27.

224. Levy, *The Jews of the Ottoman Empire*, 29.

225. Levine, *Economic Origins*, 61ff.

226. See Baron, *A Social and Religious History*, 16:275.
227. Quoted in Baron, *A Social and Religious History*, 16:280.
228. Stow, *The Jews in Rome*, 1:223–24 (no. 559).
229. Weinryb, *The Jews of Poland*, 67.
230. Weinryb, *The Jews of Poland*, 56.
231. Levy, *The Jews of the Ottoman Empire*, 26.
232. Levy, *The Jews of the Ottoman Empire*, 26.
233. Gampel, *The Last Jews*, 31.
234. Weinryb, *The Jews of Poland*, 67.
235. Weinryb, *The Jews of Poland*, 68.
236. Baron, *A Social and Religious History*, 16:250.
237. Levy, *The Jews of the Ottoman Empire*, 26.

4

Identity: Religion and Culture

The early modern Jewish experience was more than sociological. Religious belief, customs, and practices were of great importance, even if early modern Jewry may have been less homogeneous than once assumed. This chapter explores the complexities of early modern Judaism, with special attention to the attempts to create uniform codes of Jewish law, as well as the significant meaning of local and regional customs and legislation. The "flexibility" of early modern Judaism and its ability to tolerate dissent are examined closely. This chapter also introduces the production of broader literary and scholarly work, including a variety of genres created for different audiences in a host of languages. While much scholarship has debated the cultural and religious differences between **Sephardic** and **Ashkenazic** Jews, here we consider the general impact of ethnicity and cultural inheritance throughout early modern Jewry.

TRADITION AND BELIEF

In general, Jewish community was organized around the adherence of its members to a standardized and traditional body of law, the primary sources of which were the Talmud and the various medieval codifications of Talmudic law (for example, the *Mishneh Torah* of **Maimonides** and the *Arba'ah Turim* of Rabbi Jacob ben Asher). In addition, local communities were joined by the rulings of important rabbis in their **responsa**, by the *takkanot* or ordinances passed by local or on occasion regional authorities, and by the power of local or regional custom, which could often serve the same purpose as legislation.[1]

Customs

Custom was of particular importance in early modern Judaism. Customs could be local, regional, national, ethnic, or even familial. Custom could determine which view to accept when *halakhic* authorities disagreed; it could supplement existing law unable to treat new questions that arose; and, moreover, as the expression of the will of the people, it could establish new norms contrary to existing (generally only civil, not religious) law.[2] An important Jewish legal concept stipulates that customs can take the force of law and, at times, even overrule some laws.[3] This concept had particular force in the scattered communities of the fifteenth century. The important Italian legal scholar Rabbi Joseph Colon (1410/1420–1480) cited the Palestinian Talmud regarding the power of custom. Colon, commenting on an inheritance case wrote,

> We learn in the Palestinian Talmud that custom cancels law and it is written in [tractate] *Avodah Zara*, for example, that it is a permanent custom from the mouths of the sages of the place [that cancels law]; as is said in tractate *Sofrim*, no law will be permanent until it becomes the custom [of the land] and . . . [it is in this context] that it says that custom cancels law, referring to ordained custom; but custom which is not derived from the Torah is like a mistake in reasoning and how many defective customs there are.[4]

Customs were not related only to strictly religious rituals, but they also helped to define Jewish communal identity more generally. In early modern Worms, in Germany, for example, the salvation of the Jewish community was attributed to two visitors and memorialized through the custom of lighting two candles on the seventh day of Passover on behalf of their souls.[5] Similarly, certain customs as well as feasts and fasts were established to remember salvation and persecution. In Frankfurt am Main in the seventeenth century, for example, a special Purim-like celebration was established after the German rebel Vincent Fettmilch was defeated and after the Jews, who he had expelled, were allowed to return to the city.

Belief

Belief is a difficult concept to define. Indeed, we can sometimes know how people behaved or how they thought people should behave in an ideal world, and so we can attempt to derive a sense of what they believed. But belief itself is, by definition, a rather internal affair, and we must be careful not to assume that everyone thought or believed in the same way. As the growing literature on pre-modern Christianity has ably demonstrated, and as the burgeoning literature on medieval and early modern Judaism appears to indicate as well, we must be cautious against assuming religious homogeneity and consistency in the pre-modern period. As one medieval historian, John Arnold, asserts, "Even when we have more personal and individualized sources, problems remain. The fact is that historical sources are not windows that open into the minds, hearts or souls of long-dead people. They are, rather, texts: traces of their passage through the world, inflected with all kinds of complicated cultural conformities."[6] While we should not generalize too much, Arnold's conclusions about late medieval Christianity may be instructive. Arnold argues that although one can find evidence of some core tenets of the faith, Christianity was in an ongoing state of interpretation, was not static, and was not merely a linear production within a religious hierarchy.[7] Arnold contends that one way that Christians knew who they were was by understanding who they were not (they were not Jews or Muslims, for example).[8]

Many scholars reject the idea that pre-modern Jews maintained anything resembling a formal theology or dogma. Judaism, in this regard, is seen similarly to Islam as more focused on practice (ortho-praxy) than belief (ortho-doxy). There clearly are religious principles in the full spectrum of Jewish writing, however, and there were many attempts throughout the Middle Ages and into the early modern period (increasingly) to identify and discuss these principles. One very good example of this is the Thirteen Principles of faith articulated by Moses Maimonides in the twelfth century. While not everyone agreed to these principles or seriously engaged them, the scope and general focus of the principles will help us to identify some fundamental religious concepts that were of great importance (and at times frequently discussed) during our period.

The first five principles deal with God. They focus on the notion of God's existence, unity, and non-corporeality. They stipulate that God preceded everything absolutely and that He alone should be exalted, praised, and worshipped. Principles 6 and 7 refer to the existence of prophecy and to the special position of the prophecy of Moses in particular. The eighth principle establishes that the Torah is from heaven and that it is the same Torah as brought down by Moses. Further, this Torah should not be abrogated or transmuted (number 9). Principles 10 and 11 refer to human actions and their relationship to God. The former asserts that God knows and does not neglect the actions of men, the latter that He rewards and punishes people based either on their obeisance or on their violation of the Torah. The greatest rewards, according to this line of thinking, are reserved for the world to come. Principle 12 established belief in and praise for the Messiah, without, however, sanctioning any calculations for the date of his arrival. The final principle referred to the belief in the resurrection of the dead.[9]

The principles summarized here focus on the nature of God and God's relationship with men, demonstrating God's involvement in the world. In addition, the core of Jewish tradition as concretized in the unchangeable

and unique Torah, the tradition and role of prophecy, and the specific belief in the Messiah and the resurrection of the dead form the second core
component. This second core area demonstrates the centrality of the Jews
as the Chosen People and of their tradition. Notice that such a broad, almost philosophical, approach allows for a great deal of richness and diversity in actual practice, liturgy, and even belief. Even the fundamental
principles could be contested when it came to specifics. Maimonides himself had held controversial positions about resurrection at different points
in his own career. The framework of Jewish principles, combined with the
scope of various texts in need of interpretation and a web of local contexts
and individual considerations, made Judaism in our period quite elastic
in some ways and yet allowed for real continuity and sense of coherence
in many other ways.

Early modern Jewish belief, like that of "traditional" Jewish thought before it, was postulated upon the notion that God created and controlled the
world and that the Jews were His Chosen People. Moses Almosnino, for example, in a sermon he delivered in Salonika in 1568, noted,

> On my journey I saw the concrete evidence of His providence over each and
> every step. God arranged it all. I discovered that what seemed to us to be
> chance events opposing our purpose turned out to be for our good, helping us
> to accomplish our vital task. We should therefore give thanks and praise to
> God for the individual providence He bestows upon us. It may therefore be
> truly said that the tabernacle of our city testifies to glory and splendor: that His
> presence dwells among us.[10]

Jews were expected to fear God and behave according to His Law. As Isaiah Horowitz, in his *Generations of Adam*, urged, "A person is not able to
reach the crown of Torah if he has not prepared himself in fear of sin, so
that his soul and pure heart long for *devequt* with God, blessed be He."[11]
One method of achieving this fear was clearly through rebuke:[12] "These ethical words of Torah bear fruit and make an impression," Horowitz noted,
"because they enter the heart. Such learning leads to action."[13]

Observance

Jewish communal religious practices were often dictated in various communal statutes. According to the Statutes of the Scola dei Tedeschi in Rome
from 1541, for example, by which the *parnasim* gave to the rabbi full authority to make *takkanot* (ordinances), the members of the community were
obligated as follows: all members had to pray in the evening, morning, and
afternoon in the synagogue (they could do so in other places only with special permission); absence for three consecutive days resulted in a monetary
fine; a fee was involved for quitting the synagogue; and no business could

be transacted before the *shaharit* (morning) prayers. The statutes also indicated that all members must pay assessed synagogue taxes and pay all donations immediately; all needs of the synagogue were to be determined by majority vote; two *parnasim* and three counselors were to be appointed, who must take an oath of office; and no one was to speak during prayers without permission from the *parnasim*. Disputes between members had to be brought before the congregation; no member was to strike another or speak badly of him; reconciliation at the Torah must be accepted; and, in the same spirit of community, all members were to share the expenses of the communal *lulav* and *etrog*, used during the holiday of **Sukkot**.[14]

Like their neighbors, Jews developed religious beliefs and practices that were folkish or popular, in addition to the learned or normative systems that are left behind for us in legal codes and rabbinic responsa. As the scholar Shalom Sabar notes, "The reality of daily life, the deep religious beliefs of the common people, and close contacts with the host societies and their varied cultures gave rise to popular beliefs, patterns of behavior, customs and practices, and the production of religious artifacts that could not be always accounted for in the 'official' halakhic sources."[15] Among the artifacts of such beliefs were various amulets as well as different incantations intended to offer protection to individuals in a wide range of situations.

In fact, Jewish religious observance was affected by a host of factors. At times, fear of external perceptions or anti-Jewish backlash also forced Jews to alter their religious customs. The Polish rabbi Solomon Luria suggested that Jews abandon the custom of saying a blessing in the street as mourners returned from burying the dead because non-Jews would be riled up by what they saw as a public religious action.[16]

While there clearly were examples of deviance from Jewish observance and communal norms, as will be discussed below, it is likely that the vast majority of early modern Jews were engaged in traditional and communal practices. In Poland, for example, most Jews appear to have participated in communal prayer services rather than praying at home. Most obeyed an excommunication decree, with its injunctions to have no social or business contact with those under the ban. Jews appeared to obey the Sabbath, closing their businesses on Friday afternoons and Saturdays. Some Jews were clearly unwilling to take oaths on the name of Jesus.[17]

The Nature of Jewish Education

Central to Jewish belief and religious practice was education. Here we discuss the education of males; later in the chapter we consider the education of Jewish females. As we saw in the last chapter, education was at times a communal institution and at times provided for privately by individual Jewish families. The structure and focus of education could vary greatly across regions in the early modern period. In Poland, so the idealistic account of Nathan of Hannover (d. 1683) goes, each community maintained academies, in which the heads were well compensated and respected. The study of Torah was held, here, in highest esteem.[18] According to Nathan, communities gave allowances to young men in order that they might study with the academy head, and a small number of householders supported a comparatively large number of students.[19]

Nathan outlined the academic divisions of the year and he noted, "All students studied **Gemara**, the commentaries of **Rashi** and **Tosafoth**, with great diligence. Each day they studied a halachah."[20] More advanced students were engaged with the codes, especially the *Arba'ah Turim* and commentaries, as well as the writings of Isaac Alfasi (1013–1103).[21] An inspector supervised the academy and examined the students, such that "he who knew nothing of what he had studied or erred in one thing was flogged by the inspector at the command of the director, and was otherwise chastised before the boys so that he should remember to study more diligently the following week."[22]

In Amsterdam by the end of the seventeenth century, Sephardic primary education was conducted in a six-room schoolhouse. In the first class, students studied until they could read the prayers, then they studied the Pentateuch and the cantillation. The third class focused on study of the Torah with attention to translation. Rashi's (Rabbi Solomon ben Isaac, the great medieval exegete) commentary was included with each Torah portion. In the fourth class the Prophets and Writings were studied, with cantillation as well. The fifth class was Mishnaic law. Here, instruction was in Hebrew, unless Spanish was required for explanation. Focus was placed on grammatical skills as well as relevant sections of the *Shulhan Arukh*. The sixth class was the Talmudic college, or the academy of the rabbi. The focus here was on study of the Law along with the commentaries of Rashi and the Tosafot, and consultation of legal comments by Maimonides, and those from the *Tur* and the *Bet Yosef*. The school day was from 8:00 a.m. until 11:00 a.m. and 2:00 p.m. to 5:00 p.m.[23]

Where a formal community school did not exist it was incumbent upon parents to hire worthy instructors for their children. According to Rabbi Yair Hayyim Bacharach in late seventeenth-century Worms, a group of fathers should pool their resources to engage a teacher for their children according to a proper order of instruction.[24] Bacharach offered his own educational advice, namely, "You should not let your son waste his time with *Hillukim* and nonsensical hairsplitting exercises, which, I am sorry to say, are widely practiced. We find nothing of this kind with the ancients, neither in the Talmud nor in the Tosafot, although their authors were very acute thinkers."[25] Bacharach was clear that education should be directed toward obtaining true wisdom, not honor or fortune.[26] The famous Maharal of Prague, Judah

Loew, also reacted against the then current *pilpulistic* (casuistry) style—"while we cannot achieve the wisdom of the ancients, we go idly and spend the time with empty word battles"[27]—and the lack of broad learning. (He believed it a duty also to learn astronomy and chronology.)[28] The Maharal conceded that his efforts were frequently unsuccessful, because teachers say to the fathers, "'It is better if your son learns the Talmud-**Pilpul**, by which he will rise ever higher . . .' to become a great man."[29]

More advanced education that focused on study of the Talmud and codes of Jewish law was to be found in the *yeshivah* (pl. *yeshivot*), or Talmudic academy. The *yeshivah* dated back to the rabbinic period, and throughout the Middle Ages served in something of a tripartite role, as high court, educational body, and legislating body.[30] Throughout much of the Middle Ages and early modern period, the *yeshivah* was generally more of a private institution, run by an individual rabbi, who attracted and often also supported his students, in his own house. On other occasions, however, the *yeshivah* became something like a communal institution and was supported by the members of the community at large. In any event, the *yeshivah* allowed, not only for the extension of formal Jewish learning, but it also served as a training ground for the next generation of religious leaders. In a very real sense, it also created a network of scholars and a means by which to disseminate religious law and various customs and practices. The history of the *yeshivah* is a rich and important component in the development of Jewish thought and Jewish communities.[31]

New Tools and World-Views? The Impact of Printing

As we saw in the introduction, the early modern world was significantly affected by many different developments. Some of these had to do with the creation or evolution of new political, economic, and religious views. Others had to do with the more hands-on developments of technology. While the growth of global markets and increasing contact between diverse peoples forced early modern people to reassess the world around them, it also forced them to reflect on their own identities as well. The revolution of printing that began in the fifteenth century allowed radical new developments in scholarship and greater dissemination of ideas.

Printing affected the Jews in many ways, just as extensively as it did everyone else. Printing opened and expanded the circulation of texts, while at the same time allowing for a more uniform body of material for study and the circulation of new ideas and new ways of organizing knowledge. Among the first Hebrew books to be printed, by the 1470s, were the medieval exegete Rashi's commentary to the Torah and the legal compendium of Jacob ben Asher (1275–1340), *Arba'ah Turim*. During the first quarter of the sixteenth century, Hebrew printing exploded, due in part to the work of the Soncino family in Italy and Daniel Bomberg, a Christian printer originally from Antwerp. Venice became a major Hebrew printing center, though other places were significant as well: Mantua and Rome in Italy; Basle, Prague, and Augsburg, among others, in central Europe; eventually Cracow and Lublin in the East; and Constantinople, Salonika, and Fez under Ottoman rule, where Jews expelled from Spain introduced printing in the early sixteenth century.

Salonika, for example, had a Hebrew printing press in 1515 as well as public libraries and various educational institutions.[32] The city was home to important *yeshivot* (Talmudic academies) of Jacob ibn Habib and his son Levi ibn Habib (ca. 1483–1545), Joseph Taitazak (ca. 1487–ca. 1545), Samuel de Medina (ca. 1506–1589), and Isaac Adarbi (ca. 1510–1584).[33] The first Hebrew press in the Ottoman Empire, however, was in Istanbul, founded by David and Samuel Nahmias in 1493.[34] The first book published there was a copy of the *Arba'ah Turim*.[35] As we will see below in the discussion of Christian Hebraists, Hebrew printing found a ready market among Jews but also a growing market among Christian scholars interested in a wide range of Hebrew texts. In Germany, significant Hebrew publications, often revealing intriguing Jewish and Christian relations, grew in other places as well, such as Basle, Hanau, Augsburg, Freiburg, Heidelberg, Isny, Constance, and Thiengen.[36]

Codification

Codification of law was not in and of itself new to Judaism. One might, in fact, argue that the Bible and much of rabbinic literature are codes of a certain sort. Medieval Jews also codified law, as the important and widely read codes of Maimonides, Isaac Alfasi, and Jacob ben Asher attest. In the sixteenth century, however, for a variety of converging reasons, codification took on new impetus.[37] Some Jews thought it useful to codify applicable laws for a variety of reasons: because of the massive movement of Jews and the interaction of various groups and customs; the possibilities of standardizing and disseminating written works with the development of printing; as a response to non-Jewish theology; and to combat declining familiarity among many Jews with core Jewish texts in their original language.

Some Jews rejected out of hand this idea of codification, questioning the sources for the decisions included in the codes and expressing concerns that regional customs were discarded and, worse, that individuals would either make decisions without prerequisite knowledge or the act of codification would further distance Jews from the actual sources of *halakhic* reasoning, further weakening Jewish knowledge. The resistance to codification, especially in the form of Joseph Caro's *Shulhan Arukh*, was quite marked (at least initially) in Poland and Germany. In Poland, important attempts were made to make certain that Polish customs were accounted for and utilized in the codes. In addition, genuine concern was expressed for the new methods of *halakhic* decision-making that the code enabled. Especially stiff opposition was voiced by traditionalists such as Rabbi Solomon Luria (ca. 1510–1573).[38]

In Germany, many scholars also vehemently attacked the use of the *Shulhan Arukh*. Among the most outspoken critics was Hayyim ben Bezalel (ca. 1520–1588), the brother of the famous Maharal of Prague. Hayyim attacked the *Shulhan Arukh* as well as the work of Moses Isserles. He was concerned about the neglect of some authorities in favor of others, and he argued that the codes caused people to sin unwittingly, since they invited application to situations not specifically discussed. He was critical of the exclusion of German customs, he felt that a new level of leniency in *halakhic* decision-making was being introduced, and he argued that *halakhah* was being abolished in favor of unsupported customs.[39] Hayyim noted that such codification complicated the problem by which "there are many uneducated who are not worried about the ancient writings, do not even understand them, and in the meantime forget the Torah."[40] His brother, the Maharal of Prague, was also an outspoken opponent, who criticized codification for encouraging shortcuts in legal decision-making and decreasing individuals' ability to engage the actual biblical and rabbinic sources themselves.[41] He wrote that it was better to decide from the Talmud itself (relying on a collection of decisions allows one to decide without knowing),[42] "for it is as if one was invited to a 'set table' (*Shulhan Arukh*), on which stands costly dishes, but one cannot himself acquire food and drink, rather one must wait for this foreign table."[43]

Legal Decision-Making

The early modern period was replete with important Jewish legal authorities. One of the primary tools in the legal decision-making process was rabbinic responsa. Responsa were written answers by particularly learned scholars to written questions regarding religious law.[44] Generally, the responsa recorded the questions as well as the various interpretations of issues relevant to the particular problem brought forth by the respondent. The respondent typically issued a ruling or left the information in front of the inquirer for his final evaluation, especially when the inquirer was another rabbi. Responsa dealt with a very wide range of subjects, and they have increasingly been used—not without important limitations it should be noted—for researching the communal and social history of the Jews as well. The direct impact of the responsa depended primarily on the prominence of the respondent. Generally speaking, the decisions in the responsa could not be enforced on the community, outside of the influence held by the rabbi; they were merely opinions and not court decisions.

There were many important responsa writers in the early modern period. In the Ottoman Empire, for example, Joseph Taitazak (ca. 1487–1545) wrote responsa, other legal commentaries, biblical commentaries, as well as material related to philosophy. Samuel de Medina (ca. 1506–1589), known as the Maharashdam, penned over 1,000 responsa and was sent from Salonika on various communal matters. Elijah Mizrahi (ca. 1450–1526), born and raised in Constantinople, was a leading rabbinic authority of his time. He wrote more than 100 responsa, in addition to various other commentaries on traditional medieval rabbinical texts. Joseph ibn Lev (ca. 1505–1580), born in Yugoslavia but active in Salonika, authored several volumes of responsa.

One of the most renowned responsa writers of the early modern period was Zevi Hirsch Ashkenazi (1660–1718), who, although of Ashkenazic background, adopted Sephardic customs and practices after time in Salonika and Belgrade. Appointed *hakham*, a term for rabbi among some Sephardic Jews, of the Sephardic community in Sarajevo, he later spent many years in Altona outside Hamburg and then as rabbi of the Ashkenazic congregation in Hamburg. His responsa, *Hakham Zevi* (Amsterdam, 1712), offer a wide range of rabbinic opinions and also portray his personal development. In Germany, Yair Hayyim Bacharach was another intellectual giant, who authored numerous and important rabbinic responsa. Bacharach was learned in a wide range of Jewish subjects and sources, including **Kabbalah**, as well as secular fields of study. Born in Moravia, he spent much of his life in Worms. His responsa are important legal decisions, but they also throw light on the status and history of the Jewish community in Worms.

In Poland, there were some very prominent *halakhic* experts, many of whom authored important and at times ground-breaking responsa. Jacob Pollack (1460/1470–after 1522) is renowned as one of the earliest legal authorities in Poland. Originally from Germany, he moved first to Prague and then to Cracow. A student of Pollack was Shalom Shakhna (d. 1558), the *rosh yeshiva* in Lublin, an important community in the sixteenth century. Other significant early modern Polish rabbinic authorities include Solomon Luria (ca. 1510–1574), who also spent some time in Lublin; Moses Isserles (1525/1530–1572), whom we met in our discussion of the *Shulhan Arukh*; Joel Sirkes (1561–1640), who served in a number of different communities; and Aaron Koidonover (ca. 1614–1676), who also served in Germany before assuming the role of *av bet din* in Cracow.

Ethics

If one surveys broadly the intellectual output of early modern Jews, one is immediately struck by the preponderance of ethical writings. These writings included moral tales, especially, for example, of the medieval *Hasidei*

Ashkenaz (German Pietists) and various chronicles intended to strength certain behavior and mindset, such as Solomon Ibn Verga's *The Staff of Judah*.
Sermons preached in the synagogue were often later collected and printed
in written form. Yiddish was becoming an increasingly important medium
for communication, and a variety of publications in Yiddish provided Jewish education (especially in this area of ethics) as well as a host of popular
tales. Some were adaptations of non-Jewish literature, for a wide audience
that included an expanding middle class and, as some scholars maintain, a
large female readership.

The *Hasidei Ashkenaz* (German Pietists) of the Middle Ages had handed
down much of their morally infused teaching through various works, especially the *Sefer Hasidim* (Book of the Pious). That work was reprinted in the
early modern period, and a variety of tales allegedly describing the activities
of the *Hasidei Ashkenaz* circulated throughout Europe in Yiddish and, later,
in Hebrew. Often these tales provided important moral and religious instruction. At the same time, they created something of a bridge connecting
the Jews of the Middle Ages and the early modern period.[45]

While Ibn Verga's work is generally recognized as a history, its focus on
the causes for Jewish suffering evokes a powerful moral sense as well.
Among the reasons that Ibn Verga supplied for hatred of Jews were divine
anger, the sins of our fathers, natural causes that prolong the Exile because
of our lack of merit, and the slaying of Jesus. Added to these factors, however, Ibn Verga added the following moral twist. Persecution is caused in
part by jealousy or envy regarding religion, women, and money, all of
which are involved in Jewish and non-Jewish relations. In addition, Ibn
Verga argued that the people became accustomed to swearing falsely and
that some Jews developed enormous pride, which they lorded over their
Gentile neighbors, creating a good deal of animosity.[46]

Perhaps the late seventeenth-century memoirist Glückel of Hameln put it
most succinctly. Of her work, she wrote to her children the following:

> This, dear children, will be no book of morals. Such I could not write, and our
> sages have already written many. Moreover, we have our holy Torah in which
> we may find and learn all that we need for our journey through this world to
> the world to come. . . . The kernel of the Torah is, Thou shalt love thy neigh-
> bour as thyself. But in our days we seldom find it so, and few are they who love
> their fellowmen with all their heart—on the contrary, if a man can contrive to
> ruin his neighbor, nothing pleases him more. The best thing for you, my chil-
> dren, is to serve God from your heart, without falsehood or sham, not giving
> out to people that you are one thing while, God forbid, in your heart you are
> another. Say your prayers with awe and devotion.[47]

She concluded, rather pragmatically, "Above all, my children, be honest in
money matters, with both Jews and Gentiles, lest the name of Heaven be

profaned."[48] From Glückel we gain insights into the synagogue[49] and the socialization of religion. In much of the story told by Glückel, religion is presented, at least in its best and purest form, as internal religious observance and action; the dichotomy is often self versus community, and the incidence of punishment is frequently narrated. Bad things were explained, in typical medieval and pre-modern fashion, as punishments for evil actions or shortcomings.

Some significant work has been done on early modern Jewish sermons, especially by the historian Marc Saperstein. One particularly rich collection of sermons, by the Amsterdam rabbi Saul Levi Morteira is a good example of the elocutionary and moral power of the sermon. Morteira, born around 1635 in Venice, became one of the guiding rabbinic lights for the Portuguese Jews of Amsterdam.

Morteira addressed a wide range of communal issues, and much like the sumptuary laws that circulated widely in the early modern period and that attempted to curb certain forms of excessive behavior, his sermons called for moderation and improvement. According to Morteira, for example,

> This [envy] has frequently been the cause of massacres and expulsions during our own exile. Expelled from certain countries, we have arrived in others totally destitute, and God has graciously enabled us to acquire new wealth and possessions. Those who knew at first hand the circumstances of their arrival lived in peace. But after their deaths, others became arrogant, indulging in empty vanities, until the indigenous population eventually expelled them.
>
> So it is with the Jewish people. If they would willingly accept their exile, behaving moderately—rather than arrogantly overshadowing the inhabitants of the lands where they dwell—they would pass through their exile in fair condition, without suffering, until God favors the remnant of Joseph.[50]

Many Jews, even prominent ones, it seems were taken in by trends and practices surrounding them. One common shortcoming that turns up in many writings of the period is gambling. Leon Modena, the vicarious rabbi from seventeenth-century Venice, fills his autobiography with tales of his gambling addiction, as well as the financial losses brought with it. Modena writes, for example, that "during Hanukkah [December 23–20, 1598], 'Satan' duped me into playing games of chance, and by the following Shavuot [May 30–31, 1599] I lost more than three hundred ducats." After he had worked hard to repay his debts, "that same friar [a Christian clerical acquaintance] misled me into the secret company [of players of games of chance] and caused me to lose much money."[51] In his own attack on gambling, Modena concluded that it was a sin that leads one to violate all of the Ten Commandments, estranging the gambler not only from God but from his fellow men as well.[52] Much early modern Jewish literature addressed such concerns and offered suggestions and prescriptions for living a more ethical and devout life.

Another central European figure who was also associated with Kabbalah (see below) was Isaiah ben Abraham Ha-Levi Horowitz (known as Ha-Shelah ha-Kodesh, ca. 1565–1630). Born in Prague, Horowitz studied there and in Poland, before becoming head of the rabbinic court in Dubno in 1602 and later in Frankfurt am Main, where he lived from 1606 until 1614. He then returned to Prague for the remainder of his life. Horowitz authored the widely circulated *Shenei Luhot ha-Berit* (Two Tablets of the Covenant), which went through many editions. In that work, which is a commentary on the weekly portions of the Torah, he notes that he has undertaken the publication of a commentary "on the overriding nature of the commandment to observe the Sabbath," regarding which the rabbinic sages dictated that a person should "peruse the weekly portion twice in the original Hebrew, and once in an appropriate translation." While Horowitz sought to explain both the obvious and the hidden meanings of the text, he was also concerned "to pinpoint the ethical and moral content of these various portions of the written Torah."[53] This centrality of ethical-moral discussion penetrated all levels of Jewish thought and writing in the period.

Kabbalah Mysticism

Jewish cultural and religious proclivities are sometimes evident by the books early modern Jews read, discussed, or engaged. It is difficult to differentiate what more popular folks were reading as opposed to the elite, but various book inventories from Jewish community holdings or personal libraries, as well as printing petitions and permissions, do shed some light on Jewish reading interests of the period. At times these lists were maintained by the Jews themselves; at other times, they were kept by local authorities or the Inquisition. For Renaissance Italy, up until 1540, the historian Robert Bonfil has examined around forty different book lists. These lists, according to Bonfil, indicate a declining interest in philosophy in the Jewish public,[54] with the exception of Maimonides' *Guide for the Perplexed*.[55] On the other hand, kabbalistic literature seems to have grown in popularity in this period.[56]

Interest in Jewish mysticism among both Jews and Christians was well entrenched by the middle of the sixteenth century.[57] This development was due in part to internal Jewish developments, such as the circulation of copies of the *Zohar*, important advances in the mystical center of Safed, and later to the events surrounding Shabbetai Sevi in the mid-seventeenth century. In Poland as well in the second half of the seventeenth century, kabbalistic works and ideas reached remarkable popularity and were seen as eminently practical, making their way into religious discourse and everyday life in such things as amulets, which were intended to heal all sorts of maladies.[58]

Despite serious challenges to its authority, the *Zohar*, now believed to have been penned by Moses de Leon in thirteenth-century Spain, was circulating widely in the sixteenth century and filtered its way into compilations of rabbinic responsa and customs books.[59] The *Zohar* appeared in several important sixteenth-century editions, even if such printing was not always supported by key rabbinic personalities. Excerpts of the text were already being quoted by the late 1540s, even though the first printed editions did not appear until 1558–1560 in Mantua and 1559–1560 in Cremona.[60] Among more than 400 Mantuan libraries surveyed from the end of the sixteenth century, fifty-one copies of the *Zohar* could be found.[61]

While there was a significant mystical tradition within Judaism, the sixteenth century seemed to usher in a new and extremely explosive interest in Kabbalah. Fostered by the general messianism we will see below, as well as the popularization made possible by printing, the study (and practice) of Kabbalah entered a new stage in its development.

A particularly powerful discussion of Kabbalah emerged in the town of Safed in Israel. Safed became, for a period in the middle of the sixteenth century, a central meeting place for some of the leading kabbalists, whose impact would rock the edifice of traditional Judaism for centuries. Safed, which had a Jewish community as early as the thirteenth century, numbered about 300 Jewish families under Mamluk rule by the end of the fifteenth century. A wave of Sephardic immigration after 1492 and again after the conquest of the Ottomans in 1516 led to the development of a large and multiethnic Jewish community that became home to central scholars such as Rabbis Jacob Berab (who sought to reestablish a **Sanhedrin** and rabbinic ordination); Joseph Caro (author of the famed *Shulhan Arukh* (Prepared Table) but also the more mystical *Maggid Mesharim* (Preacher of Uprightness); Moses di Trani (a great *halakhist*); Isaac Luria (perhaps the most important kabbalistic thinker of the period), as well as his disciple Hayyim Vital and many others.

Safed, as we noted in chapter 2, was an important center of Jewish life. Reaching a great spiritual pinnacle in the sixteenth century, the city was home not only to thousands of Jews but also to the first printing press in the Orient and eight synagogues. Though the economic and material welfare of the community was to wane significantly by the middle of the seventeenth century, at the beginning of that century Safed, despite intense poverty, was home to many important rabbis and educational institutions. A rich ascetic and mystically oriented culture bloomed in Safed, with numerous brotherhoods and study groups holding night-time vigils, developing important new mystical themes, and seeking *devekut*, or mystical union, with God.

One central figure, Joseph Caro (1488–1575), after the Spanish expulsion, moved to Istanbul, Adrianople, Nikopol, and Salonika, studying for a time with Solomon Molkho. Known for his important legal code, Caro was one of the four scholars initially ordained by Berab (see chapter 3). Caro became a leading figure of the Safed community, attracting great numbers of students to his *yeshivah*, including Moses Cordovero and Moses Alsheikh. In addition to his legal writings and codifications, Caro also penned a mystical diary, and some of his writing is infused with messianic language and concepts.

Moses Cordovero (1522–1570) also had Spanish origins and was a teacher of the renowned Isaac Luria. His important book *Pardes Rimmonim* (Orchard of Pomegranates) was completed before he was thirty and was widely cited throughout the early modern period. Cordovero also composed an extensive commentary on the *Zohar*. Cordovero was himself an important mystical mediator. His writing stressed meditation, truthfulness, confession, non-anger, prayer, charity, focus on Torah, and a certain level of asceticism (depriving the body through such things as fasting). He wrote, for example, that "a person ought to meditate upon matters of Torah with each bite he eats in order that his food may serve as a sacrifice and his drinking of water and wine as drink-offerings."[62]

But it was Isaac Luria (1534–1572), known as Ha-Ari, the (sacred) lion, who transformed the very concept of the Kabbalah in the sixteenth century. Born in Jerusalem, Luria was raised in Egypt and settled in Safed only very late in his life. Of Luria it was written that he

> knew all the deeds of men and even their thoughts. He could read faces, look into the souls of men, and recognize souls that migrated from body to body. He could tell you about the souls of the wicked which had entered into trees and stone or animals and what sins he had committed since youth; he knew wherein a sinful man had been punished by God and would prescribe "improvements" to remove a moral blemish, and knew just when such a moral defect had been corrected. He understood the chirping of birds, and through their flight he divined strange things, as is referred to in the verse [Ecclesiastes 10:20]: "For a bird of the air shall carry the voice, and that which hath wings shall tell the matter." All of this he acquired because of the piety, asceticism, purity, and holiness that he had exercised since his youth.[63]

Although recognized as one of the giants of mystical thought, Luria left no writings, and his thinking is known largely through the writings of his disciples, principally Hayyim Vital. Luria emphasized the doctrine of *tikkun*, or repair of the cosmos. He also focused a great deal of attention on the concept of *kavana* (intention) in prayer and the performance of the commandments. Luria wedded his Kabbalah with messianic strands, with some speculating that he may have revealed himself as the Messiah had he lived longer and that the redemption was imminent, perhaps in 1575.[64]

Hayyim Vital was himself a most interesting and complicated individual, as revealed in his writings, notably his spiritual autobiography. Vital was born in Israel, perhaps in Safed, and he studied under Rabbi Moses Alsheik, later serving as Luria's primary student and the organizer of his teachings. Indeed, in 1575 twelve of Luria's disciples agreed to study Luria's teaching only from Vital. Vital was an energetic writer and penned a variety of commentaries on biblical works as well as kabbalistic works. Vital headed a *yeshivah* in Jerusalem between 1577 and 1585, before returning to Safed from 1586 until 1592. At the end of his life he lived in Damascus.

Vital propagated the idea that the soul of the Messiah transmigrates (*gilgul* in Hebrew). He emphasized the need for preparing for the messianic age through repentance, and he even fashioned himself as the Messiah son of Joseph, the supposed precursor to the final Messiah (son of David). As he wrote, regarding a dream in his autobiography,

> I [a spirit] have been sent by Heaven to reveal to him Heavenly secrets which he did not learn from his teacher z"l [his memory for a blessing], in order that he should cause the world to repent. Everything depends upon him to repair the world. I came to reveal to him matters concerning the Messiah. He is on the verge of coming. . . . During this time, many troubles will befall Damascus and it will be overturned like Sodom and Jerusalem will also be burned. Only Safed will be saved.[65]

Jewish mysticism existed and at times flourished outside of the Holy Land as well. Judah ben Bezalel Loew, or the Maharal of Prague (ca. 1525–1609) is well-known for the legend that he created an artificial being, a *golem*. The Maharal delved into many areas of learning and was a thinker of the highest order in rabbinics. He was a moralist, something of an educational reformer, learned in math and science (interested in alchemy as well, as was the fashion of the day), and he maintained connections with some of the leading scholars of his day. Loew sought to reground Jewish education logically with the development of necessary skills and sequencing of learning. According to him, "If he was entrusted through instruction in Bible with the ground rules of the religion, so the foundations were laid for the **Mishnah** and he could build upon it in order to achieve the understanding of the Talmud, then he could advance to independent research and be admitted into learned debate."[66] Loew was *Landesrabbiner* of Moravia and then the head of a *yeshivah* in Prague. He was familiar with kabbalistic concepts, which were used in his various commentaries. Loew was particularly taken with the unique nature of the Jews, whose pure essence he described in many writings.[67]

Yet, while many continued to reject kabbalistic concepts, many important kabbalistic ideas and practices made their way into traditional Jewish liturgy and observance. One example of this penetration is the popular

Lechah Dodi (Come My Beloved) for the Sabbath evening service. Composed by the kabbalist Rabbi Solomon Alkabetz, a relative of Moses Cordovero, in Safed, the song offers a refrain in which God is enjoined to meet the Sabbath presence. Throughout the stanzas, the religious message focuses on the oneness of God, the honor of the Sabbath, and an overpowering sense of redemption in a rather messianic vein.

Messianism

Messianism, like Kabbalah, received new impetus in the years after the great expulsion of the Jews from Spain. The upheaval of a central and long-standing Jewish community, combined with the mass movement of Jews and a plethora of significant world events, seemed to be the spark for a period of messianic speculation. False messiahs abounded throughout Europe, both Jewish and non-Jewish. Some, like Asher Lemlin (who mounted something of a crusade of repentance) in Germany, had a short and more regional impact. Others, like David Reubeni and Solomon Molkho touched off a domino-like effect, especially among **Marranos**. They struck the fantasy of many European leaders, who for a short time entertained their supposed burgeoning campaign against the Turks. Here, as in other areas, a growing and burning apocalyptic sense captured people across the globe, with many believing the sixteenth century as perhaps the last of earthly rule. Other pseudo-messianic figures populated the early modern topography, with dozens listed in contemporary literature.

Dramatic events and discoveries, especially those in the New World, further excited messianic speculation around the globe. The important Amsterdam rabbi Menasseh ben Israel (1604–1657), who developed a host of relationships with Christian scholars and who advocated vociferously for the readmission of Jews to England, also speculated about the meaning of the natives in America for world history. After the 1630s Menasseh, like many Christian millenarians, stressed the idea of human freedom and universal salvation. He also became increasingly taken with the story of the Ten Lost Tribes, and his explanation of their whereabouts worked to reinforce his petition for readmission of the Jews to England. In 1650, he dedicated a Latin work *The Hope of Israel* to the English Parliament. Menasseh argued, "To this opinion add an argument taken from what logicians call a simili; for he that will compare the laws and customs of the Indians and Hebrews together, shall find they agree in many things. Whence you may easily gather that the Indians borrowed those of the Hebrews (who lived among them) before or after they went to the unknown mountains."[68] He found a variety of similarities: circumcision among the Indians of the Yucatan; rending of garments in mourning by the Totons of New Spain; maintaining fires on altars by Mexicans; and certain aspects of the practice of family purity laws by Nicaraguans.[69] In a letter to John Dury in late 1649, Menasseh wrote,

> I declare that our Israelites were the first finders out of America; not regard-
> ing the opinions of other men, which I thought good to refute in a few words
> onely; and I thinke that the ten Tribes live not only there, but also in other
> lands scattered every where; these never did come backe to the second Tem-
> ple, and keep till this day still the Jewish religion, seeing all the prophecies
> which speak of their bringing backe unto their native soile must be fulfilled:
> So then at their appointed time, all the Tribes shall meet from all parts of the
> world into two Provinces, namely Assyria and Egypt, nor shall their king-
> dome be any more divided, but they shall have one Prince the Messiah, the
> Sonne of David.[70]

Much of the early modern period was replete with tales of various, false messiahs. In addition to these well-known Jewish personalities, there were rampant tales of warrior Jews, penned up in the mountains, waiting to usher in apocalyptic times. The convert Victor of Carben, for example, al-leged that Jews proclaimed, "'We still have a king the other side of Babylo-nia, in the Caspian Mountains. He is descended from the tribe of Judah. These same Jews are the Red Jews and strong. They are as many more of them than there are Christians in all of Christendom.'"[71] The myth of the Red Jews provided a powerful image for a Christian society expecting the apocalypse and fearing the very real spread of the Turks west. It simultane-ously re-enforced anti-Jewish stereotypes and the fear that the Jews were plotting, this time with military assistance, the overthrow of Christianity and dominion over the entire world.

Perhaps the best-known Jewish messianic figure, certainly of our period but perhaps in all of Jewish history, was Shabbetai Sevi. Sevi was born in Smyrna in 1626. Sevi was influenced by the *Zohar* as well as late medieval Byzantine Jewish mysticism, and like many mystics, he emphasized the use of divine names. After an extended period of semi-seclusion between 1642 and 1648, he publicly proclaimed himself the Messiah. Later, in 1665 in an apparent trance, Nathan of Gaza (1644–1680), who would become some-thing like Sevi's number 2 man and his publicity agent, made several utter-ances, including referring to Sevi as the Messiah and himself as a prophet chosen by God. Sevi apparently accepted this proclamation and in the sum-mer of that year announced that the traditional fast day of the Seventeenth of Tammuz, the beginning of a three-week period of mourning for the de-struction of the Temple, was turned into a feast day. While there was prece-dence in Jewish thought for a messianic reversion of days of sorrow to ones of joy, Sevi apparently had other questionable practices, including some re-lated to the consumption of non-kosher food. According to Nathan,

From that moment on he was clothed with the Holy Spirit and with a great illumination; he pronounced the [ineffable] name of God and performed all sorts of strange actions as seemed fit to him by reason of the mystical *tiqqun* intended by them. Those who saw him did not understand his actions, and in their eyes he was like a fool. Repeatedly he was flogged by our teachers in Palestine for his many deeds which appeared repugnant to reason, until he retired, away from men, to the wilderness.[72]

Sevi traveled to Jerusalem but was summarily expelled by the rabbis there. Still, tales of his alleged miracles grew and circulated. Sevi was credited with resurrection of the dead, for example. Eventually and fairly quickly, tales of Sevi spread across the Islamic world and throughout all of Europe. While many discounted Sevi and his accomplice, large numbers of Jews seem to have been convinced that indeed the messianic era was beginning. Though opposed by many rich and rabbinic leaders, large numbers of Jews flocked to Sevi in the cities of Aleppo, Smyrna, and Constantinople. Some have speculated that economic turmoil inflamed support for him. But Sevi also received support, though less intense and focused on the penitential aspects of messianism, in parts of the Holy Land (Gaza, Hebron, Safed), as well in the Balkans, Yemen, Morocco, and Cairo.[73] Small pockets of supporters could be found in Amsterdam, Hamburg, Ancona, Venice, and perhaps even in Frankfurt, Prague, and Vienna. The memoirist Glückel of Hameln described how her own family was caught up in the excitement, selling all their goods and preparing for a final journey to the Holy Land. She wrote,

Many sold their houses and lands and all their possessions for any day they hoped to be redeemed. My good father-in-law left his home in Hameln, abandoned his house and lands and all his goodly furniture, and moved to Hildesheim. He sent to us in Hamburg two enormous casks packed with linens and with peas, beans, dried meats, shredded prunes and like stuff, every manner of food that would keep. For the old man expected to sail any moment from Hamburg to the Holy Land. . . . But the Most High pleased otherwise.[74]

In 1666 Sevi sailed to Constantinople from Smyrna, where he was prepared to remove the crown from the Sultan and assume rule over the Ottoman state. In February of that year, he was captured by Turkish authorities, who were careful to bring him to court without harm to avoid turning him into a martyr of any kind. After being imprisoned and given the choice between death and conversion to Islam, Sevi converted. He was eventually banished to Albania, where he died in 1676.

While many followers were quite naturally devastated, some held fast to their belief in the failed messiah, especially convinced by the prophet Nathan that the Messiah had to penetrate the world of Islam in order to elevate the remaining divine sparks, save the Muslims from evil, and then usher in the messianic era. Others argued that Sevi was indeed the Messiah, but the Messiah son of Joseph, who would serve as a precursor to the Messiah son of David. While small pockets of believers continued long after Sevi's conversion and death, forming sectarian groups, such belief was frequently condemned. Sabbatians were excommunicated by the Polish Council of Four Lands in 1669.

Shabbetai Sevi has been variously evaluated in Jewish history, at times seen as insane and at other times as a pious mystical searcher. Some have seen Sevi's role as central and others the work of Nathan of Gaza. Some have attributed Sevi's development and his success to burgeoning mystical speculation, while others have stressed the various Sephardic elements, Christian similarities, or general turmoil of the age as reasons for his development and success. There was, to be sure, a wide-ranging and popular belief in the Messiah, fuelled by Christian millenarian speculation throughout the seventeenth century. There were long-seated expectations of Marrano reversion to Judaism in something of an end-of-time development. The great calamities of the seventeenth century, such as the Chmielnicki massacres, seemed to portend some grand transformation to be ushered in upon Jewish history. Sevi was something of a novelty for non-Jewish observers as well, and this episode sparked a great deal of attention from a wide range of Christian and Muslim writers.[75]

In the Ottoman Empire, some scholars have maintained, the Shabbetai Sevi debacle led to accelerated decline of the position of the Jewish community along with a growing conservativism and strengthening of rabbinic authority. Neither assertion has been proven.[76] It is clear, however, that in some places the entire episode led to anti-Jewish sentiment and stoked anti-Jewish activity. According to a Muslim chronicle from the very beginning of the eighteenth century, for example,

> In the month of Rajab of the year 1077 [1666] the Jews were overcome by the utmost depravity, for they were making preparation to leave the Yemen and join their brethren in the Holy Land and Jerusalem. They claimed that their king, the Messiah, son of David, had arisen and had restored their kingdom. They sold their belongings at a ridiculous price and prepared to depart in the path of the devil.[77]

Magic, the Supernatural, and the Jews

Throughout much of Jewish history magic and religion have been intimately connected, if not inseparable. As one of the leading writers on the subject, Joshua Trachtenberg, noted many decades ago, folk beliefs or folk religion combined with more formal or official religious practice throughout Jewish history.[78] Trachtenberg noted, "While it is difficult to dissociate the religious from the superstitious in such pious practices as fasting and charity, which as expiatory measures served to avert the evil consequences of sin, there can be no doubt that they were believed to exert a certain degree of compulsion upon the supernatural powers."[79] The author of one late fifteenth-century compendium of customs and laws, for example, noted the power that many ascribed to a particular linen shirt, which it was alleged could protect one from assault. Even when more "rational" Jews, such as Eliezer Ashkenazi (1513–1586), wrote of demons, various explanations could be devised so that Jews would not have to dismiss such notions out of hand.[80] Still, some early modern people certainly saw through some trickery disguised as magic.[81]

Jews, like other early modern people, engaged in various magical practices and beliefs. Among the most prominent was dream divination. Leon Modena, for example, wrote in his autobiography, "Anyhow, I had engaged in dream divination, using prayer without conjuration, in order to see the woman intended as my mate." Modena reported the results of his dream to his parents, who apparently did not believe it.[82] Dreams could be called upon to testify to political developments, as Rabbi Moses Almosnino wrote regarding a decree in the late 1560s in Salonika: "Thus I understood correctly the verse I had called out that night in my dream. I realized that through a true dream it was proclaimed that the entire community of Jews in Salonika is truly blessed and worthy, peerless in the exiles of this people, liberated not by their own efforts but by the Lord."[83] Palmistry was also subscribed to, as Hayyim Vital notes in his autobiography, leading him to knowledge of the good and bad choices to face him later in life.[84] Other forms of divination were also mentioned in early modern texts.[85]

The idea of reincarnation and transmigration of the soul also circulated in segments of the early modern Jewish society. The mystic Hayyim Vital and others had much to say about the subject. Rabbi Elijah Ha-Kohen of Izmir writing in 1674, noted, "God makes the soul, separated from the body, return to this world in an animal, bird, or human being in order to restore and cleanse it. This is the doctrine with which Elihu rebuked Job, telling him that he should see the kindness God does for the human soul by making it return three times into this world (Job 33:29)."[86] Further, although he had had some intrepidations about writing about this subject, he concluded, "Transmigration is not a subject that must be concealed, like the esoteric mysteries of the Torah. If transmigration were one of these mysteries, how could God have revealed it to Pythagoras, who was a Gentile?"[87]

Jews ascribed great power to words, especially the various names attributed to God. Masters of the art of utilizing these special names, known as *baalei shemot* (literally, masters of the names), appear in a great deal of early modern literature. Often they defended the Jews. A number of tales from seventeenth-century Germany, for example, describe how such figures were able to summon assistance—either angelic armed forces or the illusion of such—when attacks from non-Jewish citizens erupted.[88] There were also tales of Jews with the power to create artificial anthropoids. The Maharal of Prague was reputed to have created such a *golem* out of clay. Whether such occurred or not (and many early modern thinkers were quick to discount such ideas), the legend has circulated widely and has even been the subject of Hollywood productions.

DEVIANCE?

Deviance is a complicated subject, but it involves a variety of behaviors that somehow do not fit with established, or establishing, norms. According to the medievalist R. I. Moore, who has advanced significant theories about ideas of persecution and heresy in medieval Europe, defining individuals or groups as deviants, that is, those transgressing certain established social values or norms, is a means for controlling society and reinforcing social and communal unity.[89]

Moore, like others, notes that as medieval and early modern rulers began to assert themselves they developed a hierarchy of specialized agencies to enforce order. This led to a monopoly of legitimate violence but also to what Moore terms the rise of victimless crimes, whereby "criminals" who committed offenses against governing authority, social norms, or general morality were prosecuted and punished. Indeed, the rise of the centralized state and police ordinances have been studied by historians of early modern western Europe for many years. (Yet, it should be pointed out that the same concern over the state and proper behavior was not unique in the West.)

Another noted historian, Norbert Elias, developed in the first half of the twentieth century the concept of an historical "civilizing process" that evolved in the early modern period. Elias noted the monopolization of physical force by the state, leading to greater and more planned intervention in society and the creation of a sense of shame by those not following the dictated order. Elias argued that this civilizing process ushered in a period that favored and even forced social constraint and self-constraint.

Some monopolization of power and moral policy was felt within the Jewish communities as well, through the imposition of external non-Jewish authorities and the legislation of Jewish governing bodies. A number of regional synods and ordinances pointed both to increasingly frequent attempts to regulate Jewish behavior and to the fact that there existed a certain lack of observance of religious laws by at least some early modern Jews. According to the Frankfurt synod of 1603, for example, some Jews were engaged in the following: *shehitah* without proper authorization or knowledge; purchasing wine from non-Jews against rabbinic restrictions;[90] publishing books, at times of questionable orientation, without communal permission;[91] and purchasing milk milked by Gentiles with no Jewish witnesses. These acts point to both transgressing against legislation and social regulation.[92]

At times, internal Jewish legislation, even regarding internal religious or social behavior, was greatly affected by rules and scrutiny imposed from external non-Jewish authorities. One telling example occurred in seventeenth-century Hamburg, where the Portuguese Jewish community kept protocol books that recorded communal legislation as well as communal transgressions. These volumes, however, simultaneously served an external audience of civic legislators, who also required similar compendia from other religious minorities, most notably the Mennonites.

Mental illness could lead to deviance from social, communal, or religious norms. Some historians have seen an increase in mental illness since the seventeenth century and attributed it in part to the turbulence and anxiety of the period. In the early modern world, mental illness was often seen as contagious, and such individuals were often locked away in family houses or, increasingly by the end of our period, in institutions.[93]

Deviance could be defined as veering from accepted belief, rabbinical norms, and everyday practice. Despite some examples of Sabbath desecration, Sabbath observance was extremely important in early modern Judaism, and rarely were individuals accused of a lack of Sabbath observance (e.g., smoking, lighting a fire, carrying money). Still, in Hamburg, the Portuguese Jewish protocol book recorded various instances of Sabbath transgression.[94] While clearly the exception, some Jews were prosecuted for poor synagogue attendance. Several documents from seventeenth-century Amsterdam reveal poor Sabbath observance by at least some members of the community.[95]

There were other religious and moral transgressions as well. In a recent study of Amsterdam, the following were identified as the major communal issues of transgression: gambling (which as we have seen in the case of Leon Modena was a rather widespread concern), extra-marital and sexual relations, improper business conduct, and friction with Christians. Some men apparently transgressed the biblical injunction against shaving the beard with a razor or trimming the beard during the period of the counting of the *Omer* between the festivals of Passover and Shavuot. In the Portuguese Jewish community of Hamburg, the protocol books give evidence of various transgressions, including the circulation of "shameful writings" or books that discussed concepts that were banned by the community;[96] playing card games on holidays;[97] a Jewish man traveling with a non-Jewish woman;[98] or inviting non-Jews to religious ceremonies, such as **beritot** (circumcisions).[99] Many times transgressions that were public, and so also ran the risk of placing the community in a poor light or stirring up anti-Jewish sentiment, were punished most harshly.

Sexual misconduct was discussed in many different cases. In Amsterdam, numerous cases were mounted against Portuguese Jews who apparently attended brothels (and while there also drank non-kosher wine). Among the most common social problems in Amsterdam, writes the historian Daniel Swetschinski, were prostitution and the fathering of illegitimate children.[100] In Lublin, Rabbi Me'ir ben Gedaliah (1558–1616) complained about Jewish men having sexual relations with non-Jewish women as well as adulterous affairs with married Jewish women.[101] According to one case, assessed in the responsa of Rabbi Sirkes,

> A married woman came home with a particular male guest who was passing by the town in which the woman lived. The woman's husband was not in town. There was also no one else in the house except for an important woman who saw the two of them coming and then they vanished from her sight and she did not know where they went. Then a great fear fell upon her and she thought that maybe they went to the cellar. As quick as the blink of an eye, she heard the sound of the hinges of the cellar door and her fear increased. She went from the "winter house" to near the cellar and she heard the cellar doors close. While she was standing there, several other women came and asked whether she had seen the aforementioned woman with X, the guest, and where did they go since the cart driver will [soon] be on his way. The woman replied that she saw both of them coming to the house and then she lost sight of them. The women [who had come] said that maybe they went into the cellar and they [all] waited for them to come out. Then one woman said, "Let us light a candle and look for them in the cellar," but in the middle of her saying this the aforementioned woman came from the cellar and said that X was sitting [in] the cellar in the cold and would to drink some mead there. While she was talking X came behind her from the cellar in front of all the people standing there and they saw that the back of the woman's scarf was dirty with mud and earth of the cellar [presumably she was surprised and turned around at his approach]. Based on these things the whole city was talking about the woman who adulterated with X.[102]

Given that deviance was also diverging from communal norms and laws, the whole range of deviant behavior, as well as the communal responses to it, was related to the location and execution of authority. The *herem*, or excommunication, was used to coerce proper behavior and punish transgressive behavior. A large number of excommunications are recorded in some places for the early seventeenth century.

The Amsterdam *mahamad* constructed a constitution that gave it sweeping authority. Numerous violations could lead to excommunication from the community. These included establishing a *minyan*, or prayer quorum, outside the congregation; disobeying the orders of the *mahamad*; raising one's hand with the intention to strike a fellow Jew in or near the synagogue; arriving at the synagogue with a weapon; circumcising non-Jews without permission; speaking in the name of the Jewish community without permission; brokering divorces without permission; dealing in contraband coins; and engaging in prayer services with individuals who had never been members of the synagogue or who had left the synagogue in rebellion. Other activities were also subject to the ban. These included deriding publicly other members of the community, especially rabbis; writing letters to Spain with Jewish references that might jeopardize the receiver; printing a book without permission; and engaging Gentiles in theological discussions.

What do we make of these cases? Were they simply aberrations or do they perhaps point to some more fundamental tensions within the early modern communities? We know that the number of excommunications in some places, such as Hamburg, expanded dramatically in the seventeenth century. While such incidents may have been attributable to *conversos* returning to Judaism but not completely absorbing normative Jewish practice, such an explanation does not explain every case. The attempt to locate and enforce authority, an issue that was very much part of the broader discussion raised by the Reformation in Europe and by the political consolidation in the Ottoman Empire, clearly resonated in the communal tensions that we have already discussed in chapter 3. Can the shifting nature of authority and the challenge to tradition that marked much of the early modern period be applied to early modern Jewish history as well? Can early modern Judaism be seen as attempting to resolve a "crisis of stability?" If so, perhaps the attempts to define communal authority and the increasing policing of what would be seen as accepted norms of behavior, and eventually belief as well, help to explain what appears to be increasing deviance in early modern Judaism.

Halakhic Flexibility and the "Neutralizing Society"

Jacob Katz, who should perhaps be considered the founding father of Jewish social history, presented the Jews of the early modern period (and part of the Middle Ages as well) as somewhat transitional. He developed a notion of the Jews of this period as maintaining a certain level of *halakhic* flexibility. So, for example, Jews may have considered medieval Christians as idolaters, because of their belief in the Trinity. By Talmudic law, Jews were not allowed to do business with idolaters for a period of three days before and after the idolaters' festivals, for fear that the proceeds of such business would go to support their idolatry. Given the vast number of festivals on the Christian calendar, however, if such restrictions were applied to Jewish and Christian interactions, then the Jews would have no opportunity for business or for making a livelihood. That consideration, combined with others, allowed Jews to reassess their image of Christians and, since the high Middle Ages, to begin to see Christians as something different than idolaters.

Katz also forwarded the conception of what he termed a "neutralizing society." Before modernity, Katz argued, variations on traditional patterns of belief and practice could still be woven into the old fabric of Jewish society,[103] even as the system remained closed and uncontested. This was deviance that could be neutralized by the traditional system as opposed to deviation that could undermine the traditional system, the latter being a sign of modernity and the dissolution of the traditional Jewish society.[104]

A related concept of "tolerated dissent" argues that Jewish religious society had the capacity to absorb religious dissent in the early modern period. One very intriguing example of this apparent trend is presented by the scholar Talya Fishman, in her study of the curious and learned Rabbi Leon Modena of Venice. Modena (1571–1648) was born in Venice and raised in Ferrara. He was himself something of a renaissance man, who had great talents in rabbinic studies as well as in Italian literature. The author of important rabbinic decisions, he also wrote an intriguing autobiography that both elevated himself and described his own personal flaws and shortcomings. Modena was at once a renowned preacher (whose sermons were heard by non-Jews), as well as a writer of literature, letters, and music. Modena was involved with the non-Jewish world around him at the same time that his Jewish identity and sense of community were quite "traditional." Modena's involvement with printing expanded his circle of relations with Christians, even as it made it possible for him to develop as a scholar and circulate his own writings.

Modena, who was recognized as an important rabbinic authority, was a complex figure. He served on various rabbinic courts but was also heavily involved in secular learning. A prolific writer, it appears that Modena penned an anonymous anti-rabbinic treatise titled *Voice of the Fool*. While the first part of the treatise presents something of a traditional position, at least biblically speaking, about the nature of God and the creation of the world, the second entails a stunning critique of rabbinic law, and the third part contains a proposal for a different religious program. Based on a "rational" approach, the author argued, "For every mind to which this is acceptable—as it became acceptable to me—will stand by all the principles and worthy beliefs: Providence, Torah from Sinai, Reward and Punishment, Immortality of the Soul, and the rest, and will see them following and coming from this."[105] Torah, in this line of thinking "is instruction and teaching to orient oneself toward perfection."[106] But already at the end of the first essay, the author signals a significant diversion. He writes, "From the death of Joshua to the present, we have not merited that this holy Torah be interpreted in accord with its truth. And the congregation of Jacob to which it was given as an inheritance have erred regarding it; they constantly stumble in judgment, either by subtracting from or by adding to it."[107] With a variety of examples, the author concludes, "Under the cover of the term 'fence' and 'interpretation,' they have changed and altered almost all the commandments, skewing the intention of the arranger," instead proffering "childish particulars, difficult to perform and fulfill."[108] Fishman, in her examination of this writing and the possible motives that Modena had in producing it, concludes that early modern Jewish society was able to tolerate a certain level of internal dissent.

Whether or not this assessment of Modena and his writing is accurate, such concepts are significant, for they imply that early modern Jews were not homogenous in their belief or their practice and, even more importantly, that they defined their communities and religion in multiple and at times varying ways. Jewish religious and cultural life could be incredibly multivalent, absorbing external elements but also allowing a good deal of freedom for internal discussion and debate. In this sense, early modern Judaism was the ideal vessel for transferring a Diaspora people who had to respond to frequently difficult and changing circumstances. The modern debates about theological systems or dogma and the "genuine" ideas and ideals of the Jews are, in this regard, rather limited for understanding the early modern Jewish experience. But, it was not simply flexibility and toleration that characterized early modern Judaism. If one includes the various customs and the important role of *conversos* in the discussion of early modern Judaism, then one may have to concede that early modern Jews engaged a wide range of intellectual traditions and orientations.

Intellectual Diversity

It has been argued recently that some among the younger generation of Jews in the later Middle Ages were increasingly attracted to non-Jewish culture and learning and opposed to philosophy or complex religious rituals. Some Jewish polemic, which was ostensibly anti-Christian, was apparently intended to reinforce Jews in their faith and commitment as well. In their assessment of the polemical and highly influential fifteenth-century *Sefer ha-Nizzahon* of Yom Tov Lipmann Mühlhausen, for example, Ora Limor and Israel Yuval have argued that there is evidence of a crisis of late medieval Ashkenazic Jewry. They write that the traditional Ashkenazic structure of exegesis informed by the Tosafists and *Hasidei Ashkenaz* and revolving around "a tangled web of religious rituals, a defensive barrier to preserve its unique identity and prevent any infiltration of Christian influence," was in crisis.[109]

Added to the complexity of a customs-based and regionally diverse Judaism was the addition of a certain *converso* religiosity. Jews throughout the early modern period maintained close contacts with converts, and in the case of the Marranos, many individuals descended from such families seized the opportunity to revert to, or to experience really for the first time, Judaism. Such individuals might be extremely flamboyant, creative, and intriguing people. Often they brought unique world-views with them, worldviews that were shaped by previous life and upbringing, including the inculcation of Christian, typically Catholic, values and sensibilities. Catholic concepts such as the Eucharist and the virgin mother made their way into what we might call *converso* culture. While some former *conversos* rejected Catholic ideas, and images, others might insert the same into their Jewish worship, adding Jewish images to replace the Catholic ones that were lost. Jewish "saints," for example, replaced Catholic ones. As the historian Miriam Bodian and others have argued, the Portuguese Jews in Amsterdam, many of the early generation of whom were previously of *converso* lineage, grafted Iberian culture and mores onto a newly adopted and learned rabbinic Judaism, making for a complicated and at times internally inconsistent Jewish identity.

Whether there was more deviance from institutional and traditional rabbinic Judaism in the early modern period, or whether we simply have more writing about it, especially as Jewish communities closed in upon themselves, is hard to say. What we can say is that there are a number of rather prominent and intriguing cases of heterodoxy in the early modern period. The Marrano physician Juan de Prado (ca. 1615–ca. 1670) fled to Holland in 1655, accepting Judaism. At the center of a circle of intellectuals in Amsterdam, he interacted with Spinoza, among others, and developed some rather unsettling ideas. Only a year after his arrival in Amsterdam, he was charged with publicly criticizing the Bible, denying rabbinical tradition, and favoring Natural Law.[110] Prado was excommunicated.

An even more famous personality was Uriel da Costa (1585–1640). From a Marrano background, his family took on Judaism after a move to Amsterdam in 1615. Da Costa apparently found his reading of the Bible, which had brought him to Judaism, to be at variance with the Judaism practiced in Amsterdam, and he became an outspoken opponent of the rabbinic community. He wrote,

> After we have now explained that no other Torah and no other commentary but the written ones come from God, the so-called verbal deliveries in regard to the above mentioned can only have been mad-made. Setting aside that it means an important breach if one would give to people occasion to deviate from Moses' Torah, to explain and to offer man-made explanations instead of the ones given by God to teach to proclaim, it would result as something humane, it would mean a great denial.[111]

Da Costa also rejected the immortality of the soul, the discussion of which was a very hot topic in the seventeenth century. Previously da Costa had been excommunicated in Venice and Hamburg. Because of his writings, da Costa was again excommunicated, arrested, and fined, this time in Amsterdam. His book was burned. Although he later sought to be reconciled with the Jewish community, he could not stem his criticisms of the Jewish community or his rather deistic religious impulses. He appears to have committed suicide after a demeaning set of punishments when he tried to reconcile with the Jewish community a second time. The Venetian authorities' ban of da Costa is concerned with those free thinkers opposing the rabbinic sages. The document reads, "Among them as wisdom is considered all that is in variance to our Sages, and to the vexation of Israel do they tear down all protective walls of the Law. . . . They think themselves to be the only wise men."[112]

Spinoza and Modernity?

At the end of the early modern period we encounter perhaps the most significant deviance, that of formal separation from the Jewish community for theological reasons. [113] Here the figure of Baruch (later Benedict) Spinoza is most important. Spinoza proved to be unable to be absorbed into or neutralized by traditional Jewish society. Yet, he did not become a Christian either. He is perhaps the first visible example of a Jew to leave Judaism but not accept another formal religion, marking him, according to some scholars, as the first "modern Jew." While the restrictions of the *herem* did not lead Spinoza back into the fold, he developed a complex network of relationships with a wide range of scholars and non-traditional thinkers.

Spinoza came from a well-entrenched family in the Portuguese Jewish community in Amsterdam. He had a fairly traditional educational upbringing and may have even had some traditional *yeshivah* education. Spinoza clearly demonstrated familiarity with some key Jewish texts. He was affected by both internal and external influences as well as by some very significant independent thinking. As noted above, there was precedence among earlier Jewish figures associated with the Amsterdam community for questioning traditional biblical interpretation and communal authority.

Spinoza was educated to be familiar with various languages and classical learning and philosophy. Much of Spinoza's early work was formed and outlined in reaction to the work of Rene Descartes, which he read, discussed, and in many ways, rejected. Spinoza was not the only seventeenth-century individual to read the Bible critically, of course. A number of non-Jewish thinkers were engaged in such criticism, including the French millenarian Isaac La Peyrere (ca. 1596–1676), the English Quaker Samuel Fisher active in the last half of the seventeenth century, as well as even Thomas Hobbes (1588–1679).

There is no evidence that Spinoza sought consciously to break with the Jewish community. However, his views, which were disquieting to the *mahamad* for the doubts they might raise were probably more problematic if seen by non-Jewish citizens and authorities as examples of Jewish religious instigation. While drawing from traditional excommunication formulae, the excommunication of Spinoza was very aggressive. It read, on July 27, 1656,

> The Lords of the ma'amad, having known of the evil opinions and acts of Baruch de Spinoza, have endeavored by various means and promises, to turn him from his evil ways. But having failed to make him mend his wicked ways, and, on the contrary, daily receiving more and more serious information about the abominable heresies which he practiced and taught and about his monstrous deeds, and having for this numerous trustworthy witnesses who have deposed and born witness to this effect in the presence of the said Espinoza, they became convinced of the truth of this matter; and after all of this had been investigated in the presence of the honorable chachamim, they have decided, with their consent, that the said Espinoza should be excommunicated and expelled from the people of Israel. By decree of the angels and by the command of the holy men, we excommunicate, expel, curse and damn Baruch de Espinoza, with the consent of God, Blessed be He, and with the consent of the entire holy congregation, and in front of these holy scrolls with the 613 precepts which are written therein; cursing him with the excommunication with which Joshua banned Jericho and with the curse which Elisha cursed the boys and with all castigations that are written in the Book of the Law. Cursed be he by day and cursed be he by night; cursed be he when he lies down and cursed be he when he rises up. Cursed be he when he goes out and cursed be he when he comes in. The Lord will not spare him, but then the anger of the Lord and his jealousy shall smoke against that man, and all the curses that are written in this book shall lie upon him, and the Lord shall blot out his name from under heaven. And the Lord shall separate him unto evil out of all the tribes of Israel, according to all the curses of the covenant that are written in this book of the law. But you that cleave unto the Lord your God are alive every one of you this day. . . . No one should communicate with him, neither in writing, nor accord him any favor nor stay with him under the same roof nor come within four cubits in his vicinity, nor shall he read any treatise composed or written by him.[114]

What exactly did Spinoza think? In his famous *Tractatus Theologico-Politicus* (*TTP*), Spinoza outlined a study of Scripture that followed a methodology for the study of nature. Spinoza wrote,

> I hold that the method of interpreting Scripture is no different from the method of interpreting Nature, and is in fact in complete accord with it. For the method of interpreting Nature consists essentially in composing a detailed study of Nature from which, as being the source of our assured data, we can deduce the definitions of the things of Nature. Now in exactly the same way the task of Scriptural interpretation requires us to make a straightforward study of Scripture, and from this, as the source of our fixed data and principles, to deduce by logical inference the meaning of the authors of Scripture. In this way— that is, by allowing no other principles or data for the interpretation of Scrip-

ture and study of its contents except those that can be gathered only from Scripture itself and from historical study of Scripture—steady progress can be made without any danger of error, and one can deal with matters that surpass our understanding with no less confidence than those matters that are known to us by the natural light of reason.[115]

Spinoza differentiated philosophy and reason, which aims at truth, from theology, which seeks acts of piety and obedience. According to Spinoza, the *TTP* was intended to liberate reason from superstition, to loosen the hold of religion over weak and gullible human minds. Spinoza opposed not so much religion as the priesthood, which he saw as a tool to dominate people.

At the same time, Spinoza held miracles as unnatural events, arguing that nothing can really happen contrary to the laws of nature. In the same vein, Spinoza rejected the apparently miraculous nature of prophecy, a function of imagination according to Spinoza rather than knowledge. Spinoza rejected the notion of an unchanging and ever-enduring Bible. The role of Moses and Mosaic law was created in a particular context and for particular purposes and a clearly delimited time. Spinoza's *TTP*, with its rational and historical approach to the Bible and religion, was condemned not only by the Jewish community but also by councils and synods of the Reformed Church as "the vilest and most sacrilegious book the world has ever seen."[116]

After the excommunication, Spinoza studied at the University of Leiden, and he changed his name to Benedictus, a Latin equivalent of his Hebrew name Baruch. By the early 1660s Spinoza was known for both his allegedly atheistic beliefs and his work with optical instruments. While the former, combined with his general philosophy, would make him known for future generations, the latter, for which he was well-known, may have eventually claimed his life, as he was subjected to the dust of his profession. In 1664 Spinoza moved to a suburb of The Hague and in 1670 to The Hague itself, where he stayed until he died.

In some ways, Spinoza was both traditional and innovative. He has been described in the literature as a "God-intoxicated man" as well as a "systematic atheist." He has been seen as a "medieval" when he was Baruch and part of the Jewish community and "modern" as Benedictus with his innovative philosophy. He has been both lionized and demonized.[117] He represented an important bridge between the traditional and modern.

JEWS AND CULTURE IN THE EARLY MODERN PERIOD

What do we mean by culture, and what was culture in the early modern sense of the term? To answer these questions, it is helpful to both review recent historical scholarship as well as to listen to the voices of the early modern sources themselves. In a great many ways, early modern culture was simultaneously traditional and innovative; isolated or isolating and acculturating; reactive and an agent for change; "medieval" and "modern." Culture, throughout this chapter, is taken in a rather broad sense and helps to delineate Jewish identity and sense of self throughout our period.

The great scholar of "the civilizing process" Norbert Elias was careful to distinguish between "civilization" and "culture." For Elias, culture, in its German sense (*Kultur*), refers in its essence to intellectual, artistic, and religious developments, as opposed to political, economic, or social factors. For Elias, whereas civilization represents a process, culture refers to human products "in which the individuality of a people expresses itself."[118] In recent Jewish Studies, the concept of Jewish culture has received a good deal of, although not always consistent or focused, attention. According to one important scholar, David Biale, who has edited a massive volume on "Cultures of the Jews," culture is elastic and is itself the "practice of everyday life."[119] In a Jewish context, the notion of culture is plural, and despite the fact that Jewish culture has traditionally presumed some kind of continuity in both literary or textual and folk traditions, it does not obviate the fact that Jewish culture is multivalent.[120] In part such complexity is due to the changing contexts in which the Jews have found themselves. Biale writes, "The production of Jewish culture and identity in such circumstances can never be separated from the power relations between Jews and their neighbors."[121] For Biale, as for others, culture for Jews served to expand the limits and interpretations of Jewish law.[122] In this sense Jewish culture includes law and religion, at the same time that it is something larger and more fundamental. While not everyone will agree to such a concept, the idea proves useful as we try to understand Jewish identity and sense of self in a context that was local, regional, and global just as it was independent and closely attuned to the (non-Jewish) world in which it was set.

Arts, Sciences, and Jewish and Non-Jewish Symbiosis

Jewish involvement in science had a long tradition. But in the early modern period, Jews made important contributions to the burgeoning study of the sciences, a study that has been hailed by many as a Scientific Revolution in the late sixteenth and into the seventeenth centuries.

In both cutting-edge scientific development as well as more traditional, and what we might today label pseudo-science, Jews played an important role. Many Jews, even well-established and "traditionally minded" Jews such as Leon Modena's son in Italy and Hayyim Vital in Safed, were involved in alchemy. The quest to turn ordinary substances into gold was justified by many Christians in the early modern period by turning to alleged proof texts and examples in the Hebrew Bible. Some suspected that the biblical Abraham was learned in this discipline, as well as Isaac and Elijah.[123] The study of alchemy was also, at times, strongly linked with Kabbalah, with one of the great German scientists of the sixteenth century, the eclectic if at times path-breaking Paracelsus, seeing the study of Kabbalah as something like a prerequisite for the study of alchemy.[124]

A number of famous Jews contributed significantly to the study of science and medicine. The renowned Abraham Zacuth (1575–1642), known as Zacutus Lusitanus, was born into a Marrano family from Lisbon. In 1625 he made his way to Amsterdam where he adopted Judaism and also wrote several important medical books, particularly relating to the description of diseases. One famous personality at the end of our period was Tobias Cohen (1652–1729). Cohen was raised in Metz, France, and then sent to Cracow. He studied medicine at Frankfurt an der Oder and subsequently at the University of Padua. He served for years as a court physician in the Ottoman Empire and retired later in life to Jerusalem. Like other encyclopedic works of the period, his *Ma'aseh Tuviya* (1707) treated a range of topics such as botany and theology along with medicine. Cohen addressed the latest scientific advances, as posited by Kepler and Harvey, for example. The work, which went through multiple editions, was the only heavily illustrated Hebrew book on the topic.[125]

In the area of literature, Jews both borrowed from and contributed to the broader society in which they were steeped. Several of the leading Spanish and Portuguese writers of the sixteenth century were clearly of Marrano origins and, some have argued, used their writings as a veiled method for communicating with and even strengthening the identity of fellow Marranos.[126] Some writers of Marrano origin returned to Judaism once they left Iberia. One famous example is Daniel Levy de Barrios (1635–1701), who accepted Judaism in Amsterdam in 1674. Before his Amsterdam period, Barrios was concerned primarily with classical and pagan motifs; later his works were infused with a certain Jewish identity.[127] Barrios addressed various communal issues and also used his writing to criticize the Inquisition.[128]

Jews under Islam also accomplished a good deal. Despite great oppression in Iran, for example, some Persian Jews reached great literary heights. Inspired by his Persian context, the Jewish poet Imrani placed in verse the entire history of the Jews from the period of Moses until King Solomon. His work was written in Persian but in Hebrew script.[129]

Jews throughout Renaissance Italy were involved in theater and especially in music. In Mantua a large Jewish contingent worked in theater and was both well-known and respected for their work, often traveling into other regions to perform. In Amsterdam a vibrant theater that produced plays in Spanish existed.[130] In music, Salamone de Rossi, hailed by some later critics as one of the fathers of modern classical music, and a regular at the Mantuan court, is perhaps the best known. His sister, who went by the name Madame Europa, was a well-known performer as well. De Rossi was involved with Leon Modena, whom we have met in other contexts. Modena himself was a talented musician and perhaps even directed a music academy. Modena assisted with editing some of de Rossi's Hebrew works and wrote extensively on the question of the appropriateness of music in the synagogue.

Salamone de Rossi was a pioneer in instrumental music. Several of his contributions could be found in composite collections, and the extent of his connections in courtly circles is indicated by the dedications of his works. De Rossi's works were adjudged positively by later scholars. Indeed, de Rossi has been compared to Monteverdi, and one scholar even goes so far as to consider him the inventor of the symphony in its modern sense.[131]

What made de Rossi so controversial was the attempt to infuse this new music into the synagogue service. In 1622–1623 de Rossi published in Venice a volume of synagogue music, entitled "HaShirim asher liShelomo" (The Songs of Solomon). By that time de Rossi had at least nine printed collections to his name. While previous collections consisted of secular instrumental or Italian vocal works, usually for three to five voices, this one consisted of thirty-three Hebrew works for three to eight voices, set to biblical and post-biblical texts, and intended, in part, for use on certain occasions in the synagogue. The chief innovation of his collection was the polyphonic treatment of Hebrew texts, which broke the tradition of a single voice cantillating biblical passages in prayer.

The title of the collection proclaimed, "A new thing in the land" and "the Lord has put new songs into my mouth." Its own contents were lauded as being "composed according to the science of music" and "an orderly relationship of the voices." The collection seems to have divided the community fairly quickly. In its defense, Leon Modena advanced a number of arguments for bringing polyphony into the Hebrew tradition including the following: the composer acted under divine influence; the music was a medium for revelation; synagogue music as practiced in the Diaspora had fallen from the heights of older biblical music, for which the new songs represented a renaissance; not synagogue music, but music of the ancient Temple should be praised; and de Rossi's songs not only displayed a new form, but also in their emphasis on rejoicing, they exuded a new spirit. In his defense, Modena asked, "Should we then say that, because God has graciously given these people the knowledge of organizing music and they come to honor the Lord with it, they have committed a mortal sin? God forbid! For if it were a sin, then we should decree that the cantors should bray like donkeys and sing in unpleasant voices."[132] The songs were also clearly designed to meet the approval of any discriminating Gentiles who happened to hear them. Modena noted that because of this endeavor Jews would be evaluated positively by non-Jews for their skills and accomplishments.[133]

Participation in the Broader Cultures

In some cases, Jews were extremely involved in external culture. Some famous Jewish literary and scientific figures drew from prevailing cultural and intellectual norms and models. Others served as intermediaries between Jewish and non-Jewish culture. Elijah Levita, for example, who lived from the late 1460s until 1549, was a Hebrew philologist and grammarian who taught Hebrew to a wide circle of renowned Christians. Born in Germany, he journeyed throughout northern and central Europe, with close connections to luminaries of the age, including Guillaume Postel (the somewhat radical philosopher and millenarian), Paul Fagius, Sebastian Münster, as well as the dynamic humanist Cardinal Egidius da Viterbo, who drew an impressive array of Jewish scholars into his orbit.

One well-respected Jewish scholar was Elijah Delmedigo (ca. 1460–1497), who was praised by both Jews and Christians for his extensive philosophical knowledge. Delmedigo was versed in Islamic and Jewish, in addition to classical philosophy and was even called upon by the civic authorities in Venice to arbitrate between Italian philosophical schools. While navigating the fine line between religion and philosophy, Delmedigo assumed that religion could be interpreted according to philosophical principles; however, he retained the primacy of religion, which could contradict even what appeared to be philosophical truths.[134] Delmedigo attacked the Kabbalah, especially the argument for its antiquity, and he rejected the claim that the *Zohar* had been written by Shimon bar Yohai, citing as proof the fact that the text mentioned individuals who had lived after Shimon's death.[135] Like other important Jewish philosophers of the period, Delmedigo was responsible for the translation of key classical texts as well as some of Averroes' commentaries.

Around the world, there are examples of Jews collaborating with non-Jews, both in business as well as in intellectual endeavors. One intriguing example of a scholar who simultaneously bridged the Jewish and non-Jewish worlds, and who was simultaneously both traditional and somewhat radical was Isaac Abarbanel, who we met briefly in chapter 2. Among his innovations, methodologies, and areas of interest, two points are worth considering here. First, Abarbanel was in some sense a historical exegete, and he took many opportunities to compare the society of his own day with that of the biblical period. He had, for example, many interesting things to say about the concept of kingship in a contemporary context. Second, Abarbanel read and absorbed many elements from Christian scholars and commentators, though generally he incorporated concepts from such scholars shorn of their Christian content.[136]

A similar observation may be made with regard to many of the secular or non-Jewish historical narratives crafted by the Prague scholar David Gans

(1541–1613). Gans is an outstanding exemplar of the early modern Jewish world trapped between tradition and acculturation. David Gans was simultaneously a chronicler, an astronomer, and a mathematician. He was born in Westphalia in 1541 and studied Talmud at Bonn and Frankfurt. Later he studied under Moses Isserles in Cracow, and he held the rabbinic title *morenu ha-rav*.[137] After 1564 he settled in Prague, where he engaged in business. His well-known historical work *Zemah David* (Seed of David) was first published in 1592 but was also extensively expanded during the course of the seventeenth century. Gans' chronicle is comprised of two parts, one on Jewish history and one on general history.[138]

Although Gans studied with a number of prominent rabbis and relied heavily upon the work of earlier Jewish scholars, he was also very familiar with several German and Czech chronicles, and he stands at the crossroads of what the Columbia University historian Yosef Hayim Yerushalmi has described as the beginning of Jewish historical thinking.[139] Gans combined Jewish and non-Jewish history and historical sources, although he was aware of the tensions in combining them, and offered two parts to his book, one treating Jewish historical accounts and the other profane history.[140] Given his own interests in astronomy, as well as his contacts with great non-Jewish thinkers of the time such as Tycho Brahe,[141] and the environment of Prague with its rich Jewish intellectual tradition and personalities and the resplendent and eclectic court of Emperor Rudolph II, Gans combined Jewish interest with European stimuli.[142]

Gans' historiographical orientation is perhaps best revealed in the introduction to part 2 of *Zemah David*. Gans notes, "The words of this second part from the writings of the books of the Greeks and from other books of foreigners" were not meant to be equivalent to, or worse, uproot Jewish law and tradition.[143] But, Gans wrote, "However, I have set aside for them a section from this book in order to distinguish between the holy and the profane and not mix matters of the living God in matters of dried hay."[144] Throughout, Gans is careful to note that any statements he makes "are not against our holy Torah and not against the sayings of the sages."[145]

Gans' work was well received, in part perhaps because he did not really address "theological" issues. Gans nonetheless saw clearly that he would be attacked for his use of non-Jewish sources: "I see in advance that many will speak out against me, condemn me, and consider me sinful because I have taken material from non-Jewish writers."[146] Gans noted that other Jewish writers had utilized non-Jewish sources, however, and he asserts that Scripture itself "has allowed us to search in non-Jewish books for accounts of events which can be of some use to us."[147]

The broadly learned and vivacious Italian Jewish thinker Azariah de' Rossi also deserves attention in this regard. De' Rossi was a highly eclectic scholar and one whose work was not always positively received in rabbinic circles, although it was widely read and circulated. In the nineteenth century, de' Rossi became something of an early modern reformer for the great religious reformers, pointing, many argued, in the direction of secularization. Whatever his real orientation, it is clear that de' Rossi was extremely learned in Jewish and secular topics and that he was in many ways fairly "traditional" in his Jewish outlook. His enormous work *Meor Enayim* (Light of the Eyes) is a sprawling conglomeration of short essays on particular, and frequently unrelated, topics, exploring themes and questions that de' Rossi found particularly problematic, such as the dates for certain historical events and the nature of certain rabbinic stories. De' Rossi also discussed at length his reasons for writing, including the stimulus of the violent earthquake in Ferrara in 1570 that he himself had experienced.

De' Rossi begins the body of his work with some discussion about his scholarly methodology. While concerned that his use of Gentile sources will not be well received, de' Rossi makes the argument that a variegated and eclectic method of study is preferable to a unitary and homogenous one.[148] He asserts, "When we realize that there may be some chance of acquiring some wisdom from even an uncultivated person, we should not stand on our dignity and arrogantly spurn it. Rather, we should grasp it until it becomes ours. Then learning can issue from every place."[149] In addition, such learning is enjoyable and allows an individual to gain "sharper analytical insight."[150]

In defense of his use of non-Jewish sources, de' Rossi writes that he will not use any source that opposes or contradicts the Torah.[151] If, however, such sources can shed light on certain questions or explanations of Torah, they are valuable and should be consulted. To be considered by him, such sources need to "be made in innocence and they must have no claims whatsoever in the issue at stake."[152] Indeed, de' Rossi accepts the notion that the non-Jewish scholars he considers would have been concerned with their reputation and therefore would not have fabricated their information.[153]

One striking example of de' Rossi's scholarship is his examination of the rabbinic story of a gnat flying into the head of the Roman emperor Titus, driving him mad and eventually killing him. De' Rossi examines the various rabbinic accounts of this tale (taking full stock of the variations in these narratives), as well as medical literature (that clearly indicate that the story is, on its face value, impossible). He also examines non-Jewish historical works and finds that the dating of the story as retold by the rabbis does not mesh with actual historical events. De' Rossi concludes,

> Our sages who were truly wise, were perfectly aware that even a story such as this had no foundation, or at least not in the way they described it. And yet, it did not prevent them from representing and embellishing it with such conspicuous detail as if it had really happened in the way they had enunciated.

Their aim was to instill and infuse the people with knowledge of the goodness and justice to which they should aspire, and to impress upon their souls the purpose of morals and instruction which are requisite for us. For the sake of the glorification of God's name, they could even speak rhetorically.[154]

In another interesting departure from traditional Jewish approaches to the past, Rabbi Elijah Capsali (ca. 1483–1555), who studied in Padua, Italy, and served as rabbi in Candia after 1518, authored a history of the Jews under Venetian authority. However, he was much better known for his survey history of the Ottoman Empire that extended until contemporary times.[155] In both cases Capsali merged various Jewish and non-Jewish historical developments.

In all these cases, Jewish approaches to history and to scholarship more broadly evinced a curious development in the early modern period. While the individuals we have already met would never have forsaken Jewish sources or the primacy of Jewish personalities and events, they were quite willing to engage with non-Jewish authorities and history. While Jews of the Middle Ages often interacted with non-Jewish culture in more profound ways than they are sometimes given credit (or blame) for, some of our early modern personalities were remarkably open about their exploits, even when they understood the difficult straits that such activities could lead to.

Between Ashkenaz and Sepharad: Regional Variation and Ethnic Diversity

When we consider cultural and religious developments within the Jewish communities, it is important to keep in mind the very significant impact that regional and ethnic diversity could have. Cultural developments were experienced in different ways and at different times in varying places. Some cultural innovations penetrated some societies further than others. Certain cultural orientations mixed with traditions, customs, and historical developments differently in certain contexts. Indeed, many scholars have sought to understand the apparently extremely diverse orientations of Jews from different societies by positing fundamental divergences in world outlooks among Jews of Ashkenazic and Sephardic background. This argument has at times been vigorously forwarded.

The famous scholar Gershon Cohen, in attempting to understand differing understandings of messianism, for example, posited that Ashkenazic Jews were submissive and accepting of divine decrees, awaiting God's intervention in history and His restoration of the Jews. Ashkenazic Jews were, therefore, more willing to be martyrs and less willing to forsake their beliefs. Sephardic Jews, on the other hand, were steeped in heterogeneous cultures and had real capacity for and experience of political success. They were more willing to convert from Judaism in turbulent conditions (as they did on occasion in Spain and in Muslim lands), only to revert to their religion after political crises had passed. As such, and confident in their own powers, they were less likely to be steeped in the messianism of their Ashkenazic co-religionists.[156]

A similar interpretation regarding differing Sephardic and Ashkenazic world-views has been offered by another leading scholar. According to the historian Ivan Marcus, narratives of the past written by Sephardic Jews were mainly concerned with the rabbinic elites. Ashkenazic texts, on the other hand, generally described a broader social spectrum.[157] In the Sephardic world, there was an importance attached to uninterrupted tradition. Continuity with an earlier classical past served as the basis for Sephardic legitimacy.[158] Ashkenazic narratives, however, were focused on discontinuity in the community brought about by migration and trauma. Marcus writes, "The Ashkenazic texts seem to emerge especially at times when communal status is in decline, in comparison with an earlier time. The occasion for writing down a narrative about the past is not idle curiosity or even family pride or community self-respect but a perceived change or loss." In a sophisticated application of this observation, he argues, "The emphasis in the Ashkenazic narratives on the story of the changing holy community makes the remembered changes in the life of the community comparable to a dense, partially obscure, sacred text that requires interpretation."[159] The very essence of the Ashkenazic Jews, in the interpretation, was therefore wrapped up with the clarification of traditional religious texts through traditional religious analysis.

Whether or not such generalizations are accurate—we have, for example, evidence of Sephardic martyrs and Ashkenazic politicians—in the end it should be clear that the settlement and migration of Jews affected their religious and cultural experiences a great deal. Subjected to a range of new ideas and practices, Jews often adapted or reconsidered their own world-views. Such reconsiderations could occur at the individual as well as the communal level. Throughout most of the early modern period, Judaism and Jewish communities were able to absorb, to neutralize if we use Katz's terminology, the external. In this sense, traditional Jewish sources of authority and beliefs helped Jews to navigate changing circumstances, to adapt to the new environments in which they found themselves, and to create communities and social structures that were simultaneously able to withstand external forces while maintaining internal traditions, norms, and limits.

CONCLUSIONS

The historian Jonathan Israel argues that the various cultural and religious developments, especially since the middle of the sixteenth century, such as counter-polemic against Christianity, **Lurianic Kabbalah**, and legal codification "were, in large measure, aimed at restoring the confidence, lifting the morale, and soothing the doubts of a people reeling from immense mishaps and disasters in the recent past and now, in the face of a stepped-up bombardment of Lutheran and Counter-Reformation conversionist zeal, striving to achieve a new stability and equilibrium."[160] Israel, like others, finds an inward-looking stance of Jews (pushed as they were into ghettos beginning in the later Middle Ages and throughout the early modern period), as Jews were forced to separate themselves and yet at the same time confront non-Jewish culture and norms.[161]

Jewish religious structures were grounded in biblical and rabbinic texts as well as a tradition of rabbinic interpretation and a wide range of local and regional customs. While Judaism was, and remains in many circles, very much a religion of practice (of observing the commandments, commandments that engage every part of life), there were at the same time some fundamental principles of religious belief that shaped Jewish thought and Jewish practice. Among the most significant pillars of Judaism were discussions about God, God's relationship with the Jewish people, the status of the Torah, the role of prophecy and messianism, and the concept of resurrection of the dead. While it is notoriously difficult to know how religion was practiced or, indeed, what common people believed, the evidence we do have suggests that most Jews were "traditional" in the sense that they obeyed for the most part rabbinic and communal authority, they were familiar with and studied traditional texts and beliefs, they were involved in discussion about Jewish thought, and they attended religious worship on a regular basis.

Education was a pillar of Jewish life, and it existed at various levels. In some cases, increasingly in the early modern period, Jewish education for males was a concern of the community. On the other hand, a rich tradition of private tutoring among wealthier Jews continued. At the apex of Jewish education stood the *yeshivah*, or Talmudic academy, where high level engagement with Talmudic texts and religious codes was stressed. Especially at these high levels of religious education it was the rabbi who was the educational director of the Jewish community. On the other hand a variety of middle-range religious functionaries served the community, at times in different educational capacities. At times, private tutoring was made available to Jewish women as well, many of whom appear to have been familiar with key religious ideas and commandments. In some cases the instruction of women was in vernacular languages, though some were evidently also quite learned in the Hebrew language as well.

Printing affected Jewish education as it did Jewish and non-Jewish culture more generally. The availability of texts standardized educational curricula and discussions, at the same time that the transmission of various texts opened Jewish thinkers to a range of traditional and innovative ideas. Despite the intense discussions about, and at times opposition to, codification, the circulation of codes, notably Joseph Caro's *Shulhan Arukh* and the printing and circulation of various rabbinic responsa, dramatically impacted the legal decision-making of Jewish communities. On the one hand, such codes and decisions allowed for greater uniformity; on the other hand, they pointed to significant discrepancies in thinking, custom, and practices among the far-flung Jewish communities of the early modern period.

Among the most significant genres of Jewish writing in the early modern period aside from these religious texts were ethical writings and, increasingly, mystical writings as transmitted through Kabbalah. Key ethical treatises, some produced in the Middle Ages and others compiled in the early modern period itself, circulated widely and inundated early modern Jewish literature and thought. The number and range of kabbalistic works increased dramatically throughout our period and influenced various religious practices, at times seeping into liturgy as well. A particularly important and dynamic center of Jewish mysticism developed in the Middle Eastern city of Safed, home to some of the religious luminaries of early modern Judaism. While early modern Jewish mysticism drew from deep wellsprings of Jewish thought, it was also steeped in robust streams of Christian and Islamic mystical speculation as well.

A correlated area of mysticism was messianism, which also drew from surrounding cultural and religious developments, and took on great urgency in Jewish thought, particularly as the speeding up of changes across the globe seemed to be ushering in the end of days. There were numerous messianic figures in early modern Judaism, as there were in early modern Christianity and Islam. The most well-known, and in some ways, most significant, was Shabbetai Sevi. Shabbetai Sevi seemed poised to turn the world upside down and usher in the messianic period. Many Jews became followers and expected the messianic redemption at any moment. With Sevi's capture and conversion to Islam, those hopes and dreams were dashed, at least for most Jews.

Like Jewish mysticism and messianism, early modern Judaism engaged what we might today term the supernatural and magical. These were elements that in many ways were inseparable from religious thinking throughout the early modern period. Such was the case in all early modern religions. Various practices, such as divination, palmistry, and the use of amulets marked early modern Judaism as a religion that imbibed and adapted external practices and that was intimately centered on the practical as much as the speculative.

Not all Jews were strict adherents to "traditional" authorities and ideas. Early modern Judaism was in some ways flexible, allowing for variations in thought and to some extent even in practice. Particularly as authority became more centralized and sought after in the early modern period, we have greater insistence in Jewish sources and throughout Jewish communities that Jews behave in particular ways. It is, perhaps, not so surprising that under such conditions the examples of deviance from accepted customs or norms increased. Such deviance was due in part to human nature; some individuals always have difficulty in behaving in certain ways, no matter what the circumstances. In large measure, the deviation was due to the growing diversity of the Jewish communities themselves.

Many Marranos returning to Judaism brought non-Jewish ideas and practices with them. Intellectual speculation was spawned in part by the increased transmission of ideas through printing and confrontations of different ethnic and regional customs as Jews from different regions and backgrounds were forced to live together, further complicating Jewish thought and practice.

In general, early modern Judaism seemed to be able to absorb and, as one scholar maintains, neutralize various decentralizing trends. Yet, throughout the early modern period, and certainly by the end of the period, there were significant examples of thinking and practice that could not be held within traditional Jewish boundaries. Perhaps the best example of this was Baruch Spinoza, whose philosophy challenged traditional religious thinking in many and important ways. Spinoza was excommunicated from the Jewish community, and his ideas were also criticized by Christians, even in the midst of the notoriously tolerant Dutch society. Other changes were soon to come. In some ways traditional and in other ways innovative, modern Hasidism in central and eastern Europe, which is beyond the scope of this book, would help to further transform Judaism.

Early modern Jewish culture was not simply religious. Jews produced and engaged a wide range of literary, artistic, and scientific works. In many cases, Jewish participation in these intellectual and cultural fields was long-standing and rich. Indeed, the Jews themselves portrayed their cultural achievements as biblical and rabbinic in origin, thereby defining their contemporary efforts as a continuation of traditional Jewish endeavors. Jewish participation in broader cultural developments is exemplified by the work of Salamone de Rossi in the field of music and Azariah de' Rossi, David Gans, and Elijah Capsali in the area of history. In each of these cases, Jews engaged the non-Jewish world but interpreted it within a Jewish framework. While many would criticize the use of non-Jewish sources, the subtle arguments for their use combined with more "traditional" purposes indicates that early modern Jewish society was on the edge, navigating both traditional and innovative worlds. The interactions between Jews and non-Jews could be complex, and now we turn in chapter 5 to a deeper exploration of these relationships.

NOTES

1. See Menahem Elon, *Jewish Law: History, Sources, Principles*, trans. Bernard Auerbach and Melvin J. Sykes, 4 vols. (Philadelphia, 1994; orig., 1973), 2:881.

2. Elon, *Jewish Law*, 2:896, 904.

3. Dean Phillip Bell, *Sacred Communities: Jewish and Christian Identities in Fifteenth-Century Germany* (Leiden, Netherlands, and Boston, 2001), 159–60.

4. Bell, *Sacred Communities*, 160.

5. Shlomo Eidelberg, *R. Juspa, Shammash of Warmaisa (Worms): Jewish Life in Seventeenth Century Worms* (Jerusalem, 1991), 57.

6. John H. Arnold, *Belief and Unbelief in Medieval Europe* (London, 2005), 25.

7. Arnold, *Belief and Unbelief in Medieval Europe*, 32.

8. Arnold, *Belief and Unbelief in Medieval Europe*, 34.

9. See the translation provided in Menachem Kellner, *Must a Jew Believe Anything?* (London, 1999), 142–52.

10. Marc Saperstein, *Exile in Amsterdam: Saul Levi Morteira's Sermons to a Congregation of "New Jews"* (Cincinnati, 2005), 222.

11. Isaiah Horowitz, *The Generations of Adam*, trans. Miles Krassen (New York, 1996), 41–42.

12. Horowitz, *The Generations of Adam*, 43ff.

13. Horowitz, *The Generations of Adam*, 50.

14. Kenneth Stow, ed., *The Jews in Rome*, 2 vols. (Leiden, Netherlands, 1995), 1:210–11 (no. 526).

15. Shalom Sabar, "Childbirth and Magic: Jewish Folklore and Material Culture," in *Cultures of the Jews: A New History*, ed. David Biale (New York, 2002), 671.

16. Jonathan Israel, *European Jewry in the Age of Mercantilism, 1550–1750*, 3rd ed. (London, 1998), 34–35.

17. Edward Fram, *Ideals Face Reality: Jewish Law and Life in Poland, 1550–1655* (Cincinnati, 1997), 62.

18. Nathan of Hannover, *Abyss of Despair: The Famous 17th Century Chronicle Depicting Jewish Life in Russia and Poland during the Chmielnicki Massacres of 1648–1649 = Yeven metzulah*, trans. Abraham J. Mesch (New Brunswick, NJ, 1983), 110, 115–17.

19. Nathan of Hannover, *Abyss of Despair*, 111.

20. Nathan of Hannover, *Abyss of Despair*, 112.

21. Nathan of Hannover, *Abyss of Despair*, 113.

22. Nathan of Hannover, *Abyss of Despair*, 114.

23. In Jacob Marcus, *The Jew in the Medieval World: A Source Book, 315–1791* (Cincinnati, 1938), 378–79.

24. Franz Kobler, ed., *A Treasury of Jewish Letters: Letters from the Famous and the Humble*, 2 vols. (London, 1952), 2:561–62.

25. Kobler, *A Treasury of Jewish Letters*, 2:562.

26. Kobler, *A Treasury of Jewish Letters*, 2:561.

27. Moritz Güdemann, *Quellenschriften zur Geschichte des Unterrichts und der Erziehung bei den deutschen Juden, von den ältesten Zeiten bis auf Mendelssohn* (Amsterdam, 1968), 64.

28. Güdemann, *Quellenschriften*, 67.

29. Güdemann, *Quellenschriften*, 71.

30. See S. D. Goitein, *A Mediterranean Society: An Abridgement in One Volume*, rev. and ed. Jacob Lassner (Berkeley, CA, 1999), 264ff.

31. For discussion of the *yeshivah*, see Mordechai Breuer, "The Wanderings of Students and Scholars—A Prolegomenon to a Chapter in the History of the Yeshivot," in *Culture and Society in Medieval Jewry: Studies Dedicated to the Memory of Haim Hillel Ben-Sasson*, ed. Menahem Ben-Sasson, Robert Bonfil, and Joseph R. Hacker (Hebrew) (Jerusalem, 1989), 445–68.

32. Avigdor Levy, *The Jews of the Ottoman Empire* (Princeton, NJ, 1992), 37.

33. Levy, *The Jews of the Ottoman Empire*, 38.

34. Levy, *The Jews of the Ottoman Empire*, 38.

35. Levy, *The Jews of the Ottoman Empire*. 38.

36. On Hebrew printing, see Stephen G. Burnett, "German Jewish Printing in the Reformation Era (1530–1633)," in *Jews, Judaism, and the Reformation in Sixteenth-Century Germany*, ed. Dean Phillip Bell and Stephen G. Burnett (Leiden, Netherlands, 2006), 503–27; A. M. Haberman, *Studies in the History of Hebrew Printers and Books* (Hebrew) (Jerusalem, 1978); Marvin Heller, *The Sixteenth Century Hebrew Book*, 2 vols. (Leiden, Netherlands, 2004); Raphael Posner and Israel Ta-Shma, eds., *The Hebrew Book: An Historical Survey* (Jerusalem, 1975).

37. See Elliot Dorff, *A Living Tree: The Roots and Growth of Jewish Law* (Albany, NY, 1988).

38. Moshe Rosman, "Innovative Tradition: Jewish Culture in the Polish-Lithuanian Commonwealth," in *Cultures of the Jews: A New History*, ed. David Biale (New York, 2002), 542–45.

39. Alexander Tobias, "Hayyim Ben Bezalel," in *Encyclopedia Judaica*, 16 vols. (Jerusalem, 1971–1972).

40. Güdemann, *Quellenschriften*, 77.

41. Güdemann, *Quellenschriften*, 62–63.

42. Güdemann, *Quellenschriften*, 69.

43. Güdemann, *Quellenschriften*, 74.

44. A recent treatment of the responsa literature can be found in Peter J. Haas, *Responsa: Literary History of a Rabbinic Genre* (Atlanta, 1996).

45. See Dean Phillip Bell, *Jewish Identity in Early Modern Germany: Memory, Power, and Community* (Aldershot, UK, 2007).

46. See Michael A. Meyer, *Ideas of Jewish History* (Detroit, 1987), 110–14.

47. Glückel of Hameln, *The Memoirs of Glückel of Hameln*, trans. Marvin Lowenthal (New York, 1977), 1–2.

48. Glückel of Hameln, *The Memoirs*, 3.

49. The falling ceiling (Glückel of Hameln, *The Memoirs*, 272ff), which again teaches important moral and communal lessons.

50. Quoted in Marc Saperstein, *Jewish Preaching, 1200–1800: An Anthology* (New Haven, CT, 1989), 274.

51. Leon Modena, *The Autobiography of a Seventeenth-Century Venetian Rabbi: Leon Modena's Life of Judah*, ed. and trans. Mark R. Cohen (Princeton, NJ, 1988), 100.

52. Marcus, *The Jew in the Medieval World*, 418–21.

53. Here and above, see Isaiah Horowitz, *Shney Luchot Habrit*, trans. Eliyahu Munk, vol. 1 (Jerusalem, 1962), 1.

54. Robert Bonfil, *Jewish Life in Renaissance Italy*, trans. Anthony Oldcorn (Berkeley, CA, 1994), 275.

55. Bonfil, *Jewish Life in Renaissance Italy*, 278.

56. Bonfil, *Jewish Life in Renaissance Italy*, 278–80.

57. On women and Kabbalah, see Chava Weissler, *Voices of the Matriarchs: Listening to the Prayers of Early Modern Jewish Women* (Boston, 1998), 89ff.

58. See Rosman, "Innovative Tradition," 548ff. For Italy, see Elliot Horowitz, "Families and Their Fortunes: The Jews of Early Modern Italy," in *Cultures of the Jews: A New History*, ed. David Biale (New York, 2002), 583ff.

59. Consider *Yosef Ometz.*

60. Gershom Scholem, "Zohar," in *Encyclopedia Judaica*, 16 vols. (Jerusalem, 1971–1972).

61. Horowitz, "Families and Their Fortunes," 605.

62. *Safed Spirituality: Rules of Mystical Piety, The Beginning of Wisdom*, trans. Lawrence Fine (New York, 1984), 37.

63. Marcus, *The Jew in the Medieval World*, 258–59.

64. See Gershom Scholem, *Major Trends in Jewish Mysticism*, 3rd ed. (New York, 1954), regarding the significance of Lurianic thought.

65. Hayyim Vital in *Jewish Mystical Autobiographies: Book of Visions and Book of Secrets*, trans. Morris M. Faierstein (New York, 1999), 61–62.

66. Güdemann, *Quellenschriften*, 59.

67. See Byron Sherwin, *Mystical Theology and Social Dissent: The Life and Works of Judah Loew of Prague* (New Jersey, 1982).

68. Menasseh ben Israel, *The Hope of Israel*, ed. Henry Mechoulan and Gerard Nahon (Oxford, 1987), 118.

69. Menasseh ben Israel, *The Hope of Israel*, 118ff.

70. Kobler, *A Treasury of Jewish Letters*, 2:509.

71. Andrew Colin Gow, *The Red Jews: Antisemitism in an Apocalyptic Age 1200–1600* (Leiden, Netherlands, 1995), 250.

72. Gershom Scholem, *Sabbatai Sevi: The Mystical Messiah, 1626–1676*, trans. R. J. Zwi Werblowsky (Princeton, NJ, 1973), 136.

73. See Scholem, *Sabbatai Sevi*, passim.

74. Glückel of Hameln, *The Memoirs*, 46–47.

75. See, for example, Richard H. Popkin, "Three English Tellings of the Sabbatai Zevi Story," *Jewish History* 8 (1–2) (1994): 43–54; Giacomo Saban, "Sabbatai Sevi as Seen by a Contemporary Traveller," *Jewish History* 7 (2) (1993): 105–18; and Jetteke Van Wijk, "The Rise and Fall of Shabbatai Zevi as Reflected in Contemporary Press Reports," *Studia Rosenthalia* 33 (1) (1999): 7–27.

76. See Levy, *The Jews of the Ottoman Empire*, 87.

77. Bat Ye'or, *The Dhimmi: Jews and Christians under Islam*, trans. David Maisel, Paul Fenton, and David Littman (London, 1985), 363.

78. Joshua Trachtenberg, *Jewish Magic and Superstition: A Study in Folk Religion* (New York, 1939).

79. Trachtenberg, *Jewish Magic and Superstition.*

80. David B. Ruderman, *Kabbalah, Magic, and Science: The Cultural Universe of a Sixteenth-Century Jewish Physician* (Cambridge, MA, 1988), 55.

81. Ruderman, *Kabbalah, Magic, and Science*, 80.

82. Modena, *The Autobiography*, 90.

83. Quoted in Saperstein, *Exile in Amsterdam*, 223–24.

84. Vital in *Jewish Mystical Autobiographies*, 43.

85. Vital in *Jewish Mystical Autobiographies*, 44.

86. Quoted in Saperstein, *Exile in Amsterdam*, 309.

87. Saperstein, *Exile in Amsterdam*, 309.

88. See Bell, *Jewish Identity in Early Modern Germany*.

89. See the corpus of his work but, especially, R. I. Moore, *The Formation of a Persecuting Society: Power and Deviance in Western Europe, 950–1250* (Oxford, 1987).

90. Louis Finkelstein, *Jewish Self-Government in the Middle Ages* (New York, 1924), 260.

91. Finkelstein, *Jewish Self-Government*, 263.

92. Finkelstein, *Jewish Self-Government*, 262.

93. See Eric Middlefort, *A History of Madness in Sixteenth-Century Germany* (Stanford, CA, 1999).

94. See, for example, Isaac Cassuto, "Aus den ältesten Protokollbuch der Portugiesisch-Jüdischen Gemeinde in Hamburg: Übersetzung und Anmerkungen," in *Jahrbuch der Jüdisch-Literarischen Gesellschaft* 6 (1908): 1–54; 7 (1909): 159–210; 8 (1910): 227–90; 9 (1911): 318–66; 10 (1912): 225–95; 11 (1916): 1–76; 12 (1920): 55–118—here at 8:265.

95. See Daniel Swetschinski, *Reluctant Cosmopolitans: The Portuguese Jews of Seventeenth-Century Amsterdam* (London, 2000), 214–16.

96. Cassuto, "Aus den ältesten Protokollbuch," 6:28, 7:27.

97. Cassuto, "Aus den ältesten Protokollbuch," 6:43.

98. Cassuto, "Aus den ältesten Protokollbuch," 7:22.

99. Cassuto, "Aus den ältesten Protokollbuch," 10:241.

100. Swetschinski, *Reluctant Cosmopolitans*, 217–18.

101. Fram, *Ideals Face Reality*, 52.

102. Responsum old 98, in Fram, *Ideals Face Reality*, 51–52.

103. Jacob Katz, *Out of the Ghetto: The Social Background of Jewish Emancipation, 1770–1870* (New York, 1978; orig., 1973), 35.

104. Katz, *Out of the Ghetto*, 36.

105. Talya Fishman, *Shaking the Pillars of Exile: "Voice of a Fool," an Early Modern Jewish Critique of Rabbinic Culture* (Stanford, CA, 1997), 85.

106. Fishman, *Shaking the Pillars of Exile*, 88–89.

107. Fishman, *Shaking the Pillars of Exile*, 98.

108. Fishman, *Shaking the Pillars of Exile*, 102.

109. Israel Yuval and Ora Limor, "Skepticism and Conversion: Jews, Christians, and Doubters in 'Sefer ha-Nizzahon,'" in *Hebraica Veritas? Jews and the Study of Judaism in Early Modern Europe*, ed. Allison P. Coudert, Alison Shoulson, and Jeffery S. Shoulson (Philadelphia, 2004), 173.

110. "Prado, Juan de," in *Encyclopedia Judaica*, 16 vols. (Jerusalem, 1971–1972).

111. Uriel Acosta, *Uriel Acosta: A Specimen of Human Life* (New York, 1967), 62. See also Steven M. Nadler, *Spinoza: A Life* (Cambridge, UK, 1999), 66–73.

112. Acosta, *Uriel Acosta*, 68.

113. See the recent and outstanding biography of Spinoza by Nadler, *Spinoza*.

114. Paul Mendes Flohr and Jehuda Reinharz, eds., *The Jew in the Modern World: A Documentary History*, 2nd ed. (New York, 1995), 57.

115. Benedictus de (Baruch) Spinoza, *Tractatus theologico-politicus*, trans. Samuel Shirley, 2nd ed. (Leiden, Netherlands, 1991), chap. 7, "Of the Interpretation of Scripture."

116. According to Harry Wolfson, a leading scholar of Spinoza, Spinoza was new and daring in a number of ways. See Harry A. Wolfson, *The Philosophy of Spinoza: Unfolding the Latent Process of His Reasoning* (Cambridge, MA, 1983).

117. See Sander L. Gilman, *Jewish Self-Hatred: Anti-Semitism and the Hidden Language of the Jews* (Baltimore, 1986), 104–5; see also the introductory comments by Don Garrett in Don Garrett, ed., *The Cambridge Companion to Spinoza* (Cambridge, UK, 1996).

118. See Norbert Elias, *The History of Manners (The Civilizing Process, Vol. 1)*, trans. Edmund Jephcott (New York, 1978; orig., 1939), 4–5.

119. David Biale, "Introduction," in *Cultures of the Jews: A New History*, ed. David Biale (New York, 2002), xvii.

120. See Biale, "Introduction," xxiv.

121. Biale, "Introduction," xxii.

122. Biale, "Introduction," xxvi.

123. Bernard Suler, "Alchemy," in *Encyclopedia Judaica*, 16 vols. (Jerusalem, 1971–1972).

124. Suler, "Alchemy."

125. See David B. Ruderman, "Medicine and Scientific Thought: The World of Tobias Cohen," in *The Jews of Early Modern Venice*, ed. Robert C. Davis and Benjamin Ravid (Baltimore, 2001), 191–210.

126. See Colbert I. Nepaulsingh, *Apples of Gold in Filigrees of Silver: Jewish Writing in the Eye of the Inquisition* (New York, 1995).

127. See Miriam Bodian, *Hebrews of the Portuguese Nation: Conversos and Community in Early Modern Amsterdam* (Bloomington, IN, 1997), 74.

128. See, for example, Nadler, *Spinoza*, 145–46.

129. Levy, *The Jews of the Ottoman Empire*, 298.

130. See Yosef Kaplan, "Bom Judesmo: The Western Sephardic Diaspora," in *Cultures of the Jews: A New History*, ed. David Biale (New York, 2002), 664.

131. See Cecil Roth, *The Jews in the Renaissance* (Philadelphia, 1959), 290–99.

132. Solomon Freehof, *A Treasury of Responsa* (Philadelphia, 1963), 165.

133. See Don Harran, "Jewish Musical Culture: Leone Modena," in *The Jews of Early Modern Venice*, ed. Robert C. Davis and Benjamin Ravid (Baltimore, 2001), 225. See also Kobler, *A Treasury of Jewish Letters*, 2:416–19.

134. Jacob S. Levinger, "Delmedigo, Elijah ben Moses Abba," in *Encyclopedia Judaica*, 16 vols. (Jerusalem, 1971–1972).

135. Levinger, "Delmedigo, Elijah."

136. Avraham Grossman, "Abarbanel as Biblical Exegete," in *Encyclopedia Judaica*, 16 vols. (Jerusalem, 1971–1972).

137. Mordechai Breuer, "Modernism and Traditionalism in Sixteenth-Century Jewish Historiography: A Study of David Gans' Tzemah David," in *Jewish Thought in the Sixteenth Century*, ed. Bernard Dov Cooperman (Cambridge, MA, 1983), 54; see also Mordechai Breuer, "Introduction," in David Gans, *Zemah David*, ed. Mordechai Breuer (Jerusalem, 1983), i.

138. Gans believed the study of general history is important for a number of reasons, including his rationale that it is important that Jews will not seem to non-Jews

"like cattle that cannot distinguish between their right and left, or as though we [Jews] were all born but the day before yesterday." Cited in Meyer, *Ideas of Jewish History*, 131.

139. See Yosef Hayim Yerushalmi, *Zakhor: Jewish History and Jewish Memory* (Seattle, 1982).

140. Breuer, "Modernism and Traditionalism," 77–78. See also Salo Baron, *History and Jewish Historians: Essays and Addresses* (Philadelphia, 1964), 192, for de' Rossi's argument regarding the use of sources of Gentile origin; and see *Me'or 'Einayim* I, 75 (ca. 89). For Azariah's rationalizations, and their inherent flaws, see Lester A. Segal, *Historical Consciousness and Religious Tradition in Azariah de' Rossi's Me'or 'Einayim* (Philadelphia, 1989), 55f.

141. Breuer, "Modernism and Traditionalism," 57.

142. Breuer, "Modernism and Traditionalism," 50–53.

143. David Gans, *Zemah David*, ed. Mordechai Breuer (Jerusalem, 1983), 163.

144. Gans, *Zemah David*, 6.

145. Gans, *Zemah David*, 15.

146. Meyer, *Ideas of Jewish History*, 128; Gans, *Zemah David*, 164.

147. Meyer, *Ideas of Jewish History*, 128–29; Gans, *Zemah David*, 165.

148. Azariah de' Rossi, *The Light of the Eyes*, trans. Joanna Weinberg (New Haven, CT, 2001), 81.

149. De' Rossi, *The Light of the Eyes*, 82.

150. De' Rossi, *The Light of the Eyes*, 83.

151. De' Rossi, *The Light of the Eyes*, 86.

152. De' Rossi, *The Light of the Eyes*, 96.

153. De' Rossi, *The Light of the Eyes*, 97.

154. De' Rossi, *The Light of the Eyes*, 300.

155. See Cecil Roth, "Capsali, Elijah," in *Encyclopedia Judaica*, 16 vols. (Jerusalem, 1971–1972), and Meyer, *Ideas of Jewish History*, 19.

156. See Gershon Cohen, "Messianic Postures of Ashkenazim and Sephardim," reprinted in *Essential Papers on Messianic Movements and Personalities in Jewish History*, ed. Marc Saperstein (New York, 1992), 220, 222, for example.

157. Ivan Marcus, "History, Story, and Collective Memory: Narrativity in Early Ashkenazic Culture," *Prooftexts* 10 (1990): 379. This distinction is related to the important, if overextended, theory of Gershon Cohen, regarding the differences between Sephardic and Ashekenazic culture. Cohen argues for the notion that Ashkenazic writing reveals submissiveness and acceptance of divine decrees, until God intervenes in history and restores His people. See Cohen, "Messianic Postures of Ashkenazim and Sephardim," 220. On the other hand, Cohen argues that Sephardic writing reveals political success and confidence in its own powers (222).

158. Marcus, "History, Story and Collective Memory," 381. In this context, it might be interesting to consider the attitude toward Sephardic sources; see Eric Zimmer, *Fiery Embers of the Scholars: The Trials and Tribulations of German Rabbis in the Sixteenth and Seventeenth Centuries* (Hebrew) (Jerusalem, 1999), regarding the debate over the use of Sephardic sources in early modern Germany.

159. Marcus, "History, Story, and Collective Memory," 381.

160. Israel, *European Jewry*, 70.

161. See Israel, *European Jewry*, 60.

5

Relations with the Other

In light of the dramatic movement of Jews and Jewish communities, relations with non-Jews could be tenuous, complicated, and ever changing. This chapter, therefore, explores Jewish views of and relations with non-Jews, in both religious and popular literature as well as in daily interactions. We consider how Jews and non-Jews interacted in the early modern world and for what purposes. This chapter argues that there were many different modalities of interaction (such as political, religious, neighborly, extraordinary, etc.) and that such interaction was greatly affected by universal considerations as well as by unique local or regional complexities.

This chapter also asks how Jews were perceived and represented by non-Jews. Special attention is given to anti-Jewish thought and action and the increasing phenomena of assimilation and conversion, which though not yet common were becoming more frequent perhaps partially in response to growing toleration of Jews in society. Throughout, it is noted that Jews and non-Jews might, and often did, have very positive relationships and that it is inappropriate to dismiss the period as one bracketed simply by expulsion and emancipation. While some Jews, for example, lived in separate quarters or ghettos, even under such conditions there could be important opportunities for close relations between Jews and non-Jews.

THE BASIS OF JEWISH AND NON-JEWISH RELATIONS

The position of the Jews could vary dramatically even within the same country or geographic region. Despite negative conditions in some places, Jews living in other regions appear to have lived fairly peaceful lives.

Though Jewish communities frequently suffered restrictions or were affected by the circulation of negative stereotypes, individual Jews might have had opportunities for normal or even successful relations beyond the Jewish community.

In Amsterdam, for example, as in many other places Jews faced a combination of restrictions and freedoms. There, Jews could practice their religion but not in public or in ways that would make it too visible. Even after construction of synagogues began, the public worship of Judaism was not actually sanctioned.

Throughout the Dutch lands, various attitudes regarding the Jews existed. In this sense, the Dutch case is instructive. On the one hand, there existed a certain degree of toleration. According to Franciscus Junius (1542–1602), a French Calvinist who resided in Amsterdam for a decade and who repeated stock medieval stereotypes but in an early modern context, for example,

> they ought to be tolerated among Christians: First, because they are poor ignorant creatures, and that no man living ought to be extirpated from the earth on account of Religion, since Faith is a gift of God, and since all men are by nature our brethren. Secondly, that although the Body of the Jews is in general rejected by God, yet it is not to be inferred from thence that the particular Members of that Body are not to be tolerated among Christians: for the Church must be gathered out of both. Consequently they are to be tolerated, not only on account of Nature, but of Grace. From their unfruitful works we ought indeed to abstain. There is much said about their Synagogues, but there is nothing to be found in them that so greatly wounds the reputation of Religion.[1]

While some theologians disagreed with certain spiritual and theological aspects of Judaism, others conceded that Judaism was a far cry better than no religion at all. The fear of secularism or even anti-religious sentiment was a growing concern in some circles during the early modern period, just as institutionalized religion was increasing its hold and simultaneously being resisted. In the staunchly anti-Catholic Netherlands there was more concern with the religion of the pope than that of the Jews. Indeed, as one founding legend of the nascent Amsterdam Portuguese Jewish community indicated, a secret worship session of the Jews was discovered by the police, who prepared to haul the participants off as illegal papists. Once it was realized that the worshippers were Jews and not Catholics, however, they were not only released but even requested to pray for the city.

There could, of course, be significant differences of opinion about the toleration of Jews between civic leaders, religious leaders, and the general populace. Variations might exist among the same constituents and at different times within the same communities. Clerics in Amsterdam were rather outspoken in their opposition to the Jews, and there were also conversionary campaigns in Amsterdam as well as in other cities in the Netherlands in the 1670s. Civic leaders, however, did what they could to allow some degree of toleration for the Jews to remain in the city and practice some form of livelihood.

Still, some Christians, especially certain Protestant sectarians, identified with the Jews, seeing themselves as the new Israel—God's new Chosen People—battling the superstitious and idolatrous papists. Indeed, the Dutch national struggle against Spain was cast very much in light of the Israelites redemption from Egypt and the settlement of the Holy Land. In addition, Calvinist theologians often focused on the moralistic aspects of the Old Testament, and they identified with the biblical flood, living as they did with the constant threat of the flood waters. Still, this identification could be enlisted to support two opposing policies: expulsion and toleration.

Dutch Jews and Christians engaged with one another in daily business, and the Jews were not forced into a ghetto. In early modern Amsterdam, the Jews had no distinguishing marks to wear, were not presented with overly exaggerated characteristics or physical features, and appeared as part of society in various artistic representations.[2] In fact, everyday images of Jewish life seem to have been easily and willingly incorporated into Dutch art of the period.

Early modern Jews found Amsterdam to be a remarkably tolerant city. In addition to early rabbinic leaders, individuals outside the city marveled at the opportunities and tranquility afforded the Jews. One rabbinic writer from the early seventeenth century wrote,

> Today a tranquil and secure people dwells in Amsterdam, and the officials of the city have sought to expand the settlement and to establish laws concerning it. Among these [laws] they have allowed every man to believe in divine matters as he chooses, and each lives according to his faith, as long as he does not go about the markets and streets displaying his opposition to the faith of the residents of the city.[3]

Even when leading legal figures such as Hugo Grotius (1583–1645) pointed out the fundamental opposition of Judaism and Christianity, they rejected the exclusion of Jews, primarily because of the perceived economic value of Jewish enterprise and the possibility of eventual conversion of the Jews to Christianity. Jews were allowed a certain degree of professional flexibility.

Nevertheless, the position of the Jews in Dutch society was not always secure, and general anti-Jewish stereotypes and legislation persisted. Grotius, for example, disavowed public Jewish worship, Christian attendance at Jewish religious services, and the conversion of Christians to Judaism. Jews were to be prohibited from holding public office, sexual relations between Jews and Christians were forbidden (and both could be punished), and Jewish shops were to be closed on Sundays and Christian holidays.

INTERACTION OF JEWS AND NON-JEWS

Jewish relations with non-Jews were complex and variable. Both Jews and non-Jews legislated restrictions on interaction. But Jews also engaged non-Jewish culture, distancing themselves sometimes but acculturating or adapting at others.

Sumptuary Laws and Jewish Relations with the Broader Culture

Sumptuary laws designed by the Jews themselves were extensively circulated in the later Middle Ages and early modern period. While such laws legislated how Jews could dress and how many people might be invited to various celebrations, the laws, as well as other communal legislation, were also concerned about how Jews and Jewish behavior would be perceived by non-Jews. In Cracow in 1595 it was decreed,

> It is forbidden to go through the streets at night playing on musical instruments, nor shall anyone, whether householders, young men, or boys, shout or yell in the streets. If a person does such things, or if a fight breaks out at night, or if someone attacks a citizen or injures his home, the night-watch are required to awaken one or two of the officials who are expected to get up immediately and to admonish the people to go home.[4]

While order in the community was important, so was the concern that the Jewish community be seen as quiet, peaceful, and law-abiding. In Forli, Italy, in the early fifteenth century, sumptuary laws proscribed, "In order also to humble our hearts, and to walk modestly before our God, and not to show off in his presence of the Gentiles, we have agreed that from today, until the termination of the time already mentioned, no Jew or Jewess of the above recorded communities, towns, or villages shall be so arrogant as to wear a fur-lined jacket, unless, of course it is black."[5]

In Recife, South America, as elsewhere, relations with non-Jews were carefully considered. This was particularly true when it came to modest behavior—Jews wanted to remain under the radar as it were—but also regarding religious disputation and conversion to Judaism. According to regulation number 27 of the Minute Book, "And in view of the fact that all manner of disputations against other religions turn to our damage and prejudice, it is ordered that no person shall engage in them. And whoever happens to have fallen into this error shall be punished by the Gentlemen of the **Mahamad** as they deem best."[6] Great concern was also expressed about conversion to Judaism in a period when such action was subject to severe punishment for the individual who converted and also created a dangerous situation in which the Jewish community itself might be held responsible for such indiscretions. *Ascamot* 32 of the Recife constitution reads, "No person shall—except with the permission of the Gentlemen of the Mahamad—circumcise a stranger or admit a strange woman to the **Theuilah** [immersion in a ritual bath as part of the conversion process], under penalty of being separated from the nation and fined fifty florins."[7]

Jews of Recife were ever cognizant of the danger posed by non-Jewish neighbors and citizens and similarly made every effort to maintain a low profile. As in parts of central Europe at the same time, even Jewish celebrations were to be low-key to avoid any run-ins with Christians. The doors of the synagogue were to be closed and locked on the nights of **Simhat Torah** and **Sabat Bereshit** because "the Gentlemen of the Mahamad are cognizant of the damage that may be caused by the gatherings and riots of Goim occurring on the night of Simha[t] Tora when the synagogue is opened after the **Arvit** [evening service]."[8]

Acculturation

In the early modern period we know that Jewish culture was not simply a segregated one of the ghetto. Jews participated in the broader culture but gave it Jewish meaning. For example, central European Jews appropriated chivalric romances but substituted Jewish characters for Christian ones. Jews developed a wide range of customs (see chapter 4) and often adopted or adapted local and non-Jewish practices into their own religious practice and lives. This meant, however, that Jews developed a wide range of often divergent practices and customs, even when or if they shared basic religious ideas and principles. Indeed, the important Venetian Jew Rabbi Simone Luzatto (1583–1663) once noted, "The Jews accept various practices from the other nations in whose midst they dwell. Therefore, the ways of the Venetian Jew differ from those of the Jew of Constantinople, of Damascus and of Cairo, and all of these differ from the Jews of Germany and Poland."[9]

The historian of early modern Jewish Amsterdam Daniel Swetschinski has used the term "reluctant cosmopolitans" to describe the Jews he studied. According to him, "There is, in the final analysis, something unexpectedly Jewish and modern in these two simultaneous endeavors: the universalist, 'cosmopolitan' striving towards religious or ethical harmony and the more particularistic, 'reluctant' definition of a Portuguese Jewish identity."[10] Such a conundrum of identity, melding external and internal traditions, was not unique to Italy of the Renaissance or to cosmopolitan Amsterdam. In Poland, for example, Church and theater melodies appear to have penetrated into the synagogue,[11] though clearly with some limitations. For early modern Poland, the historian Moshe Rosman argues,

> Despite their lack of assimilation to Polish culture, Jews saw themselves functioning as part of the system. They were concerned about demonstrating the

depth of their roots in Polish soil and the legitimacy of their rights, without try-
ing to escape their Jewishness. Given the range of responses to domination
available to subordinated minority groups, they chose accommodation, es-
chewing the extremes of revolt and assimilation.[12]

In the early modern period prior, Jews already attempted to balance Jewish
identity with (non-Jewish) national or regional identity. Early modern Jews
did not fundamentally alter their religious structures, though a wide range
of religious customs and ideas were clearly affected by external developments. According to the prominent Jewish historian Ivan Marcus, Jewish
culture is itself one that actively and inwardly acculturates.[13] Such acculturation did not imply succumbing to or simply repeating the external. Far less
did it imply any kind of external transformation of Judaism or secularization.[14] Marcus concludes that non-Jewish cultures contributed a great deal
to the "innovation and development of Jewish life cycle events." "With few
exceptions," he writes, "those cultures stimulated Jews to adapt aspects of
the majority culture to existing institutions and patterns in Judaism."[15]
While not unique to early modern Jews, such innovation had tremendous
importance and was frequently discussed in the early modern period.

Similarly, the contemporary Jewish historian of Rome, Kenneth Stow, argues that early modern Jews practiced "acculturation, adding to one's cultural identity through adoption, adaptation, and modification" rather than
"assimilation, blemishing ones cultural essence through negation and
abandonment, and leading, often, to outright denial. Jewish acculturation
in sixteenth-century Rome thus required that Jewish behavior be rooted in
a set of time-honored principles simultaneously distinguishing Jews from
others, yet also sufficiently elastic to make Jews comfortable both at home
and in Roman society as a whole."[16] Stow notes that Jews could very clev-
erly adopt external concepts within a traditional, or traditional-sounding,
framework. In 1522 Rabbi Abramo Scazzocchio, for example, described an
engagement by saying that the parties had reached the stage of *teqi'at kaf*
("planting of the hand") and *kinyan*. *Kinyan* was the traditional symbolic
act signifying that a betrothal had taken place. Added to this is a novel Hebrew term "planting of the hand," a public handshake by the contracting
parties to seal the deal, imitating the Italian *impalmamento*.[17]

Other scholars, such as Robert Bonfil, caution against making too much
of any perceived distinctions between integration and acculturation. Bonfil
notes that there is a historiographical trend to see

> a picture of a Jewish society in the process of giving way to centrifugal forces
> and forsaking the distinguishing features of its Jewishness, in other words, a
> Jewish society in the grip of an impulse toward assimilation, touched off by the
> close contacts that were a consequence of the high degree of integration, as
> well as by the force of attraction exerted by Renaissance cultural values.[18]

Some Jewish book collections and libraries included a good deal of secular material. One such collection from the Finzi family in Italy included 226 Hebrew manuscripts, of which eighteen were prayerbooks, twenty-one philosophical works, and thirty-one medical treatises.[19] Other Finzi libraries included large numbers of Italian literature, such as Petrarch, and classical gems as well, such as Ovid's *Metamorphoses*.[20] In Amsterdam, we find libraries with a wide range of non-Jewish books. The library of Isaac Aboab da Fonseca, for example, contained 373 Hebrew books, in addition to 179 books in non-Hebrew languages, especially Latin and Greek. At the end of the seventeenth century in Hamburg, Rabbi Samuel Abbas, who was a native of the city, had a library of 236 Hebrew works, 421 Latin, 168 Spanish and Portuguese, 243 French, and 113 Italian volumes.[21] At the beginning of the eighteenth century, Rabbi David Nunes Torres of The Hague possessed over 1,500 non-Hebrew books, including Uriel da Costa's banned work against the immortality of the soul.[22] In each of these examples we find Jews who were **Sephardic** and perhaps more open to heterogeneous cultural influences. What is more, each of these libraries was sold at public auction, which according to the historian Yosef Kaplan suggests that "no one in the Sephardic communities followed in the footsteps of these cultivated rabbis."[23]

In contrast to the Renaissance cultural values perceived by some historians, however, Robert Bonfil asserts the pervasively Jewish and religious nature of Renaissance Italian Jews. He asserts that there was a high degree of Jewish literacy and that practically all Jewish cultural activity was based on texts written in Hebrew and unquestionably modeled on "sacred literature." If, for example, one looks at the lists of books inspected by the Mantuan Inquisition, Bonfil contends, one finds that 98 percent of the books owned by Jewish community members were what he terms "sacred literature." What is more, only 11.2 percent of libraries contained books written in Italian, constituting a mere 0.6 percent of total number of volumes. The principal literature produced by Italian Jews of the Renaissance period was works relating to Jewish law, especially rabbinic **responsa**.

Bonfil maintains that in every field, the literature produced by Italian Jews selectively imported cultural trends and values, fashionable literature and motifs, norms and conventions, and philosophical problems and solutions. Jews made attempts to "**Judaize**" anything that seemed worthy of being presented within a Jewish context, a situation that was not limited to Renaissance Italy. Yet, Hebrew culture was seen as superior to all other cultures. Indeed, the famous Jewish exegete Isaac Abarbanel, for example, saw a biblical model for the Venetian republic. Johanan Alemanno (1433–ca. 1504) found the model for the Florentine city-state in the Bible. And Messer Leon (ca. 1470/1472–ca. 1526) argued that all of Ciceronian rhetorical figures could already be found in the Bible and further that the Bible contained still more not mentioned by classical authors.

As the scholar Arthur Lesley concludes, "To assume that a minority culture that has long survived, such as that of the Jews, automatically imitates
whatever it encounters in the surrounding society both ignores the internal
dynamics of Jewish life and reduces intercultural relations to simplistic al-
ternatives of borrowing or complete originality."[24] Jews in Renaissance Italy
did not resist or ignore humanism; they chose what interested them and
disregarded the rest. Isaac Abarbanel, for example, traced the origins of classical and scientific learning to biblical sources.[25]

Early modern Jews often looked to biblical and rabbinic writings for evidence that Jews already knew particular fields of learning and then, justified
by these precedents, integrated these disciplines into Jewish discourse. According to Judah Messer Leon (ca. 1425–1495), for example,

> For when I had studied the Torah in the habitual way, I had not been able to
> fathom that it embraced the science [of rhetoric] or part of it. Only after I had
> learned, searched and mastered it [rhetoric] in all its depth from the writings
> of the Gentiles, could I visualize, when returning to he Holy Scriptures, what
> they were like. Now the eyes of my understanding were opened and I saw
> that there was, in fact, a vast difference between the pleasantness and ele-
> gance of their speeches . . . and all that is found in this [genre] among the
> rest of the nations.[26]

Jews did occasionally create a more formal relationship between traditional
Jewish and classical and "practical" secular learning. In the early modern
period we have several examples of Jewish "colleges" proposed or established for a short time for this purpose. A Hebrew document from 1564 in
Mantua, Italy, by David Provencal and his son Abraham, called for the creation of a Jewish college. The college was to serve a dual purpose. On the
one hand, it was to offer serious Jewish learning: "Thus everyone who seeks
Jewish learning and lore may turn here to our great wine cellars of Torah
and science; let him drink and forget his intellectual poverty." On the other
hand, the college was to supply professional learning that was sought after
by contemporary Italian Jews. "Why should we be inferior," Provencal asks,
"to all other peoples who have scholarly institutions and places fit for instruction in law and the sciences where students may flock and slake their
thirst?"[27] Provencal was concerned because, as he saw it, "the peoples
among whom we live are ever increasing in wisdom, understanding, and
knowledge, and in all arts, but Israel alone is isolated, desolate, poor, most
unsightly, like a lost sheep, like a flock without a shepherd."[28]

The college was to nurture the entire life of its students. It provided room
and board, and the course of study encouraged academic endeavor as well
as religious observance. The plan of study outlined for the college included
the following, in order. First, there was to be instruction in proper ideas

drawn from the Bible and rabbinic teachings, so that students would be zealous for both the "rational and the ceremonial commandments," acquire good manners and commendable virtues, and attend the synagogue for morning and evening prayers. Jewish philosophy was also covered, as was Hebrew grammar and language. In addition, Latin was taught because of its utility in relations with officials and so that students could read the sciences. If provided in the nurturing environment of the Jewish college, the Jewish student would not need to study this subject at the university and "need not waste his days and years in a university among Christians in sinful neglect of Jewish studies."[29] The combination of sacred and profane disciplines was not limited to this collegiate experiment, as several of the important chronicles such as that of David Gans and Azariah de' Rossi discussed in chapter 4 indicate.

Jewish engagement with the non-Jewish world led to Jewish adaption of non-Jewish ideas and practices. Let's consider one curious example of acculturation from south Germany, the *Hollekreisch* ceremony. In one of his responsa, the fifteenth-century Rabbi Moses Mintz wrote,

> For after the parturient who gave birth to a girl leaves her house, it is a custom to name the baby, and that naming is called *Hollekreisch*. I heard a reason from my father, may his memory be blessed, who heard from his mentors, that the meaning of *Hollekreisch* is that they cry out at that time to the [female] baby a not holy name and the same for a baby boy. For example, if the "holy" name is Samuel and the *hol* name is Zanvil, they call him Zanvil at that time etc. . . . . And *Hollekreisch* is made up of two words, *Holle* from *hol* and *kreisch*, meaning "to cry out." In other words, the *shem hol* is cried out and announced, for in the language of Lower Ashkenaz they call a cry *kreisch*.[30]

An early version of this curious custom is mentioned in the twelfth-century *Sefer Hasidim* (Book of the Pious), the thirteenth-century collection *Or Zarua* (Sown Light), Rabbi Jacob Weil's (fifteenth-century) responsa, and the seventeenth-century customs book of Juspa Hahn of Nördlingen, *Sefer Yosef Ometz*. In varying explanations, the term *hol* refers to the Hebrew term for profane and *kreisch* refers to the German for cradle or crying.

The custom has no apparent grounding in Jewish tradition, however, a similar custom was regnant among Christians during the fifteenth century, especially in south Germany. The custom was based on myths associated with a figure known as Frau Holle, a Germanic demoness known for abducting children and as something like a fertility goddess. The Christian custom was remarkably similar to the Jewish one described above.[31] Outlawed by the Christian Church in the sixteenth century, in the midst of major persecutions of alleged witches, the ceremony continued in Jewish circles, especially in south Germany well into the nineteenth century. The

Christian content and context of the ceremony, however, were stripped over time and acculturated into Jewish ritual. What is more, because of seeming parallels between Frau Holle and Lilith (of rabbinic lore), the ritual became in a sense "inherently" Jewish.[32]

It is important here, as elsewhere, to note as the historian Ivan Marcus points out that there can be a difference between Jewish culture and the actual behavior and practices of individual Jews. Sub-cultures, to use Marcus' phrase, existed and sometimes competed with one another.[33] In addition to the more obvious borrowings we have just witnessed, consider, for example, that Jews in northern Europe during the fifteenth century began to inscribe the dates of their children's births in a family Bible, a practice just emerging among Christians as well.[34] In Germany, there developed the practice of giving the father of new baby boys the honor of being called to the Torah and the use of an embroidered cloth, or wimple, to be used for holding the baby during his *brit milah*, which appears to have had some similarities with Christian baptism cloths.[35] The institution of deathbed confessions among early modern Italian Jews also seems to have mirrored nearby Christian practices.[36]

Innovative Tradition

But Jews did not simply acculturate to their surroundings.[37] Early modern Jews themselves developed a range of religious practices, often with very specific local or regional foci and variations. For example, while it had been a long-standing custom for Jews to make a pilgrimage to holy graves a month after the holiday of Passover, Jews entering the Ottoman Empire from Spain altered the practice. Instead of visiting the graves of the Palestinian sages Hillel and Shammai, they visited the grave of Rabbi Shimon bar Yohai, the individual assumed at the time to be the author of the mystical treatise the *Zohar*. Not only that, but some leading mystics, such as Rabbi Isaac Luria began to visit the grave on other special occasions or festivals as well. Other customs also developed. For example, on *Lag b-Omer*, Rabbi Solomon Luria cut his son's hair for the first time, inaugurating a now long-standing tradition.[38] To give some additional examples, while the bar mitzvah has become widespread and commonly known in our own day, the roots of much of the practice developed in early modern Germany, expanding an earlier and not fully disseminated practice, which even when it did exist did not amount to much of a life cycle event.[39] The modern-day *huppah* was in the Middle Ages nothing more than a head covering for the bride and groom; its translation into a wedding canopy was something of an innovation noted by Rabbi Moses Isserles in Poland in the sixteenth century.[40]

FORMS OF INTERACTION

Jews and non-Jews often lived in close proximity and had significant business relationships. At times there is evidence of important and long-standing social interaction. In early modern Poland, for example, friendships developed and Jews and Poles socialized, cultivated business partnerships, protected their towns together, and even traveled together.[41] Notarial documents from across the early modern world reveal various levels and types of business interactions and partnerships between Jews and between Jews and non-Jews. To give only one example, consider the case of Hayyim Saruq, a colorful personality who was active throughout the Mediterranean area in the sixteenth century. Saruq was known for patronage of Jewish printing, in addition to his political and economic roles. He imported a wide range of goods from the Ottoman Empire, and he was also involved in the purchase or ownership of various small- and medium-sized sea vessels.[42] But Saruq was involved with both Jewish and non-Jewish business partners in Venice, Constantinople, Ferrara, and Ancona. In some areas of Germany during the Thirty Years' War, some Jews fared well, and in some cases Jews succeeded as provisioners, middlemen, and court factors.

Perhaps one of the reasons leading to the readmission of the Jews to England in the mid-seventeenth century was economic. The strong medieval Jewish community in England was suddenly expelled in 1290. Despite the occasional presence of Jews in business, and perhaps the existence of secret communities of Jews, over the next three and a half centuries there was no formal Jewish presence in England. One of the vivacious Jewish rabbis of Amsterdam, Menasseh ben Israel, lobbied and petitioned (partially in a millenarian vein) in 1655 for the readmission of the Jews. He called for the readmission of the Jews; the establishment of public synagogues, cemeteries, and internal Jewish courts; and trading licenses.[43] Menasseh argued that the Jews possessed three very important qualities useful for the regent, namely, profit, fidelity, and nobleness.[44] While Menasseh himself did not live to see the Jews formally return to England, they were readmitted shortly after his petition.

Throughout the early modern period there is a good deal of evidence of close social relations between Jews and others. In the area of sexual encounters, for example, a wide range of evidence in both Christian court and Jewish communal sources can be found relating to Jewish male relations with non-Jewish females.[45] In parts of Italy, despite legislation to the contrary by both the Jewish and Italian courts, such interactions assumed a certain anticipated normalcy. In the late fifteenth-century *condotta*, or charter, Jewish bankers had it stipulated that they could not be imprisoned for more than five days if they were caught having relations with Christian women.[46]

As the historian of Italy Elliot Horowitz notes, there are several cases of such interactions taking place in the homes of Jewish procuresses, some of which were located within the Jewish ghetto.[47]

Jews and non-Jews also encountered one another throughout their daily lives and even in synagogues. Numerous ordinances from the early modern period forbid the entry of Gentiles to synagogues. In London, in 1664, for example, communal legislation ordained, "From this day henceforth no *Yahid* (individual congregant) of this *Kahal Kados* (holy community) may bring them to it, nor rise, nor move from his place to receive them, nor [persons] of any other nation that may be, in order to accompany them, or give them place."[48] It is clearly not possible to generalize the nature of daily social interaction between Jews and their non-Jewish neighbors. What can be said, however, is that based on many different historical sources such interaction was likely much more frequent and at times much more normalized than previous historical accounts or limited preserved historical sources have traditionally led us to believe.

External Religious Development and the Jews

In some parts of western Europe, notably Spain and parts of France and Italy, the early modern period witnessed a consolidation of traditional religious authority. In some cases, as in Iberia in the fifteenth century, such consolidation led to attempts to create a certain degree of religious homogeneity, culminating with the final push of Muslims out of the peninsula, the suppression of some heretical and rebel groups, and the expulsion of the Jews. In other parts of western Europe, the Protestant Reformation shattered the centuries-long homogeneity of the Christian Church. The Reformation, building from various late medieval religious developments, entailed more than simply theology. It also encouraged a wide range of social, political, and cultural transformations. According to famous sociological theories, it fundamentally altered economic development as well. It remains an open question whether or not the Reformation in the West led to the secularization and modernization that is frequently ascribed to it. There is no doubt, however, that the Reformation loosened some social and religious bonds, encouraged the questioning of established tradition, and gave new impetus to local and vernacular developments. It also fundamentally altered the function and status of the clergy, who were seen in some ways more now as moral guides and overseers rather than mediators with God. Whether directly or indirectly these trends seem to have spilled into and affected Jewish communities and Jewish discussions of authority as well.

A movement often associated with the Reformation was **"confessionalization."** Confessionalization was the creation of orthodoxies, of confessions, according to which people's lives and beliefs would be shaped. Confessionalization has been linked with the development of social discipline, but at its heart it reflected the fracturing of western European religious cultures between different denominations. Lutherans and other Protestants agreed about some Church reforms but disagreed about many others as well. In addition to Martin Luther (1483–1546), there was a wide range of important reformers, including some in the Catholic tradition, who considered various aspects of Judaism, and to some extent the Jews, in their theological discussions.

In recent years there has been a marked attempt to dislodge Martin Luther from the center of the "Reformation." Nevertheless, Luther's position regarding the Jews has remained critical. This is due in part to the large volume of Luther's writings on the Jews, in which he discussed Jews primarily as a historical people. But it is also due in part to the persistence of a perceived "*Sonderweg*" (special path of development) between the thought and recommendations of Luther regarding the Jews and the historical events since the sixteenth century, particularly the Holocaust.

Luther's vision of the Jews was largely theological and rhetorical in nature. Jews formed part of a devilish group subverting the true Church, which also helped indicate the end of days. For Luther, Jews of ancient Israel were markedly different from contemporary Jews, however, who, Luther argued, were not really Jews at all. In fact, for Luther it might be more appropriate to view Catholics or Protestants as Jews, God's new Chosen People. What is more, the concept of the Jew is largely a foil for Luther's attacks on his own society. Even in his later blandishments against contemporary Jews, Luther uses the Jews to strike out against those who he believes misuse their authority.

It has been noted that Luther's attitude toward the Jews seems to become more radical after 1538, and particularly so in his last works. It is worth pointing out, however, that Luther's later writings are highly polemical and directed against all his enemies (including the Devil, Turks, papists, radical reformers, etc.) not just the Jews; and that his later writings, for all their harshness and bitter vindictiveness, continue his earlier theological issues very logically. Still, in his early writings, Luther held out the hope of mass Jewish conversion to his religion; by the end of his life he saw this was not to be, and his anti-Jewish writing became more violent. Nonetheless, there were important continuities in Luther's thinking about the Jews.

Like other reformers, radical Protestant reformers used discussions of biblical Israel for contemporary Christian purposes. Casting themselves as the new Israelites and their resident cities as New Jerusalems, Protestants displaced Jews and, much like earlier Christian exegetes, interpreted the Old Testament in Christological fashion, focusing not on the historical Israelites but on the moral lessons to be learned from them.

Of course, there was something of a flip side to this argument. Some reformers could be more tolerant and ecumenical, even if their primary goal remained the conversion of the Jews and the supposedly accompanying Second Coming of Christ. A certain inner spirituality or piety prevailed in some circles leading to a somewhat ecumenical outlook. The radical early sixteenth-century Sebastian Franck, for example, argued in his *Paradoxa*, "Who is in one city is in the entire world; although he finds different customs, languages and clothing, the nature, heart, and the senses and the will are the same in all. All men are one Man, the difference is only external, in countenance and appearance before the world; the inner truth is with them all one and the same."[49]

In France, Isaac La Peyrere (1594–1676), famous for his biblical criticism, and at times accused of atheism, argued,

> The argument whereby Christians, by persecuting Jews, only wish to be of service to a similar excuse, that they thought they were serving God when they crucified Jesus Christ. That is why both the Jews and ourselves have substantial reason to pray to God to forgive us for our hidden faults and our unknown sins. . . . The Jews for the sin they have committed against Jesus Christ. The Gentiles, for the sin they are committing against the Jews. The one and the other sin both committed inadvertently, because of an impetuous zeal which quite often carries us to evil under the appearance of good.

In something of a messianic tone, Peyrere predicted the end of the Jews' exile.

> The latter day Jews will no longer have this black and swarthy skin color they have acquired during the Exile from the injuries of both time and men. They will change faces within this Recall, and the whiteness of their complexion will shine the same way, as the Psalmist says, as the wings, and the breast of a pigeon, an extremely white one at that. The Jews will no longer smell of mouldiness, nor of staleness. Their breath will be all sweetness. Only musk and amber will exude from their clothes and their sweat.[50]

It should be pointed out that even such "positive" and tolerant attitudes were underpinned by a basic anti-Jewish sensibility and sought primarily the conversion of the Jews.

For many others, the Jews and Judaism remained a target of negative perception. Later thinkers extended some of the anti-Jewish thought of the later Middle Ages and Reformation period. In Germany one of the most influential such figures was Johannes Eisenmenger (1654–1704). Eisenmenger rehashed older accusations of Jews murdering Christian children and well poisoning. He relied on information from converts and argued that one cannot suppose that all such accusations are untrue.

Catholics also engaged the Jews largely for apologetic purposes in battling the reformers. Indeed, Catholics frequently decried reformers as Judaizers and "rabbis."[51] The Catholic position developed from traditional medieval teachings on the Jews and the Old Testament but was also supplemented with developments from specific local contexts. In Poland, for example, one recent scholar identifies two trends in Catholic clerical attitudes toward Jews. On the one hand were the general polemic against the Talmud and Jewish exegesis as well as defense of traditional Christian notions of messianism and **supercession**. Yet, even in this context, Jews were not blamed for the death of Jesus, which was instead attributed to Christian sins. On the other hand, there also existed general support for the proliferation of blood libel accusations, general religious polemic, and later efforts at the conversion of the Jews.[52] It appears in general that there were few concerted attempts to curb anti-Jewish sentiment among the Catholic clergy in Poland until the seventeenth century,[53] when the position of the Jews began to become more favorable and expand dramatically.

Throughout much of the early modern period, however, the majority of Jews lived in the world of Islam. Under Islam, the position of the Jews remained similar to that noted for the Middle Ages in chapter 1. Violent actions and anti-Jewish feeling erupted from time to time, as Jews were seen as becoming too prominent or as having too much religious freedom.[54] In addition, just as religious extremism at times surfaced in North Africa and the Middle East during the Middle Ages, it also occurred at times during the early modern period. Indeed, by the end of the seventeenth century, the position of the Jews even within the Ottoman Empire had begun to decline in some significant ways.[55]

Even at the apex of the Jewish experience under Islam, certain basic inequalities were the norm. Jews were, as protected people, to enjoy certain rights, but they remained second-class citizens (*dhimmis*) as they had been throughout the Middle Ages. As an order to the Qadi of Istanbul from 1568 makes clear, Jewish life was to have very circumscribed boundaries:

> Whereas you sent a letter to my Threshold of Felicity, in which you informed me that Jewish and Christian men and women, among the infidels residing in the God-guarded city of Istanbul, are wearing garments of fine, fringed cloth, buying fine turbans and binding them in the style of cavalry officers and the like, wearing kaftans of atlas and cotton and other fine cloths, and adopting the same kind of shoes and slippers as Muslims, with the result that the prices of turbans, cloths, and footwear has risen beyond reach, and in which you requested that infidels be prevented from dressing like Muslims. . . .
>
> Therefore I now command that when this present [decree] arrives, you proceed in accordance with my previously sent imperial decree, and ensure that henceforth neither Jew nor Christian nor any other infidel be allowed to wear

fine clothes, as set forth above, and in contravention of my previously issued noble command.[56]

Carried out to the full letter of the Law, Islamic ruling about Jews (and Christians) could result in severe handicaps and degradation for the minority religions. As appears even from the decree above, often such strict application was lacking, and especially under Ottoman suzerainty, Jews enjoyed a good deal of freedom and opportunity.

Buttressed by traditional Islamic law, however, the position of the Jews could vary greatly depending upon the attitudes and policies of regional governors, influential clerics, and even the sultan. Severe limitations on Jews, for example, were articulated during the reigns of Bayezid II in the late fifteenth century and Murad III in the last quarter of the sixteenth century. The attitudes of these rulers, of course, were shaped by a myriad of political and economic, in addition to religious, conditions.[57]

The Political and Legal Position of the Jews

The political and legal position of the Jews could vary dramatically over time and by region. Theoretical rights and restrictions were balanced by practical discrimination and toleration, so that the position of the Jews was complicated and quickly changeable. Let's consider a few examples, from Germany and Poland under Christian rule and from Iran and the Ottoman Empire in Muslim lands.

Jews were often subject to multiple authorities. In Germany, for example, imperial, princely, civic, and Church authorities often jockeyed for control over the Jews residing in their areas and, more importantly, the revenues to be gathered from taxes paid by the Jews. The Jews often served as scapegoats or as pawns in escalating political tensions in different regions and under different political and religious environments. When, for example, city authorities contested princely authority, Jews under princely protection were targets of aggression directed at the princes.

The status of the Jews depended heavily upon local religion and politics. In Braunschweig in central Germany, for example, the declining position of the Jews in the later Middle Ages was further worsened by tensions surrounding the introduction and expansion of the Protestant Reformation in the city. The anti-Jewish teaching of Luther had, in a sense, been internalized within some circles in the city, resulting in greater marginalization of the Jews and finally their expulsion in 1546.

In Hesse, in Germany, the position of the Jews was greatly affected by the religious, economic, and political concerns of Landgrave Philip. Early in his career, at the beginning of the 1520s, Philip had sought the expulsion of the Jews in his lands. In the 1530s he sought out clerical advice about whether to tolerate the Jews. Rebutting the clerical advice not to tolerate the Jews, Philip argued that the Jews were "a noble race, from which even Christ, our Savior, was born in the flesh; so are the Apostles come from such a race, which race also is confident that God has saved it." He concluded,

> We do not find it in the Holy Scriptures or in the New Testament that we should treat the Jews so badly and could perhaps, therefore in the meantime, tolerate the Jews above all the other unbelievers, as did the old Christian emperors and bishops; but all under the condition that the Lord may also want to alleviate (as indeed the learned advice also says) his old people, and He supports us so that we be from the wild olive tree grafted in the natural branches. Therefore the Jews are above other unbelievers in order because they willingly love the Father, even if they are enemy to the Evangelist.[58]

Philip allowed the Jews to be tolerated for one or two more years; at that point, based on the Jews' behavior, he would decide whether or not to tolerate them longer in his lands. Philip then promulgated an eleven-article ordinance, the net effect of which was to strengthen restrictions against the Jews, while maintaining their ability to participate in the financial well-being of the territory. Simultaneously, the ordinance outlined how Jewish business dealings were to be administered.

While anti-Jewish stimulus throughout much of the early modern period seems to have come from the town dwellers and the common folk, there are many instances of clerical agitation against the Jews as well as anti-Jewish legislation supported by the city rulers, princes, or even kings. At a Diet in 1534, for example, the Polish Crown asserted,

> One should inhibit the Jews' unrestrained license in trading, which is most pernicious for all classes in the realm. For it has come to pass that almost all business is falling into Jewish hands. They [the Jews] adulterate all goods, especially those intended for human consumption, and in doing business with foreign lands—which no Christian is allowed to do—defraud the customs and the Treasury of our most benevolent king. There is no place which the Jews do not penetrate. Traveling to Walachia, they buy up cattle, skins, and other objects of this kind which they export outside Poland, from which arises the great scarcity of all wares here. . . . Nor are they of any use to the Commonwealth and contribute nothing to its defense. Let them display distinguishing marks according to custom. If stolen objects are found in their possession they should restore them to the owners and not enjoy therein any preferential treatment over the Christians, since they themselves are often responsible for the thefts.[59]

In other places in the early modern period, there is evidence that Jews were more favorably viewed for their service to the ruling authorities. In the late sixteenth century, the Jews of Cracow were praised for assisting the royal household during a fire, for example.[60] Indeed, much favorable legislation coexisted with the legal restrictions we have already encountered. Particularly by the end of the sixteenth century, Polish Jews seemed to have achieved more favorable status and gained some rights in court, rather extensive freedom of movement, and some freedoms related to religious worship.[61] In 1570, the Jews of Luck, for example, were granted similar rights as citizens, including the exemption from Lithuanian tolls.[62] Just as in Germany and other parts of Europe, in Poland, the legal position of the Jews could vary greatly due to local autonomy and custom as well as the at times ineffectual reach of more centralized government.

There are cases of Polish Jews taking nobles to court for slander or defamation in the early fifteenth century.[63] Polish Jews were allowed to bear arms, and in the seventeenth century were at times required to fortify their synagogues.[64] Jews took up arms with other burghers against the Cossacks—and there seems to be evidence of Jews or recently converted Jews joining the Cossack forces in some places.[65] In Poland, the Jewish oath was not preceded by derogatory language, as it was in Germany, where often Jews were forced to stand on a pigskin while taking the oath.[66]

The legal standing of Jews in Poland was founded on medieval precedents and developments. Throughout much of Poland Jews seem to have enjoyed a status akin to freemen (with settlement rights) and even nobles.[67] The 1264 Statute on Jewish Liberties in Poland, which was replicated and minimally expanded throughout the fifteenth and into the sixteenth century, illustrates the generally favorable, if often theoretically disadvantaged, legal position of the Jews in the later Middle Ages and into the early modern period. The statute is very similar in many regards to others from western Europe. At times the specific details were ignored, as more increasingly happened in the West, but nonetheless the Statute reveals that the Jews were relatively well tolerated and recognized, explaining perhaps why, despite some significant early modern attacks and setbacks, the Jewish population in Poland became dominant in world Jewry by the end of our period.

The Statute opens with a law that, in any court case involving a Jew, whether regarding property or crime, "if any Christian should accuse any of the Jews in any matter whatsoever, even a criminal matter, he shall not be admitted to testimony except with two good Christians and also with two good Jews."[68] These individuals must be of good repute with no criminal record, and they must swear on their holy scriptures, respectively. In a similar case, if a Christian sues a Jew over a security held by the Jew, stating that it was taken from him through robbery or larceny, the Jew may respond with an oath "as to the sum for which the security was pawned, and with the Jew having made expurgation, the Christian shall be obliged to pay over in reality and with effect the principal money for which the security was pawned, and also the interest accruing from the time of the obligation."[69]

In what appears as an even more remarkable piece of legislation, but was also fairly common in the high and later Middle Ages in western Europe, we find a discussion about what happens in the event that a Christian kills a Jew. The ordinance declares, "If the Jew next of kin to the slain Jew over-swears the Christian on the scroll of the Ten Commandments according to the custom of the Jews, then we will and ordain that such a Christian thus oversworn by the Jew must be punished with the imposition of death, a head for a head, and it is not to be done otherwise in this matter."[70]

Here and elsewhere the legal position of the Jews was theoretically rather strong. In general, Jews were not brought before ecclesiastical courts in cases with Christians.[71] The Statutes also condemned the accusations of Jewish ritual murder and host desecration. Article 39 stated, "We ordain by decree that [if] any Jew is to be prosecuted by any Christian alleging that the Jews of necessity annually use the blood of Christians of the sacraments of the Church of the Christians, concerning which the statutes and constitutions of Pope Innocent teach us that in such matters they are not culpable, since this is against their own law."[72] If nonetheless the accusation is brought, the Christian must support it with the testimony of three good propertied Jews "who are not infamous in character and are firm in faith."[73]

The Statute also regulated a certain level of order and authority within the Jewish community itself. Article 11 noted, "Likewise, if any of the Jews is not obedient to his own superiors, then he must pay to the lord palatine a penalty of three marks, and to the superiors a similar penalty of three marks."[74] Jews were allowed free and secure travel and were responsible for regular tolls, "just as other Christians," but nothing else.[75] Jewish homes and property were protected.[76] Synagogues were also protected from reproach, and any Christian who jeered at the synagogue was to pay the palatine a fine.[77]

Even though Jews at times experienced positive legislation under both Christian and Muslim overlords, throughout the early modern period Jews were also subject to discriminatory legislation as well. While the Jews in the Ottoman Empire often enjoyed privileges and a degree of communal freedom, Jews around the Muslim world were also persecuted. Under Shah Abbas II in Iran, Jews were forced to convert and also subjected to a wide range of regulations, barring them from having shops in the bazaar, having their oaths admissible in court, taking cover in alleyways, or wearing fine clothing.[78] A seventeenth-century Persian Jewish poet lamented the conversion and oppression of these Jews:

> We are devoid of glory and of the Torah . . .
> Although we are apparently Muslims, within our hearts we are Jews.
> Verily we do not resemble in any way the Muslims . . .
> We all feign to believe when we act as Muslims . . .

We are helpless and ailing, we have fallen upon misfortune;
It is on account of oppression that we have delivered our souls to the faith of
   the Muslims . . .
It is time to free us from the Muslim faith . . .
A thousand times, at every moment, we curse Islam . . .
Our heart and soul delight not, when we must act as Muslims . . .
They expelled us from the town [probably Isfahan] and acted toward us with
   violence;
They have made us Muslims through violence . . .
Cup after cup, I drink poison from the hand of Islam;
O that I might drink cup upon cup of wine from the hand of Judaism![79]

The restrictions and taxes imposed on Jews (and other non-Muslims, such
as Christians as well) were deemed throughout the early modern period as
a great yoke. One kabbalist from Safed noted at the end of the sixteenth
century,

> Perhaps this is an allusion to the situation that prevails in our times, for there
> is no town in the [Ottoman] empire in which the Jews are subjected to such
> heavy taxes and dues as in the Land of Israel, and particularly in Jerusalem.
> . . . The nations humiliate us to such an extent that we are not allowed to
> walk in the streets. The Jew is obliged to step aside in order to let the Gentile
> [Muslim] pass first. And if the Jew does not turn aside of his own will, he is
> forced to do so.[80]

As in Europe, Jews under Ottoman reign were subjected to heavy financial
milking. In early seventeenth-century Fez, it was rued, "Who can write the
story of our sorrow? There are taxes every day—it cannot all be told. For the
King's decrees concern only the Jews."[81] Under the threat of expulsion or
worse, Jews were forced to pay a variety of regular and extraordinary taxes.
   Jews were also persecuted in the wake of the Shabbetai Sevi debacle. We
find the following account of persecution in the Yemen in 1666:

> Then the heads of the community were imprisoned in the fortress of King
> Isma'il, after which they were taken out and brought to the torture chamber,
> where they were exposed in the hot sun. Thereupon they were stripped naked
> and hung up in the sun at the entrance to the palace in front of all the [Mus-
> lims] who passed by. These cried out, "Forsake your faith; of what use is it to
> you!"[82]

Nevertheless, Jews did have some level of security, even if as second-class
citizens and at times in tenuous positions. In 1577, for example, the Jews of
Safed petitioned the Sultan for redress from persecution by local officials,
who apparently were forcing the Jews to work on Saturday and to pay excessive amounts of tax. The Jews were also not protected from home inva-

sion by robbers, and some had been detained in prison on false charges. The Sultan called for the situation to be investigated.[83]

Still, Jews living under Ottoman suzerainty at times received state protection and even, in special cases, certain legal tax exemptions. Jews were willing and often did use the Ottoman courts, despite rabbinic and communal prohibitions.[84] As Rabbi Samuel de Medina (1506–1589) noted around midcentury, "This realm is wide open without a wall . . . and everyone anxious to do so may come in and attend to his business. . . . We Jews live under [a] sovereign who imposes no restrictions on travel or on commercial activities on his subjects."[85]

The Portuguese Jewish chronicler Samuel Usque, who wrote in the form of something of a pastoral consolation, highlighted the tragedies of Jewish history and especially the persecutions and dispersions affecting the Portuguese Jews. He had generally positive things to say about the fate of the Jews living in Ottoman lands, however. The Jews in Constantinople in 1542, for example, managed to survive false accusations that they killed a Turk. Of Salonika, Usque noted, "The majority of my children who have been persecuted and exiled from Europe and many other parts of the world have taken refuge in this city, and she embraces them and receives them with as much love and good will as if she were Jerusalem [metaphorically speaking], that old and ever pious mother of ours."[86]

In late medieval Yemen, the protection of Jews and their religious practices, especially their Sabbath observance, was linked to stories that Jews supported Muhammad in battle. The prophet was said to have decreed, "I shall grant you my protection, my covenant, my oath, and my witness to those who come after me."[87] The Jews were to be protected from "shame, insult, abuse, accusation of wrong-doing, and any disgrace." They were to have security in the market places, and they were not to forsake their religion, desecrate their Sabbath, or be prevented from praying in their synagogues or attending their schools and ritual baths.[88]

Likewise, an Italian Jew, David dei Rossi, described his travels in the Ottoman Empire during the sixteenth century. According to him, in Safed,

> The Exile here is not like in our homeland. The Turks hold respectable Jews in esteem. Here and in Alexandria, Egypt, Jews are the chief officers and administrators of the customs, and the king's revenues. No injuries are perpetrated against them in all the empire. Only this year, in consequence of the extraordinary expenditure caused by the war against Shah Tahmsap al-Sufi, were the Jews required to make advances of loans to the princes.[89]

As the early modern period progressed, particularly by the late sixteenth century, some scholars have maintained that a certain economic openness and mercantilism developed in Europe as well, allowing for more positive treatment and integration of the Jews.[90] A certain philo-semitism, albeit with real limitations, seems to have arisen during the course of the seventeenth century in parts of western Europe.[91] In many places Jewish populations developed or stabilized, and under watchful civic or regional eyes, Jewish business was allowed to develop in new ways. In Poland, Jews and Christians clearly interacted at the important trade fairs in Lublin,[92] and Jews throughout central Europe were also granted access to a host of fairs by the seventeenth century. Old anti-Jewish measures and sensibilities continued to pervade Jewish and non-Jewish relations, both theoretically and very frequently practically as well. At the same time, the period also witnessed the opening of some new opportunities for Jews, especially economically but to some extent socially as well, indicating that Jewish life might be able to take seed and grow in ways that had not before been possible.

Anti-Judaism

Despite important examples of tolerance and positive, if at times ambiguous, legal possibilities for Jews, the early modern period remained fundamentally anti-Jewish. In the West, Jews were accused of many crimes and in the East Jews remained second-class citizens.

Anti-Semitism was a late nineteenth-century concept, probably first used by the German Wilhelm Marr and other social scientists, who combined political, social, and pseudo-scientific ideas in an effort to separate Jews from civil society. Steeped in an intellectual environment in which Darwinistic notions of evolution were applied to human development, anti-Semitism was part and parcel of political thinking that differentiated human potential and status based on racial background. For the early modern period there were certainly some instances where Jews were seen as a separate race. Consider, for example, the purity of blood laws in the fifteenth century, in which familial background helped to determine civic status, or in late fifteenth- and sixteenth-century political and religious thought that cast the Jews as a unique, and inferior, race and used degrading and dehumanizing images to describe Jews. Nonetheless, anti-Semitism is largely an anachronistic concept for the early modern period. It is better to speak of anti-Judaism, which focuses on negative representations of Jews because of their religious beliefs and practices.

Whether we call it anti-Semitism or anti-Judaism, however, there are many explanations for anti-Jewish sentiment and behavior. Socio-psychological explanations focus on concepts of projected guilt and displaced aggression, the search for a scapegoat. Ethnic explanations associated marginalization, or negative representation of the Other, with perceived ethnic differences. Xenophobia ascribes anti-Jewish sentiment to broader concern over minority groups within a national or regional identity. Some scholars have posited that anti-Jewish sentiment, especially that which ascribed to

Jews ritual murder, was simply chimerical. These accusations had no basis in reality and were never actually observed but had developed into complex myths. By the end of the sixteenth century traditional accusations of host desecration and ritual murder seem to have declined precipitously, even if they would rear their head again in later centuries.

Some explanations, however, focus on alleged Jewish guilt. According to this idea, there did exist Jewish guilt for certain crimes at times, and this helps to explain why Jews were perceived poorly. Similarly, based on biblical concepts, both Jews and Christians, and to some extent Muslims as well, might posit eternal hatred between Jacob and Esau, representing Judaism and Christianity respectively, or Isaac and Ishmael, representing Judaism and Islam.

What we can say for certain is that some expressions of anti-Judaism seem to have been trans-historical, spanning different chronologies and geographical confines. In part, the Jewish concept of chosenness and separation could lead to charges of misanthropy and plotting, as they did since late Antiquity.[93] Yet some anti-Jewish expression was very much dependent upon specific conditions and could arise very differently depending on a variety of circumstances.

The anti-Jewish trends that were evident throughout Spain at the end of the fourteenth and the beginning of the fifteenth centuries are quite clear in the case of the city of Tortosa.[94] In 1346 the local cemetery was profaned, and Jews frequently suffered attacks during Holy Week (in fact, prohibitions against injuring Jews during this week had to be issued in 1369). The preaching against Jews in Tortosa was particularly virulent as a result of the disputations held in the city between 1413 and 1414 and volatile sermons against the Jews in the 1420s. Such sermons roused the local population to anti-Jewish behavior and brought about a high number of Jewish converts to Christianity. Jews could suffer at the hands of secular authorities as well. Throughout the fourteenth and fifteenth centuries we find significant emigration from royal to baronial domains by Jews seeking to avoid excessive taxation.[95]

Host desecration accusations, like the accusations of the desecration of other Christian symbols and images, were fueled by anti-Jewish sermons, popular writings, and illustrated broadsheets that circulated widely and that sent the message to the populace that could not read. Much like the modern-day comic strips, these illustrated images presented a full story, from the Jews purchasing the host, to their attempts to destroy and torture it, and their machinations whereby they sent it to other foreign Jewish communities for the same purpose. Inevitably, the illustrations also highlighted the host protecting itself, the Jews being brought to justice, and the creation of shrines or pilgrimage spots to mark the alleged miracles performed. In Passau, in southern Germany, in 1478, for example, the story was told of a certain "wanton and desperate fellow" who was "unmindful of his soul's salvation and lusting for temporal goods" and therefore brought the host to the Jews. The Jews, for their part, are described as "enemies and blasphemers of the crucified true, living God and of Mary his mother." As the text explains, "The Jews—blasphemers of God—kept the Hosts and skeptically brought them to their synagogue, seized hold of the body of Christ with their sinful hands in order to crucify him with savage eagerness and thus to test the Christian faith." In the end, the Jews were captured. Four converted to Christianity, and their penalty was relegated to death by sword as opposed to those more obstinate Jews who were burned, torn with pincers, and then burned alive.[96]

Throughout late medieval and early modern Europe Jews were accused of desecrating the Eucharist.[97] This host desecration, it was argued, simultaneously proved the deviance of the Jews—who allegedly attacked the host as if they were attacking Christ directly, either through stabbing or burning it—and demonstrated that the Jews secretly believed that which they denounced. Namely, they themselves believed the consecrated host to have changed into the body of Jesus, hence their malignant response to it. The host desecration charges allowed clerics to raise a morally upbraiding finger at Christians as well, for in these host desecration narratives it was generally through the assistance of a wayward Christian that the Jews obtained the host. It should be pointed out that, through much of this period, the Eucharist, which was established as a sacrament only at the beginning of the thirteenth century, was still not seen as "piously" as it might have been and certainly as the Church may have wanted it to be. As one skeptical modern historian notes, common Christians might sequester the host to their plot of land where they would grind it over their crops, expecting that it contained some kind of magical elixir to help them grow.[98]

In Europe, Jews were also accused of poisoning wells and ritual murder. According to the latter accusation, Jews kidnapped or bought Christian children in order to murder them and use their blood for their religious rituals. Important blood libels in Germany were played out in Endingen (1470), Regensburg (1476), Passau (1477), and Brandenburg (1520), for example. There were numerous charges of blood libel and the profanation of Christian religious objects throughout early modern Poland. More than thirty have been identified from the middle of the sixteenth through the end of the seventeenth centuries.[99] Such accusations were not unknown in Muslim lands. There is evidence of at least eighty such libels in the Ottoman Empire between the fifteenth and nineteenth centuries. Generally, such accusations were played out in areas with large Christian populations and when Christian children disappeared.[100]

While accusations of host desecration and ritual murder originated earlier in the Middle Ages, each developed further in the later Middle Ages and early modern period. The most famous case of ritual murder accusation was that of Simon of Trent, in northern Italy. That story and the subsequent re-narrations of it, including the canonization of the young victim, Simon, had a long-lasting and at times devastating effect on the Jews. According to the folksong that circulated in Germany and other places, the Jews in 1475, in their great need for Christian blood, sent for a Christian child. As in many of the cases of host desecration, a disgruntled Christian arrived in the Jewish quarter with the goods, a pious son of a cobbler. The "contemptuous Jews" then tortured and murdered the boy. The Jews allegedly used the boy's blood to bake their (Passover) bread, which was then distributed to many lands. In the end, the Jews were apprehended and brought to justice; they were punished for their use of innocent blood, and miracles occurred in the name of the martyred Simon. The accusation focused on the Jews' alleged criminal and devious acts. At the same time the accounts of the ritual murder indicted certain marginal Christians who were supposed to have assisted the Jews.

Another infamous ritual murder trial revolved around the Holy Child of La Guardia. Six Spanish *conversos* and two Jews were tried beginning in 1490 and, in late 1491, after various confessions under torture, were burned at the stake. The highly diverging confessions supposedly revealed host desecration and the murder of a Christian child (never found) in the service of Jewish sorcery. The alleged conspiracy of Jews and *conversos* no doubt inflamed already elevated tensions and concerns about alleged collusion between the two groups. The entire episode took on dramatic dimensions with the quick and lasting reverence paid to the Holy Child and the persistence of the story in a variety of literature throughout the early modern period.

Some scholars, most notably the historian R. Po-chia Hsia, have argued that the frequency of ritual murder accusations declined in the sixteenth century, in part because of the Reformation.[101] While this may be true, such accusations did continue, and in some areas such as Poland they began to increase in frequency. As with host desecration charges, even in Muslim lands Jews were not completely protected from such allegations.

Anti-Jewish Imagery and Anti-Jewish Accusations

Adding to the sense of sinister behavior was the fact that the Jews worshipped in private in a language that was not understood by most people. The entire image of Jews as a criminal and dangerous people was fed by the segregation both practiced and forced upon the Jews. Jews practiced a different religion, prayed (and often spoke) a different language, had practices that were foreign to those around them, and had connections with other Jews living abroad, making them easily associated with elements that were seen as foreign, secretive, or plotting. In the Christian West Jews were often accused of being in league with the Turks, and their semi-private existence was fodder for many legends such as the previously described myths of ritual murder and host desecration. A common theme in Christian art and literature of the early modern period, as in the Middle Ages, was Jews in the service of the Devil and the Antichrist.

Jews were frequently accused of taking undue and excessive interest on money loaned to Christians, and such accusations could not but stir anti-Jewish sentiment, especially in difficult times. This theme was frequently raised in legal documents as well as inflammatory preaching. According to the preacher Bernard of Sienna, for example,

> Money is the vital heat of a city. The Jews are leeches who ask for nothing better than the opportunity to devour an ailing member, whose blood they suck dry with insatiable ardor. When heat and blood abandon the extremities of the body to flow back to the heart, it is a sign that death is near. But the danger is even more imminent when the wealth of a city is in the hands of the Jews. Then the heat no longer flows, as it does normally, towards the heart. As it does in a plague-ridden body, it moves towards the ailing member of the body; for every Jew, especially if he is a moneylender, is a capital enemy of all Christians.[102]

We do find that some Jews were indeed unscrupulous in their interest taking. On the other hand, in most cases, Jews were allowed significant interest rates, and given the frequency of attacks and the absolution of debts by the non-Jewish governments, apparently excessive interest rates were often justified. That does not, however, change the perception that many commoners may have had, especially as they struggled economically and were forced to deal with Jewish moneylenders, individuals practicing a despised trade on the margins of society. Such concerns over usury or other forms of economic greed were, of course, not limited to Christian lands. In a related sense, in some areas, the Turkish term for miser was used for Jews, and the term Jew was often used in a negative sense in modern language.[103]

Jews were frequently represented visually in derogatory ways. Often gross physical features or demarcating clothing indicated that the individuals represented were Jews. Combined with discourse alleging criminal or deviant acts, such imagery could instill in the minds of the populace great anti-Jewish animosity. Among the most common portrayals of Jews were those that dehumanized the Jews by making them engage in disgusting acts or by associating them with animals. Jews were frequently associated with avarice and greed in many early modern visual representations. It should be noted, however, that certain characteristics were attributed to non-Jews as well. At times Polish noblemen or political figures were cast in similarly greedy veins. Peasants and other marginal individuals were depicted with exaggerated features. Even in the context of religious or political propaganda, various Christian groups could be depicted very similarly to Jews. Jews were frequently associated with pigs, with the infamous image of the *Judensau*, which depicted Jews peering into the anus and eating the defecation of the sow, pointing to alleged inhuman and disgusting acts and a certain disingenuousness from Jews who were known to avoid eating the pig for religious dietary reasons. But there were also polemical caricatures of the pope, as in one common Protestant attack depicting the pope riding a pig and holding a pile of excrement. Jesuits were pictured carrying bulging moneybags, and various Catholic theologians or reformers were depicted as a range of animals or as cronies of the Devil or devilish figures.

The imagery representing Jews in the early modern period is probably not drastically different from much of what existed in the Middle Ages. On the other hand, particularly as we approach the end of the early modern period, we begin to find more neutral or even positive depictions of Jews in some areas. Various Jewish rites and Jewish personalities, for example, were depicted in Italy, Germany, and the Netherlands with little or no animus and often with little indication that the figures represented were even Jews.

More neutral images might have developed because of increasing social and cultural interactions with Jews or the decline of various superstitious accusations against Jews. Jews themselves were perhaps increasingly the patrons of the art being produced and demanded or were accorded a more positive portrayal. Whatever the reasons, such improvements in representation were certainly not universal, and many standard anti-Jewish images and motifs continued to circulate well into modernity.

Persecution

Throughout the early modern period, Jews were subjected to various forms of harassment and violence.[104] Numerous attacks on the Jews were carried out during the sixteenth and seventeenth centuries. The historian Bernard Weinryb identifies more than fifty such attacks in early modern Poland, in a list that is probably not exhaustive.[105] Jews were also subjected to persecution under Islam. The Jews of one district in Syria, for example, were subjected to the extortions of a rebellious governor just as the Jews in Jerusalem suffered the extortions of their governor. Persecution and physical attack were not simply related to state affairs or high politics. In 1617 a convoy of Jewish merchants from Salonika was attacked, robbed, and killed by bandits.[106] Safed was attacked by rebellious Druze and Bedouins from the late sixteenth through the first half of the seventeenth century, and Jews suffered at their hands.[107] Despite general protection from the state, Jews in Ottoman lands did experience attacks by their non-Jewish neighbors, for example, in the Balkans and Anatolia.

Warfare also affected the Jews throughout the early modern world, often wreaking havoc on Jewish communities and claiming individual Jewish lives. Jews in early modern Poland suffered at the hands of robber bands, Polish soldiers, as well as various insurgents.

In Poland-Lithuania in the middle of the seventeenth century, widespread and extremely gruesome massacres of large numbers of Jews took place as part of the broader social revolution led by the infamous Bogdan Chmielnicki, the Cossack leader (1595–1657). The Cossacks attacked ruling authorities and at times associated the Jews with those authorities. Such attacks, of course, were incited by various political, economic, social, and religious agendas. As the Jewish chronicler Nathan of Hannover noted, in describing the massacre in the city of Menirov in Podolia,

> No sooner had the gates been opened than the Cossacks entered with drawn swords, and the townsmen too, with swords, lances, and scythes, and some only with clubs, and they killed the Jews in huge numbers. . . . The number of all those murdered and drowned in the holy community of Nemirov was about 6,000; these met all sorts of terrible deaths, as has already been described.[108]

Whether Nathan's account is completely accurate or exaggerated, massive numbers of Jews were slaughtered, and the event significantly impacted Polish Jewry.

While the great massacres and pogroms of the middle of the seventeenth century are generally featured in discussions of anti-Jewish persecution in Poland, a variety of anti-Jewish attacks, policies, and sentiments occurred long before that time. At least nineteen persecutions of Jews occurred in Poland in the fourteenth and fifteenth centuries, with a noticeable increase in the latter half of the fifteenth century, with concentrations in particular areas.[109] There were Black Death attacks in Cracow and Kalish in 1348–1349. The Jews of Cracow were again attacked in 1360, 1407, 1423, 1454–1455, 1463, 1477, 1494–1495, and 1498–1500. The Jews of Posen also suffered numerous attacks in 1367, 1399 (when a rabbi and thirteen other Jews were burned), 1434, 1447, and 1464. In Warsaw, Jews were attacked in 1455, 1483, and 1498.[110]

The year 1648 did not mark the end of anti-Jewish attacks either, and in fact the period of 1648–1660 is often referred to as the "Deluge." In the mid-1650s, for example, a large number of Jews in Vilna were massacred, perhaps 70 percent of the 1,300 Jewish residents, by the invading Muscovite army.[111]

In fifteenth-century Spain, on the heels of the 1391 persecutions, the position of the Jews was at times precarious. In Valencia, for example, the Jewish quarter was stormed, and more than 200 Jews were killed; most of the other Jews were forced, in spite of royal decrees to the contrary, to convert to Christianity.[112] The pogrom also had serious effects on Jewish property and created general turmoil.[113] In addition, Jews suffered from general assaults and crimes. In Trujillo, for example, cattle were stolen on what seems to be a daily basis from Jewish-owned herds. More seriously, individual Jews traveling were at times abducted and held for ransom. An entire community could be subjected to molestation as well. During the week of Easter in 1486 a faction of Christians cast stones at Jewish houses, causing much damage. Given general concerns about such attacks spiraling into social revolts, the royal authorities appear to have done what they could to stem them.[114]

Traditional anti-Jewish sentiment followed the Jews to the New World. A French Catholic priest visiting Martinique in the early 1660s bemoaned, "The Jews, the biggest and most cruel enemies of Jesus Christ, whom they Crucified, publicly exercise their religion and keep the Sabbath."[115] Jews were in some places and under certain governors permitted to practice their trades and, if out of the public eye, practice their religion as well.[116] Even those who apparently tolerated the Jews for economic reasons might seek their expulsion on the turn of a dime, however. One petition by such an administrator referred back to the "Black Code," a seventeenth-century decree against Jewish settlement:

> We wish and intend that the edict of the late king, of glorious memory . . . of April 23, 1615 [1685?], be implemented in our islands, which enjoins our officers to expel from the Islands all of the Jews who have established residence there, who as declared enemies of Christianity, we order them to depart within three months from the day of publication of the present decree, on pain of confiscation of their person and goods.[117]

Even in somewhat more tolerant political conditions, the plight of the Jews could be severe. In New Amsterdam, later to be known as New York, in 1654 the Dutch West India Company director of New Netherland, Peter Stuyvesant, wrote to the directors of the Amsterdam Chamber of the Company announcing, "The Jews who have arrived here [fleeing the Portuguese in Brazil] would nearly all like to remain here." But, he continues, he learned "that they (with their customary usury and deceitful trading with the Christians) were very repugnant to the inferior magistrates, as also to the people having the most affection for you."[118] He argued that it would be best to turn them away, concluding that they were a "deceitful race," "hateful blasphemers of the name of Christ," and suggesting that they "be not allowed to further infect and trouble this new colony."[119] The Company responded to Stuyvesant indicating that forcing the Jews out would be unfair, and in 1655 it ruled that the Portuguese Jews be allowed to "travel and trade to and in New Netherland and live and remain there, provided the poor among them shall not become a burden to the company of the community, but be supported by their own nation." They were, after all, Dutch subjects. In 1656 it was further ordered that the Jews be granted the same civic and political liberties that they had in the Netherlands but "without the said Jews becoming thereby entitled to a license to exercise and carry on their religion in synagogues or gatherings."[120]

Anti-Jewish activities exploded in the Czech lands in 1541 resulting in pogroms in many places, and the expulsion of the Jews from Bohemia, with the exception of Prague. Though even in Prague, several expulsion attempts surfaced in the middle of the sixteenth century.[121]

Anti-Jewish persecutions could be planned, but they might also be relatively spontaneous. They could erupt in almost any context. In Mantua in 1600 an elderly Jewish woman was burned for allegedly engaging in witchcraft. Two years later, seven Jewish men were hung upside down and eventually executed for allegedly staging a mocking of an itinerant Franciscan within the synagogue.[122]

While Jews generally fared better under Islam, there were embedded anti-Jewish sensibilities that manifested in daily social degradation and that flared up into more overt persecution at times. The poor treatment of Jews in Morocco is described in a document by a French writer from the late seventeenth century. According to this document,

> The Jews are very numerous in Barbary, and they are held in no more estimation than elsewhere; on the contrary, if there is any refuse to be thrown out, they are the first employed. They are obliged to work at their crafts for the king, when they are called, for their food alone. They are subject to suffering the blows and injuries of everyone, without daring to say a word even to a child of six who throws stones at them. If they pass before a mosque, no matter what the weather or season might be, they must remove their shoes, not even daring in the royal cities, such as Fez and Marrakesh, to wear them at all, under pain of five hundred lashes and being put into prison, from which they would be released only upon payment of a heavy fine.[123]

An attack on the Jewish quarter in Fez in 1465 almost wiped out the Jewish population.[124] The event was described in an Arabic letter penned by Abd al-Basit b. Khalil. The letter reports, "On the eleventh of Shawwal 869 (7 June 1465), the news arrived in Tlemcen from Fez that the great mass of people of Fez had risen up against the Jews there and had killed them almost to the last man."[125] The stated explanation for the attack was that a Jewish vizier had been appointed, who along with other influential Jews, had dominated Muslims. The author writes, "He [the ruler, Abd al-Haqq] raised the Jew to an exalted position, although he pretended to be disturbed at having need of him. This Jew remained the de facto vizier, for there was no vizier other than he, and he had the final say in the vizierate—all while remaining in his religion!"[126] "The Jews in Fez became arrogant during his tenure—even in the provinces. They came to have authority, influence, prestige, and the power to command and be obeyed."[127]

Expulsion

Expulsion, at the local, regional, or even national level, was an all too common fate for late medieval and early modern Jews. After expulsions some Jews remained close to their original homes; others, however, chose or were forced to migrate long distances and often into unfamiliar environs or foreign contexts.

The Spanish expulsion edict issued by King Ferdinand and Queen Isabella, who had united the kingdoms of Castille and Aragon in Iberia, focused heavily on the concern that, although Jews had been segregated from their former co-religionists who had since converted to Christianity, they nevertheless continued to exercise undue influence over them, leading them away from proper Christian practice.[128] According to the document,

> Because whenever some grave and detestable crime is committed by some persons of a group or community, it is right that such a college or community be dissolved and annihilated . . . and that those who pervert the good and honest living of the cities and villages, and that by contagion could injure others, be expelled from among the peoples, and even for other lighter causes that are harmful to the states, and how much more so for the greatest of the crimes, dangerous and contagious as is this one.[129]

The Jews were portrayed as corrupting the community. They were expelled and told to liquidate all their holdings.

As we noted in chapter 2, the Iberian expulsions (including Portugal and Navarre) affected a very large number of Jews and *conversos*—300,000 according to the contemporary Isaac Abarbanel, 200,000 according to other chroniclers—and have variously been attributed to the king, the queen, and certain advisers.[130]

Like the Spanish, the Portuguese in December 1496 expelled all Jews, under the penalty of death and loss of possessions. Again, the reason given for the expulsion was that the Jews caused true Christians to depart from the proper course. The alleged great evil and blasphemies of the Jews were also pointed out, as was the royal obligation to protect the Church and advance the Catholic faith. In the infamous events of 1506, New Christians, who had formerly been forcibly converted from Judaism in 1497, were attacked and massacred in Lisbon. According to a Catholic prelate's account,

> About the same time there happened a great tumult at Lisbon, raised by the fury and madness of the rabble; in this almost all the Jews, who as we before observed, had been converted to Christianity, were cruelly massacred. . . . The news of this massacre having reached the country, next day [Monday, April 20] above a thousand men from the villages flocked into the city and joined the murderers, and the slaughter was renewed.[131]

Some scholars, going so far as to write of a renaissance of fifteenth-century Spanish Jewry in some places, contend that the expulsion of 1492 was hardly inevitable. Nonetheless, there were clearly important and escalating acts of marginalization that occurred during the second half of the fifteenth century. Indeed the Cortes of Toledo had already attempted to segregate the Jews in 1479/1480, and as partial pretext for the Andalusian expulsion of 1483, Jews were accused of collaborating with the Muslims. In January 1486 the municipal council of Valmaseda in the Basque country decided to expel the Jews, following the Andalusian example. Already in 1483, however, the same council had banned marriages between resident and foreign Jews.[132] In the late 1480s and early 1490s there was a substantial increase in the taxes demanded of Jews and degeneration of the economic position of the Jews.

Jews were expelled from many places in the early modern period. In Germany, Jews were forced out of a host of cities and regions. There were significant urban expulsions in Augsburg, Vienna, Nuremberg, and Ulm in the fifteenth century, and Regensburg and Rothenberg in the early sixteenth. Important and long resonating territorial expulsions took place in Lower Austria, Wurttemberg and Würzburg in the fifteenth century, and Brandenburg and Saxony in the sixteenth. The Jews of Frankfurt and Worms, two of the most important Jewish communities in Germany in the seventeenth century, were expelled for relatively short periods (one to two years) in the midst of sinister social revolts in the second decade of the century. The Fettmilch uprising wreaked tremendous havoc on the Jewish community of Frankfurt. Many sources attest to the difficult circumstances. "They burned in our streets countless holy writings, which they found in our houses and in the synagogue."[133] During the uprising 262 Jews were killed, while vast sums of Jewish money were plundered.[134]

Since expulsion was a frequent eventuality, the position of Jewish communities was tenuous. In Italy, a number of fifteenth-century attacks and expulsions broke what at times appeared to be relative calm. For example, expulsions took place in Perugia (1485), Vicenza (1486), Parma (1488), Milan and Lucca (1489), Florence (1494), and Treviso (1509). In 1491 the synagogue in Ravenna was destroyed and the quarter pillaged.[135] In some places, however, traditional power relationships held fast, and the calls by burghers or clerics to expel the Jews were denied by ruling city councils, princes, or kings, as in Mantua and Ferrara.[136]

While we discussed the ghetto in chapter 2, a few words are in order here as well, for the creation and enforcement of a ghetto was an anti-Jewish act. This was particularly clear with the 1555 bull of Pope Paul IV "Cum Nimis Absurdum," which enforced the segregation of the Jews within the Papal States.[137] Paul's successor Pius V (r. 1566–1572) expelled the Jews from most Papal States, closed 108 synagogues, and forced the emigration of thousands of Jews, including the expulsion of some 800 Jews from Bologna.[138]

The expulsion of Jews in Poland appears to have been rare, though there was a large expulsion from Lithuania in 1495 (the Jews were allowed to return in 1503), and some individual cases of non-toleration (see also chapter 2).[139] In the Ottoman Empire, as we have already seen, the *sürgün*, while clearly part of broader political governance, was essentially an expulsion and forced migration, even if Jews appear to have been able to adapt quite well.

Marranos (New Christians), Ethnicity, Inquisition

The forced conversion of Spanish Jews at the end of the fourteenth century sparked a long and complicated history of relations between Christians, Jews, and *conversos*. The political reach of Spain and the forced baptisms of Jews in Portugal in the early sixteenth century further complicated an already confusing set of relationships.

Conversos maintained multilayered identities and religious belief systems. Many rejected Catholicism as idolatrous, believed that the Messiah would lead them to the Holy Land, and adhered to aspects of the Mosaic law. On the other hand, *conversos* identified with Iberian cultural norms. They often held Catholic-oriented ideas of personal salvation and understood their entire theological world within a Catholic context. When such *conversos* reverted to Judaism, as happened in Amsterdam, Hamburg, and parts of Italy and the Ottoman Empire, such identities might clash with more traditional rabbinic norms and concepts and create a rather complicated religious identity.[140]

It was *conversos*, not Jews, who were the real target of the Spanish Inquisition. *Conversos* were suspected of Judaizing, that is, of practicing Jewish rites or maintaining Jewish beliefs. They were seen as backsliding Christians in need of correction, coercion, or punishment. The institution of the Inquisition, itself a medieval Church invention, was intended to search out and reconcile such alleged Judaizers and other heretics, though it was not only about religion, at times demonstrating political agendas and influence. In Spain, the king and queen requested that an inquisition be established in 1477. The pope granted permission late in 1478, and the Inquisition began to operate in 1481.

Already in the 1460s an inquisition in Aragon began to investigate *conversos* in Valencia. Between 1483 and 1485 the Inquisition in Ciudad Real condemned 100 *conversos*, fifty-two at the stake, fifteen in effigy, and some through exhumation. In 1486 in Toledo alone, twenty **auto da fes** were conducted, and more than 3,300 people were sentenced.[141] While exact numbers are notoriously difficult to ascertain, it is estimated that, from the late fifteenth century into the early nineteenth century, when it ceased, the Inquisition in Spain burned almost 32,000 "heretics" and more than 17,000 people in effigy. More than 291,000 heretics were "reconciled" back to the Catholic Church.[142] In early modern Portugal, some 40,000 cases were tried, with 30,000 people condemned, over 1,800 burned at the stake, and 29,590 penanced.[143] The Inquisition also extended its reach into the New World especially in Portuguese and Spanish possessions. There the famous "Black Code" was actualized by the French King Louis XIV in 1685. The code resulted in the migration of Jews from French holdings throughout the Caribbean and Guianas.[144] Although granted a significant degree of tolerance by the Dutch, Jewish fates took a turn for the worse in areas that were taken or retaken by the Portuguese, who were fervent about rooting out any alleged Judaizing behavior.

The Inquisition in Iberia in the sixteenth century sought out suspected Judaizers, often compelling confessions through torture and thereby gathering "information" on other transgressors. In 1567, for example, in one such case, a certain Elvira del Campo was tortured in order to exact a confession. The woman cried out in pain and implored her captors to have the ropes loosened and then proclaimed that she had nothing to tell. Other torture devices were utilized, including a *porto*, which as one modern historian defines was "a sort of ladder with sharp-edged rungs." When the pain became too great, the account records, "then she said: 'Senor, I did it to observe that Law.' She was asked what Law. She said: 'The Law that the witnesses say— I declare it all Senor, and don't remember what Law it was—O wretched was the mother that bore me.'" Further exhausting torture was applied. After six months, she was freed from prison, but she was a ruined woman, impoverished with a terrible stain on her family.[145]

The Inquisition varied in scope, intensity, and focus by region and under different supervision. In Italy, the Venetian Inquisition dealt with cases related to Judaism or Judaizing directly only 5 to 10 percent of the time. Most cases treated offenses that involved the public interest. According to Brian Pullan, the great historian of Venice and the Venetian Inquisition, frequently, the activities of the Inquisition simply extended the work of the secular magistrates regarding the maintenance of public order and morality.[146] To that extent, the Inquisition was related to a host of social issues and involved the quest for authority and public conformity. As in Spain in the late fifteenth century, the Italian Inquisition was more about suspect behavior than it was about Judaism, which was not technically subject to the Inquisition or to the epithet of heresy.

Conversion

While the history of the Jews reveals apostasy throughout the ages, there appears to have been at times subtle increases in conversion during the early modern period, perhaps as social opportunities arose, as social inter-action with non-Jews became more permeable, or as Jews were forced to de-cide between conversion on the one hand and expulsion or death on the other. Many Jews, for example, were forced to convert to Christianity during the 1391 attacks in Spain. The *converso* problem in Spain actually began in the fourteenth century. In 1378 the Archdeacon Ferrant Martinez initiated a campaign of violent anti-Jewish sermons, calling for and leading to the de-struction of almost two dozen synagogues. After the forced conversions of 1391 many baptized Jews led a rather tenuous life. Many were allowed within the next two decades to revert to Judaism in Spain and as migrants in North Africa, but for various reasons many did not return to Judaism. The status of these converts was much discussed by rabbinic authorities in the fifteenth century.

Important numbers of *conversos*, however, managed to make their way into courtly and aristocratic circles. In some cases, these "New Christians" attained great wealth and political power, intermarrying with the Old Chris-tian nobility. In this new position, *conversos* appeared to be a serious threat to the old guard and traditional social order. As a result, in the middle of the fifteenth century purity of blood laws were first passed in Toledo. These laws excluded anyone of Jewish ancestry from holding municipal office in the city.

In central Europe, the Reformation, at least initially, seemed to hold out the promise of the beginning of a messianic era. In this context, some Jews did convert to Protestantism but probably not a large number. Martin Luther, who maintained high expectations early in his career for the con-version of the Jews, was disappointed at the end of his life with the actual conversion rate. Some Jews did, however, convert, and some became He-brew instructors or university professors. In some cases these early and high profile converts were touted by the Church and used as a means to encour-age other potential converts. In some cases such converts became especially harsh opponents of their former co-religionists. We will read about Jo-hannes Pfefferkorn shortly. Another early and influential convert was An-thonius Margaritha, who was born around 1490 into a rabbinical family in Regensburg. Margaritha converted to Catholicism in 1522 and later to Protestantism. He was a Hebrew lecturer in Augsburg, Meissen, Zell, Leipzig, and Vienna. He was involved in significant debates against leading Jewish personalities, most notably the **shtadlan** Josel of Rosheim.[147] Despite being castigated by the emperor himself and having some of his work banned from printing, his anti-Jewish tractate *Das Gantz Jüdisch Glaub* (The Entire Jewish Belief) served as a catalyst for anti-Jewish accusations and con-firmed generations of Christians in their anti-Jewish prejudices.

Jews converted for a variety of reasons. In some cases these reasons were related to genuine religious belief or spiritual searching. In others, conver-sion was related to the belief that a change of religion would improve their social or economic opportunities. Some conversions were undoubtedly insincere. Records in Germany indicate that some Jews converted to Christianity multiple times for the baptism money they would receive. Faced with intense persecution, some Jews had no choice but to convert. Often times these Jews traveled to far off lands, especially the Ottoman Empire, in order to revert to Judaism. In some cases they remained in the relatively more tolerant world of the East; in other cases, like a certain rabbi from Ulm, they returned to their former lands. But Jews were at times also forced to decide between conversion and death. Just as in the Crusades of the high Middle Ages, some Jews, especially in the Ukraine in the mid-seventeenth century, chose to die as martyrs committed to their faith rather than soil themselves or their descendants with conversion from Judaism.

In early modern Poland we find examples of Jewish apostasy. Some converted through force, while others apparently did so voluntarily, including several Jews among the lower social strata. As in other places during the early modern period, converts often continued to work in the same professions they had practiced as Jews and, surprising as it may sound, often continued in positive relationships with their families and former co-religionists.[148] Conversion did, on occasion, lead to professional growth as well. One Jewish musician, for example, was appointed as the king's trumpeter after his conversion.[149] Conversion could, however, strike even the leading families. One member of the well-to-do Fischel family in Cracow converted at the end of the fifteenth century.[150]

In Germany, there appears to be a noticeable, if not yet dramatic, increase in the number of converts from Judaism during the sixteenth century. Later, during the seventeenth century, an increasing number of Jews left their faith, many from the middling social class of educators.[151] Unlike in fifteenth-century Spain, in Germany there was no coordinated effort to convert Jews. There were few formal disputations. Early Christian infighting that erupted with the Protestant Reformation did not usher in large numbers of conversions, although there are examples of individual Jews converting to both Protestantism and Catholicism. Indeed, in some cases Jews moved between Christian denominations when they did not find spiritual satisfaction.

Converts, no matter how anti-Jewish they became or how well embraced within certain Christian circles, were often unable to break through the stereotypes that they carried from their birth as Jews. The fifteenth-century German convert from Judaism Victor of Carben wrote,

> And thus, says the Psalmist, one spends the entire day like a poor dog that has spent its day running and returns home at night hungry. For there are many uncharitable and ignorant Christians who will not give you but will rather show you from their doors with mockery, saying, "Look, there goes a baptized Jew."

And then others answer, "Yes, anything that is done for you is a waste. You will never become a good Christian." And thus they are mocked and insulted by the Christians from whom they expect help and solace. And they are also hated by the Jews from whom they have come. Whatever joy or pleasure that one or the other may have had is turned to unhappiness and displeasure.[152]

There are many cases of Jewish converts who went on to careers as Christian theologians or lecturers in Hebrew. Paul Staffelsteiner, born Nathan Aaron in Nuremberg before 1499, converted with his children but not his wife first to Catholicism and perhaps later to Protestantism, and he filled the long-vacant chair of Hebrew at Heidelberg in 1551, the same year that he published a German speech on the messianism of Christ. Paul Weidner (Asher Judah ben Nathan Ashkenazi) (ca. 1525–1585) was the brother of the physician and diplomat Solomon Ashkenazi and served as a physician and rector of the university in Vienna. He wrote conversionary sermons and enjoyed extensive imperial patronage, eventually obtaining the title of nobility *von Billerburg* in 1582.

After the failure of the Sabbatian movement in the late seventeenth century there may have been a spike in Jewish conversions, although the increase may have had to do with various social and political changes within Christianity as well as the concerted efforts of some missionizing operations. One such effort was led by the Lutheran minister Esdras Edzard in and around Hamburg in the last three decades of the seventeenth century. Edzard saw the mass conversion of the Jews as a precursor to the Second Coming of Christ.[153]

Conversion of an individual did not always mean conversion of an entire family, and it could lead to very complicated familial relations. Victor of Carben, for example, converted at the age of forty-nine, leaving behind his wife and children. Still, as in fifteenth-century Iberia, converts often retained close and at times cordial relations with Jews.

Christian Hebraica and Kabbalah

Throughout the early modern world there are examples of close intellectual, business, and even social interchange between Jews and non-Jews. Particularly in Christian lands, our period witnessed close collaboration between some scholars, frequently but not always, converts, in the area of Hebrew book printing and what has come to be termed Christian Hebraica and Christian **Kabbalah**.

Spurred on by the Renaissance interest in antiquity, texts, and language, a cadre of Christian scholars became widely interested in the Hebrew language and in Jewish rites. While most of these figures never approached Judaism with an unbiased understanding, many did advocate a more restrained

approach to Judaism and Jews, especially regarding the sacred texts of the
Jews and the Hebrew language. Perhaps the most renowned Christian Hebraist was Johannes Reuchlin. The German scholar, who lived between 1455
and 1522, was a Greek specialist, who began to study Hebrew before he was
twenty. Reuchlin early on encountered the grammars of Jews, such as the medieval scholar David Kimhi, as well as the early work of pioneering Christians. Becoming well versed in the language, he wrote many translations and
held important professorships in Greek and Hebrew at the University of In-
golstadt (1520–1521) and Hebrew at Tübingen (1521–1522). Reuchlin was
also particularly taken with Kabbalah, a subject that he engaged for much of
his professional career.

Reuchlin, best known for his defense of Hebrew texts against the attack
of the convert from Judaism Johannes Pfefferkorn, argued,

> Jewish commentaries should not and cannot be abandoned by the Christian
> church, for they keep the special characteristics of the Hebrew language before
> our eyes. The Bible cannot be interpreted without them, especially the Old Tes-
> tament, just as we cannot do without the Greek language and Greek grammars
> and commentaries for the New Testament, as is confirmed and indicated in
> canon law.[154]

Hebrew texts were clearly of great importance but also very complicated. As
Reuchlin pointed out, "The Talmud is idiomatically so complex . . . that not
every Jew, even if he has a good command of Hebrew, can understand it.
How could one therefore justify Christians rejecting the Talmud, when they
cannot even understand it?"[155] Perhaps more pragmatically, Reuchlin declared, "There is nothing to be gained from burning Jewish books in Germany, where the smallest number of Jews reside. For they still have other
schools of higher learning in Constantinople and in the Orient, and also in
Italy and in other kingdoms, schools where they may study freely and read
what they wish."[156] Instead, he believed that the Jews should be dealt with
gently so "we may succeed in converting them to the cause of our Mother,
the Christian Church."[157]

Reuchlin did not defend all Hebrew texts. He scorned anything that could
have been construed as anti-Christian, and his love of the language did not
lead him to an equal love of the Jews, sharing as he did the discriminatory
trends of his time. Reuchlin felt that the Jews deservedly suffered for denying the Messiah and murdering Christ.[158] Reuchlin's debate with Pfefferkorn spilled out into the larger academic circles. And even his enemy Pfefferkorn, supported by many, could never shake the accusations that
accompanied any converts from Judaism of being insincere Christians, who
with their unchangeable nature always remained Jews.

Another leading Christian humanist was Sebastian Münster (1488/
1489–1552). Münster was the best-selling Christian Hebraist before the

middle of the sixteenth century. Often accused of relying too heavily on Jewish biblical interpreters, Münster was himself, however, also affected by the anti-Jewish impetus of his age, and we find two anti-Jewish publications among his works. Münster taught Hebrew at the universities of Heidelberg and then Basle. Münster appears to have had personal academic relations with individual Jews, to whom he turned for access to Hebrew manuscripts and translations and discussions of translations from Hebrew to Aramaic.

Münster's extensive correspondence with some Jews, most notably Elijah Levita (1468–1549), were well-known and reveal a heavy influence of Judaism on his work. But his relationship to Judaism revolved around not only his scientific inquiry into linguistics and rabbinics; it seems to have had a rather more personal relationship as well. Münster apparently attended synagogue services frequently, was familiar with the practices of German Jews, and studied Jewish gravestone inscriptions in both Heidelberg and Basle. A reconstruction of Münster's library reveals that he was acquainted with more than fifty rabbinic authors.[159]

A final example of a significant Christian Hebraist is Johannes Buxtorf the Elder (1564–1629), whose work had tremendous impact well into the seventeenth century. Buxtorf maintained a rich correspondence with Jewish scholars and worked closely with several Jews. He maintained a remarkable Hebraica library and was familiar with a range of rabbinical writings. Yet, Buxtorf was also anti-Jewish in his orientation. Still, his work, especially the *Juden Schul*, became a standard work with the reputation of ethnographical genuineness that shaped subsequent Christian scholarship and perceptions.[160] Indeed, it has recently been argued that Christian ethnography of the Jews took significant strides in the sixteenth and seventeenth centuries, eventually paving the road for the more favorable representations and position of the Jews at the edge of modernity.[161]

Christian Hebraica took a special form with Christian Kabbalah. Interest in Jewish mysticism depended upon internal Christian interests but was also brokered by key Jewish intellectuals such as Elijah Levita and Elijah Loanz, who tutored Christian scholars, and by central Christian scholars as exemplified by Johannes Reuchlin. Interest in Kabbalah was not simply academic. Many mystical amulets as well as the inscriptions on them were produced by Christian artisans, for example.[162]

Christians co-opted Kabbalah in interesting ways and for a host of reasons. Some, such as Giovanni Pico della Mirandola (1463–1494), considered by some as the father of Christian Kabbalah, saw Kabbalah as another form of early philosophy that could be welded with Christian faith. Like many other Christians of his generation and later, Pico probably began his study of Kabbalah in translation. He was familiar with many classics of medieval Jewish mysticism, although he probably read most through the translation of Flavius Mithradites (fifteenth century), the famed apostate Renaissance translator of Arabic, Hebrew, and Greek texts. Pico's purpose was fairly clear, when he noted,

> I come now to those things that I have dug up from the ancient mysteries of the Hebrews and have brought forward in order to confirm the holy and Catholic faith. And lest by chance they be thought by those to whom they are unknown to be fictitious nonsense or tales about rumors, I wish everyone to understand what and of what sort they are, whence sought, by which and how famous authors they are guaranteed, and how they were stored away, how divinely inspired they are, and how necessary to us for defending religion against the rude slanders of the Hebrews.[163]

Others, like the seventeenth-century Francis Mercury von Helmont, saw Kabbalah as a means of explaining certain Christian tenets within a framework of a toleration of theological deviance and openness.[164] Ironically, perhaps, Christian use of Kabbalah led, in some circles, to Jewish criticism of Kabbalah. The entire discussion about Kabbalah pointed, in the end, to the real possibilities for Jewish and non-Jewish intellectual engagement. The common threads linking various strands of early modern mystical speculation also point to some transformations that were unique to the Jews but that were part of broader early modern culture as well.

Jewish Polemic

Jewish relations with non-Jews were, as we have seen, not always positive. Jews could engage polemic and apologetics as well. In Spain after the persecutions of the late fourteenth century, leading Jewish intellectuals, such as Hasdai Crescas and Profiat Duran, attacked certain Christian and philosophical positions. Such work was particularly significant in light of various religious disputations, most notably that at Tortosa in 1413–1414. In Italy some Jewish scholars challenged restrictive legislation of the popes and defended various Jewish laws.

Yom Tov Lipmann Mühlhausen composed *Sefer Nizzahon* (Book of Polemic) in early fifteenth-century Prague. Mühlhausen was an important rabbinic scholar, originally from Alsace, who made his way to Prague by 1389. In 1407 he was appointed "Judex Judaeorum," judge of the Jews in Prague. Mühlhausen traveled throughout Bavaria, Austria, Bohemia, and Poland, and between 1440 and 1450 he headed the rabbinical council at Erfurt. Mühlhausen defended Judaism while systematically attacking Christian views. He rejected the notion that the Messiah had already come.[165] Mühlhausen's discussion of circumcision begins with the Christians' attack on the practice and concludes with his own defense:

> The Christian mocked, saying, females who are uncircumcised have no Jewish character. They [the Christian mockers] do not know that faith does not de-

pend upon circumcision but is in the heart; circumcision does not make a Jew of one who does not believe correctly, and one who believes correctly is a Jew even if he is not circumcised, although he is guilty of one transgression. And circumcision is not possible with women.[166]

Mühlhausen insisted, however, that circumcision was a general obligation for each man, just as for Abraham, Isaac, and Jacob, each of whom circumcised himself. The covenant was to "be in the flesh" forever. Indeed, he defended the proposition forever by asserting that in the future Israel will settle in the land of Israel forever and that the kingship of the house of David will last forever.[167] Citing Isaiah 66:20 ("And they shall bring all your brethren from all the nations as an offering to the Lord, upon horses, and in chariots, and in litters, and upon mules, and upon dromedaries, to my holy mountain Jerusalem"), Mühlhausen argued that the nations of the world were to be an offering from the Jews to God, they were to be shown the way to the true faith.

Another prominent anti-Christian thinker was Isaac Orobio de Castro (1620–1687). Orobio was born in Portugal to **Marrano** parents. He was a prominent physician and a philosopher with an appointment in metaphysics at Salamanca, before being arrested by the Inquisition. He confessed, was released, and made his way to Toulouse as a professor of pharmacy. Later in 1662 he moved to Amsterdam. Another apologetic was the Karaite scholar Isaac Troki (ca. 1533–ca. 1594), who despite his Karaite emphasis on the Written as opposed to the Oral Law, also attacked certain Christian traditions and beliefs.

Jews debated Christianity in various ways. Josel of Rosheim, the great German *shtadlan* of the sixteenth century, was responsible for defending the Jews and was successful in having some expulsion edicts revoked, in limiting for a time the circulation of Luther's later inflammatory writings and in defending the Jews against the attacks in the works of the converted Jew Anthonius Margaritha.

Early modern Jews also attacked Christian dogma, especially assertions of Jesus' divinity. Throughout the medieval period Jews often considered non-Jews, especially Christians, as idolaters. While practically speaking Jews did not do so after the twelfth century, the argument still remained. In sixteenth-century Poland and Germany Christians might still be considered idol worshippers.[168] For example, according to the famous preacher in Amsterdam, Saul Levi Morteira, "None of the forms of idolatrous worship that preceded them [Christians] was as steeped in impunity and squalor as their own worship." Morteira continued, "Furthermore, look at the power of their veneration of bones and skulls of the dead. To them they burn incense, to them they bow down, before them they fall and prostrate themselves."[169]

CONCLUSIONS

Early modern Jewish relations with non-Jews could be complex, quickly changeable, and dependent upon a wide range of local conditions. Throughout much of our period toleration of the Jews did exist, often for economic or political reasons, but was generally subsumed within traditional anti-Jewish sentiment and mentality. Jews engaged with their non-Jewish neighbors in many different ways and at various levels. Daily interactions are notoriously difficult to document, but we know that Jews socialized with non-Jews and at times shared fairly positive and intimate relations. Various communal legislation and sumptuary laws frequently attempted to limit Jewish and non-Jewish relations. The repetition of these laws as well as non-Jewish evidence suggests that such laws were frequently ineffectual or overlooked.

Indeed, the cultural adaptation that many Jews practiced in various settings also appears to indicate that Jews interacted seriously with non-Jews. Such adaptation does not indicate that Jews assimilated or replaced their own practices or world-views. Jews appear to have had a remarkable ability to engage the world around them, without abandoning their own religion. Jewish engagement with non-Jewish ideas is evident in the very books Jews read, as we have noted in this chapter and at the end of chapter 4. Jews participated in the literary and scientific world in which they lived and even adopted certain Christian customs but in each case placing them within and giving them Jewish meaning.

Even when they lived in segregated quarters, Jews were not a people of the ghetto. The theological and social developments of general society impacted them. Religious reforms led sometimes to new images of or approaches to Judaism. At times such religious changes even seeped into Jewish practices and thought.

The political and legal position of the Jews varied by location and could also vary between theory and practice. At times Jews enjoyed some social, economic, and even religious freedom, always providing that such religion was practiced in private. Even when Jews teetered on the edge of expulsion they might be allowed to remain if they were thought to bring any kind of economic benefit to the region or the ruling authorities. In some cases individual rulers or authorities changed their position on the Jews after short periods of time, making Jewish existence often tentative and fragile.

Throughout the early modern period Jews remained religious and social outsiders. Particularly in Christian society, but not exclusively, Jews were accused of a range of crimes and devious behaviors. Many of these alleged crimes were related to Christian doctrines. The power of Jesus, for example, was supposedly mocked by Jews, who allegedly secured Eucharistic wafers and attacked them. Jews were accused of desecrating other Christian images as well. Jews were also accused of other crimes, such as taking excessive usury, counterfeiting coins, poisoning wells, and most heinously, the murder of Christian children for the sake of imagined Jewish rituals. There are various ways that modern historians have attempted to explain such accusations, but the net result was that Jews were seen as enemies, who sought the downfall of their host societies and who could not entirely be trusted. Such accusations often led to restrictive measures as well as to persecutions—attacks on property, expulsions, and pogroms. While Jews generally fared better in Islamic lands, such violent anti-Jewish actions could erupt anywhere and under almost any conditions, even when not sanctioned by ruling authorities.

Interaction between Jews and non-Jews could be even more complex when some Jews were forced to leave or voluntarily left Judaism. Some infamous converts became ardent opponents of Judaism and their former brethren. Even positive relations between Jews and converts could lead to trouble for the Jews. The Inquisition was primarily concerned about such positive relations through which New Christians might be led back to Judaism, a serious crime in Christian society. Converts did not always have to be engaged in negative relations with their former or new co-religionists. In many cases, converts were part of a complex intellectual and cultural milieu, serving as Hebrew instructors at universities and proofreaders at printing shops. Serving as intermediaries in these various capacities, converts and some Jews became valuable colleagues for Christian Hebraists and Christian kabbalists who eagerly read and discussed Hebrew texts and Jewish rites.

Jews were, of course, not simply idle spectators in their relations with non-Jews and in the events that unfolded around and often included them. Early modern Jews debated non-Jews and contested marginalization. They did what they could to secure political rights and social and economic privileges. They defended their religious beliefs at the same time that they questioned Christian and Islamic dogma. Jewish relations with the Other in this sense were affected by Jewish settlement and migration, by internal Jewish developments and discussions, and by the developments in broader non-Jewish society. Jews both responded to and helped create early modern society. Their experiences allow us a window into an important and transitional period of Jewish history. At the same time, early modern Jews provide a valuable means for understanding more general early modern historical experiences and development.

NOTES

1. Quoted in Daniel Swetschinski, *Reluctant Cosmopolitans: The Portuguese Jews of Seventeenth-Century Amsterdam* (London, 2000), 28–29.

2. See Steven M. Nadler, *Rembrandt's Jews* (Chicago, 2003).

3. Quoted in Miriam Bodian, *Hebrews of the Portuguese Nation: Conversos and Community in Early Modern Amsterdam* (Bloomington, IN, 1997), 63.

4. Jacob Marcus, *The Jew in the Medieval World: A Source Book, 315–1791* (Cincinnati, 1938), 195.

5. Marcus, *The Jew in the Medieval World*, 194.

6. Arnold Wiznitzer, *The Records of the Earliest Jewish Community in the New World* (New York, 1954), 67.

7. Wiznitzer, *The Records of the Earliest Jewish Community*, 69.

8. Wiznitzer, *The Records of the Earliest Jewish Community*, 83.

9. Quoted in David Joshua Malkiel, *A Separate Republic: The Mechanics and Dynamics of Venetian Self-Government 1607–1624* (Jerusalem, 1991), 233.

10. Swetschinski, *Reluctant Cosmopolitans*, 322.

11. Edward Fram, *Ideals Face Reality: Jewish Law and Life in Poland, 1550–1655* (Cincinnati, 1997), 31–32.

12. Moshe Rosman, "Innovative Tradition: Jewish Culture in the Polish-Lithuanian Commonwealth," in *Cultures of the Jews: A New History*, ed. David Biale (New York, 2002), 528.

13. Ivan G. Marcus, *The Jewish Life Cycle: Rites of Passage from Biblical to Modern Times* (Seattle, 2004), 5–6.

14. Already for medieval Europe, Ivan Marcus asserts that Jews resisted majority Christian culture and developed collective Jewish identity by what he terms "inward acculturation," "by internalizing or transforming various genres, motifs, terms, institutions, or rituals of Christian culture in a polemical, parodic, or neutralized manner." Ivan G. Marcus, "A Jewish-Christian Symbiosis: The Culture of Early Ashkenaz," in *Cultures of the Jews: A New History*, ed. David Biale (New York, 2002), 461.

15. Marcus, *The Jewish Life Cycle*, 8.

16. Kenneth Stow, *Theater of Acculturation: The Roman Ghetto in the 16th Century* (Seattle, 2001), 68.

17. Stow, *Theater of Acculturation*, 70.

18. Robert Bonfil, *Jewish Life in Renaissance Italy*, trans. Anthony Oldcorn (Berkeley, CA, 1994), 7.

19. Elliot Horowitz, "Families and Their Fortunes: The Jews of Early Modern Italy," in *Cultures of the Jews: A New History*, ed. David Biale (New York, 2002), 592.

20. Horowitz, "Families and Their Fortunes," 602.

21. Horowitz, "Families and Their Fortunes," 602.

22. Yosef Kaplan, "Bom Judesmo: The Western Sephardic Diaspora," in *Cultures of the Jews: A New History*, ed. David Biale (New York, 2002), 665.

23. Kaplan, "Bom Judesmo," 665.

24. David B. Ruderman, ed. *Essential Papers on Jewish Culture in Renaissance and Baroque Italy* (New York, 1992), 45.

25. See Arthur Lesley, "Jewish Adaptations of Humanist Concepts in Fifteenth- and Sixteenth-Century Italy," in *Essential Papers on Jewish Culture in Renaissance and Baroque Italy*, ed. David B. Ruderman (New York, 1992), 46.

26. Alexander Altmann, "Ars Rhetorica as Reflected in Some Jewish Figures of the Italian Renaissance," in *Essential Papers on Jewish Culture in Renaissance and Baroque Italy*, ed. David B. Ruderman (New York, 1992), 75.

27. Marcus, *The Jew in the Medieval World*, 382–83.

28. Marcus, *The Jew in the Medieval World*, 382.

29. Marcus, *The Jew in the Medieval World*, 384–85.

30. In Elisheva Baumgarten, *Mothers and Children: Jewish Family Life in Medieval Europe* (Princeton, NJ, 2004), 96; Moses Mintz, *Sheelot u-teshuvot* (Jerusalem, 1990–1991), no. 19.

31. See, for example, Lotte Motz, "The Winter Goddesses: Percht, Holda, and Related Figures," *Folklore* 116 (1984): 151–66.

32. See, recently, Jill Hammer, "Holle's Cry: Unearthing a Birth Goddess in a German Jewish Naming Ceremony," *Nashim* 9 (1) (2005): 62–87; Martha Keil, "Lilith und Hollekreisch—Schwangerschaft, Geburt ud Wochenbett im Judentum des deutschen Spätmittelalters," in *Aller Anfang: Geburt, Birth, Naissance*, ed. Gabriele Dorffner and Sonia Horn (Vienna, 2005), 145–72.

33. Marcus, *The Jewish Life Cycle*, 28.

34. Marcus, *The Jewish Life Cycle*, 40.

35. Marcus, *The Jewish Life Cycle*, 65.

36. Marcus, *The Jewish Life Cycle*, 199.

37. The term is used by Moshe Rosman in his "Innovative Tradition," 519–70.

38. Here and above, see Marcus, *The Jewish Life Cycle*, 77–78.

39. Marcus, *The Jewish Life Cycle*, 100–101.

40. Marcus, *The Jewish Life Cycle*, 163.

41. Fram, *Ideals Face Reality*, 30–31.

42. See Benjamin Arbel, *Trading Nations: Jews and Venetians in the Early Modern Eastern Mediterranean* (Leiden, Netherland, 1995), 95ff.

43. Marcus, *The Jew in the Medieval World*, 66–67.

44. Paul Mendes Flohr and Jehuda Reinharz, eds., *The Jew in the Modern World: A Documentary History*, 2nd ed. (New York, 1995), 10.

45. For Amsterdam, see Swetschinski, *Reluctant Cosmopolitans*.

46. Horowitz, "Families and Their Fortunes," 580

47. Horowitz, "Families and Their Fortunes," 581.

48. Kaplan, "Bom Judesmo," 654.

49. Kaplan, "Bom Judesmo," 654.

50. Cited in Myriam Yardeni, *Anti-Jewish Mentalities in Early Modern Europe* (Lanham, MD, 1990), 100.

51. See Robert Bireley, "The Catholic Reform, Jews, and Judaism in Sixteenth-Century Germany," in *Jews, Judaism, and the Reformation in Sixteenth-Century Germany*, ed. Dean Phillip Bell and Stephen G. Burnett (Leiden, Netherlands, 2006), 249–68, passim.

52. See Judith Kalik, "The Attitudes Towards the Jews in the Christian Polemic Literature in Poland in the 16–18th Centuries," in *Jews and Slavs*, vol. 11, ed. Wolf Moskovich and Irena Fijalkowska-Janiak (Jerusalem, 2003), 60–62, 73.

53. See Zenon Guldon and Waldemar Kowalski, "Between Tolerance and Abomination: Jews in Sixteenth-Century Poland," in *The Expulsion of the Jews: 1492 and After*, ed. Raymond B. Waddington and Arthur H. Williamson (New York, 1994), 166.

54. Bernard Lewis, *The Jews of Islam* (Princeton, NJ, 1984), 137–38.

55. See Lewis, *The Jews of Islam*, 147.

56. Quoted in Lewis, *The Jews of Islam*, 37–38.

57. See Lewis, *The Jews of Islam*, 49–51.

58. Philip of Hesse, in Martin Bucer, *Martin Bucers Deutsche Schriften*, vol. VII, ed. Robert Stupperich (Gütersloh, 1964), 381.

59. Quoted in Salo Baron, *A Social and Religious History of the Jews*, vols. 16–17, 2nd ed. (Philadelphia, 1976–1980), 16:133–34.

60. See Baron, *A Social and Religious History of the Jews*, 16:142–43.

61. See Baron, *A Social and Religious History of the Jews*, 16:150–51.

62. Baron, *A Social and Religious History of the Jews*, 16:186.

63. Bernard Weinryb, *The Jews of Poland*, 38.

64. Weinryb, *The Jews of Poland: A Social and Economic History of the Jewish Community in Poland from 1100 to 1800* (Philadelphia, 1973), 38–39.

65. Weinryb, *The Jews of Poland*, 39.

66. Weinryb, *The Jews of Poland*, 39.

67. Weinryb, *The Jews of Poland*, 38–39.

68. Iwo Cyprian Pogonowski, *Jews in Poland: A Documentary History* (New York, 1998), 45.

69. Pogonowski, *Jews in Poland*, 46.

70. Pogonowski, *Jews in Poland*, 48.

71. Pogonowski, *Jews in Poland*, 52.

72. Pogonowski, *Jews in Poland*, 55.

73. Pogonowski, *Jews in Poland*, 55.

74. Pogonowski, *Jews in Poland*, 47.

75. Pogonowski, *Jews in Poland*, 49.

76. Pogonowski, *Jews in Poland*, 52.

77. Pogonowski, *Jews in Poland*, 50.

78. See Avigdor Levy, *The Jews of the Ottoman Empire* (Princeton, NJ, 1992), 293–95.

79. Bat Ye'or, *The Dhimmi: Jews and Christians under Islam*, trans. David Maisel, Paul Fenton, and David Littman (London, 1985), 359–61.

80. Bat Ye'or, *The Dhimmi*, 354.

81. Bat Ye'or, *The Dhimmi*, 357.

82. Bat Ye'or, *The Dhimmi*, 362.

83. Norman A. Stillman, *The Jews of Arab Lands: A History and Source Book* (Philadelphia, 1979), 298.

84. Levy, *The Jews of the Ottoman Empire*, 18.

85. Cited in Levy, *The Jews of the Ottoman Empire*, 19.

86. Samuel Usque, *Consolation for the Tribulations of the Jews*, trans. Martin A. Cohen (Philadelphia, 1965), 211–12.

87. Stillman, *The Jews of Arab Lands*, 256.

88. Stillman, *The Jews of Arab Lands*, 256–57.

89. Stillman, *The Jews of Arab Lands*, 291–92.

90. See Jonathan Israel, *European Jewry in the Age of Mercantilism, 1550–1750*, 3rd ed. (London, 1998), 2, 32ff, for example.

91. Israel, *European Jewry in the Age of Mercantilism*, 46ff.

92. Fram, *Ideals Face Reality*, 29.

93. See Peter Schäfer, *Judeophobia: Attitudes toward the Jews in the Ancient World* (Cambridge, MA, 1997).

94. See the introduction by Yom Tov Assis in *The Jews of Tortosa 1373–1492: Regesta and Documents from the Archivo Histórico de protocols de Tarragona*, compiled by Josefina Cubelis I Llorens (Jerusalem, 1991), vi.

95. Assis, *The Jews of Tortosa*, xvif.

96. Marcus, *The Jew in the Medieval World*, 156–57.

97. See Miri Rubin, *Gentile Tales: The Narrative Assault on Late Medieval Jews* (New Haven, CT, 1999).

98. Jean DeLumeau, *Catholicism between Luther and Voltaire: A New View of the Counter-Reformation* (London, 1977).

99. Weinryb, *The Jews of Poland*, 152.

100. See Jacob Barnai, " Blood Libels' in the Ottoman Empire of the Fifteenth to Nineteenth Centuries," in *Antisemitism through the Ages*, ed. Shmuel Almog, trans. Nathan H. Reisner (Oxford, 1988), 189–94.

101. See his very important book *The Myth of Ritual Murder: Jews and Magic in Reformation Germany* (New Haven, CT, 1988).

102. Cited in Bonfil, *Jewish Life in Renaissance Italy*, 24.

103. Levy, *The Jews of the Ottoman Empire*, 40–41.

104. Fram, *Ideals Face Reality*, 33.

105. Weinryb, *The Jews of Poland*, 153.

106. Levy, *The Jews of the Ottoman Empire*, 82.

107. Levy, *The Jews of the Ottoman Empire*, 81.

108. Marcus, *The Jew in the Medieval World*, 451, 453. See other sources for further details.

109. Weinryb, *The Jews of Poland*, 46–47.

110. Weinryb, *The Jews of Poland*, table on p. 47.

111. Baron, *A Social and Religious History of the Jews*, 16:208–9.

112. See Jose Hinojosa Montalvo, *The Jews of the Kingdom of Valencia from Persecution to Expulsion, 1391–1492* (Jerusalem, 1993), 35.

113. Montalvo, *The Jews of the Kingdom of Valencia*, 230.

114. For these examples, see Haim Beinart, *Trujillo: A Jewish Community in Extremadura on the Eve of the Expulsion from Spain* (Jerusalem, 1980), 10–12.

115. Mordechai Arbell, "Jewish Settlements in the French Colonies in the Caribbean (Martinique, Guadeloupe, Haiti, Cayenne) and the 'Black Code,'" in *The Jews and the Expansion of Europe to the West, 1450–1800*, ed. Paolo Bernardini and Norman Fiering (New York, 2001), 291.

116. Arbell, "Jewish Settlements in the French Colonies," 293.

117. Arbell, "Jewish Settlements in the French Colonies," 294.

118. Mendes Flohr and Reinharz, *The Jew in the Modern World*, 452.

119. Mendes Flohr and Reinharz, *The Jew in the Modern World*, 452.

120. Mendes Flohr and Reinharz, *The Jew in the Modern World*, 453.

121. Israel, *European Jewry in the Age of Mercantilism*, 32.

122. For both, see Horowitz, "Families and Their Fortunes," 617.

123. Stillman, *The Jews of Arab Lands*, 304.

124. Lewis, *The Jews of Islam*, 149.

125. Stillman, *The Jews of Arab Lands*, 281.

126. Stillman, *The Jews of Arab Lands*, 282.

127. Stillman, *The Jews of Arab Lands*, 282.

128. See Norman Roth, *Conversos, Inquisition, and the Expulsion of the Jews from Spain* (Madison, WI, 1995).

129. For a slightly differently worded translation, see Haim Beinart, *The Expulsion of the Jews from Spain*, trans. Jeffrey M. Green (Oxford, 2002; orig., 1994), 51–52.

130. See Roth, *Conversos*; Yitzhak Baer, *A History of the Jews in Christian Spain, Volume 2: From the Fourteenth Century to the Expulsion*, trans. Louis Schoffman (Philadelphia, 1966); Haim Beinart, ed., *Moreshet Sepharad: The Sephardi Legacy*, 2 vols. (Jerusalem, 1992); and Haim Beinart, *The Expulsion of the Jews from Spain*, trans. Jeffrey M. Green (Oxford, 2002; orig., 1994). According to Ibn Verga, "Indeed, the Jews had been beloved by the kings and ministers and all their wise men, who had always respected them highly. The expulsion order only remained in effect because of the intervention of some of the common people, who claimed that ever since the Jews had arrived in the kingdom food had become more expensive, and that the Jews had usurped the positions in certain trades. The expulsion was also fostered by the priests, in order to show how saintly they were and to show the people that they wished to honor and advance the Christian religion." Quoted in David Raphael, ed., *The Expulsion 1492 Chronicles: An Anthology of Medieval Chronicles Relating to the Expulsion of the Jews from Spain and Portugal* (North Hollywood, CA, 1992), 92.

131. Marcus, *The Jew in the Medieval World*, 56, 58.

132. Roth, *Conversos*, 283.

133. *Yosif Ometz*, section 153, in Isidor Kracauer, *Geschichte der Juden in Frankfurt am Main* (Frankfurt am Main, Germany, 1925), 1:388.

134. See the excellent study of Christopher Friedrichs, "Politics or Pogrom? The Fettmilch Uprising in German and Jewish History," *Central European History* 19 (1986): 186–228.

135. Israel, *European Jewry in the Age of Mercantilism*, 6, 7.

136. Israel, *European Jewry in the Age of Mercantilism*, 7.

137. Israel, *European Jewry in the Age of Mercantilism*, 15.

138. Israel, *European Jewry in the Age of Mercantilism*, 17.

139. Weinryb, *The Jews of Poland*, 36–37, 50.

140. See Bodian, *Hebrews of the Portuguese Nation*.

141. "Inquisition," in *Encyclopedia Judaica*, 16 vols. (Jerusalem, 1971–1972).

142. Cecil Roth, "Inquisition: Statistics," in *Encyclopedia Judaica*, 16 vols. (Jerusalem, 1971–1972).

143. Roth, "Inquisition: Statistics."

144. Arbell, "Jewish Settlements in the French Colonies," 288.

145. See Marcus, *The Jew in the Medieval World*, 173–78.

146. See Brian Pullan, *The Jews of Europe and the Inquisition of Venice, 1550–1670* (London, 1997).

147. For Josel, see the important if now somewhat dated work of Selma Stern, *Josel of Rosheim: Commander of Jewry in the Holy Roman Empire of the German Nation*, trans. Gertrude Hirschler (Philadelphia, 1965; orig., 1959).

148. Weinryb, *The Jews of Poland*, 95.

149. Weinryb, *The Jews of Poland*, 94.

150. Weinryb, *The Jews of Poland*, 95.

151. See Elisheva Carlebach, *Divided Souls: Converts from Judaism in Germany, 1500–1750* (New Haven, CT, 2001).

152. Sander L. Gilman, *Jewish Self-Hatred: Anti-Semitism and the Hidden Language of the Jews* (Baltimore, 1986), 40.

153. See Carlebach, *Divided Souls*, 81–82.

154. Johannes Reuchlin, *Recommendation Whether to Confiscate, Destroy, and Burn All Jewish Books*, ed. and trans. Peter Wortsman (New York, 2000), 93.

155. Reuchlin, *Recommendation*, 90.

156. Reuchlin, *Recommendation*, 83.

157. Reuchlin, *Recommendation*, 87.

158. Erika Rummel, "Humanists, Jews, and Judaism," in *Jews, Judaism, and the Reformation in Sixteenth-Century Germany*, ed. Dean Phillip Bell and Stephen G. Burnett (Leiden, Netherlands, 2006), 20.

159. On Münster, see Dean Phillip Bell, "Jewish and Christian Historiography in the Sixteenth Century: A Comparison of Sebastian Münster and David Gans," in *God's Word for Our World: In Honor of Simon John DeVries*, ed. J. Harold Ellens, Deborah L. Ellens, Rolf P. Knierim, and Isaac Kalimi, vol. 2 (London, 2004), 141–58.

160. The best and most important study is that of Stephen G. Burnett, *From Christian Hebraism to Jewish Studies: Johannes Buxtorf (1564–1629) and Hebrew Learning in the Seventeenth Century* (Leiden, Netherlands, 1996).

161. See R. Po-chia Hsia, "Christian Ethnographies of Jews in Early Modern Germany," in *The Expulsion of the Jews: 1492 and After*, ed. Raymond B. Waddington and A. H. Williamson (New York, 1994), 223–35; Stephen G. Burnett, "Distorted Mirrors: Antonius Margaritha, Johann Buxtorf, and Christian Ethnographies of the Jews," *Sixteenth Century Journal* 25 (1994): 275–87; Yaacov Deutsch, "Polemical Ethnographies: Descriptions of Yom Kippur in the Writings of Christian Hebraists and Jewish Converts to Christianity in Early Modern Europe," in *Hebraica Veritas? Jews and the Study of Judaism in Early Modern Europe*, ed. Allison P. Coudert and Jeffery S. Shoulson (Philadelphia, 2004), 202–33.

162. Horowitz, "Families and Their Fortunes," 583.

163. Quoted in Klaus Reichert, "Pico della Mirandola and the Beginnings of Christian Kabbala," in *Mysticism, Magic, and Kabbalah*, ed. Karl Erich Grözinger and Joseph Dan (Berlin, 1995), 196–97.

164. See Allison P. Coudert, *The Impact of the Kabbalah in the Seventeenth Century: The Life and Thought of Francis Mercury van Helmont (1614–1698)* (Leiden, Netherlands, 1999).

165. Yom Tov Lipman Mühlhausen, *Sefer Nizzahon*, ed. Theodorico Hackspan (Altdorf, Germany, 1644), 94.

166. Mühlhausen, *Sefer Nizzahon*, 19–20. Quoted in Haim Hillel Ben-Sasson, *Trial and Achievement: Currents in Jewish History (from 313)* (Jerusalem, 1974), 273. In arguing with the Christian, Mühlhausen has had to revert to a Christian framework.

167. Mühlhausen, *Sefer Nizzahon*, 120–21.

168. Fram, *Ideals Face Reality*, 28. See also Phillip Dean Bell, *Jewish Identity in Early Modern Germany: Memory, Power, and Community* (Aldershot, UK, 2007).

169. Quoted in Marc Saperstein, *Exile in Amsterdam: Saul Levi Morteira's Sermons to a Congregation of "New Jews"* (Cincinnati, 2005), 276.

Conclusion

As we noted in the introduction, **periodization** in history can be complicated, frequently contested, and certainly variable, but often very useful for thinking about the past. How we slice up the past tells us quite a bit about the past but even more about ourselves. The questions we frame and the issues we thematize are more often than not outgrowths of questions and issues we face as individuals and as members of society. On the other hand, these questions and issues do not arise in a vacuum, and they cannot be addressed in one. The past, no matter how interpreted, offers sources and (multiple) contexts in which to read, understand, and interpret those sources.

The early modern period, in particular, which has in many ways been a modern invention over the past century, has recently received a great deal of scholarly attention. This has been due in part to the fact that the period is located squarely between the Middle Ages and modernity and has been presented as a transitional epoch, with important ties to what came before and after. At the same time, the early modern period is now clearly to be understood as unique. The early modern period, therefore, has been seen as simultaneously traditional and transformational. What we can say is that early modern society was remarkably rich, diverse, and complex.

Jewish history of the early modern period has benefited from the sources and methodologies available to non-Jewish historians and the non-Jewish world. At the same time, the discovery, analysis, and reinterpretation of many Jewish sources has added tremendously to what we know of early modern Jewish life. Many scholars have seen, and will no doubt continue to see, early modern Jewish history as an appendage to the Jewish Middle Ages or as primarily a precursor to modernity (consider the discussions in chapter 1 and in the introduction). Yet, the very fact that both positions seem to have strong justifications should make us pause and consider how this can be.

We have seen many themes that characterize the early modern period, the period between 1400 and 1700. Among these themes are globalization, population growth, increased social stratification, economic development, the location of and challenge to authority (communal and religious), and increasing cultural interaction. In each of these cases, early modern Jewry was both traditional and transitional. It was, as the historian Jacob Katz articulated, capable of both absorbing and neutralizing new ideas and developments without forcing its current structures to crumble within.

Jewish population and settlement patterns in the early modern period, for example, could be highly volatile. While some areas experienced significant and long-term continuity, such as in parts of the Ottoman Empire, most Jewish settlements changed dramatically over time depending on a wide range of external conditions and general Jewish migration. While pockets of Jews could be found in nearly every part of the globe, it was in central and eastern Europe and throughout the broad reaches of the Ottoman Empire that the majority of Jews resided. The solid populations of western and central Europe in the later Middle Ages migrated en masse East to the Ottoman Empire and Poland. For the early part of our period, the majority of Jews lived under Ottoman rule, continuing the long medieval tradition of Jews living under Islam but also adding large numbers of Jews as the Ottoman state expanded greatly. While the late medieval settlement of Jews in Poland was slim, by the end of the early modern period, the Polish Jewish population was becoming dominant, a trend that would continue into and help to define the modern period of Jewish history.

Early modern Jewish communities were often isolated from general society but rarely insulated or homogenous. Even when Jews were not formally segregated into a ghetto they often chose to live in close proximity with one another for various social and religious purposes. Despite such separation, however, Jews continually engaged with non-Jews in various social and business capacities. What is more, with the broad and frequent movement of Jews and the diverse experiences and backgrounds of early modern Jews, it should not be too surprising that many Jewish settlements were far from homogenous. Especially in large communities, Jews of varying ethnic, national, and cultural backgrounds formed complex and at times tension-filled societies. Often, multiple communities could develop within the same city or in close proximity, as they did in Venice.

Jews were among the most mobile of people in the early modern period, as the migratory and travel paths of some famous individuals indicate, even if they seem to have resided in some cities for long periods of time. While such mobility could lead to complex community development and structure, it was also important as a survival technique, and early modern Jews showed great tenacity and ability to adapt to changing conditions, allowing them to survive in many and frequently changing diasporas. Jewish demography informed internal Jewish religious and cultural developments as well as Jewish relations with the non-Jews around them. In each case, Jewish identity in the early modern period could be complicated.

Jews could be defined by adherence to certain fundamental religious beliefs or practices; local, regional, or ethnic customs; or definitions superimposed by non-Jewish authorities. So, for example, Karaites, who rejected the Oral Law while accepting the Written Law, could be Jews in the same way that **Marranos**, or New Christians, who were suspected of practicing Jewish rites or adhering to Jewish ideas, could be. Even when they adhered to a common body of Talmudic principles, **Ashkenazic** and **Sephardic** Jews might have very different customs and world-views.

At its heart the Jewish community was an association that bound Jews together for a range of religious but also for social, cultural, economic, and political reasons. While the specifics could vary, most communities had generally similar governing structures and tools. Communities were run by councils of laymen, which shared power with or delegated tasks to communal officials, including scribes and tax assessors. Most communities had almost formulaic rules about what tasks communal officials were charged with and how such officials (adult men, generally of a certain financial means) should be elected or appointed. While the Jewish community was theoretically ruled by majority vote, many communities were simply thinly veiled oligarchies dominated by particularly wealthy, learned, or otherwise influential families. A wide range of social institutions, such as welfare and dowering societies, were combined with more physical communal structures, such as synagogues and *mikvaot* (ritual baths), with each providing important services and outlets within the Jewish community. The community was guided in Jewish law by the rabbi. The early modern rabbinate, however, was not always monolithic, and there existed levels of rabbinic ordination and levels of authority that individual rabbis might attain. Throughout the early modern period there were conflicts among rabbis and increasingly between rabbis and powerful lay leaders. The authority of the rabbi was frequently discussed, particularly as the early modern rabbi was becoming a salaried official in many communities.

Although most Jewish communities were small, with 50 or 100 members, there were some very large Jewish communities with more than 2,000 members. In both cases, however, the internal social and economic dynamics could be extremely complex. This was especially true in multiethnic or recently forged communities. Similar social stratification and social tensions existed within the Jewish communities as they did in the non-Jewish communities surrounding the Jews. Increasingly in the early modern period an immense gulf separated the very wealthy and the poor. The number of poor Jews apparently increased dramatically in our period, due to persecution and forced migration as well as to a host of other economic and political developments. This rise in poverty has been associated with increased incidents of crime committed by Jews against other Jews as well as against non-Jews. The tremendous range of social stations within the communities was clearly reflected in the range of professions and occupations practiced by Jews. While pre-modern Jews have stereotypically been seen as money-lenders and pawn-brokers—generally forced into these poorly regarded professions because of restrictive legislation—Jews were also involved in a rich array of work that defies any easy categorization. There certainly were some professions that appear to have been common in certain regions, tailors in parts of Italy, for example, and there were some areas of endeavor that appear to have rather disproportionately large or renowned Jewish participation, such as the role of Jews in medicine or in international commerce in the early modern period.

Early modern Judaism was focused on the fulfillment of the commandments (*mitzvot*). Particularly in the course of debate with non-Jews, Jews expressed theological concepts and central guiding religious principles that shaped Jewish thought and Jewish practice. Among these were discussions about the nature and existence of God, God's relationship with the Jewish people, the status of the Torah, and the role of prophecy and messianism. While we can never thoroughly know how religion was practiced or to what extent religious norms were upheld or disregarded, let alone what common people "believed," the evidence we do have suggests that most Jews were "traditional" in the sense that they obeyed rabbinic and communal authority, were familiar with traditional texts and beliefs, were involved in discussion about Jewish thought, and attended religious worship on a regular basis.

Jewish education existed at many different levels and touched almost every Jew in some way. The wealthy generally hired tutors for their children. While that trend continued, increasingly in the early modern period Jewish education was becoming a more general communal concern. At times, informal education was made available to Jewish women as well. We have indications that many women were familiar with key religious ideas and commandments, with religious instruction being conveyed in Hebrew as well as in various vernacular languages. The Talmudic academy, *yeshivah*, represented the highest level of engagement for Jewish men with classical Jewish sources, particularly the Talmudic texts and religious codes. The *yeshivot* (plural) had their own hierarchies and internal dynamics. They created something of an international and mobile form of Jewish learning, and the rabbis these institutions produced helped to shape early modern Judaism and early modern Jewish communities.

Printing affected Jewish education as it did Jewish and non-Jewish culture more generally. The availability of texts standardized educational curricula and discussions, at the same time that the transmission of various texts opened Jewish thinkers to a range of both traditional and innovative ideas. Despite the intense discussions about, and at times opposition to, codification, the circulation of legal codes, notably Joseph Caro's **Shulhan Arukh** and the printing and circulation of various rabbinic **responsa**, dramatically impacted the legal decision-making of Jewish communities. Such codes and decisions allowed for greater uniformity, but they also revealed significant discrepancies in thinking, custom, and practices among the far-flung Jewish communities of the early modern period.

Among the most significant genres of Jewish writing in the early modern period were ethical writings and, increasingly, mystical writings as transmitted through **Kabbalah**. Both had significant influence on religious thought and practice. A particularly important and dynamic center of Jewish mysticism developed in the Middle Eastern city of Safed, which during the last half of the sixteenth and well into the seventeenth century was home to some of the most renowned Jewish religious luminaries. While early modern Jewish mysticism drew from deep wellsprings of Jewish thought, it was also steeped in robust streams of Christian and Islamic mystical speculation as well. A correlated area to mysticism was messianism, which also drew from surrounding cultural and religious developments and took on great urgency in Jewish thought, particularly as rapid changes across the globe seemed to portend the end of days. There were numerous messianic figures in early modern Judaism (as there were in early modern Christianity and Islam). The most well-known and most significant was Shabbetai Sevi. Shabbetai Sevi seemed poised to turn the world upside down and usher in the messianic period. Many Jews became followers and expected the messianic redemption any moment. With Sevi's capture and conversion to Islam, those hopes and dreams were dashed.

Like Jewish mysticism and messianism, early modern Judaism engaged what we might today term the supernatural and magical. These were elements that in many ways were inseparable from religious thinking throughout the early modern period. This was the case in all early modern religions. Various practices, such as divination, palmistry, and the use of amulets marked early modern Judaism as a religion that imbibed and adapted external practices and was intimately centered on the practical as much as the speculative.

Early modern Judaism was in some ways flexible, allowing for variations in thought and to some extent even in practice. In the midst of early modern attempts to centralize and expand authority, it is not entirely clear whether the increased references to deviating behavior are an indication that early modern Jews were challenging traditional systems and norms or whether we simply have more records of such behavior—or even if the recording of such behavior was in part a ploy of moralists and communal leaders to encourage "proper behavior."

While some deviance and tension no doubt always existed in Jewish communities, the growing diversity of the Jewish communities themselves through apostasy, reversion to Judaism, the mixing of divergent customs, and the extreme migration of Jewish populations may have aggravated this situation. In general, early modern Judaism seemed to be able to absorb and, as one scholar maintains, "neutralize," various decentralizing trends. Yet, throughout the early modern period, and certainly by the end of the period, there were significant examples of thinking and practice that could not be held within traditional Jewish boundaries. The best example of this was Baruch Spinoza, whose philosophy challenged traditional religious thinking in many and important ways and led to his excommunication from the Jewish community as well as his censure by many Christian writers.

Early modern Jewish culture was not only religious. Jews produced and engaged a wide range of literary, artistic, and scientific works. In many cases, Jewish participation in such intellectual and cultural fields was long-standing and well developed. Early modern Jewish participation in broader cultural developments is perhaps exemplified by the work of Azariah de' Rossi, David Gans, and Elijah Capsali in the area of history. Each historian seriously engaged non-Jewish sources but interpreted them within and for the purpose of understanding Jewish history. While many of their co-religionists criticized the use of non-Jewish sources, the subtle arguments employed by these scholars for using them in combination with more "traditional" purposes indicate that early modern Jewish society was, in important ways, navigating both traditional and innovative worlds.

Indeed, as we have seen, the relations between Jews and non-Jews in the early modern world were complex, changeable, and dependent upon a wide range of local conditions. Throughout much of our period, and increasingly by the seventeenth century, toleration of the Jews did exist, often for economic or political reasons. Jews engaged with their non-Jewish neighbors in many different ways and at various levels, in commercial and social relations. Some communal legislation and sumptuary laws attempted to limit Jewish and non-Jewish relations, and the repetition of these laws, as well as evidence in non-Jewish sources, suggests that Jewish interaction with non-Jews was considerable and significant.

We know from library collections as well as literary productions that many Jews engaged non-Jewish ideas and non-Jewish scholars. The theological and social developments of general society impacted early modern Jews in important ways. Religious reforms within Christianity, for example, sometimes led to new images of, and approaches to, Judaism both among non-Jews and within Jewish communities. At times such religious changes even seeped into Jewish practices and thought. Yet, early modern Jews appear to have had a remarkable ability to engage the world around them, without abandoning their own religion. Here they did not simply "neutralize" the external, but also they adapted non-Jewish ideas within a traditional Jewish framework.

Nevertheless, Jews remained religious outsiders and in both Christian and Islamic society were frequently marginalized and dominated. The political and legal position of the Jews varied by location. At times Jews enjoyed relative social, economic, and even religious freedom, always provided that they were not too public or vocal. Even when Jews teetered on the edge of expulsion they might be allowed to remain if they were thought to bring any kind of economic benefit to the region or the ruling authorities. But rulers or authorities who generally inclined to tolerate the Jews for economic reasons often changed their position or placed heavy restrictions or burdens on the Jews making Jewish existence often tentative and fragile. The power to govern the community, while generally held within the community itself, could not always withstand the attention or desires of these external non-Jewish authorities, who wanted to control the community for monetary purposes.

Particularly in Christian society, though not exclusively, Jews were accused of a range of crimes and devious behaviors. Some of these allegations stemmed from long-standing anti-Jewish religious prejudices. Jews were, for example, accused of desecrating Christian images or the Eucharist. Jews were also accused of more serious crimes, such as taking excessive usury, counterfeiting coins, poisoning wells, colluding with state enemies, and most heinously, the murder of Christian children for the sake of imagined Jewish rituals. Such accusations often led to restrictive measures as well as to persecutions, with attacks on property, expulsions, and pogroms. While Jews generally fared better in Islamic lands, even there they were accused of altering biblical texts and of collaborating with foreign enemies. In the end, violent anti-Jewish actions could erupt anywhere and under almost any conditions, even when not fully sanctioned by ruling authorities.

Interaction between Jews and non-Jews could be even more complex when some Jews were forced or voluntarily left Judaism. Some infamous converts became ardent opponents of and polemicists against Judaism. Positive relations between Jews and converts, however, could lead to trouble for both the converts and the Jews. The Inquisition, and the subsequent expulsion from Spain, was directed at Christian fears that relations between Jews and newly converted Christians would lead to a reversion to Judaism, **Judaizing** behavior, or some sort of heresy. Relations between Jews and converts were, indeed, and perhaps surprisingly, often friendly. Converts served in a sense as cultural intermediaries, forming part of a complex intellectual milieu. Some served as Hebrew instructors at universities and proofreaders at printing shops, and some became valuable colleagues for Christian Hebraists and Christian kabbalists who eagerly read and discussed Hebrew texts and Jewish rites.

Jews were, of course, not simply idle spectators in their relations with non-Jews and in the unfolding events of the time. Early modern Jews debated non-Jews and contested marginalization. They did what they could to secure political rights and social and economic privileges. They defended their religious beliefs at the same time that they questioned Christian and Islamic dogma.

Jewish relations with the world around them were affected by Jewish settlement and migration, by internal Jewish developments and discussions, and by changes and conflicts in broader non-Jewish society. Early modern Jews straddled a world that was simultaneously internal and external, traditional and transitional. Their history revealed the persistence of old anti-Jewish hostilities and new opportunities for positive interaction with the world around them. Early modern Jews were steeped in a world constructed upon rabbinic and medieval ideas and situations. At the same time, they existed within and often seriously engaged the quickly changing world around them. In this sense, Jews both responded to and helped to create early modern society. Their experiences allow us a window into an important and transitional period of Jewish history. The history of early modern Jews, therefore, provides a valuable means for understanding more general early modern historical experiences and development.

Glossary

amidah   literally "standing"; prayer also know as the Eighteen Benedictions

Arba'ah Turim   (Hebrew) "four rows"; comprehensive codification of Jewish law in four parts written by Jacob ben Asher (ca. 1270–1340)

arendars   leaseholders

arvit (or maariv)   evening service

ascamot   *See* haskamah (pl. haskamot)

Ashkenazic   term used generally to designate Jews of northwest, central, and eastern European descent

auto da fe   "act of faith"; ceremony related to inquisitorial proceedings

av bet din   head of the rabbinic court

baalei shemot   masters of the names; Jewish mystics

bimah   platform in synagogue where the Torah is read

brit (pl. beritot) milah   circumcisions

condotta   charter for Jewish community in Italy

confessionalization   the process of forming denominations according to theology in the aftermath of the Protestant Reformation

converso(s)   Christian(s) of Jewish descent; frequently accused of secretly maintaining Jewish rites; also known as anusim or Marranos

darshan   preacher

devekut (or devequt)   mystical term referring to cleaving to God

dhimmis   protected people

fattori   three chief officials in some Italian Jewish communities

gabbai (pl. gabbaim)   lay communal official; warden

gaon (pl. geonim)   "excellency"; title of heads of the two leading Babylonian academies between the end of the sixth and end of the twelfth centuries

Gemara   rabbinic traditions and teachings forming parts of the Babylonian and Palestinian Talmuds

gemilut hasadim   literally "the bestowal of lovingkindness," referring also to benevolent societies

geniza   storage area for ritual objects or texts that are no longer usable

get   bill of divorce

gilgul   transmigration of souls

golem   artificial anthropoid

hadith   a foundation of Islamic jurisprudence

hakham   scholar; term used in some Sephardic communities for rabbi

halakhah (halakhic)   Jewish law

halizah (pl. halizot)   the act of "drawing off"; renunciation of the biblical injunction to marry the widow of one's brother who has died childless (Levirite Marriage)

Hasidei Ashkenaz   German Pietists active at the end of the high and during the later Middle Ages

Haskalah   Jewish Enlightenment

haskamah (pl. haskamot)   agreement or approbation (*see also* ascamot)

herem   excommunication

herem ha-yishuv   ban on settlement

hevra kadisha   burial society

hillukim   differentiations (as part of rabbinic method of study)

huppah   wedding canopy

imposta   governing body

Judaizer (Judaizing)   individual accused of practicing Jewish rites or holding Jewish beliefs

Kabbalah   "tradition"; refers to Jewish mysticism

Kabbalah, Lurianic   form of Jewish mysticism developed by Isaac Luria in sixteenth-century Safed

kahal   community

Kahal Kados; K[ahal] K[adosh]   "holy community"

kavana   intention (generally referring to performance of *mitzvot* [commandments])

kehilla (pl. kehillot)   community

ketubah (pl. ketubot)   Jewish wedding contract

kinyan   act of acquisition according to Jewish law

Landesrabbiner   regional rabbi

lulav and etrog   four species taken on the holiday of Sukkot

Maghrebi   inhabitants of North Africa and Spain according to Arab geographers

mahamad (ma'amad)   Sephardic community council of elders

Maimonides   Moses ben Maimon (1135–1204), also known as Rambam; noted medieval philosopher and thinker

Marrano   Jews in Spain and Portugal who were converted to Christianity but secretly practiced Jewish rituals

medinah   region

Memorybooks   memorial books kept by communities that recorded general information and dates of death, particularly of prominent members; read publicly at various times of the year in the synagogue

mikvah (pl. mikvaot)   ritual bath

minyan   prayer quorum (ten adult men)

Mishnah   the Oral Law, which, together with Gemara, forms the Talmud

Mishneh Torah   important legal code of Moses ben Maimon (Maimonides, 1135–1204)

nagid   head of Jewish community under Islam

ne'eman (pl. ne'emanim)   trustee

parnas (pl. parnasim)   "presider"; religious or administrative functionary in the Jewish community

parnas ha-hodesh   parnas of the month (a rotating position among the council leaders)

periodization   the act of dividing history according to particular periods

pilpul   rabbinic casuistry

pinkas (pl. pinkasim)   community ledgers

Rashi   Rabbi Solomon ben Isaac (1040–1105) of Troyes; great medieval Jewish exegete

rav   root word (meaning great) for rabbi

Reichsthaler   Silver coin issued in the Holy Roman Empire

responsum (pl. responsa) (sheelot u-teshuvot)   (Latin [Hebrew]) "questions and answers"; answers to questions on Jewish law and observance given by halakhic and Talmudic scholars in reply to inquiries addressed to them

rosh golah   exilarch

rosh yeshiva   head of a Talmudic academy

Sabat Bereshit (Shabbat Bereshit)   first Sabbath after Sukkot, when the annual reading of the Torah enters the new cycle and the weekly portion of Bereshit (beginning of Genesis) is read

Safavid   early modern Iranian ruling dynasty

Sanhedrin   assembly of ordained scholars who served as supreme court and legislating body during Temple period

Schutzbrief   German for letter of protection

semikhah   "laying on" of hands; rabbinic ordination

semikhat haver   ordination as an associate—in some places this was equivalent to rabbinic status and in others it had restrictions on certain functions that the individual could perform

Sephardic   Jews from "Sepharad," generally referring to Jews in Spain under Islam and Christianity but also taken to refer to many Jews in the Ottoman Empire

seym   Polish court

Shabbat ha Gadol   the Sabbath that precedes Passover

shaharit   morning; referring to the morning prayer service

shammash   Sexton or beadle in the Jewish community

shehitah   method of Jewish ritual slaughter of animals and birds permitted under Jewish law

shofar   ram's horn, sounded on various religious occasions

shohet (pl. shohetim)   ritual slaughterer (*see* shehitah)

shtadlan   intercessional, generally a wealthy or high ranking member of the Jewish community placed in charge of relations with the non-Jewish authorities

Shulhan Arukh   "The Prepared Table"; sixteenth-century legal code prepared by Rabbi Joseph Caro

Simhat Torah   Jewish holiday in the fall after Sukkot, focusing on the joy of completing and initiating the annual reading of the Torah

Sonderweg   in German, "special way"; relating to Jews, the Sonderweg theory posited a direct line of anti-Jewish development from the sixteenth-century reformer Martin Luther to Adolf Hitler

Sukkot   Jewish holiday, the Festival of Booths, held in the fall after Yom Kippur

supercession   replacement of the Old with the New Testament and the Jews as the Chosen People of God by the Christians

sürgün   exile or expulsion; the forced movement of populations by the Ottoman government for various political and economic reasons

takkanah (pl. takkanot)   ordinance

teqi'at kaf   handshake as part of legal acquisition

teva(h)   holy ark in the synagogue where the Torah scrolls are kept

theuilah (tevilah)   act of immersing to restore ritual purity

tikkun   repair of the cosmos

Tosafot   "additions"; collections of commentaries to Talmud, particularly from medieval France among successors to Rashi

tovim   the "good men," generally referring to council members within the Jewish community

tudescos   Portuguese term for German Jews

Tur refers alternately to the legal code Arba'ah Turim (Four Rows) or its author Rabbi Jacob ben Asher (Baal HaTurim), 1275–1340

Yahid individual (communal or congregational member)

yeshivah (pl. yeshivot) Talmudic academy

Zohar "The Book of Splendor," a primary kabbalistic text authored in large part by Moses de Leon (ca. 1240–1305) in Spain

Suggestions for Further Reading

The field of early modern history generally, but also for Jewish Studies, is vast and has grown dramatically in the last few decades. In what follows, suggestions are offered for further English-language reading beyond the materials that are formally cited in the bibliography. These suggestions are in no way intended to be exhaustive. Rather, some English-language works that are readily accessible and likely to have direct relevance to themes in this book have been included. Much of the accessible scholarship for the early modern period is heavily weighted toward Christian Europe, and the entries that follow reflect that focus.

JOURNALS AND OTHER RESOURCES

There are numerous scholarly journals (as well as more popular ones) that publish articles related to medieval and early modern Jewish history. Among the general historical journals that regularly include such articles, see *American Historical Review, Harvard Theological Review, Sixteenth Century Journal, Past and Present,* and *Speculum.* Many journals also focus specifically on issues of Jewish history. See, for example, *Jewish History, Jewish Studies Quarterly, Jewish Social Studies, Jewish Quarterly Review, AJS Review, Shofar: An Interdisciplinary Journal of Jewish Studies, Proceedings of the American Academy of Jewish Research, Leo Baeck Institute Yearbook, Studia Rosenthalia,* and *Revue des Etudes juives.*

There also exist powerful online resources. Major Judaica libraries, such as those at Harvard University, the Jewish Theological Seminary of America, Hebrew Union College, and Spertus Institute of Jewish Studies, provide easy access to bibliographical materials for a wide range of publications. The *Encyclopedia Judaica* is now available in a CD format and is extremely valuable. The Rambi Index of Articles on Jewish Studies, Jewish National and University Library, is a wonderful tool that can assist students in locating articles in many different areas of Jewish history (the website is aleph1.libnet.ac.il/F/?func=file&file_name=find-b&local_base=rmb01).

JEWISH HISTORIOGRAPHY

The work of Yosef Hayim Yerushalmi, *Zakhor: Jewish History and Jewish Memory* (Seattle, 1982), which originated as a series of lectures, has been a catalyst for the past two decades for discussions about Jewish notions of history and memory. Other recent work on various aspects of Jewish historical writing is well represented in Shmuel Feiner's *Haskalah and History: The Emergence of a Modern Jewish Historical Consciousness* (Oxford, 2002) and the volume *The Jewish Past Revisited: Reflections on Modern Jewish Historians*, ed. David N. Myers and David B. Ruderman (New Haven, CT, 1998). See also David Biale, *Gershom Scholem: Kabbalah and Counter-History* (Cambridge, MA, 1979).

A number of broader surveys of Jewish history are available in volumes cited in the bibliography but can also be found in Martin Goodman, ed., *The Oxford Handbook of Jewish Studies* (Oxford, 2002). An older collection of articles on Jewish Studies methodology is *The State of Jewish Studies*, ed. S. J. D. Cohen and E. L. Greenstein (Detroit, 1990). It contains a variety of articles, including Ivan Marcus, "Medieval Jewish Studies: Toward an Anthropological History of the Jews" (113–27). One methodological issue that is important for early modern Jewish history is the use of rabbinic **responsa** to glean information about the social history of the Jews. A central exploration of this topic was made by Hayim Soloveitchik in a Hebrew work. For a discussion in English, see Bernhard D. Weinryb, "Responsa as a Source for History (Methodological Problems)," in *Essays Presented to Rabbi Israel Brodie on the Occasion of His 70th Birthday*, ed. H. J. Zimmels, J. Rabbinowitz, and I. Finestein (London, 1967), 399–417.

Methodologically interesting are the various comparative studies that have been produced recently. For a look at how sociology has been used, consider Michael Driedger, "Crossing Max Weber's Great Divide: Comparing Early Modern European Jewish and Anabaptist Histories," in *Radical Reformation Studies: Essays Presented to James M. Stayer*, ed. Geoffrey Dipple and Werner Packull (Aldershot, UK, 1999), 157–74.

A classic and helpful general reference work is Martin Gilbert's *The Atlas of Jewish History* (New York, 1993).

MEDIEVAL JEWISH SOCIETY AND THOUGHT

A number of surveys of medieval Jewish history have appeared within the past decade or so. The most important of these are Mark R. Cohen, *Under Crescent and Cross: The Jews in the Middle Ages* (Princeton, NJ, 1994), and Kenneth R. Stow, *Alienated Minority: The Jews of Medieval Latin Europe* (Cambridge, MA, 1992); see also Leonard B. Glick, *Abraham's Heirs: Jews and Christians in Medieval Europe* (Syracuse, NY, 1999).

Over the course of the last century an impressive array of studies was published detailing the history and development of medieval Jewish societies. One of the earliest such works was Israel Abrahams, *Jewish Life in the Middle Ages* (Philadelphia, 1920), which continues to be cited today. In the late fifties through the early seventies a number of important studies were produced, including Irving Agus' *Urban Civilization in Pre-Crusade Europe* (New York, 1965) and *Rabbi Meir of Rothenburg: His Life and His Works as Sources for the Religious, Legal, and Social History of the Jews of Germany in the Thirteenth Century* (Philadelphia, 1947), Yitzhak Baer's monumental two-volume *A History of the Jews in Christian Spain*, trans. Louis Schoffman (Philadelphia, 1966), and David Menahem Shohet's *The Jewish Court in the Middle Ages: Studies in Jewish Jurisprudence according to the Talmud, Geonic, and Medieval German Responsa* (New York, 1974).

In the area of medieval Jewish education, the work of Ivan G. Marcus and Ephraim Kanarfogel has been central. See Marcus' *Rituals of Childhood: Jewish Acculturation in Medieval Europe* (New Haven, CT, 1996) and Kanarfogel's *Jewish Education and Society in the High Middle Ages* (Detroit, 1992). A number of recent studies on family and gender have added a great deal to our understanding of the complexity of medieval Jewish life. Consider, for example, the important work of the Israeli scholar Avraham Grossman and Elisheva Baumgarten (cited in the bibliography). Mark R. Cohen, noted above, has been a significant voice in the history of medieval Jewry, and his latest work on the poor in the Middle Ages, culled from documents from the Cairo *geniza* is exemplary: Mark R. Cohen, *Poverty and Charity in the Jewish Community of Medieval Egypt* and *The Voice of the Poor in the Middle Ages: An Anthology of Documents from the Cairo Geniza* (both Princeton, NJ, 2005). An extremely important voice in the history of medieval Jewry has been that of the Hebrew University scholar Michael Toch. In addition to important demographic studies, Toch has been ground breaking in his work in Jewish economic history. For a collection of some of his essays, see his *Peasants and Jews in Medieval Germany: Studies in Cultural, Social, and Economic History* (Aldershot, UK, 2003).

In the area of Jewish thought, the topics of Hasidism and philosophy have received a good deal of attention. For the latter, Ivan G. Marcus' important study *Piety and Society: The Jewish Pietists of Medieval Germany* (Leiden, Netherlands, 1997; orig., 1981) remains central. The work of the Hasidei Ashkenaz has been discussed in a number of significant articles as well—preeminently, Haym Soloveitchik, "Three Themes in the *Sefer Hasidim*," *AJS Review* 1 (1976): 311–57. A great contemporary scholar of Jewish thought and mysticism is Joseph Dan, whose writing has been primarily in Hebrew but who has also edited a number of general works such as *Jewish Intellectual History in the Middle Ages* (Westport, CT, 1994). These works supplement and build upon the important studies of Gershom Scholem and now Moshe Idel (see below). In the area of Jewish philosophy, we have already cited the work of Colette Sirat, but mention must also be made of the older *A History of Medieval Jewish Philosophy* (New York, 1969; orig., 1940), by Isaac Husik, which is still of great value.

JEWISH RELATIONS WITH NON-JEWS IN THE MIDDLE AGES

There is a vast and important literature on Jewish relations with non-Jews in the Middle Ages. Dated, but still useful, is Joshua Trachtenberg, *The Devil and the Jews* (New York, 1961; orig., 1943). Among the most productive scholars have been Robert Chazan and Jeremy Cohen. For Chazan, see his *Barcelona and Beyond: The Disputation of 1263 and Its Aftermath* (Berkeley, CA, 1992); *Daggers of Faith: Thirteenth-Century Christian Missionizing and Jewish Responses* (Berkeley, CA, 1989); *In the Year 1096: The First Crusade and the Jews* (Philadelphia, 1996); and *Medieval Stereotypes and Modern Antisemitism* (Berkeley, CA, 1997). Cohen's work includes *The Friars and the Jews: The Evolution of Medieval Anti-Judaism* (Ithaca, NY, 1982); *Living Letters of the Law: Ideas of the Jew in Medieval Christianity* (Berkeley, CA, 1999); as well as his edited volume, *Essential Papers on Judaism and Christianity in Conflict: From Late Antiquity to the Reformation* (New York, 1991).

Important work has been produced on the legal position of medieval Jews. See, for example, Bernard S. Bachrach, *Early Medieval Jewish Policy in Western Europe* (Minneapolis, 1977); Amnon Linder, *The Jews in the Legal Sources of the Early Middle Ages* (Detroit, 1997); and Guido Kisch, *Jewry Law in Medieval Germany: Laws and Court-Decisions* (New York, 1949). Consider also William Jordan, *The French Monarchy and the Jews* (Philadelphia, 1989).

There are many important books that treat anti-Judaism generally and in the Middle Ages. Among the most generally referenced, see Gavin Langmuir, *Toward a Definition of Antisemitism* (Berkeley, CA, 1990), as well as the older but still useful Leon Poliakov, *The History of Anti-Semitism*, trans. Richard Howard, 4 vols. (Philadelphia, 2003; orig., 1966). Other fascinating studies with special foci include Lester K. Little, *Religious Poverty and the Profit Economy in Medieval Europe* (Ithaca, NY, 1978) and David Nirenberg,

Communities of Violence: Persecution of Minorities in the Middle Ages (Princeton, NJ, 1996).

Jewish and Christian relations in the Middle Ages have received a great deal of scholarly attention in the past century. James Parkes' classic *The Church and the Synagogue* (New York, 1969) is still a useful overview in some ways. Heinz Schreckenberg, *The Jews in Christian Art: An Illustrated History* (New York, 1996), originally in German, is essential and very comprehensive. More focused studies that may be of interest are as follows: Anna Sapir Abulafia, *Christians and Jews in the Twelfth-Century Renaissance* (New York, 1995); Gilbert Dahan, *The Christian Polemic against the Jews in the Middle Ages*, trans. J. Gladding (Notre Dame, IN, 1998); and John Y. B. Hood, *Aquinas and the Jews* (Philadelphia, 1995). The article by Guido Kisch, "The Yellow Badge in History," *Historia Judaica* 19 (2) (October 1957): 89–146, remains valuable.

There are also some classic works on Jewish and Muslim relations, in addition to the materials cited in the bibliography. Consider Eliyahu Ashtor, *The Jews of Moslem Spain*, trans. Aaron Klein and Jenny Machlowitz Klein, 3 vols. (Philadelphia, 1973) and Moshe Gil, *Jews in Islamic Countries in the Middle Ages*, trans. David Strassler (Leiden, Netherlands, 2004). See also *From Iberia to Diaspora: Studies in Sephardic History and Culture*, ed. Yedida K. Stillman and Norman A. Stillman (Leiden, Netherlands, 1999), which contains some articles in English.

EARLY MODERN JEWISH SOCIETY AND CULTURE

Quite a few edited volumes, which contain many exceptional essays, have appeared in the past decade. Among this group of works, the following offer important insights into many of the themes discussed in this book: Bernard Dov Cooperman, ed., *In Iberia and Beyond: Hispanic Jews between Cultures: Proceedings of a Symposium to Mark the 500th Anniversary of the Expulsion of Spanish Jewry* (Newark, DE, 1998); Robert C. Davis and Benjamin Ravid, eds., *The Jews of Early Modern Venice* (Baltimore, 2001); Benjamin R. Gampel, ed. *Crisis and Creativity in the Sephardic World 1391–1648* (New York, 1997); Michael A. Meyer, ed., *German-Jewish History in Modern Times, Volume 1: Tradition and Enlightenment: 1600–1780* (New York, 1996); Jay M. Harris, ed., *The Pride of Jacob: Essays on Jacob Katz and His Work* (Cambridge, MA, 2002); Elliot Horowitz and Moises Orfali, eds., *The Mediterranean and the Jews: Society, Culture, and Economy in Early Modern Times* (Ramat-Gan, Israel, 2002); and Robert Bonfil, ed., *The Lion Shall Roar: Leon Modena and His World* (English and Hebrew) (Jerusalem, 2003).

In the area of Jewish arts and culture in the early modern period there is a wealth of wonderful and illustrative works. Regarding the great Jewish musical figure Salamone de Rossi, see the various articles by Don Harran and now his central book *Salamone Rossi: Jewish Musician in Late Renaissance Mantua* (Oxford, 1999). In the areas of art and material culture, see the work of Therese Metzger and Mendel Metzger, *Jewish Life in the Middle Ages: Illuminated Hebrew Manuscripts of the Thirteenth to the Sixteenth Centuries* (New York, 1982), as well as the older but still influential *Hebrew Illuminated Manuscripts* (New York, 1974) by the renowned Bezalel Nakriss. Consider also the beautifully produced *Prague Ghetto in the Renaissance Period* (Prague, 1965), ed. Otto Muneles and Jan Hĕrman, as well as *Gardens and Ghettos: The Art of Jewish Life in Italy*, ed. Vivian B. Mann (Berkeley, CA, 1989), for example. While older, the voluminous *A History of Jewish Literature*, trans. Bernard Martin, 12 vols. (Cleveland, 1972–1978), by Israel Zinberg, is still a useful reference and introductory tool.

Many different studies have been produced in the area of Jewish social history, especially in the history of Jewish women and the Jewish family. Among the diverse publications are those by Chava Weissler (see the bibliography); Ariel Toaff, *Love, Work, and Death: Jewish Life in Medieval Umbria*, trans. J. Landry (London, 1996); and the article by Gershon David Hundert, "Jewish Children and Childhood in Early Modern East Central Europe," in *The Jewish Family: Metaphor and Memory*, ed. David Kraemer (New York, 1989), 81–94. See also the numerous and important articles of Howard Adelman, including "Rabbis and Reality: Public Awareness of Jewish Women in Italy during the Renaissance and Catholic Restoration," *Jewish History* 5 (1) (1991): 27–40.

EARLY MODERN JEWISH THOUGHT AND PRACTICE

The study of early modern Jewish thought, and more recently religious practice and ritual, has been remarkably rich. Many scholarly works have focused on an individual Jewish thinker or figure. While there are many such studies available, the following reflect a combination of traditional and more recent assessments of Jewish intellectuals in the early modern world. Mortimer J. Cohen, *Jacob Emden: A Man of Controversy* (Philadelphia, 1937), for example, examines the life and controversies of a rabbinic figure just beyond the scope of this book but one who was greatly affected by many of the developments narrated here. Among the works that are now considered classic, even if not accepted in their entirety, one must include Benzion Netanyahu's *Don Isaac Abravanel: Statesman and Philosopher* (Philadelphia, 1982; orig., 1972) and Cecil Roth's *A Life of Menasseh ben Israel: Rabbi, Printer, and Diplomat* (Philadelphia, 1934). Older but still important works are R. J. Z. Werblowsky, *Joseph Karo: Lawyer and Mystic* (London, 1967) and Isaac E. Barzilay, *Yosef Shlomo Delmedigo: His Life, Works, and Times* (Leiden,

Netherlands, 1974). More recent and very provocative works are David B. Ruderman, *The World of a Renaissance Jew: The Life and Thought of Abraham ben Mordechai Farissol* (Cincinnati, 1981); Eric Lawee, *Isaac Abarbanel's Stance toward Tradition: Defense, Dissent, and Dialogue* (Albany, NY, 2001); Joseph Davis, *Yom-Tov Lipmann Heller: Portrait of a Seventeenth-Century Rabbi* (Oxford, 2004); and Mark D. Meyerson, *A Jewish Renaissance in Fifteenth-Century Spain* (Princeton, NJ, 2004).

A number of stimulating works that address issues of early modern Jewish thought in broad strokes are Amos Funkenstein's collection of essays, *Perceptions of Jewish History* (Berkeley, CA, 1993); the edited volume by Isadore Twersky and Bernard Septimus, *Jewish Thought in the Seventeenth Century* (Cambridge, MA, 1987); and Jose Faur, *Golden Doves with Silver Dots: Semiotics and Textuality in Rabbinic Tradition* (Bloomington, IN, 1986). More specific foci are presented in Reuven (Robert) Bonfil, "How Golden Was the Age of Renaissance in Jewish Historiography?" *History and Theory* 27 (1988): 78–102; Joseph Davis, "The Reception of the *Shulhan 'Arukh* and the Formation of Ashkenazic Jewish Identity," *AJS Review* 26 (2) (2002): 251–76; and Marc Saperstein, *Jewish Preaching 1200–1800: An Anthology* (New Haven, CT, 1989).

In the area of Jewish liturgy, the recent compilation edited by Lawrence Fine, *Judaism in Practice: From the Middle Ages through the Early Modern Period* (Princeton, NJ, 2001), is to be complemented by older works such as Ismar Elbogen, *Jewish Liturgy: A Comprehensive History*, trans. Raymond Scheindlin (Philadelphia, 1993) and more specific studies, such as Sylvie Anne Goldberg, *Crossing the Jabbok: Illness and Death in Ashkenazi Judaism in Sixteenth- through Nineteenth-Century Prague*, trans. Carol Cosman (Berkeley, CA, 1996).

The field of Jews and science is indebted to the path-breaking work of David B. Ruderman, whose many publications include *Jewish Thought and Scientific Discovery in Early Modern Europe* (New Haven, CT, 1995) and his article "The Impact of Science on Jewish Culture and Society in Venice (with Special Reference to Jewish Graduates of Padua's Medical School)," in *Essential Papers on Jewish Culture in Renaissance and Baroque Italy*, ed. David B. Ruderman (New York, 1992), 519–53. See also Y. Tzvi Langerman, *The Jews and the Sciences in the Middle Ages* (Aldershot, UK, 1999), and more specifically Andre Neher, *Jewish Thought and the Scientific Revolution of the Sixteenth Century: David Gans (1541–1613) and His Times*, trans. David Maisel (New York, 1986). There have also been useful studies assessing various aspects of pseudo-science and medicine in Jewish history. See Raphael Patai, *The Jewish Alchemists: A History and Source Book* (Princeton, NJ, 1994) and the older Hirsh Jacob Zimmels, *Magicians, Theologians, and Doctors: Studies in Folk Medicine and Folklore as Reflected in the Rabbinic Responsa, 12th–19th Centuries* (New York, 1997; orig., 1952).

The field of magic has been treated in Jewish history as it has, increasingly, in general studies. In this area, and particularly in the area of Jewish mysticism, see the ground-breaking work of Moshe Idel, "Jewish Magic from the Renaissance Period to Early Hasidism," in *Religion, Science, and Magic in Concert and Conflict*, ed. Jacob Neusner et al. (New York, 1989), 82–117, and *Golem: Jewish Magic and Mystical Tradition on the Artificial Anthropoid* (Albany, NY, 1990). See also Stephen Sharot, *Messianism, Mysticism, and Magic: A Sociological Analysis of Jewish Religious Movements* (Chapel Hill, NC, 1982).

Much important work has been done on various aspects of messianism in Judaism. See the older work of Norman Cohn, *The Pursuit of the Millenium: Revolutionary Millenarians and Mystical Anarchists of the Middle Ages* (Oxford, 1970; orig., 1957), and the agenda setting and still relevant work of Gershom Scholem, *Major Trends in Jewish Mysticism*, 3rd ed. (New York, 1954). More recent studies have been conducted by David B. Ruderman, "Hope against Hope: Jewish and Christian Messianic Expectations in the Later Middle Ages," in *Essential Papers on Jewish Culture in Renaissance and Baroque Italy*, ed. David B. Ruderman (New York, 1992), 299–323, and Matt D. Goldish, who has authored *The Sabbatean Prophets* (Cambridge, MA, 2004) and co-edited with Richard H. Popkin, *Millenarianism and Messianism in Early Modern European Culture, Volume I: Jewish Messianism in the Early Modern World* (Dordrecht, Netherlands, 2001). In particular relation to the important figure Shabbetai Sevi, see, in addition to the classic work by Scholem cited in the bibliography, Richard H. Popkin, "Three English Tellings of the Sabbatai Zevi Story," *Jewish History* 8 (1–2) (1994): 43–54; Giacomo Saban, "Sabbatai Sevi as Seen by a Contemporary Traveller," *Jewish History* 7 (2) (1993): 105–18; and Jetteke Van Wijk, "The Rise and Fall of Shabbatai Zevi as Reflected in Contemporary Press Reports," *Studia Rosenthalia* 33 (1) (1999): 7–27. The field of Jewish mysticism owes a great deal to the labors and products of Joseph Dan (for example, his *Jewish Mysticism and Jewish Ethics* [Seattle, 1986]) and Moshe Idel, as in his *Kabbalah: New Perspectives* (New Haven, CT, 1988).

JEWS AND NON-JEWS IN THE EARLY MODERN WORLD

The literature on Jewish and non-Jewish relations in the early modern world is vast. Among accounts that examine broader themes, consider the important work of Jacob Katz, such as *The "Shabbes Goy": A Study in Halakhic Flexibility*, trans. Yoel Lerner (Philadelphia, 1989; orig., 1983), in addition to the volumes cited in the bibliography. Consider David Biale's survey *Power and Powerlessness in Jewish History* (New York, 1986). See also more recently, the edited collection by Mark D. Meyerson and Edward D.

English, *Christians, Muslims, and Jews in Medieval and Early Modern Spain: Interaction and Cultural Change* (Notre Dame, IN, 2000), and for Germany the important *In and Out of the Ghetto: Jewish-Gentile Relations in Late Medieval and Early Modern Germany*, ed. R. Po-chia Hsia and Hartmut Lehmann (Cambridge, UK, 1995).

A good deal of material has been published related to Jewish and Christian relations during, and as a result of, the Reformation. Most recently there is Dean Phillip Bell and Stephen G. Burnett, eds., *Jews, Judaism, and the Reformation in Sixteenth-Century Germany* (Leiden, Netherlands, 2006). For various aspects of the Protestant Reformation, see the still classic article by Haim Hillel Ben-Sasson, "The Reformation in Contemporary Jewish Eyes," *The Israel Academy of Sciences and Humanities Proceedings* 4 (12) (Jerusalem 1970); Abraham David, "The Lutheran Reformation in Sixteenth-Century Jewish Historiography," *Jewish Studies Quarterly* 10 (2) (2003): 124–39; Mark U. Edwards, *Luther's Last Battles: Politics and Polemics, 1531–1546* (Ithaca, NY, 1983); Scott H. Hendrix, "Toleration of the Jews in the German Reformation: Urbanus Rhegius and Braunschweig (1535–1540)," *Archiv für Reformationsgeschichte* 81 (1990): 189–215; the case study of Erika Rummel, *The Case against Johannes Reuchlin: Religious and Social Controversy in Sixteenth-Century Germany* (Toronto, 2002); and for the possible impact of Jewish thought on Christian reform, Louis I. Newman, *Jewish Influence on Christian Reform Movements* (New York, 1925). One of the most important scholars of the pre-Reformation period was Erasmus. On his position regarding the Jews, see Shimon Markish, *Erasmus and the Jews*, trans. Anthony Olcott (Chicago, 1986). In the area of Catholic thought and the Jews, see Kenneth R. Stow, *Catholic Thought and Papal Jewry Policy, 1555–1593* (New York, 1977), and the provocative essay by Amnon Raz-Krakotzkin, "Censorship, Editing, and the Reshaping of Jewish Identity: The Catholic Church and Hebrew Literature in the Sixteenth Century," in *Hebraica Veritas? Christian Hebraists and the Study of Judaism in Early Modern Europe*, ed. Allison P. Coudert and Jeffrey S. Shoulson (Philadelphia, 2004), 125–55. The work of Yosef Kaplan is essential: see, for example, his *From Christianity to Judaism: The Story of Isaac Orobio de Castro* (Oxford, 1989; orig., 1982).

The study of Christian Hebraism is a well-established field that continues to generate very stimulating and fruitful scholarship. See the pioneering work of Jerome Friedman, *The Most Ancient Testimony: Sixteenth Century Christian-Hebraica in the Age of the Renaissance Nostalgia* (Athens, OH, 1983). Most recently, see David B. Ruderman and Giuseppe Veltri, eds., *Cultural Intermediaries: Jewish Intellectuals in Early Modern Italy* (Philadelphia, 2004). An older example of scholarship is Eric Zimmer, "Jewish and Christian Hebraist Collaboration in Sixteenth Century Germany," *Jewish Quarterly Review* 71 (1980–1981): 69–88. The perception and discussion of Jews and Judaism in the early modern world has received important attention, especially since R. Po-chia Hsia's essay "Christian Ethnographies of Jews in Early Modern Germany," in *The Expulsion of the Jews: 1492 and After*, ed. Raymond B. Waddington and A. H. Williamson (New York, 1994), 223–35. See, now, Yaacov Deutsch, "'A View of the Jewish Religion'—Conceptions of Jewish Practice and Ritual in Early Modern Europe," *Archiv für Religionsgeschichte* 3 (2001): 273–95, and "Polemical Ethnographies: Descriptions of Yom Kippur in the Writings of Christian Hebraists and Jewish Converts to Christianity in Early Modern Europe," in *Hebraica Veritas? Jews and the Study of Judaism in Early Modern Europe*, ed. Allison P. Coudert and Jeffery S. Shoulson (Philadelphia, 2004), 202–33.

There are numerous studies on the political position of the Jews in various early modern contexts. Consider the examples of Eric Zimmer, *Jewish Synods in Germany during the Late Middle Ages (1286–1603)* (New York, 1978) for Germany and Stefanie B. Siegmund, *The Medici State and the Ghetto of Florence: The Construction of an Early Modern Jewish Community* (Stanford, CA, 2006) for Florence. See also Benjamin Ravid, "From Yellow to Red: On the Distinguishing Head-Covering of the Jews of Venice," *Jewish History* 6 (1–2) (1992): 179–210, and "The Legal Status of the Jews in Venice to 1509," *Proceedings of the American Academy for Jewish Research* 54 (1987): 169–202.

In the area of early modern Jewish and Christian polemic and debate, the work of Haim Hillel Ben-Sasson and Daniel J. Lasker remain classic. See Ben-Sasson, "Jewish-Christian Disputations in the Setting of Humanism and Reformation in the German Empire," *Harvard Theological Review* 59 (1966): 369–90, and Lasker, *Jewish Philosophical Polemics against Christianity in the Middle Ages* (New York, 1977). Recent and provocative studies include those of Marc Michael Epstein, *Dreams of Subversion in Medieval Jewish Art and Literature* (University Park, PA, 1997) and Franco Mormando, *The Preacher's Inner Demons: Bernardino of Siena and the Social Underworld of Early Renaissance Italy* (Chicago, 1999).

ANTI-JUDAISM IN THE EARLY MODERN WORLD

Among the many significant studies of anti-Judaism in the early modern period, the work of R. Po-chia Hsia stands out in many respects. See his stimulating *The Myth of Ritual Murder: Jews and Magic in Reformation Germany* (New Haven, CT, 1988); *Trent 1475: Stories of a Ritual Murder* (New Haven, CT, 1992); "The Usurious Jew: Economic Structure and Religious Representations in an Anti-Semitic Discourse," in *In and Out of the Ghetto: Jewish-Gentile Relations in Late Medieval and Early Modern Germany*, ed. R. Po-chia Hsia and Hartmut Lehmann (Cambridge, UK, 1995), 161–76; and "Witchcraft, Magic, and the Jews in Late Medieval and Early Modern Germany," in *From Witness to Witchcraft: Jews and Judaism in Medieval Christian Thought*, ed. Jeremy Cohen (Wiesbaden, Germany, 1996), 419–33. The work of Carlo Ginzburg has been methodologically innovative. In this context, see his *Ecstasies: Deciphering the Witches' Sabbath* (New York, 1991; orig., 1989). See also Joseph Shatzmiller, *Shylock Revisited: Jews, Moneylending, and Medieval Society* (Berkeley, CA, 1990) as well as the very intriguing *Shakespeare and the Jews* (New York, 1996) by James Shapiro.

In a number of meticulous and important studies, Stephen G. Burnett has examined restrictions on Jews in the area of printing. In addition to his important work on Johannes Buxtorf, see his articles "Hebrew Censorship in Hanau: A Mirror of Jewish-Christian Coexistence in Seventeenth Century Germany," in *The Expulsion of the Jews: 1492 and After*, ed. Raymond B. Waddington and Arthur H. Williamson (New York, 1994), 199–222; "Dialogue of the Deaf: Hebrew Pedagogy and Anti-Jewish Polemic in Sebastian Münster's *Messiahs of the Christians and the Jews* (1529/39)," *Archive for Reformation History* 91 (2000): 168–90; and "The Regulation of Hebrew Printing in Germany, 1555–1630: Confessional Politics and the Limits of Jewish Toleration," in *Infinite Boundaries: Order, Disorder, and Reorder in Early Modern German Culture*, ed. Max Reinhart and Thomas Robisheaux (Kirksville, MO, 1998), 329–48.

In a more general vein, see Gavin Langmuir, *Toward a Definition of Antisemitism* (Berkeley, CA, 1990) and Shmuel Almog's edited volume, *Antisemitism through the Ages*, trans. Nathan H. Reisner (Oxford, 1988).

On the theme of alleged image desecration see Eric M. Zanfran, "An Alleged Case of Image Desecration by the Jews and Its Representation in Art: The Virgin of Cambron," *Journal of Jewish Art* 2 (1975): 62–71. For ritual murder accusations, see in addition, Alan Dundes, ed., *The Blood Libel Legend* (Madison, WI, 1991) and Christopher Ocker, "Ritual Murder and the Subjectivity of Christ: A Choice in Medieval Christianity," *Harvard Theological Review* 91(1998): 153–92.

Some works focus on anti-Judaism in specific areas or historical contexts. Consider, for example, Heiko A. Oberman, *The Roots of Antisemitism in the Age of Renaissance and Reformation*, trans. James I. Porter (Philadelphia, 1984; orig., 1981). Many books have explored the representation, often negative, of Jews in Christian art. An excellent overview is Heinz Schreckenberg, *The Jews in Christian Art* noted above. Also useful, but contested in some circles, is Ruth Mellinkoff, *Outcasts: Signs of Otherness in Northern European Art of the Late Middle Ages*, 2 vols. (Berkeley, CA, 1993). On the theme of the *Judensau*, see the old but still essential Isaiah Schachar, *The Judensau: A Medieval Anti-Jewish Motif and Its History* (London, 1974).

For discussions on various expulsions of the Jews, see *The Expulsion of the Jews: 1492 and After*, ed. Raymond B. Waddington and Arthur H.

Williamson (New York, 1994), as well as Elisheva Carlebach, "Between History and Myth: The Regensburg Expulsion in Josel of Rosheim's *Sefer Ha-Miknah*," in *Jewish History and Jewish Memory: Essays in Honor of Yosef Hayim Yerushalmi*, ed. Elisheva Carlebach, John M. Efron, and David N. Myers (Hanover, NH, 1998), 40–53.

The Inquisition has received a good deal of scholarly attention, though not always scholarly agreement. Among the most important works of the past couple decades must be included the following: Henry Kamen, *Inquisition and Society in the Sixteenth and Seventeenth Centuries* (Bloomington, IN, 1985) and Stephen Haliczer, *Inquisition and Society in Early Modern Europe* (London, 1987). Contested, but still of value, is Norman Roth, *Conversos, Inquisition, and the Expulsion of the Jews from Spain* (Madison, WI, 1995).

Regarding the tense and evocative world of conversion, see, among others, Martin Muslow and Richard H. Popkin, eds., *Secret Conversions to Judaism in Early Modern Europe* (Leiden, Netherlands, 2004). The work of Eleazar Gutwirth has also been important. See his "Conversions to Christianity amongst Fifteenth-Century Spanish Jews: An Alternative Explanation," in *Sholom Simonsohn Jubilee Volume: Studies in the History of the Jews in the Middle Ages and Renaissance Period*, ed. Daniel Carpi et al. (Tel Aviv, Israel, 1993), 97–121. One of the most important scholars of the past decades has been Yosef Hayim Yerushalmi. Yerushalmi has published widely; for the topics here, see his *From Spanish Court to Italian Ghetto: Isaac Cardoso: A Study in Seventeenth-Century Marranism and Jewish Apologetics* (New York, 1971) and *The Lisbon Massacre of 1506 and the Royal Image in the Shebet Yehudah* (Cincinnati, 1976). For the end of our period and in to modernity, consider the work of Todd M. Endelman, *Jewish Apostasy in the Modern world*, ed. Todd M. Endelman (New York, 1987), as well as more generally his *The Jews of Britain, 1656 to 2000* (Berkeley, CA, 2002).

Bibliography

Acosta, Uriel. *Uriel Acosta: A Speciman of Human Life*. New York, 1967.

Adler, Elkan Nathan, ed. *Jewish Travellers: A Treasury of Travelogues from Nine Centuries*. 2nd ed. New York, 1966.

Altmann, Alexander. "Ars Rhetorica as Reflected in Some Jewish Figures of the Italian Renaissance." In *Essential Papers on Jewish Culture in Renaissance and Baroque Italy*, ed. David B. Ruderman, 63–84. New York, 1992.

Arbel, Benjamin. *Trading Nations: Jews and Venetians in the Early Modern Eastern Mediterranean*. Leiden, Netherlands, 1995.

Arbell, Mordechai. "Jewish Settlements in the French Colonies in the Caribbean (Martinique, Guadeloupe, Haiti, Cayenne) and the 'Black Code.'" In *The Jews and the Expansion of Europe to the West, 1450–1800*, ed. Paolo Bernardini and Norman Fiering, 287–313. New York, 2001.

Arnold, John H. *Belief and Unbelief in Medieval Europe*. London, 2005.

Assis, Yom Tov. *The Jews of Tortosa 1373–1492: Regesta and Documents from the Archivo Histórico de protocols de Tarragona*, compiled by Josefina Cubelis I Llorens. Jerusalem, 1991.

Avron, Dov. "Poznan (Posen)." In *Encyclopedia Judaica*. 16 vols. Jerusalem, 1971–1972.

Baer, Yitzhak. *A History of the Jews in Christian Spain, Volume 2: From the Fourteenth Century to the Expulsion*, trans. Louis Schoffman. Philadelphia, 1966.

Balaban, M. "Die Krakauer Judengemeinde-Ordnung von 1595 und ihre Nachträge." *Jahrbuch der Jüdisch-Literarischen Gesellschaft* 10 (1913): 296–310; 11 (1916): 88–114.

Bar-Itzhak, Haya. *Jewish Poland: Legends of Origin: Ethnopoetics and Legendary Chronicles*. Detroit, 2001.

Barnai, Jacob. "'Blood Libels' in the Ottoman Empire of the Fifteenth to Nineteenth Centuries." In *Antisemitism through the Ages*, ed. Shmuel Almog, trans. Nathan H. Reisner, 189–94. Oxford, 1988.

Baron, Salo. *History and Jewish Historians: Essays and Addresses.* Philadelphia, 1964.

———. *The Jewish Community: Its History and Structure to the American Revolution.* 3 vols. Philadelphia, 1942.

———. *A Social and Religious History of the Jews.* Vols. 16–17. 2nd ed. Philadelphia, 1976–1980.

Bashan (Sternberg), Eliezer. "Nagid." In *Encyclopedia Judaica.* 16 vols. Jerusalem, 1971–1972.

Baskin, Judith, ed. *Jewish Women in Historical Perspective.* Detroit, 1991.

Battenberg, J. Friedrich. *Die Juden in Deutschland vom 16. bis zum Ende des 18. Jahrhunderts.* Munich, 2001.

Baumgarten, Elisheva. *Mothers and Children: Jewish Family Life in Medieval Europe.* Princeton, NJ, 2004.

Beinart, Haim. *The Expulsion of the Jews from Spain,* trans. Jeffrey M. Green. Oxford, 2002 (orig., 1994).

———, ed. *Moreshet Sepharad: The Sephardi Legacy.* 2 vols. Jerusalem, 1992.

———. "Saragossa." In *Encyclopedia Judaica.* 16 vols. Jerusalem, 1971–1972.

———. *Trujillo: A Jewish Community in Extremadura on the Eve of the Expulsion from Spain.* Jerusalem, 1980.

Bell, Dean Phillip. "Confessionalization in Early Modern Germany: A Jewish Perspective." In *Politics and Reformations: Studies in Honor of Thomas A. Brady, Jr.,* ed. Peter Wallace, Peter Starenko, Michael Printy, and Christopher Ocker. Leiden, Netherlands, forthcoming.

———. "Jewish and Christian Historiography in the Sixteenth Century: A Comparison of Sebastian Münster and David Gans." In *God's Word for Our World: In Honor of Simon John DeVries,* ed. J. Harold Ellens, Deborah L. Ellens, Rolf P. Knierim, and Isaac Kalimi, 141–58. Vol. 2. London, 2004.

———. *Jewish Identity in Early Modern Germany: Memory, Power, and Community.* Aldershot, UK, 2007.

———. *Sacred Communities: Jewish and Christian Identities in Fifteenth-Century Germany.* Leiden, Netherlands, and Boston, 2001.

Benbassa, Esther. *The Jews of France: A History from Antiquity to the Present,* trans. M. B. DeBevoise. Princeton, NJ, 1999.

Benedict, Philip. "Introduction." In *Early Modern Europe: From Crisis to Stability,* ed. Philip Benedict and Myron P. Gutmann, 11–30. Newark, DE, 2005.

Benedictow, Ole J. *The Black Death, 1346–1353: The Complete History.* Wiltshire, UK, 2006 (orig., 2004).

Ben-Sasson, Haim Hillel. "Council of the Lands: Structure of Leadership." In *Encyclopedia Judaica.* 16 vols. Jerusalem, 1971–1972.

———, ed. *A History of the Jewish People.* Cambridge, MA, 1994 (orig., 1976).

———. "Poland: Internal Jewish Life." In *Encyclopedia Judaica.* 16 vols. Jerusalem, 1971–1972.

———. *Trial and Achievement: Currents in Jewish History (from 313).* Jerusalem, 1974.

Berger, David, ed. and trans. *The Jewish-Christian Debate in the High Middle Ages.* Philadelphia, 1979.

Biale, David, ed. *Cultures of the Jews: A New History.* New York, 2002.

———. "Introduction." In *Cultures of the Jews: A New History,* ed. David Biale, xvii–xxxiii. New York, 2002.

Bireley, Robert. "The Catholic Reform, Jews, and Judaism in Sixteenth-Century Germany." In *Jews, Judaism, and the Reformation in Sixteenth-Century Germany*, ed. Dean Phillip Bell and Stephen G. Burnett, 249–68. Leiden, Netherlands, 2006.

Bodian, Miriam. *Hebrews of the Portuguese Nation: Conversos and Community in Early Modern Amsterdam*. Bloomington, IN, 1997.

Bonfil, Robert. "Aliens Within: The Jews and Antijudaism." In *Handbook of European History 1400–1600: Late Middle Ages, Renaissance and Reformation*, vol. 1, ed. Thomas A. Brady Jr., Heiko A. Oberman, and James D. Tracy, 263–302. Leiden, Netherlands, 1996.

———. *Jewish Life in Renaissance Italy*, trans. Anthony Oldcorn. Berkeley, CA, 1994.

———. *Rabbis and Jewish Communities in Renaissance Italy*, trans. Jonathan Chipman. London, 1993 (orig., 1979).

Bornstein-Makovetsky, Leah. "Jewish Leadership and Ottoman Authorities during the Sixteenth and Seventeenth Centuries." In *Ottoman and Turkish Jewry: Community and Leadership*, ed. Aron Rodrigue, 87–121. Bloomington, IN, 1992.

Bossy, John. *Christianity in the West, 1400–1700*. Oxford, 1985.

Bowman, Steven. *The Jews of Byzantium (1204–1453)*. Alabama, 1985.

Braden, Jutta. *Hamburger Judenpolitik im Zeitaliter lutherischer Orthodoxie (1590–1710)*. Hamburg, Germany, 2001.

Breuer, Mordechai. "Introduction." In David Gans, *Zemah David*, ed. Mordechai Breuer, i–xxxiii. Jerusalem, 1983.

———. "Modernism and Traditionalism in Sixteenth-Century Jewish Historiography: A Study of David Gans' Tzemah David." In *Jewish Thought in the Sixteenth Century*, ed. Bernard Dov Cooperman, 49–88. Cambridge, MA, 1983.

———. "The Position of the Rabbinate in the Leadership of the German Communities in the Fifteenth Century" (Hebrew). *Zion* 41 (1–2) (1976): 47–67.

———. "The Wanderings of Students and Scholars—A Prolegomenon to a Chapter in the History of the Yeshivot." In *Culture and Society in Medieval Jewry: Studies Dedicated to the Memory of Haim Hillel Ben-Sasson*, ed. Menahem Ben-Sasson, Robert Bonfil, and Joseph R. Hacker, 445–68 (Hebrew). Jerusalem, 1989.

Bronner, Fred. "Argentina: Colonial Period." In *Encyclopedia Judaica*. 16 vols. Jerusalem, 1971–1972.

Burnett, Stephen G. "Distorted Mirrors: Antonius Margaritha, Johann Buxtorf, and Christian Ethnographies of the Jews." *Sixteenth Century Journal* 25 (1994): 275–87.

———. *From Christian Hebraism to Jewish Studies: Johannes Buxtorf (1564–1629) and Hebrew Learning in the Seventeenth Century*. Leiden, Netherlands, 1996.

———. "German Jewish Printing in the Reformation Era (1530–1633)." In *Jews, Judaism, and the Reformation in Sixteenth-Century Germany*, ed. Dean Phillip Bell and Stephen G. Burnett, 503–27. Leiden, Netherlands, 2006.

Carlebach, Elisheva. *Divided Souls: Converts from Judaism in Germany, 1500–1750*. New Haven, CT, 2001.

Cassuto, Isaac. "Aus den ältesten Protokollbuch der Portugiesisch-Jüdischen Gemeinde in Hamburg: Übersetzung und Anmerkungen." In *Jahrbuch der Jüdisch-Literarischen Gesellschaft* 6 (1908): 1–54; 7 (1909): 159–210; 8 (1910): 227–90; 9 (1911): 318–66; 10 (1912): 225–95; 11 (1916): 1–76; 12 (1920): 55–118.

Certeau, Michel de. *The Practice of Everyday Life*, trans. Steven Rendall. Berkeley, CA, 1984.

Chazan, Robert. *European Jewry and the First Crusade*. Berkeley, CA, 1987.

Clossey, Luke. "Early Modern World." In *The Berkshire Encyclopedia of World History*, ed. William Hardy McNeill et al., 592–98. Great Barrington, MA, 2005.

Cohen, Gershon. "Messianic Postures of Ashkenazim and Sephardim." Reprinted in *Essential Papers on Messianic Movements and Personalities in Jewish History*, ed. Marc Saperstein, 202–33. New York, 1992.

Cohen, Mark R. *Poverty and Charity in the Jewish Community of Medieval Egypt*. Princeton, NJ, 2005.

Cohen, Martin A. "Latin America: Colonial Period." In *Encyclopedia Judaica*. 16 vols. Jerusalem, 1971–1972.

Collins, James B., and Karen L. Taylor. *Early Modern Europe: Issues and Interpretations*. Oxford, 2006.

"Colonial American Jewry, 1654–1776: English Period, 1664–1776." In *Encyclopedia Judaica*. 16 vols. Jerusalem, 1971–1972.

Cooperman, Bernard Dov. "Ethnicity and Institution Building among Jews in Early Modern Rome." *AJS Review* 30 (1) (2006): 119–45.

Coudert, Allison P. *The Impact of the Kabbalah in the Seventeenth Century: The Life and Thought of Francis Mercury van Helmont (1614–1698)*. Leiden, Netherlands, 1999.

Coudert, Allison P., and Jeffery S. Shoulson, eds. *Hebraica Veritas? Jews and the Study of Judaism in Early Modern Europe*. Philadelphia, 2004.

Cygielman, Arthur. "Cracow (Kazimierz)." In *Encyclopedia Judaica*. 16 vols. Jerusalem, 1971–1972.

David, Abraham. *To Come to the Land: Immigration and Settlement in Sixteenth-Century Eretz-Israel*, trans. Dena Ordan. Tuscaloosa, AL, 1999.

Davis, Natalie. *Women on the Margins: Three Seventeenth-Century Lives*. Cambridge, MA, 1995.

Delumeau, Jean. *Catholicism between Luther and Voltaire: A New View of the Counter-Reformation*. London, 1977.

De' Rossi, Azariah. *The Light of the Eyes*, trans. Joanna Weinberg. New Haven, CT, 2001.

Deutsch, Yaacov. "Polemical Ethnographies: Descriptions of Yom Kippur in the Writings of Christian Hebraists and Jewish Converts to Christianity in Early Modern Europe." In *Hebraica Veritas? Jews and the Study of Judaism in Early Modern Europe*, ed. Allison P. Coudert and Jeffery S. Shoulson, 202–33. Philadelphia, 2004.

Dinur, Ben-Zion. *Israel and the Diaspora*. Philadelphia, 1969.

Dorff, Elliot N. *A Living Tree: The Roots and Growth of Jewish Law*. Albany, NY, 1988.

Dubnow, Simon. *History of the Jews in Russia and Poland from the Earliest Times until the Present Day*, trans. I. Friedländer. 3 vols. Philadelphia, 1916–1920.

———. *An Outline of Jewish History*. 3 vols. New York, 1925.

Dunlop, Douglas Morton. "Rhadanites." In *Encyclopedia Judaica*. 16 vols. Jerusalem, 1971–1972.

Eells, Hastings. *Martin Bucer*. New Haven, CT, 1931.

Eidelberg, Shlomo. *R. Juspa, Shammash of Warmaisa (Worms): Jewish Life in Seventeenth Century Worms*. Jerusalem, 1991.

Eisenbeth, Maurice. *Le judaïsme nord-africain*. Paris, 1932.

Elias, Norbert. *The History of Manners (The Civilizing Process Vol. 1)*, trans. Edmund Jephcott. New York, 1978 (orig., 1939).

Elon, Menahem. *Jewish Law: History, Sources, Principles*, trans. Bernard Auerbach and Melvin J. Sykes. 4 vols. Philadelphia, 1994 (orig., 1973).

Encyclopedia Judaica. 16 vols. Jerusalem, 1971–1972 (cited throughout according to the CD-ROM version).

Finkelstein, Louis. *Jewish Self-Government in the Middle Ages*. New York, 1924.

Fischel, Walter Joseph. "India: Early Phase." In *Encyclopedia Judaica*. 16 vols. Jerusalem, 1971–1972.

Fishman, Talya. *Shaking the Pillars of Exile: "Voice of a Fool," an Early Modern Jewish Critique of Rabbinic Culture*. Stanford, CA, 1997.

Fletcher, Joseph F. *Studies on Chinese and Islamic Inner Asia*, ed. Beatrice Forbes Manz. Brookfield, VT, 1995.

Flynn, Maureen. "The Charitable Activities of Confraternities." Reprinted in *Early Modern Europe: Issues and Interpretations*, ed. James B. Collins and Karen L. Taylor, 101–20. Oxford, 2006.

Foa, Anna. *The Jews of Europe after the Black Death*. Berkeley, CA, 2000.

Foster, William, ed. *Early Travels in India 1583–1619*. Oxford, 1921.

Fram, Edward. *Ideals Face Reality: Jewish Law and Life in Poland, 1550–1655*. Cincinnati, 1997.

Frattarelli Fischer, Lucia. "Urban Forms of Jewish Settlement in Tuscan Cities (Florence, Pisa, Leghorn) during the 17th Century." In *Papers in Jewish Demography 1989*, ed. U. O. Schmelz and S. DellaPergola, 48–60. Jerusalem, 1993.

Freehof, Solomon. *A Treasury of Responsa*. Philadelphia, 1963.

Friedrichs, Christopher. "Politics or Pogrom? The Fettmilch Uprising in German and Jewish History." *Central European History* 19 (1986): 186–228.

Gampel, Benjamin R. *The Last Jews on Iberian Soil: Navarrese Jewry 1479–1498*. Berkeley, CA, 1989.

———. "A Letter to a Wayward Teacher: The Transformation of Sephardic Culture in Christian Iberia." In *Cultures of the Jews: A New History*, ed. David Biale, 389–447. New York, 2002.

Gans, David. *Zemah David*, ed. Mordechai Breuer. Jerusalem, 1983.

Garcia-Arenal, Mercedes, and Gerard Wiegers. *A Man of Three Worlds: Samuel Pallache, a Moroccan Jew in Catholic and Protestant Europe*, trans. Martin Beagles. Baltimore, 2003.

Garrett, Don, ed. *The Cambridge Companion to Spinoza*. Cambridge, UK, 1996.

Gelber, Nathan Michael. "Brest-Litovsk." In *Encyclopedia Judaica*. 16 vols. Jerusalem, 1971–1972.

Gerber, Jane. *The Jews of Spain: A History of the Sephardic Experience*. New York, 1992.

Gilman, Sander L. *Jewish Self-Hatred: Anti-Semitism and the Hidden Language of the Jews*. Baltimore, 1986.

Glanz, Rudolf. *Geschichte des niederen jüdischen Volkes in Deutschland: eine Studie über historisches Gaunertum, Bettelwesen und Vagantentum*. New York, 1968.

Glückel of Hameln. *The Memoirs of Glückel of Hameln*, trans. Marvin Lowenthal. New York, 1977.

Goffman, Daniel. "Jews in Early Modern Ottoman Commerce." In *Jews, Turks, Ottomans: A Shared History, Fifteenth through the Twentieth Century*, ed. Avigdor Levy, 15–34. Syracuse, NY, 2002.

Goitein, S. D. *A Mediterranean Society: An Abridgement in One Volume*, rev. and ed. Jacob Lassner. Berkeley, CA, 1999.

Golb, Norman. "Exploring the Cairo Geniza for New Light on the History of the Jews of Medieval Europe." In *Cairo's Ben Ezra Synagogue: A Gateway to Medieval Mediterranean Life*, ed. Jacob Lassner, 25–39. Chicago, 2001.

Goldstone, Jack A. "The Problem of the 'Early Modern' World." *Journal of the Economic and Social History of the Orient* 41 (3) (1998): 249–84.

Gow, Andrew Colin. *The Red Jews: Antisemitism in an Apocalyptic Age 1200–1600*. Leiden, Netherlands, 1995.

Graetz, Michael. "Zur Zäsur zwischen Mittelalter und Neuzeit in der jüdischen Geschichte." In *Schöpferische Momente des europäischen Judentums in der frühen Neuzeit*, ed. Michael Graetz, 1–18. Heidelberg, Germany, 2000.

Graupe, Heinz Mosche, ed. *Die Statuten der drei Gemeinden Altona, Hamburg und Wandsbek: Quellen zu jüd. Gemeindeorganisation im 17. u 18. Jahrhundert*. 2 vols. Hamburg, Germany, 1973.

Grossman, Avraham. "Abarbanel as Biblical Exegete." In *Encyclopedia Judaica*. 16 vols. Jerusalem, 1971–1972.

———. *Pious and Rebellious: Jewish Women in Medieval Europe*, trans. Jonathan Chipman. Hanover, NH, and London, 2004.

Güdemann, Moritz. *Quellenschriften zur Geschichte des Unterrichts und der Erziehung bei den deutschen Juden, von den ältesten Zeiten bis auf Mendelssohn*. Amsterdam, 1968.

Guldon, Zenon, and Waldemar Kowalski. "Between Tolerance and Abomination: Jews in Sixteenth-Century Poland." In *The Expulsion of the Jews: 1492 and After*, ed. Raymond B. Waddington and Arthur H. Williamson, 161–75. New York, 1994.

Guldon, Zenon, and Karol Krzystanek. "The Jewish Population in the Towns on the West Bank of the Vistula in Sandomierz Province, 16th–18th Centuries." In *The Jews in Old Poland, 1000–1795*, ed. Antony Polonsky, Jakub Basista, and Andrzej Link-Lenczowski, 322–39. London, 1993.

Guldon, Zenon, and Jacek Wijaczka. "The Accusation of Ritual Murder in Poland 1500–1800." *Polin* 10 (1997): 99–140.

Gutwirth, Eleazar. "Towards Expulsion: 1391–1492." In *Spain and the Jews: The Sephardi Experience 1492 and After*, ed. Elie Kedourie, 51–73. London, 1992.

Haas, Peter J. *Responsa: Literary History of a Rabbinic Genre*. Atlanta, 1996.

Haberman, A. M. *Studies in the History of Hebrew Printers and Books* (Hebrew). Jerusalem, 1978.

Hacker, Joseph R. "Jewish Autonomy in the Ottoman Empire: Its Scope and Limits. Jewish Courts from the Sixteenth to the Eighteenth Centuries." In *The Jews of the Ottoman Empire*, ed. Avigdor Levy, 153–202. Princeton, NJ, 1994.

———. "The 'Sürgün' System and Jewish Society in the Ottoman Empire during the Fifteenth to the Seventeenth Centuries." In *Ottoman and Turkish Jewry: Community and Leadership*, ed. Aron Rodrigue, 1–65. Bloomington, IN, 1992.

Hammer, Jill. "Holle's Cry: Unearthing a Birth Goddess in a German Jewish Naming Ceremony." *Nashim* 9 (1) (2005): 62–87.

Harran, Don. "Jewish Musical Culture: Leone Modena." In *The Jews of Early Modern Venice*, ed. Robert C. Davis and Benjamin Ravid, 211–30. Baltimore, 2001.

——. *Salamone Rossi: Jewish Musician in Late Renaissance Mantua*. Oxford, 1999.

Heller, Marvin. *The Sixteenth Century Hebrew Book*. 2 vols. Leiden, Netherlands, 2004.

Hirschberg, H. Z. *A History of the Jews in North Africa*. 2 vols. Leiden, Netherlands, 1974–1981.

Holtz, Barry W., ed. *Back to the Sources: Reading the Classic Jewish Texts*. New York, 1984.

Horowitz, Elliot. "Families and Their Fortunes: The Jews of Early Modern Italy." In *Cultures of the Jews: A New History*, ed. David Biale, 573–636. New York, 2002.

Horowitz, Isaiah. *The Generations of Adam*, trans. Miles Krassen. New York, 1996.

——. *Shney Luchot Habrit*, trans. Eliyahu Munk. Vol. 1. Jerusalem, 1962.

Hsia, R. Po-chia. "Christian Ethnographies of Jews in Early Modern Germany." In *The Expulsion of the Jews: 1492 and After*, ed. Raymond B. Waddington and A. H. Williamson, 223–35. New York, 1994.

——. *The Myth of Ritual Murder: Jews and Magic in Reformation Germany*. New Haven, CT, 1988.

Inalcik, Halil. *The Ottoman Empire: The Classical Age 1300–1600*. London, 2000 (orig., 1973).

"Inquisition." In *Encyclopedia Judaica*. 16 vols. Jerusalem, 1971–1972.

Israel, Jonathan. *European Jewry in the Age of Mercantilism, 1550–1750*. 3rd ed. London, 1998.

Jewish Mystical Autobiographies: Book of Visions and Book of Secrets, trans. Morris M. Faierstein. New York, 1999.

Kalik, Judith. "The Attitudes Towards the Jews in the Christian Polemic Literature in Poland in the 16–18th Centuries." In *Jews and Slavs*, vol. 11, ed. Wolf Moskovich and Irena Fijalkowska-Janiak, 58–78. Jerusalem, 2003.

Kaplan, Yosef. "Bom Judesmo: The Western Sephardic Diaspora." In *Cultures of the Jews: A New History*, ed. David Biale, 639–69. New York, 2002.

——. "The Place of the Herem in the Sefardic Community of Hamburg during the Seventeenth Century." In *Die Sefarden in Hamburg I*, ed. Michael Studemund-Halevy, 63–88. Hamburg, Germany, 1994.

Katsh, Abraham I. "Colonial American Jewry, 1654–1776: Dutch Period, 1654–1664." In *Encyclopedia Judaica*. 16 vols. Jerusalem, 1971–1972.

Katz, Jacob. *Exclusiveness and Tolerance: Studies in Jewish-Gentile Relations in Medieval and Modern Times*. New Jersey, 1983 (orig., 1961).

——. *Out of the Ghetto: The Social Background of Jewish Emancipation, 1770–1870*. New York, 1978 (orig., 1973).

——. *Tradition and Crisis: Jewish Society at the End of the Middle Ages*, trans. Bernard Dov Cooperman. New York, 1993 (orig., 1958).

Katz, Nathan. *Who Are the Jews of India?* Berkeley, CA, 2000.

Keil, Martha. "Lilith und Hollekreisch—Schwangerschaft, Geburt und Wochenbett im Judentum des deutschen Spätmittelalters." In *Aller Anfang: Geburt, Birth, Naissance*, ed. Gabriele Dorffner and Sonia Horn, 145–72. Vienna, 2005.

Kellenbenz, Hermann. *Sephardim an der unteren Elbe: Ihre wirtschaftliche und politische Bedeutung vom Ende des 16. bis zum Beginn des 18. Jahrhunderts*. Wiesbaden, Germany, 1958.

Kellner, Menachem. *Must a Jew Believe Anything?* London, 1999.

Kirshenboim, Shiomshon Leib. "Lublin." In *Encyclopedia Judaica*. 16 vols. Jerusalem, 1971–1972.

Kobler, Franz, ed. *A Treasury of Jewish Letters: Letters from the Famous and the Humble*. 2 vols. London, 1952.

Kracauer, Isidor. *Geschichte der Juden in Frankfurt am Main*. Frankfurt am Main, Germany, 1925.

Lesley, Arthur. "Jewish Adaptations of Humanist Concepts in Fifteenth- and Sixteenth-Century Italy." In *Essential Papers on Jewish Culture in Renaissance and Baroque Italy*, ed. David B. Ruderman, 45–62. New York, 1992.

Levine, Hillel. *Economic Origins of Antisemitism: Poland and Its Jews in the Early Modern Period*. New Haven, CT, 1991.

Levinger, Jacob S. "Delmedigo, Elijah ben Moses Abba." In *Encyclopedia Judaica*. 16 vols. Jerusalem, 1971–1972.

Levy, Avigdor, ed. *The Jews of the Ottoman Empire*. Princeton, NJ, 1992.

———, ed. *Jews, Turk, Ottomans: A Shared History, Fifteenth through the Twentieth Century*. Syracuse, NY, 2002.

———. *The Sephardim in the Ottoman Empire*. Princeton, NJ, 1992.

Levy, Habib. *Comprehensive History of the Jews of Iran: The Outset of the Diaspora*, ed. Hooshang Ebrami, trans. George W. Maschke. Costa Mesa, CA, 1999.

Lewis, Bernard. *The Jews of Islam*. Princeton, NJ, 1984.

Lieberman, Victor. "Transcending East-West Dichotomies: State and Culture Formation in Six Ostensibly Disparate Areas." Excerpts reprinted in *Early Modern Europe: Issues and Interpretations*, ed. James B. Collins and Karen L. Taylor, 419–29. Oxford, 2006.

Liebman, Seymour B., and Harold Lerner. "Mexico: Colonial Period." In *Encyclopedia Judaica*. 16 vols. Jerusalem, 1971–1972.

Litt, Stefan. *Protokollbuch und Statuten der Jüdischen Gemeinde Friedberg (16.–18. Jahrhundert)*. Friedberg, Germany, 2003.

Maimon, Arye, Mordechai Breuer, and Yacov Guggenheim, eds. *Germania Judaica. Volume III: 1350–1519, Part 3*. Tübingen, Germany, 2003.

Malino, Frances. *The Sephardic Jews of Bordeaux: Assimilation and Emancipation in Revolutionary and Napoleonic France*. Alabama, 1978.

Malkiel, David Joshua. *A Separate Republic: The Mechanics and Dynamics of Venetian Self-Government 1607–1624*. Jerusalem, 1991.

Marcus, Ivan G. "History, Story, and Collective Memory: Narrativity in Early Ashkenazic Culture." *Prooftexts* 10 (1990): 365–88.

———. "A Jewish-Christian Symbiosis: The Culture of Early Ashkenaz." In *Cultures of the Jews: A New History*, ed. David Biale, 449–516. New York, 2002.

———. *The Jewish Life Cycle: Rites of Passage from Biblical to Modern Times*. Seattle, 2004.

Marcus, Jacob. *Communal Sick-Care in the German Ghetto*. Cincinnati, 1947.

———. *The Jew in the Medieval World: A Source Book, 315–1791*. Cincinnati, 1938.

Menasseh ben Israel. *The Hope of Israel*, ed. Henry Mechoulan and Gerard Nahon. Oxford, 1987.

Mendes Flohr, Paul, and Jehuda Reinharz, eds. *The Jew in the Modern World: A Documentary History*. 2nd ed. New York, 1995.

Meron, Orly Caroline. "Demographic and Spatial Aspects of Jewish Life in the Duchy of Milan during the Spanish Period, 1535–1597." In *Papers in Jewish Demography 1989*, ed. U. O. Schmelz and S. DellaPergola, 37–47. Jerusalem, 1993.

Meyer, Michael A. *Ideas of Jewish History*. Detroit, 1987.

———. "Where Does the Modern Period of Jewish History Begin?" *Judaism* 24 (1975): 329–38.

Middlefort, Eric. *A History of Madness in Sixteenth-Century Germany*. Stanford, CA, 1999.

Mintz, Moses. *Sheelot u-teshuvot*. Jerusalem, 1990–1991.

Modena, Leon. *The Autobiography of a Seventeenth-Century Venetian Rabbi: Leon Modena's Life of Judah*, ed. and trans. Mark R. Cohen. Princeton, NJ, 1988.

Montalvo, Jose Hinojosa. *The Jews of the Kingdom of Valencia from Persecution to Expulsion, 1391–1492*. Jerusalem, 1993.

Moore, R. I. *The Formation of a Persecuting Society: Power and Deviance in Western Europe, 950–1250*. Oxford, 1987.

Motz, Lotte. "The Winter Goddesses: Percht, Holda, and Related Figures." *Folklore* 116 (1984): 151–66.

Mühlhausen, Yom Tov Lipman. *Sefer Nizzahon*, ed. Theodorico Hackspan. Altdorf, Germany, 1644.

Muir, Edward, and Guido Ruggiero, eds. *History from Crime*, trans. Corrada Biazzo Curry, Margaret A. Gallucci, and Mary M. Gallucci. Baltimore, 1994.

Murphey, Rhoads. "Jewish Contributions to Ottoman Medicine." In *Jews, Turks, Ottomans: A Shared History, Fifteenth through the Twentieth Century*, ed. Avigdor Levy, 61–74. Syracuse, NY, 2002.

Nadler, Steven M. *Rembrandt's Jews*. Chicago, 2003.

———. *Spinoza: A Life*. Cambridge, UK, 1999.

Nadov, Mordekhai. "Pinsk." In *Encyclopedia Judaica*. 16 vols. Jerusalem, 1971–1972.

Nathan of Hannover. *Abyss of Despair: The Famous 17th Century Chronicle Depicting Jewish Life in Russia and Poland during the Chmielnicki Massacres of 1648–1649 = Yeven metzulah*, trans. Abraham J. Mesch. New Brunswick, NJ, 1983.

Nepaulsingh, Colbert I. *Apples of Gold in Filigrees of Silver: Jewish Writing in the Eye of the Inquisition*. New York, 1995.

Patai, Raphael. *Tents of Jacob: The Diaspora—Yesterday and Today*. New Jersey, 1971.

Pogonowski, Iwo Cyprian. *Jews in Poland: A Documentary History*. New York, 1998.

Pollak, Michael. *Mandarins, Jews, and Missionaries: The Jewish Experience in the Chinese Empire*. Philadelphia, 1980.

Popkin, Richard H. "Three English Tellings of the Sabbatai Zevi Story." *Jewish History* 8 (1–2) (1994): 43–54.

Posner, Raphael, and Israel Ta-Shma, eds. *The Hebrew Book: An Historical Survey*. Jerusalem, 1975.

"Prado, Juan de." In *Encyclopedia Judaica*. 16 vols. Jerusalem, 1971–1972.

Pullan, Brian. *The Jews of Europe and the Inquisition of Venice, 1550–1670*. London, 1997.

Rabin, Dov. "Grodno." In *Encyclopedia Judaica*. 16 vols. Jerusalem, 1971–1972.

Raphael, David, ed. *The Expulsion 1492 Chronicles: An Anthology of Medieval Chronicles Relating to the Expulsion of the Jews from Spain and Portugal*. North Hollywood, CA, 1992.

Ravid, Benjamin. "From Geographical Realia to Historiographical Symbol: The Odyssey of the Word *Ghetto.*" In *Essential Papers on Jewish Culture in Renaissance and Baroque Italy,* ed. David B. Ruderman, 373–85. New York, 1992.

Reichert, Klaus. "Pico della Mirandola and the Beginnings of Christian Kabbala." In *Mysticism, Magic, and Kabbalah,* ed. Karl Erich Grözinger and Joseph Dan, 195–207. Berlin, 1995.

Reuchlin, Johannes. *Recommendation Whether to Confiscate, Destroy, and Burn All Jewish Books,* ed. and trans. Peter Wortsman. New York, 2000.

Richards, John F. "Early Modern India and World History." *Journal of World History* 8 (2) (Fall 1997): 197–209.

Rohrbacher, Stefan. "Die jüdischen Gemeinden in den Medinot Aschkenas zwischen Spätmittelalter und Dreißigjährigem Krieg." In *Jüdische Gemeinden und ihr christlicher Kontext in kulturräumlich vergleichender Betrachtung von der Spätantike bis zum 18. Jahrhundert,* ed. Christoph Cluse, Alfred Haverkamp, and Israel J. Yuval, 451–63. Hanover, Germany, 2003.

Rosensweig, Bernhard. *Ashkenazic Jewry in Transition.* Waterloo, ON, 1975.

———. "Taxation in the Late Middle Ages in Germany and Austria." *Diné Israel: An Annual of Jewish Law, Past and Present* 12 (1984–1985): 49–93.

Rosman, Moshe. "Innovative Tradition: Jewish Culture in the Polish-Lithuanian Commonwealth." In *Cultures of the Jews: A New History,* ed. David Biale, 519–70. New York, 2002.

Roth, Cecil. "Ashkenazi, Solomon." In *Encyclopedia Judaica.* 16 vols. Jerusalem, 1971–1972.

———. "Capsali, Elijah." In *Encyclopedia Judaica.* 16 vols. Jerusalem, 1971–1972.

———. *A History of the Jews in England.* Oxford, 1941.

———. *History of the Jews in Venice.* New York, 1975.

———. "Inquisition: Statistics." In *Encyclopedia Judaica.* 16 vols. Jerusalem, 1971–1972.

———. *The Jews in the Renaissance.* Philadelphia, 1959.

———. "Nasi, Joseph." In *Encyclopedia Judaica.* 16 vols. Jerusalem, 1971–1972.

Roth, Norman. *Conversos, Inquisition, and the Expulsion of the Jews from Spain.* Madison, WI, 1995.

Rothkoff, Aaron. "Semikhah: Controversy on the Renewal of the Semikhah." In *Encyclopedia Judaica.* 16 vols. Jerusalem, 1971–1972.

Rubin, Miri. *Gentile Tales: The Narrative Assault on Late Medieval Jews.* New Haven, CT, 1999.

Rubinstein, Avraham. "Lvov (Lemberg)." In *Encyclopedia Judaica.* 16 vols. Jerusalem, 1971–1972.

———. "Warsaw." In *Encyclopedia Judaica.* 16 vols. Jerusalem, 1971–1972.

Ruderman, David B., ed. *Essential Papers on Jewish Culture in Renaissance and Baroque Italy.* New York, 1992.

———. *Kabbalah, Magic, and Science: The Cultural Universe of a Sixteenth-Century Jewish Physician.* Cambridge, MA, 1988.

———. "Medicine and Scientific Thought: The World of Tobias Cohen." In *The Jews of Early Modern Venice,* ed. Robert C. Davis and Benjamin Ravid, 191–210. Baltimore, 2001.

Rummel, Erika. "Humanists, Jews, and Judaism." In *Jews, Judaism, and the Reformation in Sixteenth-Century Germany*, ed. Dean Phillip Bell and Stephen G. Burnett, 3–31. Leiden, Netherlands, 2006.

Saban, Giacomo. "Sabbatai Sevi as Seen by a Contemporary Traveller." *Jewish History* 7 (2) (1993): 105–18.

Sabar, Shalom. "Childbirth and Magic: Jewish Folklore and Material Culture." In *Cultures of the Jews: A New History*, ed. David Biale, 671–729. New York, 2002.

Safed Spirituality: Rules of Mystical Piety, The Beginning of Wisdom, trans. Lawrence Fine. New York, 1984.

Saperstein, Marc. *Exile in Amsterdam: Saul Levi Morteira's Sermons to a Congregation of "New Jews."* Cincinnati, 2005.

———. *Jewish Preaching, 1200–1800: An Anthology*. New Haven, CT, 1989.

Schäfer, Peter. *Judeophobia: Attitudes toward the Jews in the Ancient World*. Cambridge, MA, 1997.

Scheindlin, Raymond P. "Merchants and Intellectuals, Rabbis and Poets: Judeo-Arabic Culture in the Golden Age of Islam." In *Cultures of the Jews: A New History*, ed. David Biale, 313–86. New York, 2002.

Scholem, Gershom. *Major Trends in Jewish Mysticism*. 3rd ed. New York, 1954.

———. *Sabbatai Sevi: The Mystical Messiah, 1626–1676*, trans. R. J. Zwi Werblowsky. Princeton, NJ, 1973.

———. "Zohar." In *Encyclopedia Judaica*. 16 vols. Jerusalem, 1971–1972.

Schwarzfuchs, Simon R. "Antwerp." In *Encyclopedia Judaica*. 16 vols. Jerusalem, 1971–1972.

———. "Spain: Conversos." In *Encyclopedia Judaica*. 16 vols. Jerusalem, 1971–1972.

Segal, Lester A. *Historical Consciousness and Religious Tradition in Azariah de' Rossi's Me'or 'Einayim*. Philadelphia, 1989.

Shaw, Stanford J. *The Jews of the Ottoman Empire and the Turkish Republic*. New York, 1991.

Sherwin, Byron. *Mystical Theology and Social Dissent: The Life and Works of Judah Loew of Prague*. Rutherford, New Jersey, 1982.

Shmuelevitz, Aryeh. *The Jews of the Ottoman Empire in the Late Fifteenth and the Sixteenth Centuries: Administrative, Economic, Legal, and Social Relations as Reflected in the Responsa*. Leiden, Netherlands, 1984.

Shulman, Nisson E. *Authority and Community: Polish Jewry in the Sixteenth Century*. New York, 1986.

Shulvass, Moses. *The Jews in the World of the Renaissance*, trans. Elvin I. Kose. Leiden, Netherlands, 1973.

Sirat, Colette. *A History of Jewish Philosophy in the Middle Ages*. New York, 1985.

Slutsky, Yehuda. "Kiev: The Jewish Community before 1667." In *Encyclopedia Judaica*. 16 vols. Jerusalem, 1971–1972.

Spinoza, Benedictus de (Baruch). *Tractatus theologico-politicus*, trans. Samuel Shirley. 2nd ed. Leiden, Netherlands, 1991.

Starn, Randolph. "Review Article: The Early Modern Muddle." *Journal of Early Modern History* 6 (3) (2002): 296–307.

Stern, Selma. *The Court Jew: A Contribution to the History of the Period of Absolutism in Central Europe*. Philadelphia, 1950.

——. *Josel of Rosheim: Commander of Jewry in the Holy Roman Empire of the German Nation*, trans. Gertrude Hirschler. Philadelphia, 1965 (orig., 1959).

Stillman, Norman A. *The Jews of Arab Lands: A History and Source Book*. Philadelphia, 1979.

Stow, Kenneth R. *Alienated Minority: The Jews of Medieval Latin Europe*. Cambridge, MA, 1992.

——, ed. *The Jews in Rome*. 2 vols. Leiden, Netherlands, 1995.

——. *Theater of Acculturation: The Roman Ghetto in the 16th Century*. Seattle, 2001.

Suler, Bernard. "Alchemy." In *Encyclopedia Judaica*. 16 vols. Jerusalem, 1971–1972.

Swetschinski, Daniel. *Reluctant Cosmopolitans: The Portuguese Jews of Seventeenth-Century Amsterdam*. London, 2000.

Taylor, Karen L., and James B. Collins. "Introduction: Interpreting Early Modern Europe." In *Early Modern Europe: Issues and Interpretations*, ed. James B. Collins and Karen L. Taylor, 1–5. Oxford, 2006.

Teller, Adam. "The Laicization of Early Modern Jewish Society: The Development of the Polish Communal Rabbinate in the 16th Century." In *Schöpferische Momente des europäischen Judentums in der frühen Neuzeit*, ed. Michael Graetz, 333–49. Heidelberg, Germany, 2000.

——. *Living Together: The Jewish Quarter of Poznań in the First Half of the Seventeenth Century* (Hebrew). Jerusalem, 2003.

Tobias, Alexander. "Hayyim Ben Bezalel." In *Encyclopedia Judaica*. 16 vols. Jerusalem, 1971–1972.

Toch, Michael. "The Jewish Community of Nuremberg in the Year 1489: Social and Demographic Structure" (Hebrew). *Zion* 45:60–72.

Trachtenberg, Joshua. *Jewish Magic and Superstition: A Study in Folk Religion*. New York, 1939.

Ulbrich, Claudia. *Shulamit and Margarete: Power, Gender, and Religion in a Rural Society in Eighteenth-Century Europe*, trans. Thomas Dunlap. Boston and Leiden, Netherlands, 2004.

Ulbricht, Otto. "Criminality and Punishment of the Jews in the Early Modern Period." In *In and Out of the Ghetto: Jewish-Gentile Relations in Late Medieval and Early Modern Germany*, ed. R. Po-chia Hsia and Hartmut Lehmann, 49–70. Cambridge, UK, 1995.

Ullmann, Sabine. *Nachbarschaft und Konkurrenz: Juden und Christen in Dörfern der Markgrafschaft Burgau*. Göttingen, Germany, 1999.

Usque, Samuel. *Consolation for the Tribulations of the Jews*, trans. Martin A. Cohen. Philadelphia, 1965.

Van Wijk, Jetteke. "The Rise and Fall of Shabbetai Zevi as Reflected in Contemporary Press Reports." *Studia Rosenthalia* 33 (1) (1999): 7–27.

Weil, Jacob. *Sheelot u-teshuvot*. Jerusalem, 1958–1959 (orig., 1549).

Weinryb, Bernard D. "The Beginnings of East-European Jewry in Legend and Historiography." In *Studies and Essays in Honor of Abraham A. Neuman, President, Dropsie College for Hebrew and Cognate Learning, Philadelphia*, ed. Meir Ben-Horin, Bernard D. Weinryb, and Solomon Zeitlin, 445–502. Leiden, Netherlands, 1962.

——. *The Jews of Poland: A Social and Economic History of the Jewish Community in Poland from 1100 to 1800*. Philadelphia, 1973.

——. "Texts and Studies in the Communal History of Polish Jewry." *Proceedings of the American Academy for Jewish Research* 19 (1950): 77–98.

Weissler, Chava. *Voices of the Matriarchs: Listening to the Prayers of Early Modern Jewish Women*. Boston, 1998.

Whaley, Joachim. *Religious Toleration and Social Change in Hamburg 1529–1819*. Cambridge, UK, 1985.

Wiznitzer, Arnold. "Brazil: Colonial Period." In *Encyclopedia Judaica*. 16 vols. Jerusalem, 1971–1972.

——. *The Records of the Earliest Jewish Community in the New World*. New York, 1954.

Wolfson, Harry A. *The Philosophy of Spinoza: Unfolding the Latent Process of His Reasoning*. Cambridge, MA, 1983.

Wyrozumski, Jerzy. "Jews in Medieval Poland." In *The Jews in Old Poland, 1000–1795*, ed. Antony Polonsky, Jakub Basista, and Andrzej Link-Lenczowski, 129–35. London, 1993.

Yardeni, Myriam. *Anti-Jewish Mentalities in Early Modern Europe*. Lanham, MD, 1990.

Ye'or, Bat. *The Dhimmi: Jews and Christians under Islam*, trans. David Maisel, Paul Fenton, and David Littman. London, 1985.

Yerushalmi, Yosef Hayim. *Zakhor: Jewish History and Jewish Memory*. Seattle, 1982.

Yuval, Israel. "Heilige Städte, heilige Gemeinden—Mainz als das Jerusalem Deutschlands." In *Jüdische Gemeinden und Organisationsformen von der Antike bis zur Gegenwart*, ed. R. Jütte and A. P. Kustermann, 91–101. Köln, Germany, 1996.

Yuval, Israel, and Ora Limor. "Skepticism and Conversion: Jews, Christians, and Doubters in 'Sefer ha-Nizzahon.'" In *Hebraica Veritas? Jews and the Study of Judaism in Early Modern Europe*, ed. Allison P. Coudert, Alison Shoulson, and Jeffery S. Shoulson, 159–80. Philadelphia, 2004.

Zimmels, Hirsch Jacob. "Isaac ben Sheshet Perfet." In *Encyclopedia Judaica*. 16 vols. Jerusalem, 1971–1972.

Zimmer, Eric. *Fiery Embers of the Scholars: The Trials and Tribulations of German Rabbis in the Sixteenth and Seventeenth Centuries* (Hebrew). Jerusalem, 1999.

——. *Harmony and Discord: An Analysis of the Decline of Jewish Self-Government in Fifteenth-Century Central Europe*. New York, 1970.

Zunz, Leopold. *The Sufferings of the Jews during the Middle Ages*, trans. A. Löwy. New York, 1907.

Index

Page numbers in italics refer to illustrations.

Abarbanel, Isaac, 9, *77, 78,* 177, 197,
    198, 221
Abbas, Rabbi Samuel, 197
Abbas, Shah II, 64, 209
Abraham, 27, 175, 231
Abrahams, Israel, 8
academies, 148. *See also yeshivah*
acculturation, 194, 195–200
Adarbi, Isaac, 150
Adrianople, *37, 38, 59,* 157. *See also*
    Edirne
adultery, 166
agriculture, 57, 129
Albania, 161
alchemy, 158, 174–75
Alemanno, Johanan, 197
Aleppo, 62, 161
Alexandria, *37, 38, 59,* 62, 211
Alfasi, Rabbi Isaac, 131, 148, 150
Algeria, 42
Algiers, 36, *37, 38, 59,* 63
Alkabetz, Rabbi Solomon, 159
Almohads, 27
Almoravid Berber conquest, 30
Almosnino, Rabbi Moses, 146, 163
Alsace, 53, 230

Alsheikh, Rabbi Moses, 157, 158
Altona, 79, 80, 81–82, 124, 152
Amsterdam, *59,* 65, 78, 154, 219, 231;
    Ashkenazic immigrants, 112;
    conversos in, 223; deviance of
    religious practices in, 166, 170; early
    community and founding of, 111,
    192; excommunications and fines
    in, 171; Jewish communal
    governance in, 96, 99, 115, 118,
    166; library in, 197; Polish Jews in,
    56; Portuguese Jews in, 52, 80, 170;
    professions in, 127, 129, 130, 131;
    rabbinic leadership in, 118, 159,
    201; restrictions and tolerance in,
    192, 193, 197; reversion to Judaism
    in, 175; Sephardic and Ashkenazic
    Jews in, 110, 117, 148; settlement
    in, *37, 38, 47,* 50–51, 73; support
    for Shabbetai Sevi in, 161;
    synagogues in, 112–13, *114;* theater
    in, 175
amulets, 147, 156, 183, 229, 245
Anatolia, 58, 62, 217
Ancona, 161, 201; boycott of port of,
    78

281